'The growth of business analysis has led to m...........ng
BA practices yet little information is available ....ies
a new light on business analysis from a service perspective; providing a timely and
comprehensive 'How to guide' for anyone wanting to achieve a sustainable and enduring
BA service. Reading this book will provide everything you need from establishing a new
BA service, to continuous improvement of established practices, and how to measure
them effectively. A must have for any organisation.'

Lynda Girvan, *Senior Business Analyst and Head of BA Profession, CMC Partnership Consultancy Ltd. and co-author of "Agile and Business Analysis"*

'Business analysis has evolved as a discipline, but as many business analysts will attest, there are obstacles to overcome. Often the role is misunderstood, and having a strong team and strong role identity is crucial. This practical and insightful guide provides concrete steps to avoid "role ambiguity", and will help senior business analysts and leaders to clearly set-up, manage and measure the success of their BA service. It explores different service models, highlighting the importance of adapting models to fit the context. The book discusses tricky but crucial areas such as value co-creation and the BA value proposition, and many other useful topics besides. The addition of inspirational case studies shows the types of concrete results that can be achieved.

This book will be of interest not only to those who hold formal leadership roles, but also those who seek to set up their own informal inter- or intra-organisational communities of practice. Written by two notable thought-leaders, I consider this book to be essential reading for anyone serious about setting up or running a BA service. Highly recommended.'

Adrian Reed, *Principal Consultant at Blackmetric and author of "Business Analyst"*

'This book contains a wealth of information and models to help BA leaders understand what their organisation needs from the BA function. The use of models and frameworks works particularly well; using an abstract concept to make sense of a concrete situation is, after all, the core of business analysis.

This book also recognises the need to understand leadership as a distinct skillset, which is often overlooked within BA functions as many managers are promoted on the basis of technical excellence and may have little help developing their management competence.

Whilst there are lots of ideas included in the book, I was particularly heartened that the importance of organisational context runs strongly throughout; this is not a "one size fits all" instruction manual, but rather a rich source of views and concepts to help BA leaders make the right choices for their own organisations. This book is recommended reading for anyone who has, or aspires to, a BA leadership role.'

Michelle Shakesheff, *Head of Business Analysis, Close Brothers*

'This is the book business analysts have been waiting for. A comprehensive toolkit for the modern business analyst covering everything from the BA service, through recruitment, performance and standardisation.

The chapters on business analysis culture and improving service quality are especially relevant in our modern work environment.

This book is suitable for all levels of business analysts, from those new to the profession, to the most experienced leaders in the industry. Tangible, relevant and clear case studies demonstrate the effective business analysis in action. Essential reading for any business analyst.'

Sandra Leek, *Senior Business Analyst and IIBA UK BA of the Year 2014*

'Debra and Christina have cleverly crafted this insightful guide to encompass all the facets of a high performing business analysis capability by using the wealth of its very own toolkit.

With the customer firmly at the forefront, this book is packed with practical innovative frameworks, templates and guidelines that you could introduce tomorrow and make an immediate impact to the quality of your BA value proposition.

Whether you're a BA leader, a BA professional or simply a recipient of Business Analysis services, this book brings overdue clarity on how a high performing, modern day Business Analysis capability should be structured, operated and promoted on a day-to-day basis.'

Ian Richards, *Head of Business Analysis, Capita People Solutions & IIBA UK BA of the Year 2016*

'This book covers the final steps to become a successful business analyst in an organisation by approaching the business analysis service with a business analysis lens. It is a real addition to the existing set of resources that mainly focus on the business analysis techniques and shows you how to apply and establish a solid way of working in an organisation.

It can be a real struggle to set your standards as a team of business analysts in an organisation, this book gives a clear overview of the steps you can take to create a professional and mature business analysis service.

This book will be my guide on assignments where I am asked to form a business analysis team or implement business analysis as a service. Where before I had to rely on my own experience, skills and common sense this book will help me with a framework for business analysis service. Christina and Debra have covered every angle and approached the BA service with a BA view and with a broad set of business analysis techniques. A real addition to my toolkit.'

Geertje Appel, *Business Analyst and Trainer, Le Blanc Advies*

'An important new work describing a Business Analysis Service Framework which can be applied within any organisation, concentrating on the challenges facing the definition and operation of a Business Analysis Service, and proposing options to address these.'

Dr Terri Lydiard, *Director, Teal Business Solutions Limited*

'This book is a much needed book for the BA world! It provides everything and more to be able to understand (and where needed) to implement a BA Service. It combines both theories with practical applications, tools and techniques, which provide the reader with so much more than just theory. A must have book for those wanting to expand their knowledge of BA services and the profession.'

Joanna Solecki, *Business Analysis and Business Change Professional and IIBA UK North Vice-Chair*

DELIVERING BUSINESS ANALYSIS

BCS, THE CHARTERED INSTITUTE FOR IT

BCS, The Chartered Institute for IT, is committed to making IT good for society. We use the power of our network to bring about positive, tangible change. We champion the global IT profession and the interests of individuals, engaged in that profession, for the benefit of all.

Exchanging IT expertise and knowledge
The Institute fosters links between experts from industry, academia and business to promote new thinking, education and knowledge sharing.

Supporting practitioners
Through continuing professional development and a series of respected IT qualifications, the Institute seeks to promote professional practice tuned to the demands of business. It provides practical support and information services to its members and volunteer communities around the world.

Setting standards and frameworks
The Institute collaborates with government, industry and relevant bodies to establish good working practices, codes of conduct, skills frameworks and common standards. It also offers a range of consultancy services to employers to help them adopt best practice.

Become a member
Over 70,000 people including students, teachers, professionals and practitioners enjoy the benefits of BCS membership. These include access to an international community, invitations to a roster of local and national events, career development tools and a quarterly thought-leadership magazine. Visit www.bcs.org/membership to find out more.

Further information
BCS, The Chartered Institute for IT,
First Floor, Block D,
North Star House, North Star Avenue,
Swindon, SN2 1FA, United Kingdom.
T +44 (0) 1793 417 424
F +44 (0) 1793 417 444
(Monday to Friday, 09:00 to 17:00 UK time)
www.bcs.org/contact
http://shop.bcs.org/

DELIVERING BUSINESS ANALYSIS
The BA Service handbook

Debra Paul and Christina Lovelock

bcs
The
Chartered
Institute
for IT

Published by BCS Learning and Development Ltd, a wholly owned subsidiary of BCS, The Chartered Institute for IT, First Floor, Block D, North Star House, North Star Avenue, Swindon, SN2 1FA, UK.
www.bcs.org

Paperback ISBN 978-1-780174-68-6
PDF ISBN 978-1-780174-69-3
ePUB ISBN 978-1-780174-70-9
Kindle ISBN 978-1-780174-71-6

Ebook available

British Cataloguing in Publication Data.
A CIP catalogue record for this book is available at the British Library.

Publisher's acknowledgements
Reviewers: John Burns, Michelle Shakesheff
Publisher: Ian Borthwick
Commissioning editor: Rebecca Youé
Production manager: Florence Leroy
Project manager: Sunrise Setting Ltd
Copy-editor: Denise Bannerman
Proofreader: Barbara Eastman
Indexer: Matthew Gale
Cover design: Alex Wright
Cover image: Thinkstock @ gemredding
Typeset by Lapiz Digital Services, Chennai, India
Printed and bound in the UK by Henry Ling Limited, at the Dorset Press, DT1 1HD

CONTENTS

LIST OF FIGURES AND TABLES

AUTHORS

Dr Debra Paul is the Managing Director of Assist Knowledge Development Ltd (AssistKD), a training and consultancy company specialising in business analysis and business and solution architecture. Debra jointly edited and authored the publication, *Business Analysis*, and is also the co-author of *Agile and Business Analysis*, *Business Analysis Techniques* and *The Human Touch*. Debra conducted doctoral research into the role of the business analyst and developed the Business Analysis Service Framework.

Debra is a regular speaker at business seminars and IS industry events. She has been a keynote presenter at business analysis conferences, delivering presentations such as 'Business Analysis: The Third Wave' and 'Business Analysis: Relevance and Recognition'. Debra is a founder member of the BA Manager Forum, a networking organisation for senior BAs and BA managers and was the chief architect of the BCS Advanced Diploma in Business Analysis.

Christina Lovelock is a passionate BA leader with many years' experience of managing and developing business analysts. She has built and managed BA services in several organisations, ranging in size from 3 to 120 business analysts.

She holds the BCS International Diploma in Business Analysis and is an Oral Examiner for the diploma.

Christina is an active member of the BA professional community. She regularly attends and speaks at business analysis events and conferences in the Yorkshire Region, across the UK and internationally. She is also a director of the national BA Manager Forum.

Christina is committed to the development of the BA profession, has introduced entry-level BA roles into her organisations and was lead employer for the National BA Apprentice Standard. Supporting people to become motivated and professional BAs has been a source of happiness and pride throughout her career.

FOREWORD

Business analysis and the role of the practising business analyst have developed over the last 20 years but, as an objective observer and colleague, the profession has always seemed to lack a well-defined place in the world. Over this time, there appear to have been regular, if not continuous, discussion and questioning (often involving the BAs themselves) about what exactly a business analyst does and what is the real rationale and focus of the role.

A new profession will always need to evolve and, along the way, numerous questions will arise about the profession – this must be considered a vital part of any healthy development path. Answers to these questions have to be well-founded, based upon deep understanding and focused on the fundamental objectives of the profession rather than alighting upon the 'shiny toy' of the moment. This book offers the answers to many of the fundamental questions about business analysis and reveals the opportunities for the profession to be established as an internal service provider that exists to offer benefit to organisations.

This start point for the book is to scrutinise current thinking about the business analyst role to uncover the core principles and then to build from these principles to define the necessary building blocks of good practice. Significantly, a service-based approach is advocated and clearly defined for business analysis, which is a something of an advance in thinking about this profession. However, the rewards resulting from adopting the service view are likely to be multi-fold and permanent.

Case studies bring the extensive research to life with leading practitioners sharing insights from their valuable experiences and strategies. The nature of 'value' is discussed, highlighting how this term should be used carefully – readers should expect to leave refreshingly well informed on this subject.

An initial review of the contents page is reassuring as it demonstrates the comprehensive nature of this book. Further positive news is that the book is founded in solid research and combines this with offering highly practical guidance on perennial issues such as leadership, recruitment and capability development.

Any profession that is progressing towards maturity will need to achieve important milestones along the way. This book, in providing an indispensable handbook for the thoughtful BA leader, supports the achievement of a significant milestone in the development of business analysis. It provides tangible guidance that will help to overcome the challenges, ambiguities and issues that are likely to be encountered and uses business analysis techniques wherever possible to illustrate the points made. Surpassing expectations and delivering true 'delighters' (see Chapter 10) along the way.

When passionate and knowledgeable people write about the subject in which they have invested their professional lives, giant steps can be made. This book demonstrates a leap forward for the entire business analysis community and reading it will benefit anyone working within this important profession.

Lawrence Darvill, Director, BA Manager Forum

ACKNOWLEDGEMENTS

This book could not have been written without the support and assistance of many people. In particular, we would like to thank: our case study BA leaders Kim Bray, Matt Eastwood, Michael Greenhalgh, Sandra Leek, Terri Lydiard, Jamie Toyne, Ian Richards and Charlie Payne for offering valuable experiences and insights into BA leadership work; Debbie's colleagues at AssistKD, James Cadle and Martin Pearson, for reviewing and suggesting improvements, and Andrew Watkinson and Tom Anstiss for their visualisations of our models and frameworks; Tina's BA colleagues at the University of Leeds and within the NHS for being willing to try new ideas and continuously improve the BA Service; Ian Borthwick and Becky Youé from BCS Learning & Development for their advice and guidance throughout this process; Lawrence Darvill and the BA Manager Forum members who gave us information and ideas on the nature of a BA Service; our early reviewers, Katharine Smith and Michelle Shakesheff for their invaluable suggestions; and last but definitely not least, our partners Alan Paul and Andy Broomhead for their constant support, advice and frequent delivery of much-needed sustenance.

ABBREVIATIONS

3S	Succinct, Sincere, Specific
AI	artificial intelligence
APMG	Association for Project Management Group
BA	business analysis
BABOK®	Business Analysis Body of Knowledge
BAM	business activity model
BAMF	Business Analysis Manager Forum
BAMM	Business Analysis Maturity Model
BASF	Business Analysis Service Framework
BAU	business as usual
BCS	BCS, The Chartered Institute for IT
BEAR	Behaviour Effect Alternative Result
BPMN™	Business Process Model and Notation
BRAIN	used as an acronym to define five types of influencing style: Bridging, Rationalising, Asserting, Inspiring and Negotiating
BSC	Balanced Scorecard
CASE	Computer Aided Software Engineering
CATWOE	Customer, Actor, Transformation, Weltanschauung (or world view), Owner, Environment
CES	Customer Effort Score
CIA	Control, Influence, Accept
CMMI	Capability Maturity Model Integration
CoP	Community of Practice
CPPOLDAT	Customer, Product, Process, Organisation, Location, Data, Applications, Technology
CRUD	Create, Read, Update, Delete
CSAT	customer satisfaction
CSF	critical success factor
CSI	continual service improvement
DFD	data flow diagram
DMN™	Decision Model and Notation

DOWN-TIME	used as an acronym to define the Lean Six Sigma eight types of waste: Defects, Over-production, Waiting, Non-used talent, Transportation, Inventory, Motion, Extra-processing
DSDM	Dynamic Systems Development Method
EI	emotional intelligence
ERD	entity relationship diagram
HR	human resources
IIBA	International Institute of Business Analysis
IET	Institution of Engineering and Technology
IMIS	Institute for the Management of Information Systems
IREB	International Requirements Engineering Board
IS	information systems
ISO	International Organization for Standardization
itSMF	IT Service Management Forum
JIT	just in time
KM	knowledge management
KPI	key performance indicator
MoSCoW	must have, should have, could have, want to have but won't have this time
NES	Net Easy Score
NPS®	Net Promoter Score
PESTLE	Political, Economic, Socio-cultural, Technological, Legal, Environmental
PMO	Project/Programme/Portfolio Management Office
PMI	Project Management Institute
POPIT™	People, Organisation, Processes, Information and Technology
RACI	Responsible, Accountable, Consulted, Informed
RCT	Randomised Coffee Trial
SBI	Situation Behaviour Impact
SDLC	software development life cycle
SFIA	Skills Framework for the Information Age
SIP	Service Improvement Plan
SIPOC	suppliers, inputs, processes, outputs, customers
SLA	Service Level Agreement
SME	subject matter expert
SSADM	Structured Systems Analysis and Design Method
SSM	Soft Systems Methodology
SWOT	strengths, weaknesses, opportunities, threats
TA	Talent Acquisition
TCQ	Time Cost Quality

TQM	Total Quality Management
UAT	user acceptance testing
UI	user interface
UML®	Unified Modelling Language
UX	user experience
(V)MOST	(Vision) Mission, Objectives, Strategy, Tactics
VP	value proposition
WIP	work in progress
WSJF	weighted shortest job first
WTE	whole-time equivalent (also known as FTE, full-time equivalent)

GLOSSARY

BA leader: A role that may be undertaken by individuals with a range of job titles, where the holder is ultimately responsible for directing and delivering the BA Service.

BA Service Framework: A framework that defines the key services to be offered to customers by business analysts. Each of the services is defined in terms of its activities, techniques and value proposition.

BA 3rd Wave: A model that represents the development of business analysis as a specialist discipline. The three waves are: bridging (1st Wave), challenging (2nd Wave) and advising (3rd Wave).

Buddying: A supportive connection between individuals not necessarily relating to seniority or experience. Buddying can help with personal development and performance improvement in a less formal way than mentoring or coaching.

Coaching: A coach deals with a person's tasks and responsibilities, has a specific agenda or development approach, has a focus on improving a person's job performance and may be the person's line manager.

Conversion rates: A metric used in recruitment to understand the percentage of applications that are 'converted' into interviews and actual appointments of new business analysts.

Emotional intelligence: Emotional intelligence is the measurement of an individual's abilities to recognise and manage their own emotions and the emotions of other people, both individually and in groups.

Growth mindset: Describes the attitude that intelligence and abilities are variable factors that can be influenced through learning, effort, training and practice.

High-level requirements dilemma: The erroneous belief that high-level requirements for a project or product are synonymous with 'scope', leading to a cycle of unclear scope and the inability to define and agree the requirements.

Mentoring: Provides access to knowledge and experience within a supportive professional relationship. A mentor is usually at a more advanced career stage than the person being mentored.

Performance management: The process of defining and monitoring the work of individuals or a team to ensure the best possible results.

Persona: A profile of a user of a product or service. It is usually a short, specific description of a fictional character that represents a group of users.

Pipeline approach: Ensuring that BA skills are being developed at a variety of levels within the organisation to deliver a cost-effective BA Service and minimising the impact of people leaving the team.

Process inventory: A master repository of key information about processes, including identifiers, owners, stakeholders, inputs, outputs and goals. Also known as a process catalogue.

Quality Management Cycle: An iterative framework used to establish and track business analysis quality to allow continual improvement of business analysis processes and products.

Randomised Coffee Trial (RCT): Individuals who do not know each other (or have not worked together) are paired up randomly and encouraged to arrange a real or virtual coffee break. They discuss their roles, their work, previous experience, ideas and inspiration – anything they wish.

Review triangle: Provides a representation of the different levels and types of review that may be conducted (self, peer, stakeholder).

Shrink-to-fit: This concept relates to having a framework for business analysis or BA templates that are tailorable and scalable. For example, a template that contains many options or prompts for consideration, but, when used, unnecessary sections can be removed.

Skills development framework: A framework setting out the skills required by a given domain, and the levels of competency required to apply the skills.

T-shaped business analyst: A representation of the skills that professional business analysts need to develop. The horizontal row of the T-shape is used to define the generic personal and business skills that form the basis for effective interactions with stakeholders. The vertical column of the T-shape is used to define the 'deep' skills that are specific to anyone conducting business analysis work.

Template amnesty: The process of gathering all examples of standards and approaches in use by BAs, to understand the breadth of uses and information, before moving forward with an agreed consistent set of standard outputs.

Toolkit approach: Equipping individuals with the knowledge to use a wide variety of BA tools and techniques and the confidence and experience to select and apply the most appropriate tool for the situation.

Value fallacy: No entity, whether an enterprise, internal function or a software product, can state that they 'deliver value', as value has to be co-created with the recipient.

Work package: A document used to agree and record the business analysis work to be carried out, the boundaries, activities and outputs/deliverables.

PREFACE

All organisations face external pressures that require informed decisions to be made about proposed investments and business change solutions. Business analysis is the professional discipline that aims to help businesses respond to these pressures by evaluating the feasibility of proposed investments, defining requirements, delivering relevant change solutions and ensuring that any changes are deployed effectively.

The concept of 'service' is becoming increasingly recognised in today's business world with the customer experience being at the heart of a service offering, and this applies whether the customers are internal to the organisation, external or both. Not only do customers want to be able to ensure that anything they purchase offers benefits when deployed, they also want to feel that the experience of purchasing and obtaining the service meets their personal engagement needs.

The service offered by business analysts is focused on ensuring that business problems are well defined and address actual issues, and that business solutions offer valuable outcomes and do not result from 'vanity' or 'panic' projects. Current developments in technology and business working practices have caused business analysts to be under pressure to take on new tasks, work in different ways and even justify why a business analysis team should exist. Therefore, the need to clarify the business analysis service offering, communicate the value proposition and ensure that a team of highly skilled practitioners is available to deliver the service, has never been more relevant. Establishing this service requires leadership of the highest order.

Business analysis evolves continuously, requiring ongoing consideration and clarification of each of the following concepts:

- offering the business analysis proposition (business analysis as a **service**);
- being a business analyst (business analysis as a **role**);
- doing business analysis (business analysis as an **activity**)

We have written this book because we want to extend and progress the business analysis discussion. For too long, conversations have focused on the 'what does a BA do?' question rather than 'why do we have business analysis?' Understanding business analysis as a service addresses this question and provides a clarity that is long overdue. Accepting that business analysis is a service requires consideration and definition of the BA service portfolio and the means of establishing a high-performing team to deliver the BA Service.

A set of highly skilled business analysis practitioners working independently across an organisation does not offer the same potential for business value as a coordinated and consistent service that is managed, measured and able to improve. Any organisation wishing to establish a business analysis capability needs to define, communicate and deploy three fundamental concepts: the portfolio of services offered by the BA Service, the nature of the business analyst role and the proficiency requirements of the individuals who will carry out the business analysis activities.

The BA leader must possess a skill set that extends beyond that of a practising business analyst and should appreciate the nature of 'service' and how a service function should operate. This book has been written to support those in business analysis leadership positions, whether they are running an internal practice or coordinating a dispersed community, and whether working with employed business analysts or a mix of external and internal staff. We discuss the various areas of work conducted by BA leaders and identify the techniques that we find useful in a variety of leadership situations. There is no 'one-size-fits-all' approach for the BA Service so various options and approaches are explored, which ensure the delivery of business analysis is appropriate for the business context.

Our aim with this book has been to provide a handbook for anyone who wishes to build, lead or influence a BA Service. It covers the topics and techniques that can support the promotion and development of business analysis services and the business analysts who deliver them. We hope that reading this book will help to ensure that the BA Service is better understood, not only by leaders and practitioners but also by the customers who wish to engage with business analysis in the pursuit of their business and organisational goals.

1 INTRODUCING THE BA SERVICE

INTRODUCTION

Business analysis is a professional discipline that aims to ensure that work systems are investigated, requirements are clarified, and proposed business and IT changes are evaluated. Business analysis, when conducted by skilled practitioners, can help organisations to spend investment funds with focus and insight.

Many books explore business analysis. Typically, these books are aimed at individual business analysts, with the objectives of improving business analysis skills and knowledge, and offering frameworks and techniques for conducting business analysis. The extensive readership of these books reflects the increasing number of business analysts who wish to apply professional standards to their work.

However, in many organisations, there are teams or communities of business analysts who wish to feel part of a distinct profession devoted to business analysis practice. These business analysts understand that it is possible to have a business analysis career. They recognise that there are colleagues who are new to business analysis and they are prepared to offer support and mentoring to help them. In many organisations, grading structures exist for business analysts, required skills and competency levels are defined, training is delivered, and tool support is obtained.

Unlike other business analysis publications, this book is not aimed at the practice of business analysis but at the delivery of the business analysis service within organisations. It is relevant for anyone who is leading a business analysis team, representing business analysis within an organisation, or wishing to develop the role and reputation of business analysis across a wider community.

The aim of this book is to offer a resource that will encompass the areas that should be considered when establishing a business analysis service and to provide advice and guidance for anyone working within a business analysis context.

This chapter explores one of the key issues facing business analysis – the lack of understanding that surrounds the business analyst role, where problems lie if this is not addressed, and how this can limit recognition of the advantages business analysis can offer. Clarifying the role is of primary importance to anyone working within or leading a business analysis service. This chapter explains four key topics that underlie the formation and development of any team established to offer a Business analysis (BA) Service:

- the nature of the BA Service;
- situating the BA Service;

- the problems associated with role ambiguity;
- the development pathway for the business analyst role and the BA Service.

BUSINESS ANALYSIS AS A SERVICE

Different organisations use different terminology to refer to their business analysts. In practice, a team of business analysts may be referred to by any of the terms shown in Figure 1.1.

Figure 1.1 Possible titles for the Business Analysis Service

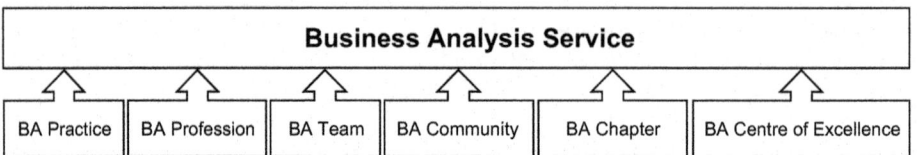

The terms used to identify a group of business analysts within an organisation will be influenced by a number of factors:

- size of the organisation;
- number of business analysts;
- how long the business analyst role has existed within the organisation;
- level of support and sponsorship for business analysis;
- development methodology in use;
- legacy structures and reporting lines, structures and re-structures;
- organisational conventions for other disciplines;
- industry influences;
- senior management influences.

Table 1.1 shows the implications of the terms often used to refer to a business analysis team.

Throughout this book, the generic term 'the BA Service' is used to refer to any team, community, group, function or department where there are business analysts who offer business analysis services. This reflects the importance of viewing business analysis as an internal service that provides skills and knowledge and has the potential to support the organisation such that beneficial outcomes are realised. The nature and characteristics of the service approach are discussed further in Chapter 2.

Table 1.1 Titles for business analysis teams that are in frequent use

Name	Implications
BA Practice	Medium–large (20–100+) number of BAs. Usually identified within the organisation structure. There is likely to be a recognised head of BA practice in place, who is likely to have responsibility for all business analysts.
BA Profession (or Professional Group)	Medium–large (20–100+) number of BAs. Likely that professions/groups for other disciplines also exist (e.g. design, testing, etc.). May be identified within the organisation structure or may be represented within a matrix approach.
BA Team	Small (<20) number of BAs. Usually identified within the organisation structure and the BA team leader is likely to have responsibility for all business analysts.
BA Community (or Community of Practice)	Any size. Usually indicates a voluntary network within the organisation. Open to BAs and those carrying out business analysis. Leadership roles in relation to the practice may be on a voluntary basis.
BA Chapter	Any size. If an organisation is using an Agile delivery approach, it is likely that chapters for other disciplines also exist (e.g. design, testing, etc.).
BA Centre of Excellence	Small (<5) number of individuals responsible for BA standards and guidance. Identified within the organisation structure, but unlikely to have a leader with responsibility for all BAs.

THE COMMUNITY OF PRACTICE CONCEPT

The Community of Practice (CoP) concept has been defined as follows:

> Communities of Practice are groups of people who share a concern, a set of problems, or a passion about a topic, and who deepen their knowledge and expertise in this area by interacting on an ongoing basis.
>
> Wenger, McDermott and Snyder, 2002

The CoP concept is at the heart of the development of the BA Service. The essence of a CoP is that it enables individuals to engage in discussions and information exchanges that they find beneficial. This may operate within a specific governance structure where there is a centralised team, or may be a topic-specific group where individuals are able to share their knowledge and concerns from across different line management structures.

It is not necessarily the case that a CoP is formed within just one organisation. Some CoPs bring together individuals from different organisations, both large and small, and the CoP members may originate from various locations or disciplines. Whichever is the case, the key focus is the desire to develop a community that is able to share knowledge, ideas and concerns regarding a particular shared interest.

Many organisations have applied the CoP concept to develop internal CoPs and these are typically concerned with a specific discipline such as project management, software testing or business analysis. When an organisation sets up a business analysis CoP, it is usually because the organisation has recognised that there is a need to develop further understanding of the business analyst role and the part business analysts play in information systems and business change projects. The CoP tends to be led by an experienced business analysis manager – probably supported by other experienced business analysts – with the authority to establish the community and provide a business analysis service that will meet the organisation's needs.

Cross-organisational CoPs may also be formed because of the wish to share insights and experiences related to a particular area of interest. Sometimes, these may originate from legal entities such as charities or professional bodies; sometimes they may be set up because a small group of individuals believe there is a potential benefit to be gained from doing so. The cross-industry BA Manager Forum (www.bamanagerforum.org) is a good example of a CoP that originated when a small group identified the need for a networking forum for business analysts in leadership and managerial roles.

A CoP is not the same as an organised team that is focused on delivering service. While a CoP offers many benefits, these are not sufficient to deliver a BA Service that offers customers a relevant portfolio of services, defined activities and standards, and professional personnel who hold the required skills.

SITUATING THE BA SERVICE

Internal services, such as business analysis, payroll, procurement and internal audit, may be situated within the organisation structure as distinct functional areas or may be subsumed within other functions. For example, the payroll function may be the responsibility of the human resources (HR) or the finance functional area. However, many of these internal services are well understood and, as a result, are relatively easy to place within the organisational structure.

The BA Service does not benefit from this clarity and, as a result, many different governance structures are found within organisations.

The range of BA Service structures

The line management structure within an organisation for the BA Service has been a topic of ongoing debate for many years, if not decades. This debate has taken place within both the wider business analysis community and individual organisations. The 'to centralise or decentralise' decision seems to be considered in most organisations – typically, every 2–3 years. Where a centralised BA Service is established, the pendulum often swings toward decentralisation within a few years. Conversely, where a decentralised model has been applied and business analysts are established within individual business areas, the decision is then made to build a centralised team.

The major reason for changing a centralised team to one that is decentralised, or vice versa, tends to depend upon the advantages and disadvantages that are perceived for each of these models. These are summarised in Table 1.2. There are several possible reporting lines for a BA Service that is based within a centralised function. For example:

- **within an IT division:** where the primary focus is on the development, delivery and maintenance of software, and the management of the technical infrastructure;
- **within a transformational change function:** where the primary focus is on the definition, delivery and deployment of business change programmes.

Where a BA Service is decentralised, the business analysts are based within operational business areas, either in teams or as individuals. The business analysts provide services specific to the particular domain and they are likely to be highly knowledgeable about the work conducted.

These three structures offer certain advantages and disadvantages, as shown in Table 1.3.

Table 1.2 Centralisation vs. decentralisation of business analysis teams

Centralised BA team	Decentralised BA teams
Advantages	**Advantages**
• Strong basis for role clarity	• Continuous access to business stakeholders enables development of working relationships
• Clearly identified line management with responsibility for business analysis work	
• Seniority of the BA leader enables access to senior stakeholders	• Business analysts embedded within the business domain, resulting in improved domain knowledge and understanding
• Clear governance of the community of business analysts and their work processes	
• Unique definition of standards	• Business analysis standards, tools and work processes more easily adapted to the requirements of the business domain
• Consistency of business analysis approaches and tool usage	
• Ease of communication across the business analysis community	• Business analysts have greater buy-in and awareness of the business domain objectives
• Community of Practice 'team spirit'	
• Regular opportunities for knowledge sharing with business analyst colleagues about new innovations and trends	
• Increased opportunity for business analysis career pathway	

(Continued)

Table 1.2 (Continued)

Centralised BA team	Decentralised BA teams
Disadvantages	**Disadvantages**
• Limits opportunities to build relationships with business stakeholders	• Weak basis for role clarity; increased chance of role ambiguity
• Reduced access to business domain, resulting in less domain knowledge and understanding	• Tendency for inconsistency through the application of numerous business analysis standards, tools and work processes
• Business analysts removed from the objectives of the business domain	• Lack of overarching business analysis governance
• Perceived 'management overhead' and increased costs	• Reduced access to senior stakeholders
	• Difficulties in building Community of Practice 'team spirit'
	• Limited opportunities for knowledge sharing with business analyst colleagues about new innovations and trends
	• Business analysts become subject matter experts (SMEs) and may lose business analysis skills

While these structures may apply as the sole organisation structure for the BA Service within an organisation, in large organisations combinations may be applied. This could result in the following structures:

- **Hub and spoke:** a centralised team that sets standards and offers community leadership coupled with decentralised teams located within individual business areas.
- **Specialised:** two or more specialist business analysis teams, each of which is based in a different division or business area (for example, a technical BA team within IT, a business-focused BA team as a separate group within business change).
- **Federalised:** a loosely linked set of business analysis teams, each of which is based in a business area or IT team.

It is also possible that business analysis is not conducted by a specialist BA Service but carried out in a more ad hoc manner.

Organisations may also adopt different approaches to the governance and standardisation of business analysis work. For example, a centralised team may have a single reporting line for the business analysts and defined standards for the business

Table 1.3 Advantages and disadvantages of different organisational structures

Within IT function: centralised BA function	Within business change function: centralised BA function	Within business division: decentralised BA function
Advantages	**Advantages**	**Advantages**
• BAs have good knowledge of software development	• BAs have a holistic viewpoint regarding problems and opportunities	• BAs may have in-depth knowledge of the services offered by the business function
• BAs have close relationships with IT colleagues	• BAs have good understanding of business in general and also of the drivers for change	• BAs are able to develop working relationships with stakeholders from the business function
• BAs are able to develop and share specialist knowledge and skills	• BAs are able to develop and share specialist knowledge and skills	
• BA team operates as a centralised, specialist community that may facilitate links with other specialist BA communities	• BAs operate as a centralised, specialist community that may facilitate links with other specialist BA communities	
Disadvantages	**Disadvantages**	**Disadvantages**
• BAs may focus on technical rather than business solutions	• BAs may lack confidence or experience when proposing or defining IT solutions as part of a more holistic solution	• BAs may have fragmented approach to business analysis work
• BAs may be perceived as systems analysts rather than having a holistic focus	• BAs may lack understanding of the trends and possibilities from the use of automation	• BAs may have limited ability for knowledge sharing across the BA community
• BAs may have limited understanding of the business services offered by the organisation	• BAs may have limited understanding of the business services offered by the organisation	• BAs may become divorced from the wider business analysis community and may lose the opportunity to learn about trends and new developments

analysis work; a decentralised structure may consist of several dispersed teams with no formal coordination or governance, but there may be an informal business analyst community.

Therefore, the way in which business analysts are deployed and managed within organisations varies considerably. These different approaches result in a variety of organisational structures where business analysis is delivered. Example structures are shown in Figure 1.2.

Figure 1.2 Example organisational structures for the BA Service

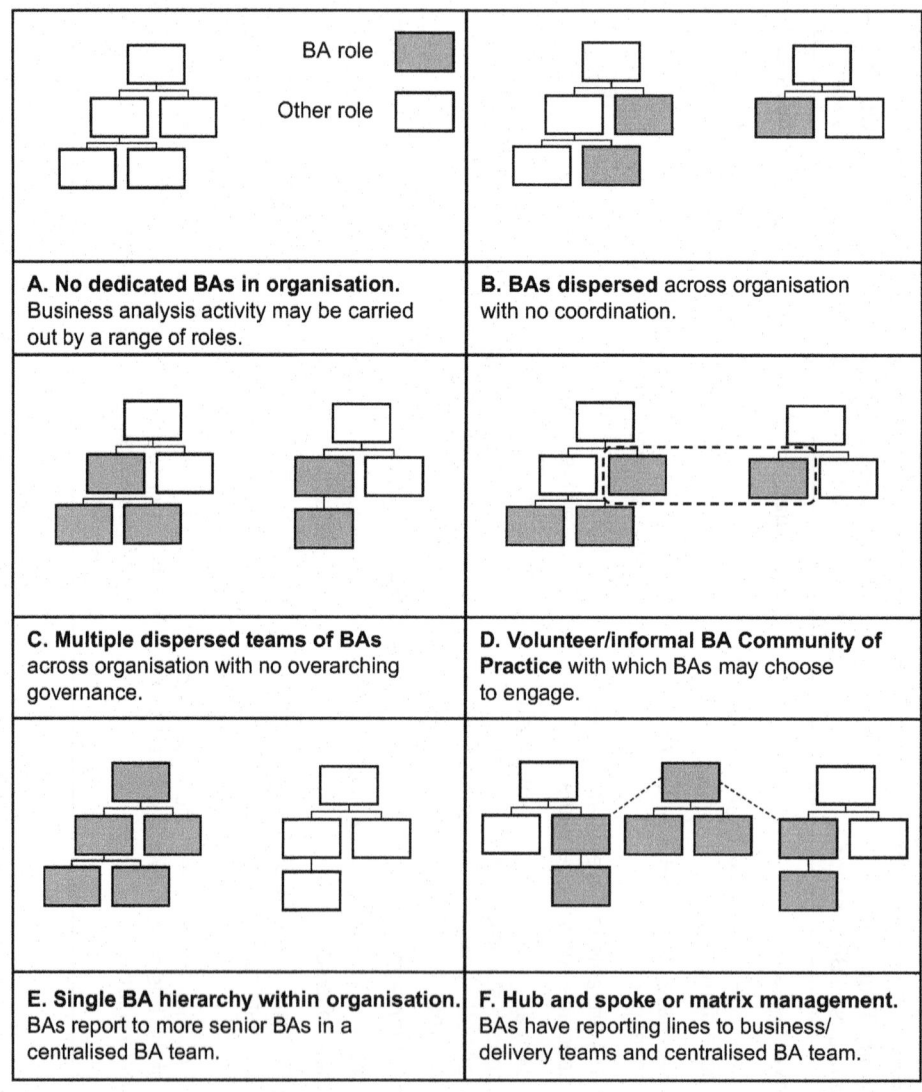

A. No dedicated BAs in organisation. Business analysis activity may be carried out by a range of roles.

B. BAs dispersed across organisation with no coordination.

C. Multiple dispersed teams of BAs across organisation with no overarching governance.

D. Volunteer/informal BA Community of Practice with which BAs may choose to engage.

E. Single BA hierarchy within organisation. BAs report to more senior BAs in a centralised BA team.

F. Hub and spoke or matrix management. BAs have reporting lines to business/ delivery teams and centralised BA team.

Whatever the structure used for the BA Service, it is important that the business analysis work is organised so that it is conducted with efficiency and effectiveness. Any BA leader is responsible for ensuring that the business analysts are supported in their work and that this contributes to the success of the organisation. The structure applied may result in an overarching head of business analysis or there may be several senior business analysts, each leading a team. Whatever situation applies, the service offered by the business analysts needs to be clearly defined so that it offers a basis for the establishment and development of a BA Service that can focus on enabling organisational improvements.

THE ROLE OF THE BUSINESS ANALYST

The concept of a 'role' originates from roles defined within the theatrical world. Roles are defined through character descriptions and scripts, and the actors are provided with direction, enabling them to perform the roles successfully. A similar situation may be perceived within the business world. Individuals are allocated to defined roles and these individuals are advised of their responsibilities when performing the role and are expected to do this effectively. However, business 'actors' aren't usually given a script to follow – they are expected to understand what is required of them and behave accordingly. In some roles, there is significant clarity of definition – in particular about the required outcomes. For example, management accountants have specific areas of responsibility, so they will know what is expected from their role. Within the information systems (IS) industry, established roles such as the project manager or software developer have considerable clarity regarding their responsibilities and the desired outcomes from their work.

These roles have a longevity, with a strong basis in research and practical experience. However, for newer roles, clarity may be lacking and the responsibilities and outcomes unclear. The business analyst role is a good example of a role where these issues have arisen.

Role clarity and ambiguity

Role clarity has been defined as follows:

> The extent to which individuals clearly understand the duties, tasks, objectives and expectations of their work roles.
>
> Henderson, Stackman and Lindekilde, 2016

A clear role definition helps individuals to understand what they are required to do to when performing their role. Role ambiguity occurs where the information required to perform a job or task is not available. Unlike a scripted theatrical role, roles within a business context are often ill-defined, resulting in ambiguity regarding what work should be done and how that work should be executed. This means that the expectations required to drive the required role behaviour are poorly defined and work effectiveness is likely to decrease. Many role definitions do not offer the clarity that is needed to drive effective performance. This is particularly important for the business analyst role, as lack of clarity about roles has been identified as a factor that can risk the success of software development projects (Jiang and Klein, 1999).

The impacts that may arise from role clarity and role ambiguity are summarised in Figure 1.3.

Figure 1.3 The differences between role clarity and role ambiguity

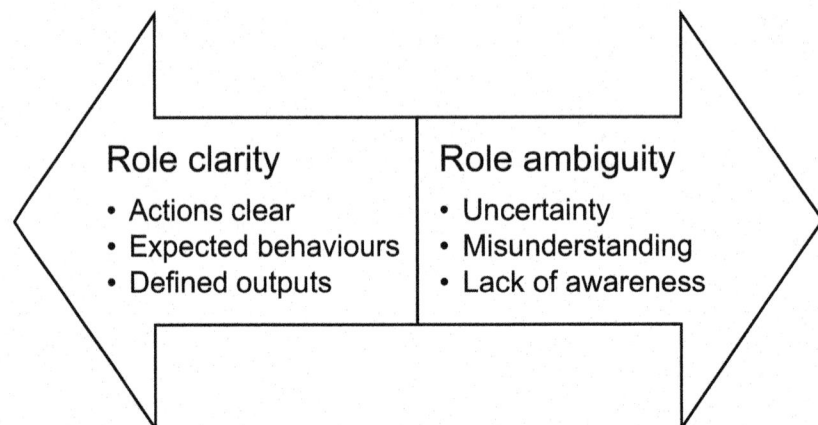

Research has shown that it is difficult to have role clarity when a role is complex and involves working within a complex team structure (Henderson, Stackman and Lindekilde, 2016). Given the variety and complexity of many IS roles, including the business analyst role, it is to be expected that difficulties arise when attempting to clarify them. However, the clear advantages of a well-defined role support the need for role clarity regarding business analysis.

The impacts on business analysis from role clarity and ambiguity are shown in Table 1.4.

Clarity of role definition also helps business actors to identify with a role and adopt the behaviours required of that role. Role identity occurs when an actor identifies with a role, wants to apply the expected behaviours and is motivated to perform the work of the role well. An actor may also identify with the community of actors responsible for the work of a role, and this sense of common cause can also improve performance and motivation. However, this requires agreement by individuals regarding the work conducted by the role and the behaviour adopted by the role participants.

Role consensus and conflict

Role consensus concerns the extent to which people agree on the behaviours associated with, and expected from, a role. Role conformity concerns the extent to which there is compliance with the expected behaviours. Where there is role clarity, there is a basis for role consensus and role conformity. This can also lead to something that is vital for the

Table 1.4 Comparison of role clarity and role ambiguity regarding business analysis

Role clarity	Role ambiguity
• Aligned expectations between business analysts and stakeholders	• Lack of understanding of the business analyst role
• Clear actions and behaviours when conducting business analysis work	• Misaligned expectations between what the business analyst believes should be done and what is required by stakeholders
• Defined business analysis outputs and deliverables	
• Appreciation for the contribution made by business analysts	• Limited awareness of business analysis and the contribution business analysts may make to change and IS projects
• Recognition of the importance of business analysis at an executive level	• Poor recognition of business analysis at an executive level

success of the BA Service – a sense of role identity. In other words, business analysts are confident about their place regarding business change initiatives and the relevance of the work that they do.

Both role consensus and role conformity are more likely to occur when an individual works within a team or project where the behaviour may be observed. This is enhanced when there is a designated authority within the team or project who has the power to impose penalties or issue performance reports if the observed behaviour is not as expected or required.

It is also important to achieve consensus about what the role entails between the role performers and the role beneficiaries or customers. Business analysis customers may operate at a number of levels within an organisation. They may be executives or managers who represent the needs of the organisation, or they may be the business staff who occupy operational roles and are required to utilise software or apply processes. Whatever the level or position of the customer, if someone is working with a business analyst there should be a mutual understanding of what the business analyst is expected to do. A lack of clear role definition can cause incongruence in mutual understanding and this may result in discrepancies where the customer party has a set of behavioural expectations from the role, but the role participant does not fulfil them. This is typically because neither party understands the other's expectations (see also Appendix 11).

Where actors have incompatible expectations regarding the behaviours to be demonstrated by role participants, this can lead to role conflict, which can contribute to performance and commitment issues within organisations. Role conflict and role ambiguity may increase tension when performing a role and can contribute to low levels of job satisfaction.

Role ambiguity and the BA Service

A further potential impact from role ambiguity or a lack of clarity is that it may affect the entire community of role performers – the 'role set'. Role performers who do not understand the role, or what is expected of them, risk diminishing the reputation of the entire community. Research (Paul, 2018) has shown that where a practitioner does not perform a particular role in line with the expectations of colleagues or stakeholders, there is a risk that the performance is deemed to be unsatisfactory. The perceptions of poor performance on the part of some role participants may contribute to perceptions of poor performance regarding the entire role set.

Unfortunately, a member of a role set perceived to offer limited or poor performance in the role can lead to the entire role being dismissed. Within the context of a business analysis team, a business analyst who does not understand what is expected and how to perform the required role is likely to cause stakeholders to dismiss the entire business analyst role. Comments such as 'we employed a business analyst on the project, but they didn't contribute a great deal' are typical. The paradox regarding the role set concept is that this does not work the other way around; that is, when a business analyst meets or exceeds expectations by delivering excellent results. The tendency here is for the stakeholders to compliment the individual and hold this person in high regard without recognising the actual role the individual is undertaking. This paradox is summed up in Figure 1.4.

Figure 1.4 The impact of performance on the role set

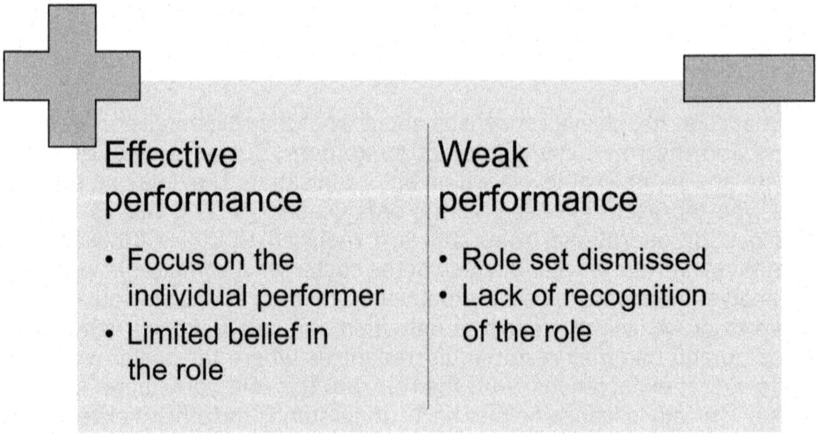

Effective performance	Weak performance
• Focus on the individual performer • Limited belief in the role	• Role set dismissed • Lack of recognition of the role

The problems of role ambiguity, lack of conformance and poor performance can apply to a particular role set both within an organisation and more widely across different companies. Therefore, a lack of role clarity regarding business analysis will result in a lack of recognition of the contribution business analysts may offer. The relationship between role clarity and role recognition is summed up in Figure 1.5, showing that as the clarity of the role definition is improved, the recognition of the role within an organisation is likely to increase.

Figure 1.5 The relationship between role clarity and role recognition

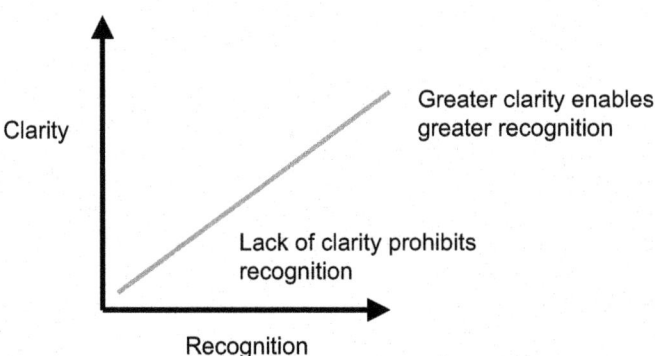

THE 3RD WAVE MODEL FOR BUSINESS ANALYSIS

The 3rd Wave model (Paul, 2013) offers an overview representation of the role of the business analyst. This model, shown in Figure 1.6, reflects the development of the role since its inception over three decades ago and highlights the overall service and value proposition offered by business analysts.

Figure 1.6 The 3rd Wave model for business analysis

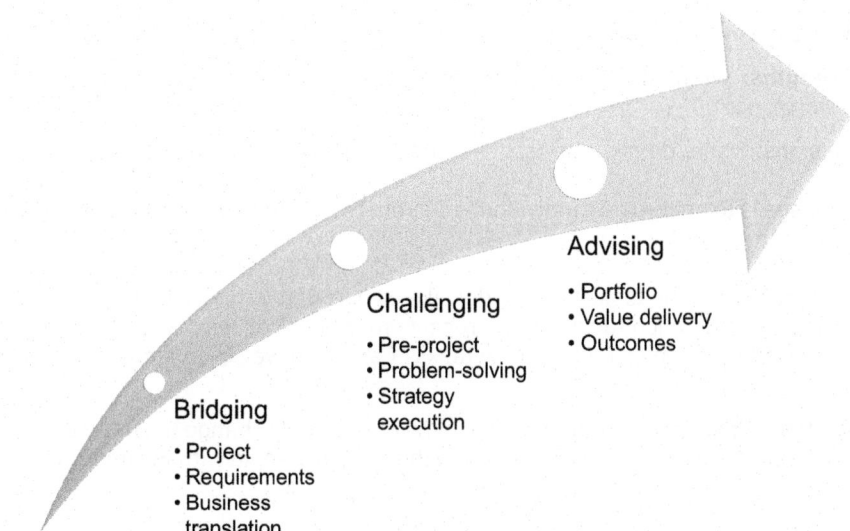

The 1st Wave of business analysis: bridging

The original view of business analysis was that a business analyst performed a bridging role, ensuring that business staff were able to articulate their needs for a new system.

The business analyst role was a development of the original systems analyst role, which was focused on the development of an IT system. The business analysis work began once a project had been clearly defined and scoped, so there was little room to extend or change the project. The primary focus when playing a bridging role was on translating business needs into defined requirements.

Over time, however, the role developed because business analysts identified that there was a problem with beginning the analysis activity after the project had been scoped and defined. This problem was reflected in an increasing recognition of the need to analyse situations prior to defining a project, to ensure that not only was the project undertaken in the right way but also that the 'right thing' was done.

The 'job crafting' concept

In 2010, *Harvard Business Review* (Wrzesniewski, Berg and Dutton, 2010) published an article about the concept of 'job crafting' and the opportunities this offers to anyone who is in a role and feels 'stuck' because they cannot see a means of moving elsewhere. Job crafting refers to the ability of individuals to develop their roles instead of moving to another role or organisation. People tend to do this when they have identified dissatisfaction with the job they perform and wish to identify how they might improve their jobs and increase their job satisfaction. While not termed 'job crafting', this approach was adopted by business analysts working during the era of the 3rd Wave when many began to be dissatisfied by the limitations of the role and sought additional responsibility.

An individual seeking to apply job crafting begins by considering three personal aspects:

1. **Motives:** why am I performing this role and what am I seeking to achieve?
2. **Strengths:** what skills do I have that enable me to demonstrate effective performance?
3. **Passions:** where do my interests lie that keep me engaged and committed?

The next stage is to analyse the individual's current role by thinking about another three elements:

1. **Tasks:** what are the tasks that I undertake as part of my role? Which tasks take up most time and which tasks should receive more time or less time? Can I change the tasks I perform or take on new tasks? Can I remove some tasks from my job role?
2. **Relationships:** who do I interact with in my role? Could I change the nature of these interactions or interact with others? Are there some people with whom I could stop interacting?
3. **Perceptions:** can I reframe my role so that it has a different focus? Can I influence others to perceive my role differently?

Job crafting is particularly relevant to business analysis, as the role has such a broad landscape and must adapt to a wide range of situations. The 'job crafting' concept has been applied successfully by some business analysts to develop their role and contribute more successfully to their organisations.

The 2nd Wave of business analysis: challenging

The need to apply 'job crafting' to business analysis grew from dissatisfaction with the initial 'bridging' role. Many business analysts identified that they should be involved at an earlier stage in a change initiative if that initiative was to have a strong basis for further work.

The 2nd Wave of business analysis moved the role to one where challenge was at the heart of the work. This didn't mean that business analysts blocked change but that they questioned assumptions and a hasty focus on solutions. The business analysts were concerned with investigating business situations to uncover the root causes of problems and thereby ensure that the fundamental problems were addressed, rather than just the manifest symptoms.

This 'early engagement' business analysis work developed using a job crafting approach. It focused on ensuring that projects were initiated from a firm basis. In some circumstances, this meant that a project was not set up at all when business analysts identified that a proposed change was unfeasible, would not deliver the proposed benefits or would not meet the business need.

The 3rd Wave of business analysis: advising

The development of business analysis standards, and confidence amongst some business analysts that they had a unique set of skills to contribute, ensured that the business analyst role developed further. This resulted in the '3rd Wave', where a business analyst would advise senior stakeholders and prioritise analysis activity across a change portfolio.

The three waves of business analysis reflect standard practice but are necessarily defined at an outline level. Describing a business analyst as an 'advisor' – or stating that business analysts perform a 'bridging' role – does not help resolve the role clarity issue defined earlier in this chapter. Each wave states the overall intent rather than the business analysis service or value proposition. This is because the 3rd Wave model reflects what business analysts say about their work to other business analysts.

While the model helps to achieve clarity, it does not specify the service offered by business analysts and does not enable understanding amongst stakeholders beyond the business analysis community. A service view of business analysis has the potential to address the role ambiguity issue by clarifying the following elements:

- the value proposition for business analysis (why the BA Service exists);
- the service portfolio offered by the business analysis function (what the BA Service does);
- the standards applied by business analysts (how the BA Service conducts the business analysis work).

This clarification is provided in Chapter 2 through the definition of the Business Analysis Service Framework (BASF). The BASF also provides a basis for defining services, activities and value propositions in line with organisational standards. This may result in tailored services that utilise the methods and tools employed within an organisation. Similarly, the services provide a basis for creating a business analyst role definition or, where applicable, role definitions for specialist business analyst roles.

CHALLENGES FACING THE BA SERVICE

Research carried out by the BA Manager Forum (www.bamanagerforum.org) in 2018 highlights some of the challenges facing the BA Service. The results showed consensus emerging in some areas, with many BA leaders identifying that their organisations could be operating the BA Service in a more effective way. Areas surveyed were:

- the governance and reporting lines for business analysts;
- the reporting line for leaders of a BA Service;
- the size of the BA Service within organisations;
- the job titles held by leaders of a BA Service;
- the level of demand for business analysts and the extent of additional capacity required;
- the BA Service structure.

The infographic shown in Figure 1.7 summarises the information gained from this survey and identifies the issues raised.

CONCLUSION

There are many contexts in which business analysis can support organisations as represented in the 3rd Wave model discussed in this chapter. However, without a central definition of the role, the potential for role ambiguity is extremely high. Issues with role ambiguity can result in a reduced sense of role identity amongst practitioners and increases the likelihood that there will be limited recognition of a role by fellow professionals and a lack of awareness of the benefits the role can offer. This has the potential to limit the extent to which a BA Service is able to support an organisation, so needs to be addressed by BA leaders at an early stage in the development of their teams.

A relevant, understandable definition of business analysis and the business analyst role will support engagement with project and business stakeholders. A service view can provide a strong basis for defining a role so the adoption of a service approach to business analysis, and the establishment of a BA Service, can improve the recognition and engagement of business analysis within organisations. Chapter 2 describes the Business Analysis Service Framework, which is intended to offer a basis for clarifying the business analyst role. The rest of this book then explores how a BA leader may develop a BA Service and describes the areas that need to be addressed in order for this to be done.

Figure 1.7 Infographic of BA Manager Forum research conducted in 2018

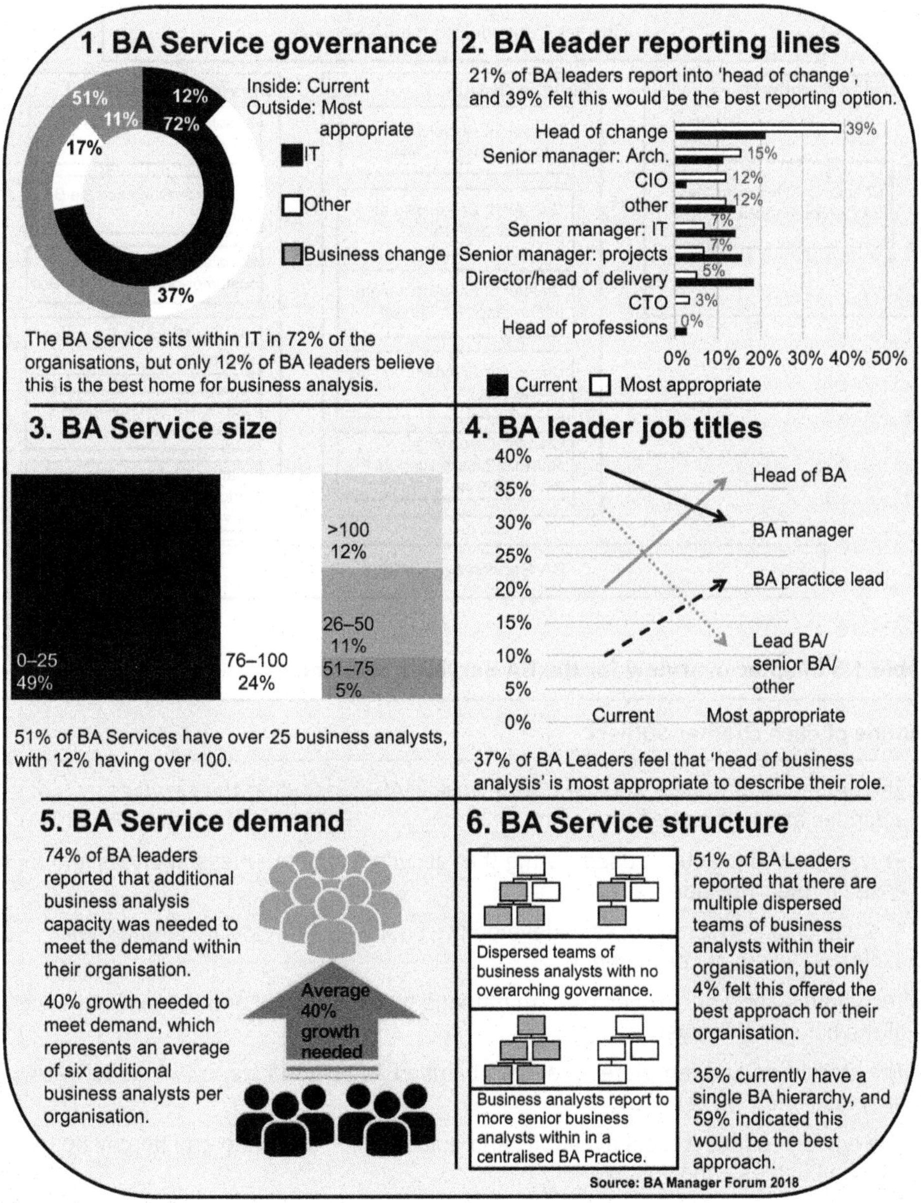

1. BA Service governance

51% 12%
11% 72%
17%

37%

Inside: Current
Outside: Most
appropriate

■ IT

□ Other

▨ Business change

The BA Service sits within IT in 72% of the organisations, but only 12% of BA leaders believe this is the best home for business analysis.

2. BA leader reporting lines

21% of BA leaders report into 'head of change', and 39% felt this would be the best reporting option.

Head of change — 39%
Senior manager: Arch. — 15%
CIO — 12%
other — 12%
Senior manager: IT — 7%
Senior manager: projects — 7%
Director/head of delivery — 5%
CTO — 3%
Head of professions — 0%

0% 10% 20% 30% 40% 50%

■ Current □ Most appropriate

3. BA Service size

>100
12%

26–50
11%
51–75
5%

0–25
49%

76–100
24%

51% of BA Services have over 25 business analysts, with 12% having over 100.

4. BA leader job titles

40%
35%
30%
25%
20%
15%
10%
5%
0%

Current   Most appropriate

Head of BA

BA manager

BA practice lead

Lead BA/
senior BA/
other

37% of BA Leaders feel that 'head of business analysis' is most appropriate to describe their role.

5. BA Service demand

74% of BA leaders reported that additional business analysis capacity was needed to meet the demand within their organisation.

40% growth needed to meet demand, which represents an average of six additional business analysts per organisation.

Average
40%
growth
needed

6. BA Service structure

51% of BA Leaders reported that there are multiple dispersed teams of business analysts within their organisation, but only 4% felt this offered the best approach for their organisation.

Dispersed teams of business analysts with no overarching governance.

35% currently have a single BA hierarchy, and 59% indicated this would be the best approach.

Business analysts report to more senior business analysts within in a centralised BA Practice.

Source: BA Manager Forum 2018

The remaining chapters, and the topics they cover, are shown in Figure 1.8 and described in outline in Table 1.5.

Figure 1.8 Structure of this book

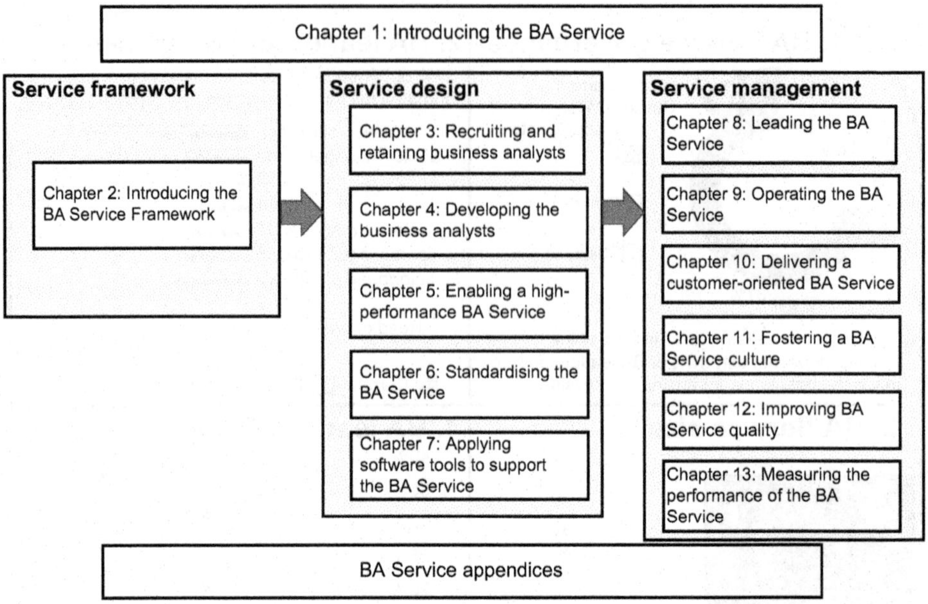

Table 1.5 Chapter overview for the BA Service handbook

Outline of each chapter subject

2: The definition of the BA Service Framework (BASF) including the services, activities and techniques.

3: Processes and practices used during the recruitment of business analysts and to assist in their retention.

4: The use of skills frameworks to develop the business analysts, including their skills and levels of competency.

5: Techniques and approaches used to manage the BA Service and the performance of the business analysts.

6: The standards and templates that may be used to aid consistency when delivering business analysis services.

7: The types of support tools available, and guidance for selecting and deploying tools used in business analysis work.

8: Guidance for BA leaders on approaches and techniques that may be used when leading a BA Service.

9: Guidance for operating the BA Service, including managing demand for business analysis resources.

(Continued)

Table 1.5 (Continued)

Outline of each chapter subject

10: The different categories of business analyst customer and techniques to engage with customers.

11: A range of frameworks that may be used to analyse and embed a service culture within the BA Service.

12: A range of frameworks and standards used to embed quality performance within the BA Service.

13: Metrics and approaches that may be applied to measure the performance of the BA Service and identify areas for improvement.

Appendices: A range of example standards and templates used by the BA Service.

2 INTRODUCING THE BA SERVICE FRAMEWORK

INTRODUCTION

Business analysis is a very broad discipline, encompassing numerous frameworks and techniques, and supporting a wide variety of business situations. It is accurate to describe it as a 'portfolio' role; however, the breadth of the portfolio raises difficulties with defining the business analyst role clearly.

Chapter 1 explained the issues that may arise when the business analyst role is not clearly defined, such as a lack of role clarity on the part of stakeholders and a lack of role identity on the part of business analysts. Many people think analytically about business situations and problems, applying techniques such as impact, risk or option analysis in order to help reach workable solutions. Therefore, without a clear business analyst role definition, it can sometimes appear that anyone is able to perform business analysis.

A discussion held during the BA Manager Forum in November 2017 confirmed this impression, concluding that business analysis is at risk because 'anyone can wear the badge' and that sometimes those with 'the badge' perform business analysis without the required expertise. This is a theme that seems to have emerged within the business analysis community and has raised concerns because of the potential impact upon the reputation and recognition of the business analysis contribution to organisational success. Chapter 5 discusses some specific unhelpful behaviours that have been exhibited by business analysts.

Chapter 1 explained how poor performance by an individual can have a detrimental impact on the reputation of an entire discipline. While a lack of role clarity and identity are not the sole reasons for these behaviours, they do not help and on occasion may prove to be the root cause of the problems. Therefore, we need to define the business analyst role clearly if we are to build a role identity, ensure role clarity for customers, colleagues and other stakeholders, and address unacceptable behaviour and poor performance.

Regarding business analysis as a service, applying the principles of service science should provide this much-needed clarity. A service view offers a basis for clarifying the business analyst role through defining the service portfolio for business analysis, the value proposition for each service, and the activities and techniques required to conduct each service. It should also ensure that business analysts can share a common language that helps them to understand their relevance to business change and IT projects and to perform their work effectively.

This chapter explores a service view of business analysis and covers the following topics:

- the nature of service and service science;
- the 'value fallacy' and the need for value co-creation;
- the Business Analysis Service Framework.

THE NATURE OF SERVICE

The nature of service has been the subject of much research over the last few decades. An emerging area of academic theory on the matter concerns Service Science, Mathematics, Engineering and Design (abbreviated to Service Science). Research into this area has examined what is meant by the term 'service' and how this may be delivered to customers. A succinct definition of 'service' provided by Service Science researchers is:

the application of competences for the benefit of another.

Vargo and Akaka, 2009

This book explores several aspects of this definition within the context of business analysis, in particular:

- the competences, such as knowledge and skills, that are required of business analysts;
- the application of business analysis competences when conducting business analysis;
- the benefits that may be achieved from the delivery of business analysis services;
- the beneficiaries of business analysis services.

The rationale for a BA Service definition

Stakeholders who initiate or work on business change projects are highly likely to work with business analysts. However, the work that the business analysts are required to do can vary significantly. The problems associated with role clarity mean that issues can occur when there is not a clear understanding of what business analysts do and the contribution they can make to a proposed business change initiative. Issues that often arise when business analysis is not understood or recognised are as follows:

- A change initiative is set up without due consideration of the problem to be addressed and the feasibility of proposed actions. In such situations, business analysis is not undertaken or is only done in a limited way. For example, a change is requested and a project is set up without questioning whether or not the change offers the desired outcomes and if there are other options available. In other words, the focus is on doing the thing right, but not necessarily doing the right thing (to paraphrase Drucker[1]).

1   Drucker, P. Available from: www.bl.uk/people/peter-drucker

- Limitations are placed upon the ways in which business analysts conduct their work. For example, business analysts are asked to document requirements without being given any authority to apply their analytical skills, merely being required to record the requirements as they are described.

- Senior stakeholders focus too much on the implementation of software solutions. For example, a software product is selected without any business analysis and understanding of the business need.

- The project team also focuses on the IT solution without a recognition of the broader business context. For example, the assessment of the business readiness for the IT system is not conducted.

The history of IT is littered with examples of projects where the outcomes were not predicted or beneficial, and the issues listed above are typical reasons why this has occurred. All of these situations require business analysis if the risks of failure are to be overcome. However, the challenge faced by business analysts is to ensure that stakeholders understand what they can offer, so that a project is not initiated without their involvement.

A defined service portfolio, with stated value propositions, is helpful for both project stakeholders and the internal business analysis team. From a stakeholder perspective, it offers the opportunity for them to understand which business analysis services are available, how a particular service may be of benefit and, in overview, how the business analysis work would be performed. Within the business analysis community, it offers a basis for developing and establishing a professional business analysis community and effective service provision. Essentially, it provides a means of communicating why business analysis helps organisations and what business analysts can do.

The Business Analysis Service Framework

Empirical research conducted over a five-year period (Paul, 2018) identified that business analysts work on a variety of assignments and projects. The work may be conducted at an early stage in the business change life cycle, whereby the analysts investigate problems or potential opportunities to see if there is a need for a change programme or IS development project. Other assignments may be more specific such as to define the requirements for a particular change initiative or to improve specific processes.

The research culminated in the development of the Business Analysis Service Framework (BASF), which identified six services that may be offered by business analysts. These services, and associated objectives, are shown in Figure 2.1.

This framework is intended to provide a BA Service with a basis for defining the portfolio of services to be offered to an organisation.

THE NATURE OF VALUE

Service Science has clarified the nature of value – in particular, what is meant by the term 'value' and how 'value' is achieved. In the past, value has been said to be 'delivered',

Figure 2.1 The Business Analysis Service Framework (BASF)

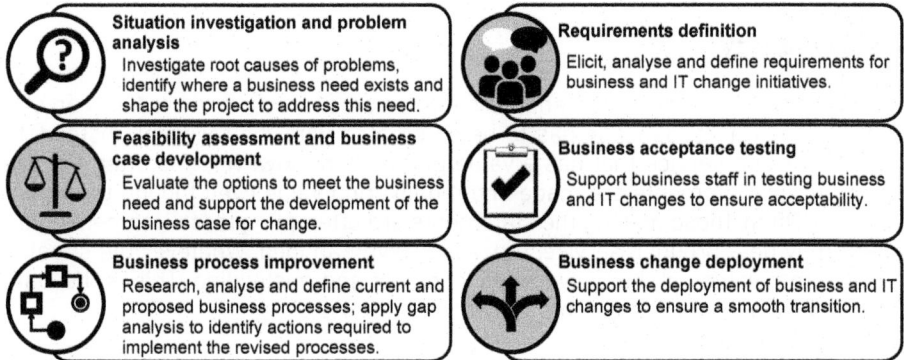

implying that value automatically results from the delivery of a product or service. This is contradicted by Service Science proponents who suggest that customers have to make use of what is delivered (whether in the form of purchased products or services) in order to realise value for themselves or their organisation.

This view challenges the assertions made regularly within the IT and business change industry that state that value may be delivered as a result of a product or service being delivered. Instead, Service Science suggests that tangible products are just the means through which a service is provided. This perspective states that value may only be realised if use is made of the products. For example:

* A person may purchase an expensive piece of equipment that has a very high specification but only realises value from this purchase if the item is used and the features exploited.

* A person may obtain tickets for a concert but only realises value by attending, and enjoying, the concert. If the person is given tickets to a concert that is of no interest, and so decides not to attend, the delivery of the tickets will generate no value whatsoever.

If this logic is applied to business analysis, the service deliverables offered by business analysis work may be seen as a means of supporting customers and enabling them to realise a valuable outcome. Although business analysis is needed as a basis for value realisation, the business analysis activities and deliverables do not, in themselves, deliver value. Where business process changes or requirements for a new IT system are analysed and documented, there is an opportunity for value to result but this is only where the defined process changes and requirements are exploited through being implemented. The business analysis artefacts are only valuable to the extent that they are used to achieve outcomes that may enable the realisation of value.

A further aspect of this logic concerns the involvement of a customer in deciding what product or service is required and which features it should offer. If a product or service is delivered to a customer but is not what is required, the prospects for realising value are very slim.

The delivery of value has been contrasted with the offering of a value proposition (Lusch and Nambisan, 2015), and it has been suggested that it is not possible for organisations to deliver value – rather, that they are limited to offering a value proposition.

The value fallacy

No entity, whether an enterprise, an internal function or a software product, can state that it 'delivers value', as value has to be co-created with the recipient; instead, the entity can provide service that has a value proposition. However, it is often the case that inaccurate statements are made about delivering value even though this cannot be justified. Often, those making the statements are attempting to 'sell' something and the item may be a product, service, process or even an idea. Whatever the situation, a promise that value will be delivered is incorrect and misleading. This is the 'value fallacy' and includes the statements shown in Figure 2.2.

Figure 2.2 Comments on value delivery – the value fallacy

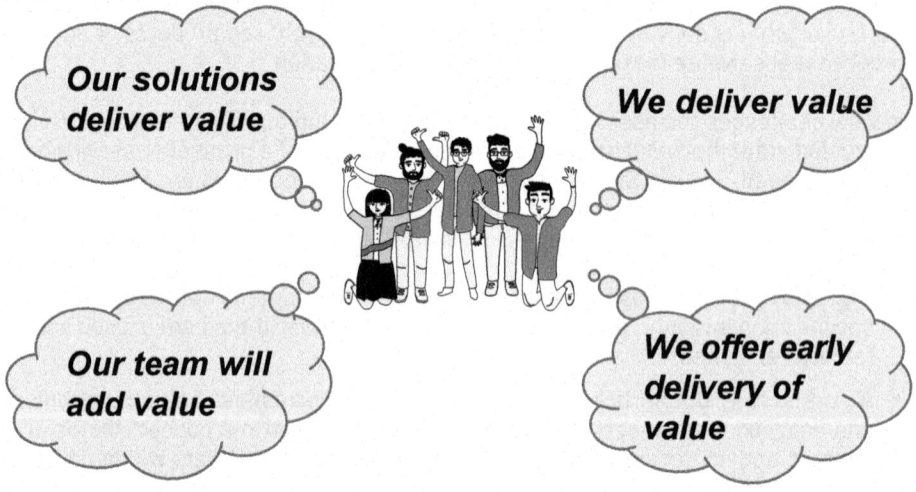

Statements such as those shown in Figure 2.2 are often used within business and IS change projects. A typical example concerns the frequent assertions that the application of Agile will deliver value. Another example is the claim that the delivery of software will result in the delivery of value. Both are promises that cannot be guaranteed and they risk raising customer expectations that will not be met. Such statements also have implications for business analysis because the focus is placed on software delivery rather than the holistic work system that encompasses all elements of the POPIT™ model: People, Organisation, Processes, Information and Technology.

It is important to recognise and understand that value cannot be delivered but is realised from the use of a product or service. In other words, value is not realised by the receipt of goods or the delivery of a service but by the uses to which they are put. Within a business and IS change context, the delivery of software will not create value for an organisation. It is only when it is used and, through this use, enables improvements or savings, that benefits are realised.

Rather than assuming that value is delivered through the exchange of products or services (this is sometimes called **value-in-exchange**), it is more accurate and helpful to focus on the realisation of value through the use of the delivered products or services (known as **value-in-use**). Examples abound of software products that have been developed or purchased, often at significant expense, yet are used to only a limited degree, if at all. There is no justification for claiming that value has been delivered by these products.

Value co-creation

The realisation of value is achieved through a process of collaboration between those requiring the value and those delivering the service or product. This is known as 'value co-creation'. If this concept is applied to business analysis, it is possible to identify three phases of value co-creation. These are shown in Figure 2.3.

Figure 2.3 The business analyst and value realisation

These value co-creation phases are described in Table 2.1.

These three phases summarise the essence of the value proposition offered by the BA Service and the means of achieving value realisation for its customers.

The value proposition for the BA Service

Value propositions state the characteristics of the value that is offered to connect those offering a service with the possible beneficiaries. A defined value proposition offers clarity and sets an expectation for potential customers. It provides a basis for customers to understand how the business analysis service could be of benefit to them and, thereby, encourages engagement between a customer and a service provider. Engagement between a service supplier (for example, the BA Service) and a service customer (for example, an organisation and its stakeholders) is vital to co-create the value required from a service.

Table 2.1 Stages of business analysis collaboration

1. Collaborating to identify where value might be achieved	This business analysis work is concerned with services such as investigating problematic or opportunity-offering business situations and uncovering root causes of problems. Business analysts need to work collaboratively with business stakeholders to understand where action is needed to improve problem situations and grasp opportunities
2. Collaborating to develop a solution that offers value	This business analysis work is concerned with defining requirements at different levels of abstraction, from enterprise-wide to individual software features, and designing holistic solutions that address all aspects of the POPIT™ model. Business analysts should also be involved in solution development work, supporting business staff in ensuring that their requirements are fulfilled, challenging assumptions and received wisdom, and clarifying business rules
3. Collaborating to ensure that value is realised	This business analysis work is concerned with acceptance testing and deployment of business change solutions. Business analysts have to collaborate closely with their business and technical stakeholders to ensure a smooth transition and the usage of the new solution

Equally important is the clarification of the roles involved in value co-creation if misaligned expectations on the part of the stakeholders are to be avoided. This is a key issue for the BA Service as explained in Chapter 1. The lack of a clear definition of the business analyst role has the potential to create incompatible role expectations and to diminish the recognition of the BA Service and the important role business analysts can play in helping organisations to succeed in today's dynamic business and technological world.

Fundamentally, a value proposition is a statement of what is offered to customers by an organisation or service provider. There are several frameworks for creating a value proposition; two popular frameworks are discussed below.

A value proposition (VP) may be examined through the lens of several elements, as shown in Figure 2.4.

These elements are defined within a business analysis context in Table 2.2.

An alternative view of a value proposition is offered by Osterwalder and Pigneur (2010) who describe a value proposition using the attributes shown in Figure 2.5.

Figure 2.4 Attributes of a value proposition (Paul, Cadle and Yeates, 2014, reproduced with permission from AssistKD)

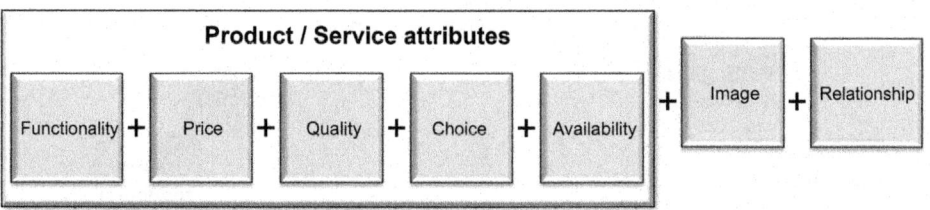

Table 2.2 Attributes of a BA Service value proposition (1)

VP attribute	Contribution to business analysis value proposition
Functionality	The business analysis services offered and why they are needed; the beneficial outcomes that result from business analysis
Price	The cost of business analysis services and why this is justified given the potential risks and costs of failing to conduct business analysis
Quality	The quality standards applied when conducting business analysis
Choice	The different levels of business analyst from entry to expert, and the corresponding levels of ambiguity and complexity that they are able to handle
Availability	The availability of business analysts to work on change projects
Image	The impact business analysis has on the reputation of the enterprise
Relationship	The impact business analysis services have on the relationship with internal and external customers

These elements are defined from a business analysis perspective within Table 2.3.

The two approaches to defining a value proposition offer different attributes. However, there is commonality between the two sets of attributes as reflected in Table 2.4.

If the attributes offered in Tables 2.2 and 2.3 are reviewed within the BA Service context, it is possible to identify how selected elements would provide the basis for an overarching value proposition statement. The statement may differ from organisation to organisation and these tables may be used to support the customisation of each value proposition.

Figure 2.5 Attributes of a value proposition (based on Osterwalder and Pigneur, 2010)

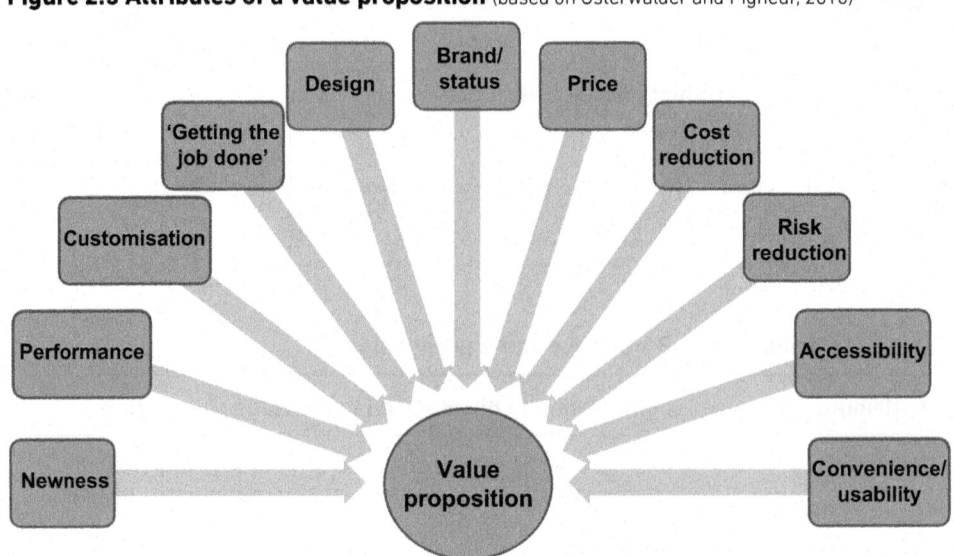

Table 2.3 Attributes of a BA Service value proposition (2)

VP attribute	Contribution to business analysis value proposition
Newness	The ability of business analysts to offer an objective and innovative perspective on a business situation
Performance	The business analysis services offered and why they are needed; the beneficial outcomes that result from business analysis. The level of quality and skill offered by business analysts
Customisation	The ability of business analysts to tailor their approach to the particular situation and to ensure that proposed options are also relevant to the context
'Getting the job done'	The skills offered by business analysts to ensure that business changes are holistic and enable an organisation to work effectively; the collaboration with stakeholders to ensure that the right things are done
Design	The improvements in product or service design that result from business analyst involvement
Brand/status	The impact business analysis has on the image presented by the enterprise and its change projects
Price	The reduction in the costs associated with business change/IT projects that result from business analysts being involved when relevant

(Continued)

Table 2.3 (Continued)

VP attribute	Contribution to business analysis value proposition
Cost reduction	The avoided or decreased costs resulting from business analysis work
Risk reduction	The avoided or mitigated risks resulting from business analysis work
Accessibility	The improved level of accessibility to products and services that result from business analysis work
Convenience/usability	The improved levels of convenience and usability that result from business analysis work

Table 2.4 Commonalities of the two sets of VP attributes

Paul et al. attribute	Osterwalder and Pigneur attribute	Aspects of the value proposition of a product or service
Functionality	Accessibility	The features offered
	Convenience/usability	
Price	Price	The expenditure concerns
	Cost reduction	
	Risk reduction	
Quality	Performance	The level of quality provided
Choice	Customisation	The extent to which options are available
Availability	'Getting the job done'	The support for achieving the desired outcome
Image	Newness	The impacts on the reputation of the purchaser
	Brand/status	
Relationship	Design	The stakeholder perceptions generated

An example value proposition for a BA Service could be defined as:

Collaborating with business stakeholders to define, develop and deploy innovative, relevant and effective business change solutions in order to co-create beneficial outcomes that result in business value.

While a value proposition for business analysis may be helpful as an overview, the portfolio offered by the BA Service necessitates the identification of value propositions for each service within that portfolio. This offers a further dimension to the BA Service and clarifies the value each service within the BASF offers organisations.

Table 2.5 states the value propositions for each of the business analysis services within the BASF.

Table 2.5 Value propositions for each of the BASF services

Service	Value proposition
Situation investigation and problem analysis	State a clear definition of the problem to be addressed and the business needs to be met. Define the scope of the work to achieve this. Where a project is relevant, in outline, clarify the investment objectives and business benefits to be achieved by the project
Feasibility assessment and business case development	Define the rationale for a proposed business change, generate, describe and evaluate the options to achieve the business requirements, and quantify and/or describe the investment objectives and predicted business benefits
Business process improvement	Define the required enabling changes through describing and redesigning business processes, and identifying the actions to be undertaken to deploy the improved processes
Requirements definition	Define the required enabling changes through eliciting, analysing, describing and managing requirements for business and IT changes at the level of detail relevant to the context
Business acceptance testing	Collaborate with stakeholders to support business acceptance of the solution
Business change deployment	Collaborate with stakeholders to support the deployment of the required business changes and enable their adoption
Stakeholder engagement	Support the achievement of business and IS project success through stakeholder collaboration, communication and effective stakeholder relationship management

APPLYING THE BASF

Each service within the BASF sets out 'what' a BA Service may offer its customers. This needs to be supplemented by a definition of 'how' the work to deliver the services may be conducted. The BASF has been defined in terms of the activities required to carry out the service and the technique categories that should be considered.

The BASF activities

The BASF activities are defined at a sufficiently generic level such that they may be adapted or customised for an internal BA Service Catalogue. The extent to which each activity is conducted, and the team structure adopted when carrying out an activity, requires further definition. This is in recognition of the range of business analyst contexts and the different approaches and frameworks applied on IS and business change projects.

The widespread application of Agile software development, and the extension of some of the concepts, principles and techniques such that they are applied to holistic business change projects, sometimes manifests itself in a dismissal of analytical work. For example, requirements definition is sometimes dismissed as inappropriate when business analysts are working within an Agile development environment. However, experienced analysts recognise the importance of ensuring that a project is doing the right thing as well as doing the thing right. Too often, they encounter situations where the focus is on delivering something even if this runs the risk of being costly and inappropriate. These business analysts recognise the need to understand the requirements and appreciate that the level will vary according to the context. Sometimes, just the general business requirements need to be defined before proceeding to an evolutionary solution development process. On other occasions, precision may be essential as specific functional and non-functional requirements need to be defined, using a combination of narrative and diagrammatic documentation. Business analysis within an Agile context is described in depth in the BCS publication, *Agile and Business Analysis* (Girvan and Paul, 2017).

Table 2.6 sets out each service and the activities that may be conducted during the provision of the service. The varying nature of organisations and business situations requires business analysts to use their experience and judgement when deciding on the exact approach to be adopted. Essentially, the focus needs to be on undertaking the service activities that will achieve the desired outcomes for the organisation. The exact activities will depend on a combination of factors, including organisational standards, industry trends, the expertise of the business analysts and the characteristics of the situation.

Table 2.6 BA service portfolio and activities

Service name	Service activities
  Situation investigation and problem analysis	1. Investigate the situation and the problem or opportunity 2. Understand the strategic context for the situation 3. Identify and articulate the business needs 4. Define the problem 5. Define the scope of the business and IS project 6. Define the rationale for rejecting a project proposal

(Continued)

31

Table 2.6 (Continued)

Service name	Service activities
 Feasibility assessment and business case development	1. Generate and describe options to resolve the problem 2. Remove unviable options 3. Identify and analyse impacts and risks for each option and what may be done about them 4. Identify and analyse costs and benefits for each option 5. Evaluate financial, technical and business feasibility of options 6. Evaluate alignment of options with strategic goals 7. Support comparison and selection of solution
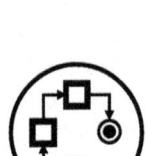 Business process improvement	1. Model existing processes 2. Define required (new or revised) processes 3. Identify gaps between existing ('as is') and required ('to be') processes 4. Analyse gaps between existing and required processes 5. Identify and analyse business process measures 6. Identify actions to implement new processes 7. Ensure alignment between IT systems and processes
 Requirements definition	1. Define requirements definition approach and quality standards 2. Elicit and interpret the requirements 3. Record requirements 4. Build models and prototypes to represent the requirements 5. Collaborate and communicate with internal stakeholders in the business and IT functions, and external stakeholders to clarify requirements 6. Analyse, prioritise and assure the quality of the defined requirements 7. Support stakeholder review of requirements 8. Conduct user analysis and profiling 9. Ensure that requirements are aligned with project scope and strategic business goals 10. Establish traceability of requirements from the business need to the solution

(Continued)

Table 2.6 (Continued)

Service name	Service activities
 Business acceptance testing	1. Agree scope for testing activity 2. Define test scenarios and test cases 3. Provide support to stakeholders when testing for business acceptance
 Business change and IT deployment	1. Assess business readiness 2. Support transition planning 3. Support the adoption of the IT and business changes 4. Develop and deliver training in the new IT and business systems 5. Support the benefits and post-implementation reviews 6. Support the realisation of the business benefits

The business analysis research used to create the BASF also identified an auxiliary service that cuts across each of the BASF services and focuses on working effectively with stakeholders. The importance of a customer orientation for the BA Service is discussed in Chapter 10.

The activities required to engage with stakeholders are defined in Table 2.7. These activities reflect the need to engage effectively with stakeholders.

The nature of stakeholder engagement is often misinterpreted as a need to build amicable relationships. However, given that the value proposition for business analysis is concerned with supporting organisational success, stakeholder engagement requires a facilitative approach that may also involve challenging and negotiating. These different aspects are reflected in the list of activities.

Stakeholder engagement has been defined as a separate service because the activities may be performed to support any of the primary six services. However, in some organisations a service may be offered that focuses on a particular stakeholder engagement service. A typical example concerns facilitation, which is sometimes viewed as a particular service that may be applied to workshops, meetings, forums and focus groups.

The BASF technique categories

Business analysis is a highly skilled discipline and has the potential to contribute to business and IT projects. The context for business analysis work is varied and often

Table 2.7 Auxiliary BASF service and the activities conducted

Service name	Service activities
 Stakeholder engagement	• Challenge and inform stakeholders • Negotiate stakeholder conflicts • Engage with stakeholders • Communicate with stakeholders verbally and in writing • Support stakeholders • Facilitate meetings and workshops and record outputs

ambiguous. Therefore, it is rarely the case that the same approach can be applied to all business analysis work so the professional business analyst has to possess a range of skills. These skills often involve the use of specific business analysis techniques, which are standard ways of working that help in the conduct of an activity.

The 'T-shaped Professional' framework provides a basis for identifying the broad range of skills required of business analysts and is discussed in Chapter 4. Each business analysis service requires a business analyst to carry out several activities, each of which may be enabled by the application of techniques. However, the techniques that are helpful will differ according to the specific context. There are numerous techniques available to the business analyst; the BCS publication *Business Analysis Techniques* (Cadle, Paul and Turner, 2014) lists 99 techniques and the toolkit seems to expand daily.

Given the number and variety of techniques within the business analysis toolkit, the BASF describes technique *categories* rather than listing each individual technique. Table 2.8 sets out the technique categories that are used frequently by business analysts and were identified during the research conducted into business analysis. The BCS *Business Analysis Techniques* publication provides additional information about the application of these techniques and also suggests additional techniques that are useful to business analysts.

There are numerous techniques that apply to each technique category and several categories may be relevant to an individual service. The technique categories that are most relevant to each business analysis service are shown in Table 2.9.

Each of the techniques results in the creation of a deliverable or contributes towards this. Some of the deliverables are intrinsically linked to the technique. For example, data modelling results in the production of a data model. Others are likely to contribute to a variety of deliverables and the exact nature will depend upon the situation and the standards applied in the organisation. For example, the use of a facilitated workshop to investigate a situation may result in the production of a range of deliverables, including a mind map, business process model, rich picture and use case diagram. Chapter 6 discusses the different standards and templates that may be applied to business analysis work.

Table 2.8 BASF technique categories and techniques

Technique category	Description
Agile development	**Objectives:** To apply Agile principles to a software development project; to govern the work of an Agile software development project
	Explanation: Agile software development projects adopt techniques and ceremonies that align with the Agile philosophy and principles. There are established techniques that are used to apply Agile effectively
	Techniques: Product/solution backlog, Kanban Board, daily stand-up, retrospective, sprint/iteration
Business case development	**Objectives:** To identify, define and evaluate options for business change; to ensure that there is a financial case for a proposed change
	Explanation: Business case development techniques are concerned with the analysis of options to address business problems or realise business opportunities. This is necessary to ensure that an organisation is going to invest financial and other resources in viable projects. These techniques consider four aspects relevant to options: the costs, benefits, impacts on the organisation, and risks. They also examine the likely business acceptance of an option
	Techniques: Cost/benefit analysis, investment appraisal, force-field analysis, risk analysis, benefits review, impact analysis, business impact assessment
Data modelling	**Objectives:** To represent the data required by an organisation or business area to support the delivery of services to customers (internal or external); to represent the business rules inherent in the structure of the data
	Explanation: Data models provide a view of an information system from a data perspective. They may be developed at different levels of granularity. For example, an information concept or domain view consisting of high-level areas or a detailed data model encompassing elements such as data groupings, relationships between the groupings, business rules and individual data items. There are two major modelling approaches used to represent data or information. These are entity relationship modelling and class modelling. While they represent similar concepts, there are differences in the ways those concepts are modelled and in some of the detail represented
	Techniques: Entity relationship diagram, class diagram, data definition, domain definition

(Continued)

35

Table 2.8 (Continued)

Technique category	Description
Environment analysis	**Objectives:** To analyse the external business environment over which the organisation has little, if any, control; to analyse the factors within the organisation that must be considered when deciding on the strategy to respond to external factors
	Explanation: Environment analysis techniques provide a rigorous basis for developing a strengths, weaknesses, opportunities, threats (SWOT) analysis. However, this may result in a large number of factors to be considered in each quadrant of the SWOT and a degree of prioritisation is often required. The strengths and weaknesses are the internal factors that will help to determine the strategic choices available to an organisation. The opportunities and threats are the external factors facing the organisation; these need to be distinguished from the strategic choices made on the basis of the SWOT
	Techniques: Political, Economic, Social, Technological, Legal, Environmental (PESTLE) analysis, Porter's 5-forces, SWOT analysis, Balanced Scorecard, critical success factor, key performance indicator
Gap analysis	**Objectives:** To examine a current and target state in order to determine where there are differences; to identify the actions required to move from a current or target state
	Explanation: Analysing the differences between current and target states might involve examining different representations of these states. For example, a popular approach is to compare 'as is' and 'to be' business process models; an alternative is to use a business activity model (BAM) as a conceptual view of a possible future state that may be compared with a representation or description of a current situation. Frameworks such as the POPIT™ model help to structure the gap analysis
	Techniques: Gap analysis, 'as is' and 'to be' comparison, BAM, POPIT™ model
Implementation	**Objectives:** To prepare affected business areas for the implementation of business changes; to deploy business changes successfully; to review the business change processes and outcomes
	Explanation: Implementation of business changes requires comprehensive planning and preparation. Typically, this includes consideration of areas such as communication, training, infrastructure set-up and data migration
	Techniques: Training needs analysis, training material development, Customer, Product, Process, Organisation, Location, Data, Applications, Technology (CPPOLDAT), post-implementation review

(Continued)

Table 2.8 (Continued)

Technique category	Description
Investigation	**Objectives:** To explore situations with the aim of uncovering issues, problems, opportunities and other relevant information; to clarify the root causes of problems
	Explanation: Investigation techniques are concerned with understanding a situation from a holistic standpoint. Information that may initially seem irrelevant – such as the climate of a business area or ad hoc comments – is gathered and noted in case it illuminates the root causes of problems or helps to identify opportunities for change. A variety of techniques are available to business analysts when investigating situations. Many of these techniques overlap with those used during requirements elicitation. However, the application, stakeholders and focus are different in line with the often-ambiguous and vague business situations that the business analysts encounter
	Techniques: Interview, workshop, survey, observation, focus group, document analysis, prototyping, wireframing
Problem definition	**Objectives:** To identify the root cause of a business problem that is to be addressed by the BA Service; to create a statement setting out a clear definition of the problem
	Explanation: Problems that are identified to require investigation and resolution are often found to be symptoms or manifestations of an underlying problem. Business analysts are required to investigate situations, challenge statements and take a holistic view in order to identify the root causes of problems and ensure that these are addressed
	Techniques: Rich picture, mind map, problem statement, Ishikawa (fishbone) diagram, five whys, context diagram, brainstorming/brainwriting, Post-it™ exercise
Process modelling	**Objectives:** To represent processing conducted by an organisation or business area to deliver services to customers (internal or external); to provide a diagrammatic view that is a basis for improving business processes
	Explanation: Process models provide a view of an information system from a process perspective. They may be developed at different levels of granularity. For example, an organisational view of the value chain consisting of high-level activities or a cross-functional diagram showing detailed elements such as process flows, actors, decisions and tasks. The fundamental aspects of process modelling techniques are very similar, as they show activities or tasks and the flows between them. However, the level of detail represented will differ depending upon the context, and the modelling notation is variable depending upon the standard adopted within an organisation or by the BA Service

(Continued)

Table 2.8 (Continued)

Technique category	Description
	Techniques: Business process model, swimlane diagram, Business Process Model and Notation (BPMN) diagram, business process map, decision modelling, value chain, activity diagram, event analysis
Requirements engineering	**Objectives:** To elicit tacit and explicit information from stakeholders regarding their requirements; to analyse this information with a view to understanding and recording why something is needed, what is needed, when it is required and who requires it
	Explanation: Different levels of requirements may be required for a project. For example, a senior executive may request a feature at an overview level of definition; this may need to be explored in further detail with operational business staff. Different techniques may be applied when recording requirements. These techniques record different aspects of the requirements and may be applied at different levels of detail
	Techniques: Requirements elicitation (see Investigation category), requirements analysis, prioritisation, traceability matrix, requirements catalogue, change control, version control
Stakeholder management	**Objectives:** To identify stakeholders with concerns relevant to a proposed business change; to analyse stakeholders' levels of power and interest, and their values, beliefs and priorities; to determine stakeholder communication and management approaches relevant to the situation
	Explanation: Stakeholder management techniques are an essential part of the business analysis toolkit because of the volume and range of stakeholders likely to be interested or affected by proposed business changes. These techniques help to ensure that stakeholders are not overlooked and that their concerns are understood, considered and addressed where possible
	Techniques: Customer, Actor, Transformation, Weltanschauung (or world view), Owner, Environment (CATWOE), root definition, worldview analysis, stakeholder wheel, stakeholder map, power/interest grid, social network analysis, Responsible, Accountable, Consulted, Informed (RACI)
System requirements specification	**Objectives:** To create a detailed specification of the requirements to be delivered by an information system; to provide a basis for the development of an information system

(Continued)

Table 2.8 (Continued)

Technique category	Description
	Explanation: Some systems development projects require detailed specification of the requirements and, in some organisations, business analysts may conduct or contribute to this work. For example, this may be for specific features or for non-functional requirements such as security and access. Techniques defined by the Unified Modelling Language (UML) are often used to provide a detailed level of specification
	Techniques: Sequence diagrams, state charts, Create, Read, Update, Delete (CRUD) matrix
User acceptance testing (UAT)	**Objectives:** To design and conduct test scenarios with a view to identifying where a product fails to meet the needs of the business user; to support the business user community in ensuring that a product is of a sufficient level of quality to be accepted for deployment
	Explanation: The confirmation that a product is acceptable is the responsibility of the business users. However, business analysts are often required to support the business users during user acceptance testing. This requires planning of the approach to the UAT and deciding the techniques and data that will be used during this process
	Techniques: User acceptance scenario, test case
User role modelling	**Objectives:** To explore the customer community, in particular the business user, to identify and clarify the requirements of a particular user role; to explore concerns specific to user roles with defined characteristics and needs
	Explanation: User role modelling helps to understand the perspectives, viewpoints and needs of different categories of customer
	Techniques: Use case diagram, scenario, user story, persona, user experience (UX) diagram, storyboard, empathy map, customer journey

THE BASF AND THE PORTFOLIO BUSINESS ANALYST

The BASF offers a definition of the portfolio to be offered by the BA Service and serves to clarify what business analysts do, the activities they perform and the techniques they might use to conduct business analysis work. This portfolio of services reflects the breadth of business analysis that has extended over the decades since it began to be recognised as a distinct discipline. This is reflected in the 3rd Wave model discussed in Chapter 1.

Much of the development of business analysis is due to a recognition, primarily within the business analysis community but increasingly by other related disciplines, that

Table 2.9 BASF services and technique categories

Technique category \ Service	Situation investigation and problem analysis	Feasibility assessment and business case development	Business process improvement	Requirements definition	Business acceptance testing	Business change deployment
Agile development				X	X	
Business case development		X				
Data modelling	X	X		X		
Environment analysis	X	X				
Gap analysis		X	X			
Implementation						X
Investigation	X		X	X		
Problem definition	X					
Process modelling			X	X		
Requirements engineering	X	X		X		
Stakeholder management	X	X	X	X	X	X
Systems requirements specification				X		
User acceptance testing					X	
User role modelling	X		X	X		X

some of the issues associated with the failure of IS projects may be avoided if analysis activity is conducted.

Particular examples include the following:

- a lack of analysis at an earlier stage in a project, resulting in a failure to identify the real problem to be addressed by the project;
- only limited evaluation of proposed solutions in order to assess the financial and business feasibility;
- a focus solely on the software product without considering the business environment into which it is to be delivered;
- a hasty move towards a 'solution' without consideration of the real problem to be addressed and whether there are other options.

However, it is not necessarily the case that all business analysis activity is effective. Where there is a lack of understanding of the business analyst role, there may be a failure to recognise the competences required to conduct business analysis effectively, which may result in assumptions that other professionals, for example, project managers or product owners, possess business analysis competences when, in practice, this is not the case. Where such assumptions are made, the analysis activity may be lacking and the opportunity to avoid the issues listed above may be lost.

The variety of situations where business analysis is beneficial crosses sectors, domains and business functions. The increasing awareness of the opportunities offered by a digital transformation perspective, for example to use technology and analytics to extend and personalise services offered to an organisation's customers, has also raised further recognition that business analysis is essential in today's complex business world. This combination of factors has resulted in business analysts specialising within specific business domains or industries and has raised questions about the possible fragmentation of the role.

The BASF offers an alternative approach to fragmentation by providing a basis for business analysts to review and plan their career paths on a service portfolio basis. It may be that an individual business analyst wishes to offer a personal portfolio comprising a sub-set of the business analysis services required by the organisation. For example, the requirements definition, business process improvement and business change deployment services.

A portfolio approach to a business analysis career will help business analysts to contextualise their experience and skills and direct their future career progression. It will also help to ensure that they can focus on the skills and techniques in which they need to be proficient if they are to offer the services within their portfolio.

THE BUSINESS CASE FOR THE BA SERVICE

The benefits offered by business analysis have to be clarified if a business case is to be made for the establishment of a BA Service within an organisation. While a value proposition sets out an intended beneficial outcome, it is sometimes necessary to examine the BA Service through a more detailed lens and set out a business case for its existence.

Two key components of a business case for the BA Service are as follows:

- the costs associated with running the BA Service;
- the benefits accrued from a BA Service.

These components are considered below.

Costs of a BA Service

The quantified costs associated with establishing and maintaining a BA Service will vary from one organisation to another. However, the areas of cost may be generalised across organisations. A helpful approach to determine these areas of cost is to consider a BAM for a BA Service; this is set out in Figure 2.6.

Figure 2.6 Business activity model for the BA Service

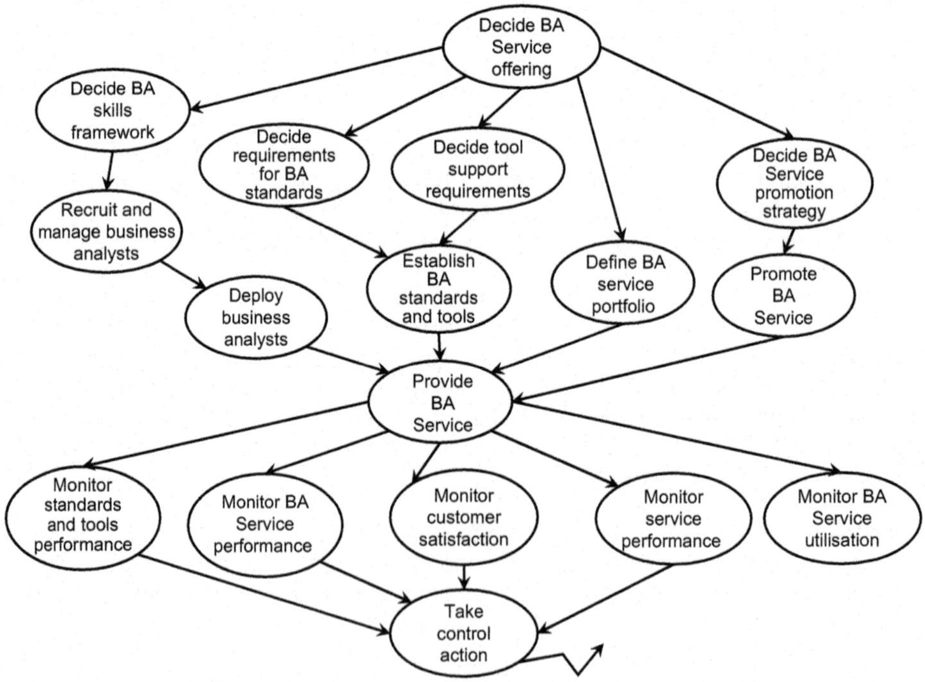

This model provides a basis for identifying the costs associated with establishing and maintaining a BA Service. Each business activity may be analysed to identify the elements that are required to establish the activity and the costs they will attract. For example, the activity 'Recruit and manage BAs' may require the definition and deployment of the following elements:

- policies and processes for recruitment, appraisal and performance review, performance management;

- BA job descriptions;

- training and mentoring in staff recruitment, appraisal and management.

Each of these elements may be analysed to identify the costs that will be incurred to establish this activity; for example, by estimating the effort required to develop the policies and processes identified.

This diagram also forms the basis for a gap analysis between this future view and the existing situation; this helps to identify the costs that would be incurred when setting up a BA Service. For example:

- Some activities may not be in place, so defining the elements required to establish those activities, and the costs of those elements, may be determined.

- Some activities may be partially in place because elements such as a skills framework or relevant support tools are already available and in use.

Comparing the current status of the BA Service with this BAM will help to identify the activities where costs will accrue and investment is required.

Benefits of a BA Service

Benefits from establishing a BA Service may be identified by looking at the four categories of benefit defined by Ward and Daniel (2012):

- **Observable benefits** that are not predicted in advance and may not be quantified financially. However, they may be observed following the introduction of the change. The observable benefits that may accrue from the introduction of a BA Service encompass:

  - improved consistency of approach;

  - increased clarity of service offering and value proposition;

  - improved clarity of the business analyst role resulting in greater coherence between stakeholder expectations and the business analysis work.

- **Measurable benefits** that may not be predicted in advance but may be quantified financially following the introduction of the change. The measurable benefits that may accrue from the introduction of a BA Service encompass:

  - reduced time to perform business analysis activities due to standardisation of approach and deliverables, and clear guidance on how to conduct the activities;

  - increased quality of business analyst deliverables, resulting in less rework, due to the introduction of a standardised approach to personal development and performance management.

- **Quantifiable benefits** that may be predicted in advance of a change but cannot be quantified financially. The quantifiable benefits that may accrue from the introduction of a BA Service encompass:

  - increased reputation for business analysts within an organisation;

  - improved definition of requirements for new products or systems;

  - easier adoption of new products or systems by business staff.

- **Financial benefits** that may be predicted and quantified in advance of the introduction of a change. The financial benefits that may accrue from the introduction of a BA Service encompass:

  - reduced spending on unproductive software products and change initiatives that will fail to address the root cause of a problematic situation (due to greater rigour in the investigation of change initiatives);

  - reduced costs associated with stakeholder involvement in change projects;

  - increased efficiency of business processes, resulting in lower costs of service or product delivery;

  - increased realisation of business benefits from a business change initiative.

An alternative way of considering the benefits from a BA Service is to evaluate the services offered by the business analysts in the light of the achievement of business benefits. The Benefits Dependency Network is a framework developed by Ward and Daniel that sets out the deliverables and dependencies that together lead towards the realisation of business benefits. The dimensions of the Benefits Dependency Network are:

- **Investment objectives:** what the business wishes to achieve from an information system investment.

- **Business benefits:** the positive advantage obtained by the organisation from an information system investment.

- **Business changes:** new ways of working adopted by the organisation.

- **Enabling changes:** one-off changes that provide a means of implementing the information system and business changes.

- **IT enablers:** the changes to the information systems and technology that are required to enact the enabling and business changes.

An overview of the Benefits Dependency Network is shown in Figure 2.7.

The contribution of the BA Service to the realisation of business benefits may be perceived by relating the portfolio of services to the elements shown in Figure 2.7. The relationships are as follows:

- Situation investigation and problem analysis: clarify the **investment objectives** and **business benefits** to be realised through providing a clear definition of the problem to be addressed, the business needs to be met and the scope of the project to achieve this.

Figure 2.7 Overview of the Benefits Dependency Network (after Ward and Daniel, 2012)

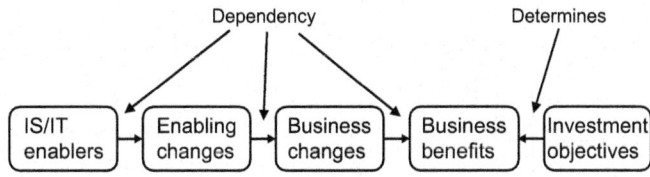

- Feasibility assessment and business case development: clarify the **investment objectives** and **business benefits** in further depth by defining the rationale for a proposed business change and generating, describing and evaluating the options.

- Business process improvement: define the required **enabling changes** through describing and redesigning business processes, and identifying actions required for their improvement.

- Requirements definition: define the required **enabling changes** and **IT enablers** through eliciting, analysing and describing requirements for business and IT changes.

- Business acceptance testing and business change deployment: clarify and enable the required **business changes, enabling changes** and **IT enablers** through collaborating with stakeholders to support business acceptance of the solution and enable its adoption.

Table 2.10 summarises the relationships between the dimensions of the Benefits Dependency Network and the business analysis services.

There are many benefits that may be realised from establishing a BA Service, both tangible and intangible. It is also possible to relate the business analysis services to the Benefits Dependency Network and thereby clarify how business analysis can support the realisation of business benefits predicted from a change initiative.

Table 2.10 The business analysis services and their relationship to the Benefits Dependency Network (adapted from Paul, 2018)

BASF services / Benefits Dependency Network	Situation investigation and problem analysis	Feasibility assessment and business case development	Business process improvement	Requirements definition	Business acceptance testing	Business change deployment
Investment objectives	X	X				
Business benefits	X	X				
Business changes			X		X	X
Enabling changes				X	X	X
IT enablers				X	X	X

CONCLUSION

The elements described in this chapter clarify the why, what and how of the BA Service, as follows:

- the value proposition for business analysis (why the BA Service exists);
- the service portfolio offered by the BA Service (what the BA Service does);
- the standards applied by business analysts (how the BA Service conducts the business analysis work).

The business analyst role is subject to ambiguity and this has previously led to a lack of role identity and role clarity. In turn, this has had an impact upon customer expectations from business analysis and has resulted in a lack of recognition of the value that may be offered by business analysts.

This chapter has described the BASF, which advocates a defined portfolio of services that the BA Service may offer to customers. This portfolio also clarifies the value propositions for these services and the work activities to be undertaken by business analysts in the delivery of these services.

The BASF is intended to improve role clarity and enable increased recognition of business analysis by customers, colleagues and other stakeholders. It is also intended to offer opportunities for the standardisation of business analysis work and to provide a basis for identifying the benefits that may accrue from establishing a BA Service.

3 RECRUITING AND RETAINING BUSINESS ANALYSTS

INTRODUCTION

All organisations need to take the time to consider their recruitment and retention approach for business analysts. The demand for business analysis skills and experienced business analysts continues to increase and the market is often competitive and fast moving, with good candidates having a range of options available. Public, private and third sector organisations, across many business domains and industries, are looking to business analysis to improve project delivery, business efficiency and strategic clarity.

Attracting and retaining the right business analysts for an organisation takes planning and continued effort from the BA Service leadership. This needs to sit within an overall strategy for building and developing the BA Service, so it cannot be handed over to the HR or recruitment specialists. Figure 3.1 sets out the different activities within the recruitment and retention cycle that need to be considered when taking a strategic approach to building the members of the BA Service.

Figure 3.1 Business analyst recruitment and retention cycle

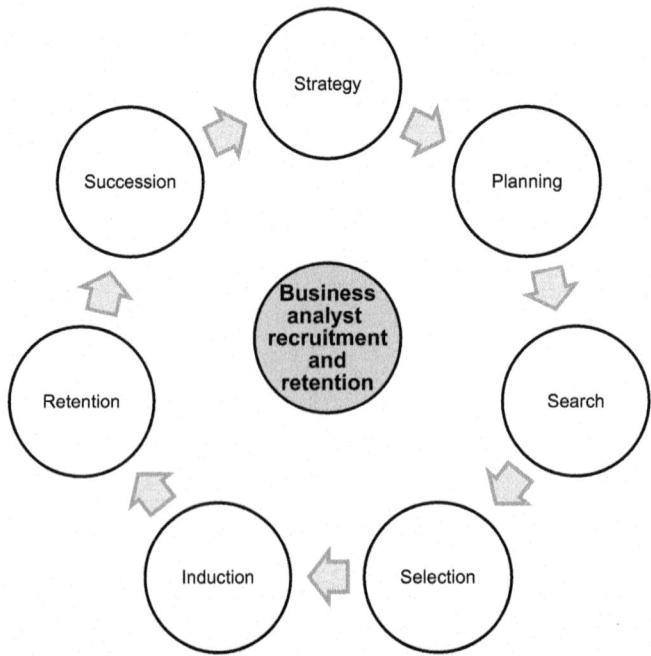

Recruitment decisions have a major impact on the delivery of the BA Service. Therefore, all elements of the business analyst recruitment and retention cycle, shown in Figure 3.1, need to be considered carefully. This chapter discusses the elements of this cycle in turn and presents various options and approaches that may apply to the different situations encountered within a BA Service.

RECRUITMENT STRATEGY

Many organisations will have an overarching recruitment strategy to guide managers. However, the BA Service has unique constraints and challenges that need to be considered and understood if the recruitment process is to be successful. Factors such as the local candidate market, competing employers, the need for particular business analysis skills and level of experience required, will all contribute to the approach to business analyst recruitment (see Appendix 2). The factors that will influence a business analyst recruitment strategy are represented in Figure 3.2.

Figure 3.2 Factors influencing the business analyst recruitment strategy

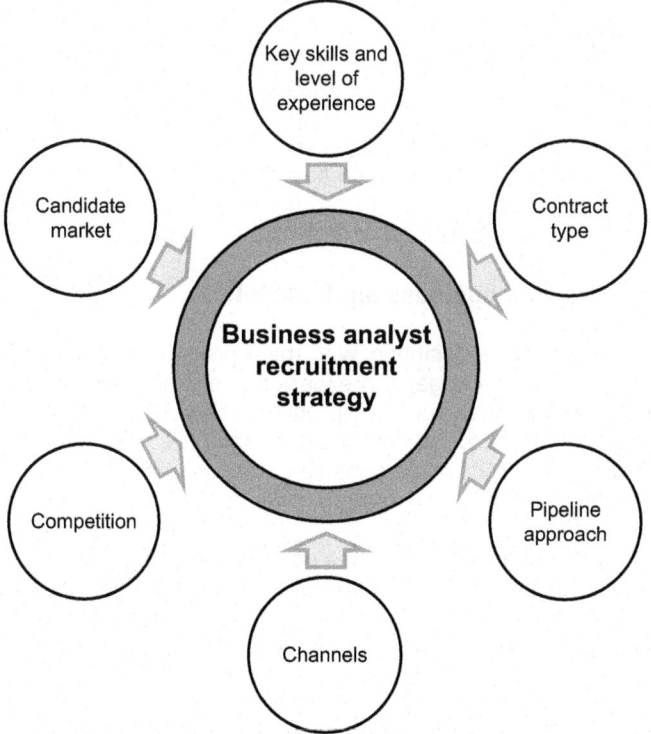

It is important to understand the context within which the BA Service is operating, and the business needs of customers, to determine a recruitment strategy that will best address the requirements for the specific BA Service. For example, if the Service needs to deploy business analysts very quickly and cost is not a barrier, employing contractors is likely to be the most appropriate option; if domain knowledge is critical to a particular project, internal recruitment within the organisation will be necessary; if the BA Service is struggling to keep pace with market salaries but is able to invest in development, an organic growth (pipeline) approach should be considered.

The needs of both the organisation and the BA Service will change over time, so they should be reviewed at regular and relevant intervals. A new BA Service may wish to invest initially in more senior business analysts to establish the Service quickly and deploy business analysts that require less training or support. Once the Service is established, it may be possible to recruit additional business analysts who are less experienced but can work alongside and be supported in their development by senior colleagues; this is discussed in Chapter 5.

Changes to organisational needs, the growth of the BA Service and the natural attrition of individual business analysts will cause vacancies to arise. It is possible that the make-up of the BA Service may be changed under such situations, which provides an opportunity to consider or re-consider the roles that are required to deliver the business analysis service portfolio. For example, are like-for-like roles required to replace departing business analysts or are new business analyst roles required to enhance the BA Service portfolio?

PESTLE analysis is a technique that is familiar to many business analysts when considering the external factors that will impact upon an organisation. The technique may also be used to consider a business area or function such as the BA Service within the context of a recruitment exercise. The PESTLE analysis in Table 3.1 identifies possible influences that may impact upon business analyst recruitment, which would need to be considered when developing a recruitment strategy. The PESTLE factors are outside the control of the organisation or business function under consideration.

Identifying the required business analyst skills

Business analysis is a broad discipline, with most practitioners having strengths and preferences in some areas and gaps in experience or knowledge in other areas. For example, many business analysts have process analysis experience, but far fewer have data analysis experience. Job descriptions may require 'all round' strengths, but the recruitment process needs to emphasise the skills and relevant experience most needed by the BA Service and its customers, given the current situation.

The BASF described in Chapter 2 sets out a portfolio of services that may be delivered by the BA Service. This portfolio is elaborated to identify the activities performed and techniques applied when delivering each business analysis service. Therefore, the BASF offers a basis for considering the skills required of business analysts within a particular BA Service. In addition to these analytical skills – the 'professional' skills of a business analyst – it is also important to identify other areas of skill – the 'personal' and 'business' skills. These three areas represent the holistic skill set required of a business analyst and are defined in detail in Chapter 4. They are described in overview in Table 3.2.

Table 3.1 PESTLE analysis to identify influences on business analyst recruitment

External factor	Considerations
Political	These may be external factors, such as political issues that are causing uncertainty for the BA Service, or they may be political factors within the organisation, but outside the BA Service, such as organisational policies or structures
Economic	These may be external factors, such as market salaries and industry trends, or may be factors such as recruitment budgets imposed on the BA Service by the organisation
Socio-cultural	These may be external factors, such as the availability of business analysis work in the local area, or internal factors such as the staff profile requirements defined for the organisation
Technological	These may be external factors, such as technological developments relevant to the business domain, or internal factors such as the technology that is available to support recruitment
Legal	These factors are likely to be external, such as employment, immigration/sponsorship and equality and diversity legislation
Environmental	These may be external factors, such as transport links and desirability of location and internal factors such as organisational policy on employee travelling distances

Table 3.2 The three skill areas required of business analysts

Skill area	Description
Personal qualities	These skills are not specific to business analysis, but are important for developing and progressing in any business environment. Assessing a person's ability to communicate, build relationships and work in a team are key to determining the right candidate. The best business analyst on paper may not be the best in practice. A common recruitment outcome is selecting a candidate with the required personal qualities who can be supported to develop their professional techniques and business knowledge
Professional techniques	These are specific to business analysis and differentiate business analysts from other roles. They include techniques such as stakeholder analysis, business modelling and requirements engineering
Business knowledge	This helps the business analyst to understand the organisation, business domain and sector. It includes knowledge of organisational structure and specific domain knowledge (e.g. regulation and legislation). This can also relate to skills and knowledge of business operations, such as business finance and business case development

(Continued)

Table 3.2 (Continued)

Skill area	Description
	Relevant sector experience is often advantageous for business analysts, but in many cases this can be gained while in the role, as an individual with strong business analysis skills should be able to pick up a new business domain relatively quickly. Attempting to recruit only those with sector experience cuts down the potential candidate pool, drives up the value of certain types of experience in the local job market and inhibits learning from other sectors. When sector experience or specific business knowledge is felt to be a priority, this opens the option to recruit internally and develop business analysis skills (see the next section on the recruitment pipeline)
	In large, complex or highly specialist organisations, experience of working within the organisation may be considered a priority. Again, this points to the option to recruit internally and develop business analysis skills

The business analyst skill set can be broken down into three areas of competency, each of which needs to be assessed by the selection process. The importance placed on each area of business analysis competency will vary from one organisation to another and between business analyst roles and grades.

Research carried out by the UK Business Analysis Manager Forum (BAMF, 2012) found broad agreement that all three skill areas are required of business analysts but, for more senior business analysts, at least half of the skill set is attributed to personal qualities. The breakdown defined by the BAMF for the senior analysts is represented in Figure 3.3.

However, the breakdown will vary between organisations and will also depend upon the nature of the role conducted by a business analyst. For example, when working within a change deployment service, the likelihood is that the personal qualities will be at the forefront, irrespective of the grade of the analyst. The key is that all three skill areas are given due consideration when developing a recruitment strategy for the BA Service and planning a specific recruitment exercise.

The BA Service can also prioritise skills in terms of what is essential at the outset, and what can be developed in individuals over time. It is far easier to support and train analysts in professional techniques such as process modelling than to develop personal qualities such as stakeholder management and facilitation skills.

The recruitment pipeline

Organisations are competing to recruit experienced business analysts, so it is important to expand the pool of business analysts, particularly those with sufficient talent and potential. This can be achieved by implementing a 'grow your own' (Lovelock and Wilford, 2014) or 'pipeline' approach, whereby individuals are recruited based on their aptitude

Figure 3.3 The three business analysis skill areas

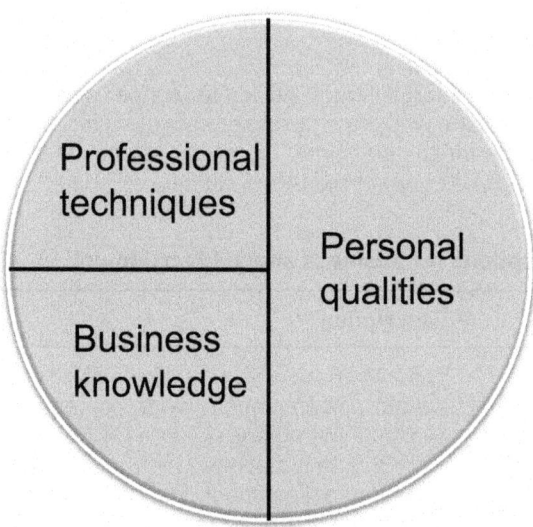

and attitude rather than their knowledge and experience. This approach requires BA leaders to make a commitment to develop and support individuals with the required personal qualities that will enable them to become good business analysts.

If business analysis is to be a widely recognised career option, there needs to be more clearly defined entry routes (or 'pipelines') into the profession, with an increased number of opportunities to start a coherent career in business analysis. Figure 3.4 highlights several potential entry points.

Figure 3.4 Pipeline options for entry into business analyst roles

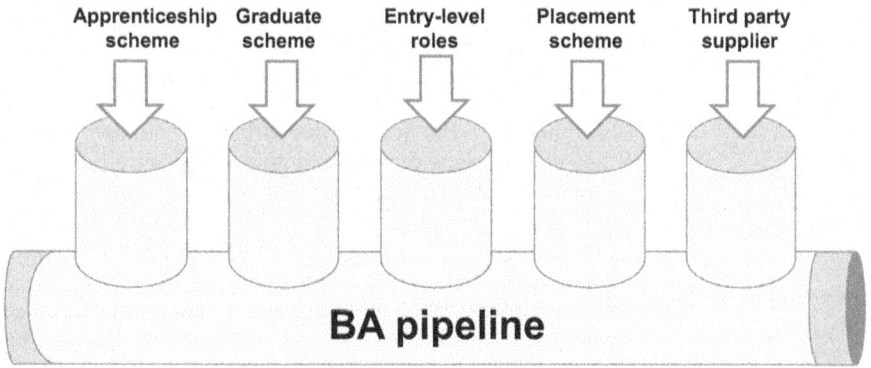

Each pipeline option focuses on a different target market of candidates. This offers a number of options to BA leaders when recruiting business analysts into the BA Service. These options are described in Table 3.3.

Recruiting younger workers

The adoption of a pipeline approach may introduce younger workers into the BA Service. Younger workers are people who are entering employment for the first time or entering their chosen profession for the first time. Typically, this means a younger worker may be anyone up to the age of 24 years old (ACAS Guidance, 2016).

Table 3.3 Pipeline options for business analyst recruitment

Pipeline option	Description
Apprenticeships	The Information Systems Business Analysis Apprentice standard is an industry-wide apprenticeship that is available in England under a UK Government scheme with BCS, the Chartered Institute for IT, providing the end-point assessment. The content of the scheme was devised by business analysis practitioners and, as a result, is extensive and rigorous. The scheme provides the opportunity to re-train existing staff or attract and develop new candidates. Taking this approach can lead to long-term commitment from apprentice business analysts, as they are provided with a wide-ranging entry into business analysis. The scheme may also offer benefits to more senior business analysts, as it provides opportunities to offer mentoring and support the development of apprentices. Organisational benefits include demonstrating corporate social responsibility and providing a cost-effective workforce (CIPD, 2017)
Graduate Scheme	Specific business analyst graduate entrant schemes or organisation-wide graduate schemes that feature business analysis as a rotation or placement. There will be initial costs associated with the creation of a scheme, then the ongoing cost of recruitment and training (usually on an annual cohort cycle). Business analyst graduate schemes often attract motivated individuals who are quick learners. With the appropriate direction and development, they can produce quality business analysis outputs. However, not all graduates finishing the scheme will stay with the organisation on completion. While the attrition rate is likely to be higher than for apprentices, graduate schemes offer benefits as they allow graduates at an early point to decide if business analysis is a career they wish to follow. Such schemes can also contribute to the provision of a cost-effective BA Service

(Continued)

Table 3.3 (Continued)

Pipeline option	Description
Third-Party Supplier	Some organisations provide recruitment, training and support for recent graduates, ex-forces personnel or people who have been out of the job market for various reasons. Individuals are placed on a client site using a consultancy model, with the opportunity to transfer from a successful engagement to a permanent role. This allows organisations without the requisite internal infrastructure to access a talent pipeline approach and gain benefits quite quickly. This approach is more expensive than direct graduate salaries but avoids many of the internal cost overheads. Contractual obligations relating to individuals who take up long-term roles with the organisation once the initial contract term is completed, need to be clearly articulated and agreed by both parties
Entry-level roles	Some organisations recruit individuals who have experience of work, possibly indirectly related to business analysis and with appropriate transferable skills, but who do not have any significant experience of business analysis work
	Advertised entry-level roles in business analysis may be attractive to internal and external candidates. They can provide a development route from areas of the organisation that are outside IT and business change. This may include support desk analysts, call centre operators or individuals from business teams who have encountered business analysts and wish to move into this discipline. This approach has the potential to extend the market of potential candidates and requires the recruitment approach to be targeted to those with the necessary interpersonal skills or specific business knowledge who can then learn the professional business analysis techniques
Placement scheme	Placement schemes provide the opportunity to host university students within the workplace, either as an internship (three months) or a year in industry (9–12 months). Having a rolling programme of placements ensures that there will always be capacity at this level, but the individual will change. Placements work best where there is a backlog of projects or work packages that can be assigned and completed without complex dependencies, as this ensures that work can be delivered effectively within the time frame. In some cases, a placement may lead to a permanent post, so it provides a post-graduate recruitment opportunity

Additional considerations may be needed when recruiting younger workers, such as:

- the use of different recruitment channels;
- the application of a 'new to work' induction process that provides information and guidance in addition to a standard induction;
- clear articulation of the workplace conventions and unwritten rules;
- clear articulation of workplace expectations (for younger workers and those supporting them);
- particular attention to workplace health and safety, which may be unfamiliar to younger workers;
- an emphasis that learning is two-way, and that they have skills and knowledge to share, even though they are relatively inexperienced workers.

Contract types

The market for business analysts is an important factor to be considered when an organisation is developing its strategy for delivering the BA Service. Typically, a BA Service hires both employed and contracted staff and will operate using one or more of the following models:

- **Permanent employee:** business analysts who are employed by the organisation on an ongoing (permanent) basis.
- **Fixed-term contract:** business analysts whose terms and conditions are typically the same as permanent staff, but with a specified end date.
- **Contractor:** usually business analysts engaged on an agreed 'day-rate' for a specific purpose or length of time.
- **Consultant:** business analysts employed by an external organisation that is engaged to provide a team or individuals to work on a specific work package, project, business deliverable or period of time.

The combination of contracts used to deliver the BA Service varies from organisation to organisation and there are no fixed ratios that will work in every situation. Some organisations use all permanent staff, some supplement the permanent staff with fixed-term or contractor business analysts, some rely mainly on contractor business analysts, and so on. The appropriate use and split of these arrangements will be influenced by several factors such as:

- cost;
- timescales for recruitment and deployment;
- certainty and clarity of ongoing funding streams;
- flexibility to scale-up or shrink the BA Service team at short notice;
- level of availability or scarcity of business analysis skills in local market;
- level of seniority or experience required of individual business analysts;
- need for specific or specialised experience or skill set.

Table 3.4 highlights some of the advantages and disadvantages of different employment models.

Table 3.4 Employment models

Type	Time	Cost	Quality (experience)
Permanent employee	Lengthy recruitment timescales probable More difficult to scale-up/down in short time frame	Set by organisation and market factors Investment in ongoing training and development	Provides the opportunity to have a defined career path, incorporating different grades of business analyst and reflecting increasing levels of experience
Fixed-term contract	Lengthy recruitment timescales probable Provides opportunity to resource a fixed period of work There may be legal responsibilities regarding end of contract and contract lengths that need to be considered	Set by organisation and market factors Investment in ongoing training and development	May be less attractive to good candidates, as it provides the uncertainty of a contract role without the level of financial reward Opportunity to have grades/levels that reflect experience and provide a career path for business analysts
Contractor	Can usually be sourced quickly Easier to scale-up/down within a short time frame	Daily rate is often higher than permanent salaries but does not include many employment costs such as pensions, equipment and training	Higher levels of experience expected Can use to address a specialised skill or knowledge gap
Consultant	Can usually be sourced quickly	Daily rate is often much higher than permanent salaries but does not include many employment costs such as pensions, equipment and training	Significantly higher levels of experience usually expected Can use to learn from elsewhere, solve problems or drive change followed by knowledge transfer into the organisation

RECRUITMENT PLANNING

The plan for the recruitment campaign needs to reflect the perspective of the recruiting organisation such as policies and processes to be adhered to, activities required, timescales, dependencies and who will be involved. The plan must also consider the following questions regarding potential candidates: Who are they? What will attract them to the role? What are the best routes to reach them?

Timescales

There are two main options for timescales relating to the search stage: setting a specific deadline or 'closing date' and reviewing all applications after that date; or, looking at applications as and when they are received and moving to the next stage when sufficient applications (by quality or quantity) have been received. Job advertisements are typically published for about two weeks. This duration could be longer if using a bespoke application form and shorter if using CVs as a first stage assessment tool.

With both approaches it is important to have planned interview dates and time slots, as panel member availability and room availability often provide logistical challenges and cause delays.

Urgency

BA leaders often find themselves in a position of reactive recruitment to address an urgent business need. When planning 'urgent' recruitment, it may be necessary to consider the following questions:

- Is it really urgent? How do we know? Are there alternatives?

- Do we have other ways to address the need than via recruitment? (see Chapter 9, Prioritising demand).

- How might we compromise our business analyst recruitment strategy to meet urgent timescales? (For example, accept a less-experienced candidate, offer a higher salary, use a contract business analyst, use recruitment agencies and incur higher recruiting costs.)

- What shortcuts might we take in the recruitment process? (For example, use of CVs rather than an application form, allow shorter advert/search time, only consider candidates who are immediately available.)

- Who wants to be involved in recruitment versus who needs to be involved? Who will prioritise the time to shortlist candidates and interview at the earliest opportunity?

Beware of making poor recruiting decisions due to perceived urgency and pressure. When the heat of the urgent situation has subsided, customers of the BA Service and the business analyst recruiting lead tend to agree that it is better to experience a short wait for the right candidate than to address the impact of an inappropriate appointment.

Approvals

Financial and managerial approvals may need to be secured before the search stage can be initiated. This will be much easier to obtain if a recruitment strategy is in place and has agreement in principle from those who can allow the recruitment activity to start. Approvals may be needed in relation to:

- increasing the budget or headcount of the BA Service;
- acceptable pay scales and salaries;
- job descriptions and person specifications to ensure organisational alignment;
- format, wording and publication of advertisements;
- use of recruitment specialists.

As approval processes could introduce delay to the process, the BA Service needs to be proactive in these areas.

Recruitment information pack

There are a number of pieces of information that are required to support the recruitment process. The pack is likely to include:

- the advertisement;
- the job description;
- the person specification;
- a set of interview questions.

In most cases it is possible to have a generic information pack that can be tailored for a specific business analyst recruitment. It is useful to review these documents and keep them up to date on a regular basis so that a reactive or urgent recruitment is not delayed unnecessarily.

Re-use of the recruitment pack also promotes consistency across recruitment campaigns and, as this means each campaign does not have to start from scratch, offers an efficient approach for each business analyst recruitment exercise. It is useful to consider the candidate experience at this stage by assessing the quality, quantity and format of information made available.

Efficient recruitment

The recruitment process can be made more effective and efficient, but this can only be achieved if a baseline is established and ongoing measurements are taken. During the planning stage it is useful to set the metrics that will be tracked. Key metrics concern the number of applications, conversion rates and timescales (see Chapter 13, Recruitment metrics).

Recruitment attraction factors

Business analyst candidates who are considering a new role will evaluate two aspects:

- **the push** (things they do not like about their current role and organisation);
- **the pull** (attraction factors about a new role or organisation).

Table 3.5 shows the general considerations that apply to the attraction of any role and also a number of considerations that relate specifically to the BA Service. These specific factors are almost always the questions business analysts ask at interview.

Table 3.5 Attraction factors for business analyst roles

General considerations	Remuneration (pay, bonus, pension)
	Flexibility
	Culture
	Reputation
	Location
	Working environment
	Organisation stability
BA-specific considerations	BA Service maturity
	BA Service culture
	BA career path
	Training and development
	Types of projects and opportunities
	Position of the BA Service within the organisation
	BA working practices (e.g. development methodologies, notation standards and support tools)

Approach to attracting business analysts

An effective business analyst recruitment campaign can be achieved through the investment of the appropriate time and effort by the BA Service and does not always come down to a question of money spent on the campaign. There are a number of key questions business analyst recruiting leads can consider and address to increase the likelihood of a successful recruitment campaign. These are listed in Table 3.6.

SEARCH

This stage of the recruitment process relates to ensuring that appropriate candidates are aware of the role within the organisation.

Recruitment channels

BA recruiting leads need to think creatively about how to reach the best candidates and they should not expect that using one channel will provide consistently good candidates. It may be necessary to have a coordinated recruitment campaign that utilises several channels simultaneously to signpost potential candidates to the organisation and role. The range of recruitment channels is described in Table 3.7.

Table 3.6 Planning effective business analyst recruitment

Key questions	Detail
Are the job descriptions clear and informative?	Lengthy job descriptions with pages of candidate criteria can be counter-productive. It is important to focus on the core expectations, outcomes and relationships for the role. The criteria should be streamlined by grouping and reducing where possible
Are job titles in keeping with the market?	Ensure that job titles reflect market trends. Candidates may have automated alerts for specific key words or job titles. It is helpful to consider whether a job title is too specific or too generic
Is the salary appropriate for the level of skills and experience required?	Ensure that salaries are in step with the market and that additional benefits are clearly highlighted
	If the salary cannot be changed, it may be necessary to consider reviewing the expectations of candidates for the role
What channels can be used to reach potential candidates?	The recruitment channel may need to be tailored to the particular skills or experience being sought
	There may be the potential to incentivise existing employees to make referrals and recommendations (see 'Recruitment channels')
Are the benefits of the role and the organisation highlighted explicitly?	This is a two-way selection process; candidates need reasons to decide to submit an application and accept a role (see 'Recruitment attraction factors')
Is the language used appropriate and inclusive?	Ensure that the language used in advertisements and job descriptions is professional, balanced and inviting
	This is the opportunity to sell the role to attract the best candidates. It can be very useful to seek input from recruitment experts
Is the recruitment process clear?	Ensure that the process for recruitment and selection is conveyed clearly to candidates, especially those candidates who are from outside the organisation or sector
Is communication working well?	Consider making the process as engaging as possible by reviewing the tone of written communications and offering a personal contact point for any queries regarding the role
	Review the use of standard and automated emails; they may not be suitable, sufficiently informative or provide a good impression of the organisation

(Continued)

Table 3.6 (Continued)

Key questions	Detail
Do the processes encourage or discourage applicants?	Avoid lengthy waiting periods between the recruitment stages, as they provide an opportunity for a candidate to receive further job offers
	Consider whether the process is supporting candidate needs as well as organisation needs. For example, the use of lengthy bespoke application forms versus use of CVs; or, the use of fixed interview dates versus flexibility to accommodate candidates' commitments
How can existing business analysts be involved in the recruitment process?	Business analysts currently employed by the organisation can help by making referrals and recommendations via professional networks and social media. These may include quotes or testimonials about the role and the working environment. If appropriate, videos or photos can help to present a positive image of the role and the environment. They may also play a role in the business analyst selection process

Table 3.7 Business analyst recruitment channels

Channel	Description
Organisation job site	Most organisations have a jobs-listing or careers section on their own website. Using this as the only recruitment channel assumes that candidates are aware of the organisation as a potential employer of business analysts and are actively looking for roles. Therefore, this channel may yield limited results if it is the sole approach used. The organisation's site may be used in conjunction with other channels as the focal point candidates are directed to
	Unlikely to incur cost
Industry- and sector-specific sites, profession-specific sites, general CV/job sites	Sites relevant to business analysis will have an audience of current professionals considering a new role
	Sites relevant to an industry or sector will have an audience with relevant domain knowledge who may be interested in becoming a business analyst
	General job-listing sites will have a wide audience with varying levels of experience
	May incur cost

(Continued)

Table 3.7 (Continued)

Channel	Description
Print and online newspapers/industry magazines/journals	This is a way of reaching 'passive' candidates who are not necessarily looking for a role but may consider the right opportunity
	Timing and timescales need to be considered for these channels, as there may be time delays (such as restrictions on when advertisements can be posted) or time restrictions (including minimum and maximum lengths of time for advertisements)
	Likely to incur cost
Organisation newsletters, email updates	Using both internal and external communications channels is a way to reach individuals who already know something about the organisation and may be interested in joining it
	Likely to incur little cost
Social media	Can be promoted by organisations (corporate social media accounts) or by individuals to raise awareness of the roles and benefits of working for an organisation
	May incur cost
Existing staff and their professional networks	Encourage existing business analysts to share links to the advert or social media posts with their professional networks
	Many people find roles through people they know and may appreciate the opportunity to find out about an organisation before submitting an application to work there
	Some organisations have an employee referral scheme (using bonuses, extra holiday or other incentives) for referring someone who is subsequently appointed
	May incur cost
Job fairs	Attending local and national job fairs aimed at different audiences (school leavers, graduates, experienced professionals) can raise awareness of an organisation and the roles that are available. This channel also provides a direct means of communicating with potential candidates
	Job fairs are likely to have set dates with long lead-in times, so recruitment timescales need to be designed around each event
	May incur cost

(Continued)

Table 3.7 (Continued)

Channel	Description
Networking events such as conferences and business seminars	Networking events encourage existing business analysts and professionals from related disciplines to see the organisation in a positive light and may prompt them into applying to work there
	May incur cost if sponsoring or hosting an event
Open days	Open days offer an opportunity for recruitment by showcasing the work of the organisation to all potential candidates. While this may attract some unsuitable candidates, some candidates may perform better in person than on paper, so an open day would enable them to engage with the BA Service team and potentially progress within the recruitment process. This channel is particularly attractive if the organisation is looking to recruit a number of different roles at the same time
	Likely to incur cost
Local university links	It is possible to work with university careers teams to participate in events and advertise via careers websites. This channel is likely to require an investment of time, and university term times and activity cycles will need to be considered
	May incur cost
Recruiters	See the discussion below regarding the use of recruitment specialists
	Will incur cost

Use of recruitment specialists

The use of recruitment specialists is a source of ongoing debate amongst BA leaders and is generally driven by positive or poor experiences of individuals – sometimes it helps, sometimes it doesn't. There are number of factors that contribute to each of these outcomes.

Recruitment or Talent Acquisition (TA) specialists sometimes have a specialist business analysis division, or particular individuals who focus on recruiting business analysts. These specialists should have a good understanding of the role and the qualities of a good business analyst, although this will need to be tailored to the specific needs of the recruiting organisation. They should provide insight to the local market, access to a range of candidates – including those who may not be actively looking for roles – as well as communication channels to a large number of active candidates. The relationship with one or more specialist business analyst recruiters can become a strategic partnership for a BA Service that faces a high volume of recruitment.

Recruiters who do not specialise in business analysis may struggle to understand what is needed, so may put forward candidates who are unsuitable. Agreements with recruiters that are open to broad interpretation sometimes drive unhelpful behaviour, such as, 'might as well put this CV forward', where the suitability of candidates is open to compromise. This causes the recruiting lead to spend unnecessary time and effort reviewing unacceptable CVs or interviewing inappropriate candidates.

Tracking of appointable candidates put forward by recruitment partners, keeping regular contact with recruiters and agreeing the requirements and expectations will provide a means of evaluating the service they provide. This will also help to ensure that the benefits from using recruitment agencies continue to outweigh the costs incurred, which may be significant.

Asking the questions posed in Table 3.6 will help to obtain the most benefit from the specialist advice offered. It is also a good idea to ask recruiters what else the BA Service might do to attract suitable candidates.

Larger organisations may have internal recruitment specialists, and it is equally important for the BA Service to cultivate this working relationship. Both internal and external recruitment specialists should advocate the use of a recruitment strategy meeting before initiating a business analyst recruitment campaign to understand what is really required and to agree the relevant channels, approach and time frame.

Top tips for working with recruitment specialists:

- Look for organisations that specialise in business analysis or individuals who specialise within a more general recruitment organisation.
- Take up references for the recruiter from other BA Service functions in other organisations.
- Invest time in the relationship; help them to understand the needs and expectations of the BA Service to get the best results.
- Use management information about success rates to have evidence-based discussions.
- Use their knowledge and advice to improve the BA recruitment process.

SELECTION APPROACH

The business analyst recruitment and selection approach must allow the recruiting lead to:

- provide the opportunity for the organisation to select the candidate, and the candidate to select the organisation;
- identify candidates who really are business analysts, regardless of previous job titles or stated knowledge and experience;

- assess whether there is a shared understanding of what constitutes business analysis;

- understand both the breadth and depth of the candidate's previous business analysis experience;

- look for the specific skills and experience that the BA Service needs;

- look for the skills and qualities that differentiate a competent business analyst from a great business analyst.

The selection process

Having an assessment process with multiple phases increases the likelihood of selecting the right candidate for the role. Figure 3.5 represents a typical selection process.

Each stage of the process is described in more detail in Table 3.8.

Figure 3.5 Business analyst selection process

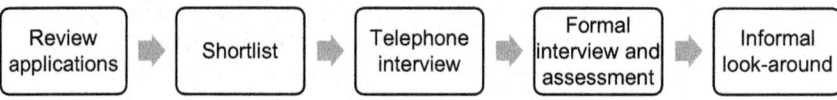

Table 3.8 Stages of the selection process

Selection stage	Description	Outcome
Review applications	A set of criteria should be defined in advance of this stage in order to ensure that the review of the applications is consistent and in line with the needs of the BA Service. This is typically carried out by the BA recruiting lead but may include others in the form of a review/ shortlisting panel	Recruiting lead has an initial view of candidate suitability
Shortlist applications	Having applied the assessment criteria, a shortlist of the most suitable candidates should be identified (by the recruiting lead or a panel)	Manageable number of suitable candidates

(Continued)

Table 3.8 (Continued)

Selection stage	Description	Outcome
Interview candidates via telephone/ technology	A set of key questions or topics should be defined for the telephone interviews. These are likely to be relatively short (in comparison with the formal interviews) and are designed to ensure that those who progress to formal interview are the most promising candidates	Increased confidence that a face-to-face interview will be a useful investment of time for both the candidate(s) and the organisation
Conduct formal (face-to-face) interview with candidates	This may involve more than one interviewer and will explore a defined set of topics that are designed to explore each candidate's experience, knowledge and level of expertise. A formal interview session is also likely to include an assessment; for example, a discussion of a test scenario, a presentation on a specific topic or an exercise to apply a technique	Recruiting lead has a good understanding of candidate suitability for the role Candidate understands the role and organisation
Offer informal visit	Staff who join an organisation need to 'fit' with the culture. An informal visit offers the opportunity for both the candidate(s) and the organisation to ensure that they will be able to work within the team	Successful candidate(s) accept the business analyst role

The first three stages may be conducted internally or by a recruitment agency; this will vary according to the channel chosen for attracting candidates. Depending on the level of standardisation set by the organisation for the recruitment process, one or more of these phases may be dropped. For example, an informal visit may be too time-intensive for the business analyst recruiting lead and candidates, so it may be decided to progress to an offer without this stage.

The recruitment process adopted should demonstrate that the same level of rigour and financial control is in place as with other types of expenditure; the financial commitment associated with recruitment is often far more significant than other types of expenditure, plus the impact of a poor process leading to a poor decision can be extremely costly.

Organisations that need to be more responsive or are struggling to recruit business analysts may need to adopt a more flexible, less formal approach. More proactive organisations may use an 'always recruiting' model, where they do not place advertisements when specific vacancies arise but are always willing to accept or make initial approaches. Clarity needs to be provided to potential candidates on the reasoning behind ongoing recruitment. For example, this may be due to the growth of the BA Service and increasing volume of work or may result from the expansion of the organisation itself. However, organisations who are in constant recruitment mode can cause concern with candidates, as this may suggest cultural issues resulting in a high turnover of staff.

Whatever the selection process adopted by an organisation, there are a variety of selection tools available to the recruiting lead. Table 3.9 describes the advantages and disadvantages of the available selection tools.

Table 3.9 Selection tool evaluation

Selection tool	Advantages	Disadvantages
CV	Candidates have them to hand	Best CV does not always equate to best candidate
		Difficult to assess breadth and depth of experience
Application form	Standard format makes shortlisting easier for the organisation	Candidates reluctant to commit time required to complete application forms in a buoyant market
	Allows more objective comparison between candidates and comparison to person specifications	
Telephone/ online Interview	Less time commitment for organisation and candidate (cost and time effective)	Usually require face-to-face interview as well, so adds a step to the process
	More immediate engagement with the candidate, who can more easily make time to be available for a phone interview	Lack of visual prompts/body language and facial expressions
		Technology limitations
	Useful to aid shortlisting of large number of candidates	
Face-to-face interview	Visual prompts such as body language and facial expressions provide a more rounded basis for assessment	Can be time-consuming and cause delays
	Allow more in-depth discussion	Can be difficult to distinguish candidates who are good at interviews from candidates who are good business analysts
	Candidate becomes more informed about the working environment	Candidates can prepare for a competency-based interview with carefully crafted and rehearsed answers

(Continued)

Table 3.9 (Continued)

Selection tool	Advantages	Disadvantages
Assessment via tasks, tests and presentations	Enables the assessment of business analysis skills rather than just discussing them Most reliable ways to verify competence	Can be time-consuming for organisation and may deter candidates
Assessment centre	Good for assessing aptitude and attitude for less experienced business analyst roles	Can be costly and time-consuming Timescales and commitment may deter candidates
References	Due-diligence on candidate employment history	May not provide much detail/ likely to be subjective

The assessment approaches available to business analyst recruiting leads are described in further detail in Table 3.10.

Table 3.10 Assessment approaches for recruiting business analysts

Assessment approach	Description
Presentation	Candidates may be asked to pre-prepare a presentation for the interview panel. This is a useful way to assess a business analyst, as both the format and content of the candidate's prepared presentation gives a good insight into their style and approach. It is important to set limits regarding the use of technology, time available and number of slides. Candidates can sometimes prepare the presentation at the expense of preparing for the interview as a whole
Task	Setting the candidate a previously unseen task to complete within a set time frame. This might include creating a process diagram for a given scenario, role-playing a requirements elicitation session, analysing a written scenario, or preparing a short presentation on a given topic. Candidates can be fearful of an invitation to undertake an unknown task they cannot prepare for, but flexibility and the ability to adapt and respond to a situation are pivotal for a business analyst role. A task provides a good opportunity to see a demonstration of a candidate's business analysis skills
Test	There is a growing use of online assessments prior to interview that reveal additional information about a candidate. These can focus on different areas, such as knowledge of business analysis or psychometric tests

(Continued)

69

Table 3.10 (Continued)

Assessment approach	Description
Certification	Many organisations now incorporate attainment of professional certification into their assessment process; in particular, for roles above a certain level of seniority. Professional certification demonstrates a specific level of business analysis competence as well as a commitment to personal development and professional direction. It provides a degree of certainty that candidates and recruiting managers have a mutual understanding of standard business analysis services, language and practices. This is discussed further in Chapter 4. Where good candidates have not attained desired certifications, it is still possible to assess their knowledge of the topics encompassed by the certifications and to evaluate their willingness to undertake the requisite study and examinations
Interview questions	The breadth of interview questions should cover all three elements of the business analyst role: personal qualities, professional techniques and business knowledge. Part of the recruitment planning process aims to ensure that the appropriate weighting in terms of number of questions and time is allocated to the elements that are most critical for the role. The questions selected should trace back to the business analysis recruitment strategy (see Appendix 2), so that specific skills and knowledge that have been prioritised by the BA Service are being examined
	Many organisations use 'competency-based' interview questions that focus on real examples from the candidate's past experience and relate to specific areas of skill or knowledge that are needed to be successful in the advertised role. 'Values-based' interview questions can use a similar format ('tell me about a time when…') but concentrate on the candidate's approach, outlook and motivations, and can help to identify if the candidate shares the same values as the organisation
	Possible follow-ups to the main questions should be identified, as they can help to achieve more of a conversational style of interview. Additional follow-up questions may also arise from the information provided by the candidate
	It is important to think about how answers to questions will be evaluated, in terms of both content and delivery format. For example, what would be the elements of a good answer in relation to this role? What negative indicators would cause concern and point to the need for further questioning?

Table 3.11 sets out an example interview question plus the following:

- possible follow-up questions;
- questions to be considered when evaluating the format of the answer;
- questions to be considered when evaluating the content of the answer;
- positive indicators regarding the candidate's performance;
- negative indicators regarding the candidate's performance.

Table 3.11 Example of competency-based questions and evaluation

Example question: Can you tell me about a time when you had to gain agreement from a group of senior stakeholders?

Follow-up questions:

How did you approach the situation?

What did you have to produce?

Who else was involved?

What was the outcome?

What would you do differently in hindsight/what did you learn from this situation?

Format evaluation	Content evaluation
Was the question answered?	Were the person's own role and actions clearly described?
Was the answer clear and concise?	
Was a specific situation described or a general/hypothetical answer given?	What was the level of 'seniority' involved?
Was the situation easy to follow?	What was the significance of the agreement?
Was the length of answer sufficiently detailed/too detailed?	Was anything produced (presentations, papers, etc.) or driven by conversations?
	What was the person's attitude towards others involved?
	Did the approach suit the situation?
Positive indicators	Situation sufficiently complex that it cannot be resolved in a single conversation
	Proactive, prepared
	Tailoring of approach for different stakeholders
	Collaborative approach
	Understanding of different perspectives

(Continued)

Table 3.11 (Continued)

Format evaluation	Content evaluation
Negative indicators	Situation very simple/easily resolved
	Stakeholders not sufficiently senior
	Other people actually gained the agreement; candidate is a bystander
	Poor attitude towards stakeholders
	No tailoring of communication and influencing styles
	No learning/reflections from the experience

There is no single right answer to a question of the type shown in Table 3.11, but there are elements that make the answer stronger or weaker. Business analysts with different levels of experience would answer this question very differently, and each answer could be assessed as 'meets', 'above' or 'below' the level expected for this role. It is also common to use a numerical scoring approach to differentiate answers with greater precision.

An experienced business analyst recruiting lead may be applying this recruitment assessment process automatically. Articulating the elements of the process explicitly enables other members of the BA Service to become involved in, and potentially lead, recruitment campaigns as this provides a means of applying consistent evaluation across candidates and across different recruitment campaigns.

Panels

Panel interviews usually make up some part of the interview process, even where one-to-one interviews also feature. Selecting the right panel is an important part of the interview process to ensure that a number of different perspectives are represented and that a fair process is applied. Panels of two or three members typically provide a balance of different viewpoints without intimidating candidates. A possible composition for an interview panel is shown in Table 3.12.

Table 3.12 Constitution of an interview panel for a business analyst role

Panel member	Description	Considerations
Business analyst recruitment lead (hiring manager)	This may be a number of different roles depending on the structure of the BA Service	Should bring consistency to different recruitment rounds
		Ultimately responsible for recruiting decisions but needs to be able to listen to different viewpoints

(Continued)

Table 3.12 (Continued)

Panel member	Description	Considerations
Business analysts	Existing members of the BA Service	Useful to get perspective of practicing business analyst
		May have less interview experience
		Candidates find it useful to ask them questions about the role
Customers	Business and IT staff who interact with the BA Service and who have some likelihood of working with the individual appointed	Opportunity to get buy-in from the customer and build trust in the BA Service
		Selecting which customers to involve may be contentious
		Customers may have short-term view about an individual's suitability for their project rather than longer-term view of suitability for the BA Service
		May be inclined to prioritise business knowledge or skills candidates hold that fill other project gaps
Independents	Someone who is from an entirely separate business area	Able to give an impartial view, as unlikely to be affected by the outcome of the recruitment
	Low likelihood of working with the individual appointed	May have limited experience of the business analyst role
Recruitment specialists	Internal or external partners whose role includes interviewing on a regular basis	Able to give wider viewpoint, how candidates measure against other (non-business analyst) roles at a similar level
		Able to advise on selection process
Senior managers	Someone from a senior management level who has responsibility for, or interest in, the BA Service	Useful to demonstrate to candidates and existing business analysts that senior managers are invested in the BA Service
		May be difficult for them to make time available, plan well in advance and have a stand-in in case manager is not available

It is useful to agree the roles of each panel member, remind all members of interview etiquette and agree that it is the responsibility of the panel to:

- get the best from candidates;
- keep to time;
- be fair to all candidates;
- conduct themselves in a manner that reflects well on the organisation and leaves a good impression, even if a candidate is not appointable.

It is also important to discuss beforehand that if there are no appointable candidates, then no one should be offered the role and to agree that this is an acceptable outcome. This helps to avoid 'best of a bad bunch' syndrome, where the panel feels inclined to appoint the best candidate, even if the standard is low, in order to avoid a 'failed recruitment'.

Bias in recruitment

Unconscious bias refers to the process of forming quick opinions about a situation or person without being consciously aware of it. Biases are essentially mental shortcuts that use knowledge about social situations, attitudes, cultures, emotional reactions and many more aspects of daily life.

In recruitment, unconscious bias can significantly affect decision making. While it is important to be able to use experience and professional judgement to assess applicants, problems can arise when decisions are influenced too heavily by biases in the form of assumptions, expectations, preferences and stereotypes.

Organisations now generally accept that conscious and unconscious bias are almost always present in their employees and therefore in the recruitment process. Raising awareness of unconscious bias is the first step to helping people to address bias. Other steps that may be taken are:

- using an anonymised application form or CV process;
- creating diverse interview panels;
- using structured interviews and standard questions for all candidates.

Recruiting leads should challenge their own preconceptions of 'organisational/team fit', the 'ideal candidate' and the first impressions gained. They should also guard against 'recruiting in their own image' and where possible, seek views from trusted colleagues who may be able to offer a different perspective.

Feedback to candidates

Candidates are likely to have invested a significant amount of time in the recruitment process and if they are unsuccessful, they should be given the opportunity to obtain honest and constructive feedback. It is important to ensure that providing constructive feedback is built into the recruitment process. One way to approach to this is for the panel to agree a few points of feedback on each candidate during the interview process. These points should be captured on a separate sheet so that the feedback can be discussed easily with candidates at a later stage.

Appointable candidates also value feedback on their interview technique and any concerns or outstanding queries the panel may have. Therefore, the interview feedback approach may also be relevant to them as they start their new role.

Feedback on the recruitment process

Business analysts who have been recently appointed, or who have turned down an offer, are a great source of feedback on the attraction and selection approach adopted. To collect feedback on the process, the business analyst recruiting lead needs to:

- design and embed a process to seek feedback;
- consider the most appropriate mechanism (for example, a telephone call or short online survey);
- be prepared to act on any feedback received.

Questions used to explore the candidate experience of the recruitment process can be both qualitative and quantitative. For example:

- What attracted to you apply?
- What factors influenced your decision?
- How would you rate the experience of going through this process (1–5)?
- What could have made a difference for you?
- How can the experience be improved for future candidates?

Improving the candidate experience of recruitment may not necessarily require significant changes to the process (which are often set at an organisational level). Making minor adjustments to how the process is applied can lead to a much better, more engaging, experience.

INDUCTION

An effective employee induction process improves both retention and performance, and will help new employees to become familiar with their role. The induction (or on-boarding) process should give new business analysts the information and tools they need to do their job from the outset, so that they are contributing to delivering the BA Service as soon as possible. This is beneficial to the new business analyst, existing business analysts and customers.

The BA Service should develop specific induction materials in addition to any organisation-wide information. The additional materials should include a business analyst welcome pack and a business analysis induction checklist. For more information on this subject, see Appendix 3.

Business analyst welcome pack

The welcome pack provides an opportunity to introduce the person to the business analyst role, the BA Service and the organisation, and to begin with positive messages and clear direction in order to foster a sense of belonging.

The pack should contain information such as:

- the mission and strategy for the BA Service;
- the BA service portfolio (see Chapter 2) and key projects and assignments;
- BA Service Improvement Plan (see Chapter 12);
- information on business analysis standards and templates (see Chapter 6);
- information about the use of and support for the business analysis tools and technology (see Chapter 7);
- the business analysis dashboard (see Chapter 13);
- key contacts within the organisation and the BA Service;
- organisation charts;
- the business analyst job description for the role.

The welcome pack could be made available as a virtual or physical pack and should be provided on the first day. There are benefits to a physical pack, such as the person feels that effort has been made for them, the pack can support conversations in an informal environment away from desks and it can be used as a reference point if waiting for IT equipment to be made available and accessible. It is also useful to share the pack electronically for future reference and to provide access to any links provided.

Some organisations also provide new employees with branded items such as mugs, stationery, lanyards, bags or water bottles as part of the welcome pack, which can be a positive way to greet new members of staff.

Business analyst induction checklist

Creating a checklist is a useful way to ensure that the induction process is applied consistently and nothing is missed inadvertently (see Table 3.13 and Appendix 3).

People and process

The amount of information involved in starting in a new role or joining a new organisation can be overwhelming and, to new joiners, it may seem that they are on a treadmill working their way through a standard process. Given this, it is helpful to consider people as individuals, as well as ensuring that the process is applied. This 'human approach' will help those joining the organisation to build relationships, and feel a part of the team, from the outset.

Table 3.13 New business analyst induction checklist

Before start date	First day	First few weeks/months
Agree start time	Outline the plan for the day	Continue appropriate introductions
Consider location, equipment and access	Agree finish time	Arrange regular check-in sessions
Prepare BA welcome pack	Conduct welcome activities and introductions	
Follow organisational processes; for example, HR or payroll	Discuss working practices and culture	Set clear objectives and discuss progress
	Discuss organisational requirements, including health and safety	Discuss and agree training, support and development

Human factors to consider as part of induction are:

- keep in touch at periodic intervals if the new joiner has to work through a long notice period, and perhaps send an invitation to any suitable business analysis meetings or events;
- send a new job card before they start;
- make customers and other business analysts aware of the new joiner's name and start date before they begin working at the organisation;
- send information to explain logistics such as parking, entry, desk arrangements, kitchens, lunch and drinks;
- arrange who will have lunch with them on the first day;
- assign a buddy for them (see Chapter 5).

The induction process is not just for a new business analyst to learn about the organisation and the role; it should be a two-way process. It allows BA leaders get to know the person and understand their preferences, strengths and areas for development. It provides a mechanism to check that things are progressing as expected, address any concerns and set the tone for a successful ongoing relationship.

The induction process also provides the opportunity to get a fresh perspective, as new business analysts may be invited to share any thoughts and observations on the BA Service – in particular, its processes and ways of working.

RETENTION

In a competitive market and having previously put a great deal of effort into recruitment, organisations need to continually review the reasons why their most effective business analysts would want to stay. Retention factors are generally in line with the recruitment attraction factors listed in Table 3.5, but also include:

- the level of communication and openness within the BA Service and organisation;
- how business analysts feel about their manager and the organisation more widely;

- the extent to which business analysts feel engaged with the organisation and have the ability to shape and influence the BA Service and the work they do;

- the social aspects;

- the level of clarity about the business analyst role and recognition of their work;

- the fairness of opportunity, evaluation and reward within the organisation and the BA Service;

- career development and progression opportunities available to business analysts.

Different perspectives on business analyst career development are discussed in the rest of this section.

BA career pathway

There is no standard business analysis career pathway (Reed, 2018). People enter business analysis from a range of backgrounds and progress in different ways both within and outside the profession. There is also a wide range of job titles in use across different organisations. Despite this variety, a pattern has emerged in recent years that reflects a generic career path within a BA Service of sufficient size and maturity to have a range of business analyst grades. This pathway is shown in Figure 3.6.

Figure 3.6 Career path trajectory for business analysts

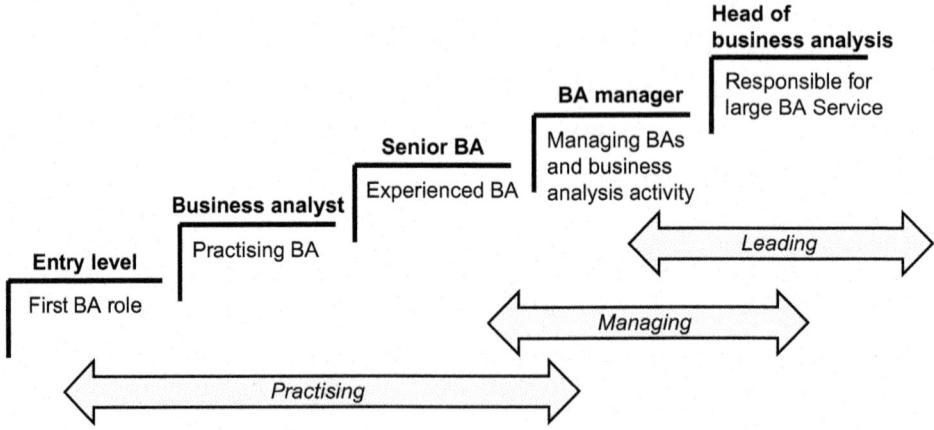

This career pathway facilitates an 'expert leader' approach (Goodall, 2012), where the person is an experienced practitioner of the discipline they are leading. This is especially important for roles with high levels of ambiguity, such as business analysis (see Chapter 1), as there is a need to advocate for and exemplify the role in order to help bring clarity for those doing the role and the customers of the service. Where a BA Service has the benefit of an expert leader, the level of maturity of the BA Service is increased (Artz, Goodall and Oswald, 2016).

The Level 5 leadership model was developed by Jim Collins (2001). This is a useful model to refer to in relation to the business analysis career path and is shown in Figure 3.7. There are a number of comparisons that can be made between the two models:

- The first step for any business analyst role is to be able to demonstrate and evidence being a highly capable individual.

- Practising business analysts (that is entry level, business analysts and senior business analysts from Figure 3.6) can be considered Highly Capable Individuals, Contributing Team Members or neither of these depending on their attitude, behaviours and performance.

- Highly capable business analysts who operate independently and autonomously may feel ready for a management role; this model highlights the need to become a Contributing Team Member (Level 2) before aiming to progress to a management role.

- Expectations of a senior business analyst may lie at either Level 2 or 3 depending on the organisation and structure of the BA Service; this needs to be clear when recruiting new business analysts to the team and for existing post holders.

- Both head of business analysis and BA manager roles may allow people to operate in the Effective Leader (Level 4) space. However, there is no consistent Level 5 Executive role that offers a clear progression route for business analysts.

Figure 3.7 Five levels of leadership (adapted from Collins, 2001)

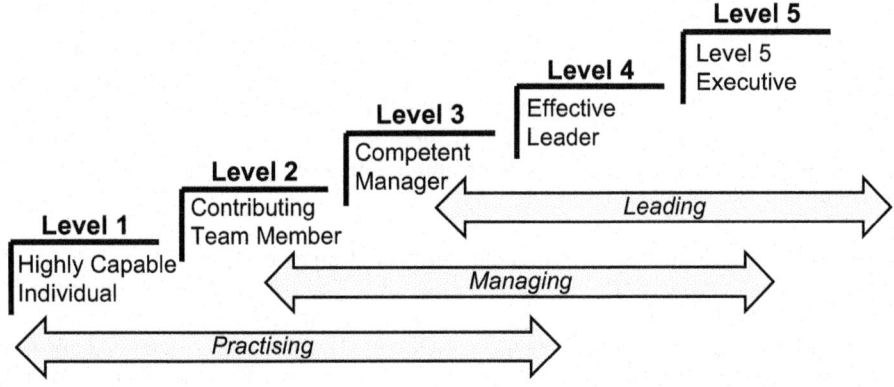

Generalist versus specialist analysts

Business analysts can move into a general business analyst role from a range of specialist analyst roles. Equally, business analysts with general experience in the role can find an analysis specialism they enjoy and wish to focus on. Three possible specialisms and the range of roles within them are listed in Table 3.14.

Table 3.14 Analysis specialisms

Business specialisms	Data specialisms	IT specialisms
Business development analyst	Business intelligence analyst	Agile business analyst
Business improvement analyst	Data analyst	Applications analyst
Business process analyst	Financial analyst	Configuration analyst
Business systems analyst	Information analyst	Digital business analyst
Change analyst	Management information analyst	Implementation analyst
Operations analyst	Performance analyst	IT business analyst
PMO analyst	Reporting analyst	Release analyst
Process analyst	Transformation analyst	Requirements analyst
Process improvement analyst		Security analyst
Procurement analyst		Solution analyst
Quality assurance analyst		Systems analyst
Research analyst		Technical business analyst
Risk analyst		Test analyst
Strategy analyst		UAT analyst
Supply chain analyst		Web analyst

When planning recruitment into the BA Service, it may be necessary to consider whether specialist roles and job titles are needed, or whether targeted recruitment can ensure that individuals with the right skills are attracted without the need to reduce the scope of the role.

If specialist roles are introduced, consideration must be given to how they fit with the business analyst career path shown in Figure 3.6. The introduction of multiple job descriptions at multiple levels requires a significant management overhead and may result in other disadvantages such as reduced flexibility of the workforce and confusion amongst customers. Chapter 1 discussed the issues that arise from role ambiguity, including a lack of certainty regarding what the role can offer and how the work will be performed.

Where legacy specialist roles and job titles exist, it may be appropriate to undertake a rationalisation exercise to standardise job descriptions and titles as far as possible.

Business analyst career options

All business analysts have the option to change both their role and their organisation. This means that there are four positive options for BA leaders to discuss with their business analysts, and they are shown in Figure 3.8. It is key to the success of the business analysis profession that individual analysts are choosing to be part of the profession and do not simply remain in a business analyst role because they feel they have no other options. Even with the appropriate training and support, not all practitioners will enjoy or excel at business analysis. Further, not all business analyst roles are the same and moving to a business analyst role in a different organisation may make better use of an individual's skills and experience.

The BA Career Options model (Lovelock, 2018), shown in Figure 3.8, indicates that, at any point in time, there are four possible career paths for business analysts. These paths involve changing or committing to the role and changing or committing to the organisation.

Figure 3.8 BA Career Options model

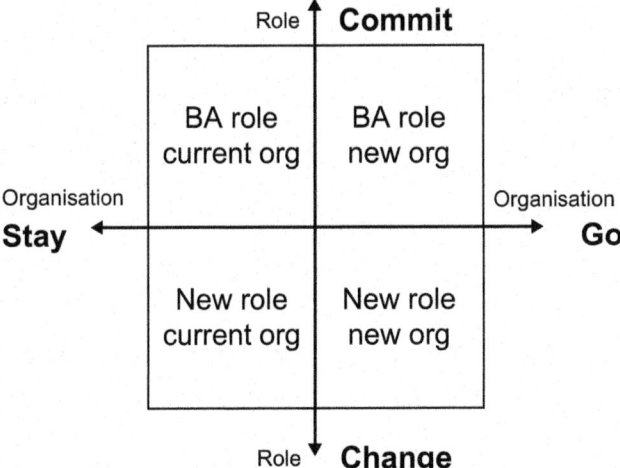

The four options identified in this model are:

- **BA role/current organisation:** commit to learn and develop from the existing business analysis work and exploit the opportunities provided.

- **BA role/new organisation:** continue business analysis career and identify a new organisation that demonstrates the appropriate attraction factors. This could include becoming a contract business analyst working on a freelance basis.

- **New role/current organisation:** discuss and pursue new roles within the organisation that match existing skill set and aspirations.

- **New role/new organisation:** identify roles or organisations that demonstrate the appropriate attraction factors. These may utilise and build on the business analysis skill set.

Where business analysts look to progress outside the business analysis profession, there are several roles and disciplines that they commonly pursue. These are shown in Table 3.15.

Table 3.15 Business analyst career development into related disciplines

Discipline	Relevance
Business change	Allows the business analyst to build on existing relationships, experience of change management and the business analysis skill set
Business architecture	Allows the business analyst to build on existing analytical skills and toolkit
Programme management	Allows the business analyst to build on project and programme experience and shape and steer programme delivery
Product ownership/ management	Allows the business analyst to build on specific product knowledge to steer and champion the ongoing development of that product

SUCCESSION PLANNING

The BA Service must acknowledge that the business analysis skill set is often in high demand, both for other roles within the organisation and by other organisations. It is likely that high-performing business analysts will want to progress either internally or by moving to a role elsewhere. Consideration of the following questions helps to build succession planning into recruitment and development decisions, thereby reducing the impact of change:

- Which roles/individuals have the biggest impact on service delivery?
- Do we have individuals who could lead the BA Service if the current leader moves on?
- How are we supporting new business analysts to be able to move into more senior roles?
- How is knowledge shared so we avoid single points of dependency?
- Do we have appropriate roles that provide a business analyst career path within the organisation?
- Do we have appropriate links and routes outside the BA Service to help retain good people within the organisation?

Addressing these questions allows the BA Service to minimise the impact of individuals moving on and maximise the likelihood that good business analysts will be able to stay. A succession planning process is shown in Figure 3.9.

There may not be set time frames for the succession planning process, but it is important to be alert to the need to replace business analyst posts and pursue succession planning on an ongoing basis.

Figure 3.9 Business analysis succession planning process

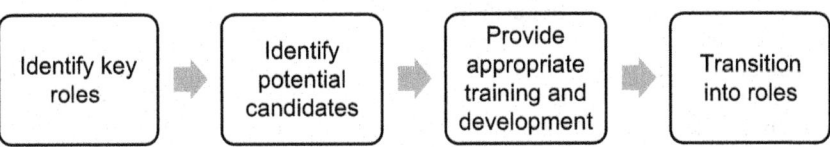

The succession planning process may be applied in a number of different situations. Key roles which may need to be replaced must to be identified. Typically, there will be business analysts at various stages of professional development so that more senior roles may be filled internally. However, succession planning is equally applicable when replacing business analysts on key projects and assignments, so it does not necessarily imply progression in terms of grade or pay scale. Potential candidates need to be identified so that their professional development can be supported and managed. This may be with reference to the T-shaped professional skills and the skills development framework discussed in Chapter 4.

The concept of transition for business analysts covers ensuring the following areas:

- that business analysts are ready and helped to progress to new roles;
- that appropriate handover and knowledge transfer occurs when a business analyst is leaving the BA Service or organisation;
- that transition activities occur when a business analyst is moving to a new piece of work or project.

Transition plans and activities exist to minimise the risk and impact of change for the business analyst and the customer, and to minimise the impact on the operation and reputation of the BA Service. Table 3.16 presents a set of transition scenarios that are likely to occur frequently once a BA Service reaches a certain size. Transition processes need to be smooth and repeatable if these different scenarios are to be handled successfully.

Table 3.16 Business analysis transition scenarios

Scenario	Description
A business analyst is progressing internally to another role within the BA Service	The business analyst can be caught between two roles, expected to cover the new role and at least part of the old role. Transition planning needs to consider if there is anyone to take over the work, any documentation needed and the time frame for the transition. It should also include any support required to help the business analyst move to the new role

(Continued)

Table 3.16 (Continued)

Scenario	Description
A business analyst is progressing internally to a role outside the BA Service	The transition plan could set out a phased release to the new role; it needs to consider if there is anyone who might take over the existing role and the likely timescale for the arrival of a replacement. There may be agreement with the new area that the business analyst might be available to answer questions or to provide support for a set period
A business analyst is leaving the organisation	The transition plan for the notice period duration should focus on: • what is realistic to complete in the time frame (acknowledging the potential for overestimating)? • which handover activities to other people can be completed? • what must be documented?
A business analyst is moving to a new project and is handing over to another business analyst	It must be made clear to customers that the BA Service is providing a skill set and specific business analysis services, and the individual providing those services may need to change over time This may not be a popular decision with either the business analyst or the customer, and the reasons behind the move may or may not be made public Where possible, the two business analysts should work alongside each other. This will help to build the new business analyst's confidence and help to establish credibility with the customer. Where no overlap is possible, a placeholder handover to a third person, such as a business stakeholder, senior business analyst or other relevant role, may be considered
A business analyst is moving to a new project, no business analyst will be assigned going forward	This may not be a popular decision with either the business analyst or the customer, but the reasons behind the move (typically funding or priority) should be communicated and discussed It may be the case that there is little business analysis work to do at this point and that other people are able to carry out the tasks and activities the business analyst had been doing If the business analyst is handing over to business stakeholders, they should be given the opportunity to shape any documentation or materials prepared during the handover

Top tips for transition planning:

- Communicate with customers about the business analyst who is leaving, any handover arrangements and the timescales for the handover should be put in place.

- Working alongside another person is usually the most effective method of handover.

- People typically overestimate what they can achieve in the transition period.

- The activities and deliverables the business analyst is involved in should be considered, and prioritised and re-assigned where possible. It should be acknowledged and agreed with customers that some things may be stopped or paused.

- Summary handover documents with links and signposting to other sources and key contacts is often more effective than lengthy documentation.

CONCLUSION

Recruitment and retention are a huge factor in the successful delivery of the BA Service. BA leaders need to understand the internal and external influences on the candidate market and design a business analyst recruitment strategy that takes these factors into account. Understanding the pipeline for new recruits is a key element of the recruitment strategy.

Planning the recruitment approach helps to ensure that the recruitment process is undertaken efficiently and adheres to the required timescales and selection criteria. However, recruitment is a two-way process, and the needs and expectations of the candidate, and the organisation, must be aligned to achieve the best possible recruitment outcome.

A well-defined and thoughtful induction process that provides the information specific to the BA Service will enable new recruits to engage with their business analyst roles quickly. A welcome pack and induction checklist will help to ensure a smooth induction of new business analysts.

Recruitment can be expensive, so retention of staff should be a key concern for the BA leader. It is particularly important that retention factors are considered where there is a shortage of business analysts or a competitive market for business analysis skills.

There are various career options available to business analysts and exploring development pathways can help to retain and motivate them. Business analysis skills can offer a wide range of opportunities both for career progression within the BA Service and to other roles. Therefore, succession planning needs to take place to minimise the risk of losing key business analysis skills and to lessen any impact on the reputation of the BA Service.

CASE STUDY 1: RECRUITING IN A COMPETITIVE MARKET

Ian Richards, Capita

The BA skill set is highly in demand by employers, with a buoyant market for both contract and permanent BAs. Ian Richards is Head of Business Analysis for Capita People Solutions, was the International Institute of Business Analysis (IIBA) UK BA of the year in 2016 and has been recruiting BAs for many years. He notes: 'It's not an employer's market. Good candidates have options and you have to move quickly.'

Recruitment can be time-consuming, and Ian was able to use a recruitment agency successfully to do initial sourcing and shortlisting of candidates. Ian said, 'This worked because we had built up a relationship over a number of years, and they really knew the skills and experience we were looking for.'

The interview process typically has two stages. It starts with a technical interview, which focuses on demonstrating the skills and competencies for the role. This is followed by a further opportunity to meet, to learn more about the candidate and discuss the organisation and role in more detail. Existing members of the team are involved in panels, which allows them to feel invested in the new BAs from the start.

Ian stresses the point that the interview is a two-way process, where the candidate is also making a decision about whether the role and organisation are right for them: 'We want to make sure that people have a good experience of our recruiting process. If they don't, they will share the experience with others!' Ian also includes discussion of different types of assignments, clients and development approaches, to ensure that the candidates have clear expectations of the role.

Attitude and professionalism are key, and a significant element of this is the BA's approach to professional development. Ian said, 'I want to understand if this is just a job for them, or if they have a passion for business analysis. I want to see a commitment to professional development – how are you making yourself the best BA you can be?' The best candidates are able to demonstrate self-awareness; they know where they need to develop, and they are keen to learn and improve.

Salary is always going to be a key factor in recruitment, and Capita are careful to benchmark against market salaries, but also highlight other aspects they know are important to candidates. Factors such as a vibrant BA community, meaningful and interesting work, a focus on professional development and organisational commitments such as diversity, inclusion and personal wellbeing all help to attract BAs.

The size of the team allows Capita to have a clear BA career structure in place, starting with a graduate scheme. This is a core element of their recruitment strategy, as it provides people with the opportunity to develop and progress internally.

Ian sees recruitment as fundamental to the type of team you want to build and the service you provide, particularly for a professional services organisation. BA leaders should try to 'enjoy recruiting, as meeting people and asking questions is part of the BA skill set!'.

4 DEVELOPING THE BUSINESS ANALYSTS

INTRODUCTION

Business analysts enter the role via many different routes. While some follow the 'developer to IT analyst' route, many become business analysts having worked in generic business operations roles or even specialisms such as accountancy, auditing or legal roles. Some business analysts work to improve business processes without the formal recognition that they are conducting business analysis. However, whatever the route to move into business analysis, it is undoubtedly the case that the broad range of frameworks and techniques with which business analysts need to be proficient present development challenges.

This chapter discusses some key elements of providing a development ecosystem for business analysts within a BA Service. These elements are:

- the T-shaped professional business analyst;
- skills development frameworks;
- the service view of skills development;
- the BA Service as a learning organisation.

THE T-SHAPED PROFESSIONAL BUSINESS ANALYST

The T-shaped professional concept can help to support the development of business analysts. A T-shaped professional is required to have broad generic skills (the horizontal row of the T) and deep specialist skills (the vertical column of the T) that are relevant to their chosen profession. Therefore, these skills will vary according to the requirements of each profession. Presentational and written communication skills are examples of the generic skills that are likely to be required by those working within service professions, such as business analysts.

Gorman suggests that the generic skills of the T-shaped Professional should focus on interactional skills, which are defined as:

The ability to interact with someone from another disciplinary community.
Gorman, 2010

This is the case for the BA Service. One of the key services identified in Chapter 2 concerns 'stakeholder engagement' and reflects the need for business analysts to interact with their colleagues from other disciplines and business stakeholders on a regular basis. These interactions may occur for several reasons; for example:

- to present options to address a business problem;
- to elicit information or requirements;
- to produce a written business case setting out the justification and recommendations for a proposed project.

Interactions that are concerned with stakeholder engagement require two generic skill sets: the personal skills that support effective interaction and communication with stakeholders; and the business domain skills that enable the business analysts to 'speak the business language'.

Personal skills

The concept of the T-shaped professional may be used when analysing and defining the skills required of business analysts. The generic interactional skills may be represented within the cross-bar of the T-shape. Therefore, the personal qualities required of a business analyst may be viewed as forming part of the horizontal element of the business analyst T-shape. Research by Paul (2018) has identified eight key areas of personal skills and these are represented within the T-shape cross bar shown in Figure 4.1.

Figure 4.1 The personal skills of the T-shaped business analyst

Personal skills	
Assertiveness	Innovation
Communication	Negotiation/conflict management
Facilitation	Presentation
Influencing	Relationship building

This entire set of skills are needed to work effectively with stakeholders and range from standard communication and presentation skills, to more exacting skills such as influencing and negotiation. Many of these skills are applicable to a range of professional disciplines, in addition to business analysis, when these disciplines need to work with different stakeholders. However, some of the personal skills identified, such as facilitation and innovation, are particularly relevant to the business analyst role and could be described as specialist skills offered by business analysts.

The relevance of each business analyst personal skill shown in Figure 4.1 is explained in Table 4.1.

Some people possess excellent interpersonal skills. They seem to have a natural facility for engaging with colleagues, delivering presentations and facilitating meetings.

Table 4.1 Personal skills of a business analyst

Personal skill	Relevance to business analysts
Assertiveness	Stakeholders, sometimes those at a senior level, often suggest ideas or change initiatives. Sometimes they identify 'the problem' or even 'the solution to the problem'. Business analysts must be able to challenge such suggestions or comments to clarify the root cause of problems and to ensure that the identification of the solution has not been based on assumptions, sales promises or incomplete information. Challenging stakeholders and questioning their suggestions may be daunting for some business analysts. However, it is a necessary part of the role and requires the business analyst to possess a sufficient degree of assertiveness. It is also important to ensure that assertiveness is not confused with aggressive behaviour, as this can be counter-productive
Communication	The ability to communicate is essential for any role with responsibility for working with stakeholders. In the case of business analysis, the responsibility is to understand what is said, listen actively and ask questions in order to elicit accurate information. The information may be tacit (not recognised and difficult to articulate) rather than explicit (known and clearly defined), placing an additional onus upon the analyst to communicate effectively
Facilitation	Facilitation skill is a key element within the business analyst skill set and is essential when delivering several of the BA services. The ability to facilitate discussions, meetings or workshops requires ongoing development and practice. This skill underpins much of business analysis work, whether redesigning business processes, analysing situations, eliciting requirements or defining the scope of a solution
Influencing	Analytical skills often result in the business analyst identifying where an approach will not be effective or where there is a more beneficial alternative. However, stakeholders may be unwilling to change their views or amend their ideas. In these situations, business analysts must be able to influence the stakeholders so that they are more open to discussion, challenge and the consideration of alternative ways forward. These situations can be difficult to handle. Therefore, influencing is a skill that is often developed through extensive experience of working with stakeholders, often those at a senior level

(Continued)

Table 4.1 (Continued)

Personal skill	Relevance to business analysts
Innovation	The identification of alternative options is a key aspect of several of the business analysis services. This requires business analysts to be able to think creatively and innovatively, possibly through applying techniques that assist this thinking process. An innovative mindset is critical for the digital business analyst who needs to have the ability to consider the possibilities offered by technology that will enable the organisation to offer additional or personalised services to customers, typically beyond the identified requirements
Negotiation/ conflict management	Negotiating with stakeholders, for example, about requirements and solutions, is often needed when conducting business analysis. Additionally, there is always the prospect of such negotiations developing into conflicts that require careful management
Presentation	Presentation skills are required of most people working in business and this is certainly the case for business analysts. They may be called on to deliver presentations in many different situations and to a range of audiences. Good presentation skills are needed to carry out all of the services within the BA service portfolio
Relationship building	It is important that business analysts build good working relationships with stakeholders. The collaborative nature of business analysis depends upon business analysts having good relationships with their stakeholders; for example, when eliciting information or managing conflicting perspectives. It is well-established that the existence of rapport between individuals helps them to work in an atmosphere of trust and support

However, even where this is the case, the most successful communicators, presenters or facilitators understand that improvement is always possible, and that well-founded techniques and frameworks can help to further develop these skills.

Developing personal skills can be difficult, as this often relies on core personal qualities such as confidence and resilience. However, it is possible to improve personal skills through learning and applying relevant rules, techniques, processes and frameworks. For example:

- The ability to communicate in writing may be improved through learning fundamental rules of grammar.

- The ability to manage negotiation and conflicts may be developed through applying frameworks, such as the Thomas-Kilmann Conflict MODE Instrument (see Chapter 10), and Ury and Fisher's (2012) Principled Negotiation process.

- The ability to deliver presentations is enhanced through careful preparation, application of standard approaches such as the 4As (Aim, Audience, Appearance, Arrangement) (Thomas, Paul and Cadle, 2012) and gaining experience within different presentational contexts (such as providing information to colleagues, delivering training sessions or presenting at industry seminars).

The recognition that improvement is possible and desirable is an important first step in the development of interpersonal skills. This then needs to be followed by a process that encompasses learning, application and reflection. An approach to learning, Triple Loop learning, is discussed later in this chapter.

Business skills

T-shaped business analysts are required to have the ability to interact with, and provide the required information for, those who represent their business domain. To do this effectively, business analysts need to have knowledge and skills relevant to the business domain in addition to the personal skills described above.

Most stakeholders expect business analysts to be able to discuss their issues with sufficient understanding of the terminology, legal framework, key processes and so on. Business analysts who do not have the ability to do this can find that their credibility is significantly undermined and this may damage their stakeholder relationships.

Business skills cover a wide range of areas – such as business finance or legal issues – but in overview are concerned with the knowledge and understanding of two key aspects:

- **The business domain within which the business analyst works.** This area of business skill is likely to be specific to a sector of the economy, organisation or line of business. While many business analyst roles require knowledge and understanding of the particular business domain, it is sometimes the case that this is not an 'essential' skill for recruitment purposes. Some BA leaders believe that business domain knowledge can be learnt when working within the domain environment. However, the requirement is likely to be for this learning to be completed at speed!

- **Generic business understanding.** This can be a difficult area in which to gain competence as it typically requires experience and genuine interest in how organisations and their finances work. Many BA leaders express concerns about the lack of business acumen and commercial awareness of business analysts. A well-worn quote is: 'a business analyst should be able to assess how many products (cups of coffee, books, cars, etc.) we would need to sell to pay for a proposed change'. In addition to business acumen concerning business finance, business analysts should also be able to understand aspects such as organisational structures, business models and cultures. All of these topics fall within this skill area.

Business skills also fall within the 'horizontal' skills required of the T-shaped business analyst. This is represented in Figure 4.2.

Figure 4.2 The personal and business skills of the T-shaped business analyst

Personal skills		Business skills
Assertiveness	Innovation	Business domain understanding
Communication	Negotiation/conflict management	Generic business understanding
Facilitation	Presentation	
Influencing	Relationship building	

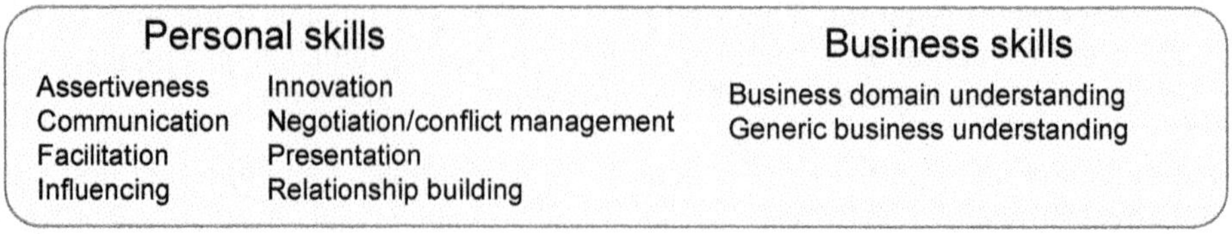

Professional, analytical skills

The professional skills of the business analyst are extensive and concern analytical thinking and the techniques that support analytical thinking. These are the 'deep' specialist skills that are specifically relevant to the T-shaped business analyst and distinguish a business analyst from other roles. They are the core skills of the business analyst, without which it is not possible to conduct the role with any degree of proficiency. There are numerous techniques, so they have been categorised and described in Chapter 2; they are represented in the vertical leg of the T-shape, which is shown in Figure 4.3.

Figure 4.3 The T-shaped business analyst

Personal skills		Business skills
Assertiveness	Innovation	Business domain understanding
Communication	Negotiation/conflict management	Generic business understanding
Facilitation	Presentation	
Influencing	Relationship building	

Professional skills

Agile development
Analytical thinking
Business case
development
Data modelling
Environment
analysis
Gap analysis
Implementation
Investigation
Problem definition
Process modelling
Requirements
engineering
Stakeholder
management
Systems
requirements
specification
User acceptance
testing
User role modelling

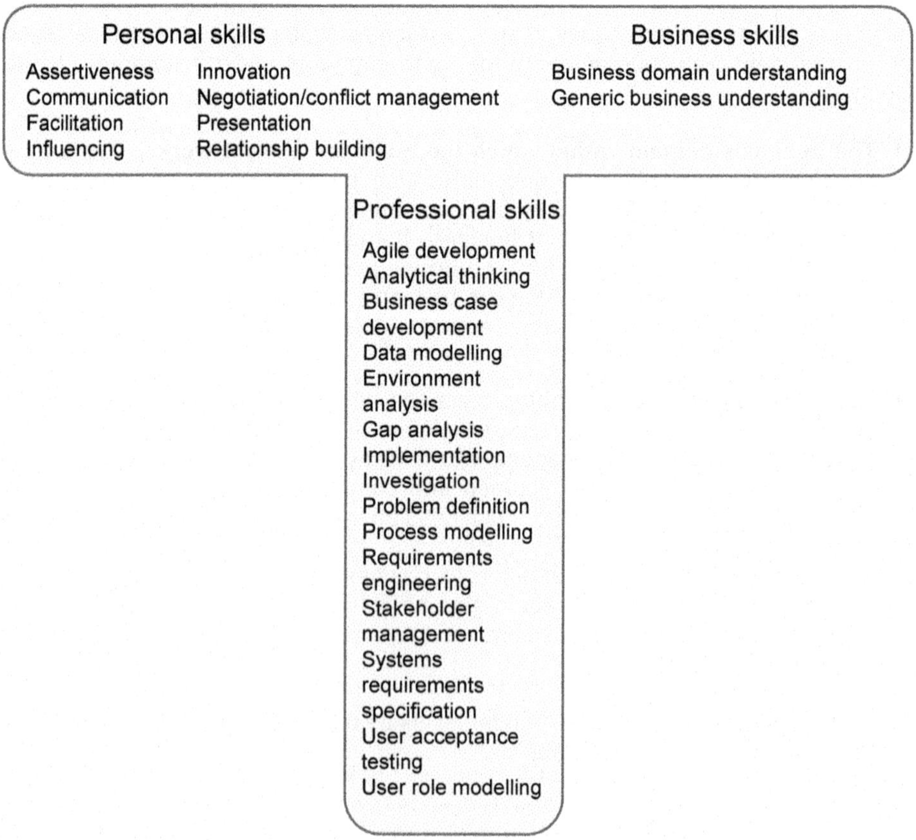

This T-shaped view of the business analyst demonstrates the extensive set of skills, techniques and knowledge required to perform business analysis work. The range and variety of skills and techniques may be viewed as a toolkit from which business analysts may select the 'right tool for the job'. It is important for business analysts to be able to identify when a skill or technique will help to meet a particular need or address a specific situation.

The extent of the business analysis toolkit may help to explain the difficulties encountered by less experienced business analysts when working within a context where their role lacks clarity. However, the definition of business analysis as a catalogue of service offerings, as defined in Chapter 2, may help to alleviate this situation as it will bring clarity regarding the activities and skills relevant to a specific assignment.

SKILLS DEVELOPMENT FRAMEWORKS

The BA service portfolio described in Chapter 2 and the business analyst T-shaped definition outline above may be adapted to meet the needs of an organisation and can support the creation of a skills development framework.

A skills development framework offers a more detailed view than a T-shaped professional definition because it defines each skill in detail and at a number of levels of competence. Some skills development frameworks also include references to development approaches such as training, certification and personal learning. They may also provide career pathways, indicating the skills required to work at different levels and the minimum requirement for an individual to be promoted to a new role.

Skills development frameworks underpin the managerial activities conducted by anyone in a leadership role. They provide a basis for managerial work conducted across the staff responsibilities landscape as shown in Figure 4.4.

Figure 4.4 Staff responsibilities landscape supported by skills development framework

A strong skills development framework can be a highly effective tool when developing business analysts. However, it is important to recognise that while it offers a basis for staff development, it does not replace the need for judgement and thoughtful application.

Table 4.2 provides further detail on the application of a skills development framework to the staff responsibilities landscape.

Table 4.2 Application of a skills development framework

Management task	Use of skills framework
Recruitment	The framework provides a basis for identifying the criteria required of a new recruit. This enables recruiting leads to be clear about what is required when communicating with professionals supporting the recruitment, such as HR professionals or external recruitment agencies, and conducting interviews. This approach is discussed further in Chapter 3
Career and skills development	The framework identifies the required skills and competency levels for each grade within a role and provides a basis for assessing an individual business analyst's skill set, identifying gaps and suggesting areas for development. Information supporting personal development, such as training approaches, certification and personal learning, may also help with career progression
Appraisal and performance management	The framework provides a basis for the appraisal of a business analyst's performance; it helps to identify whether the person is meeting the skills requirements of the role at the relevant grade, and where further opportunities for development might lie
	Skills development frameworks typically cover different types of skill; the standard three categories of professional/ analytical, personal and business skills are often used. This means that attitudinal requirements may be identified within the personal skills category and any issues may be highlighted and addressed. The framework should describe the skill requirements at increasing levels of competence, so it can help to identify the business analysts capable of performing at a more senior level. The definition of the skills and competency levels that apply to different grades and roles provides a strong basis for assessing potential candidates for promotion and specific advice about what they need to do to gain promotion
Removal	The framework helps to clarify where a business analyst does not possess the skills needed for the role and may be better suited to another discipline or possibly a different organisation. The skills categories within a skills development framework can help to identify where there are issues with performance. For example, some business analysts may have excellent professional skills but may struggle to achieve the personal skill requirements

Chapter 3 explored approaches to business analyst recruitment, including the use of a skills development framework to define competence-based criteria for use when evaluating different candidates for a role. This chapter considers the management task concerned with business analyst career and skills development. The appraisal and performance management and removal tasks are discussed in Chapter 5.

Skills development frameworks support these management tasks by providing information on the following areas:

- skill definitions across three skill categories;
- detailed definitions of the required levels of competency for each skill;
- skill requirements at different grades;
- personal development resources such as training courses, self-study materials and support from colleagues;
- certifications recognised and recommended within the organisation.

Industry skills development frameworks

Skills development frameworks may be based upon industry skills frameworks, such as the Skills Framework for the Information Age (SFIA (www.sfia-online.org/en)), or may be developed by an organisation. SFIA is published by the SFIA Foundation, a not-for-profit organisation that is run by a board composed of representatives from several professional organisations. These organisations are BCS, the Chartered Institute for IT, the itSMF (IT Service Management Forum), the IMIS (Institute for the Management of Information Systems) and the IET (The Institution of Engineering and Technology).

SFIA offers a reference model that is made up of definitions of a comprehensive suite of skills that are relevant for anyone working within information systems and digital transformation. The SFIA design is intended to be straightforward to apply, independent of technology and approach, and based upon the practitioner experience. It is intended to offer an adaptable set of definitions that may be configured to suit the needs of organisations applying SFIA.

The skills are grouped into seven categories, each of which is formed of two or more sub-categories, as shown in Table 4.3.

Seven levels of responsibility are defined within SFIA. These are: 1 – Follow; 2 – Assist; 3 – Apply; 4 – Enable; 5 – Ensure, Advise; 6 – Initiate, Influence; 7 – Set Strategy, Inspire, Mobilise. Each level is defined in terms of generic attributes of autonomy, influence, complexity, knowledge and business skills.

There are 102 skills defined within SFIA. Each skill is described in overview and then at a number of levels of responsibility. For example, the business analysis skill is defined at levels 3–6; the business process improvement skill is defined at levels 5–7. When using SFIA to define a role, it is typically the case that a role profile may be formed of skills from a variety of categories and sub-categories, and there may

Table 4.3 SFIA categories and sub-categories

SFIA category	Sub-categories
Strategy and architecture	Information Strategy, Advice and Guidance, Business Planning and Strategy, Technical Planning and Strategy
Change and transformation	Business Change Implementation, Business Change Management
Development and implementation	Systems Development, User Experience and Installation, Integration
Delivery and operation	Service Design, Service Transition, Service Operation
Skills and quality	Skill Management, People Management, Quality and Conformance
Relationships and engagement	Stakeholder Management, Sales and Marketing

be different levels of different skills. For example, there may be a role description that consists of:

- business analysis, level 4;
- business process improvement, level 5;
- business modelling, level 3;
- benefits management, level 5.

BCS have also developed an extended version of SFIA known as SFIA*plus* (www.bcs.org/develop-your-people/develop-your-team-or-organisation/sfiaplus-it-skills-framework). This framework incorporates the skills definitions from SFIA but provides additional information about areas such as techniques, training and study resources. SFIA*plus* offers extensive information and is an extremely helpful resource for developing the BA Service. However, SFIA*plus* is only available to BCS members.

The IIBA offers a competency framework that provides descriptions of skills required by business analysts. The skills are described at five levels of proficiency: strategist; expert; skilled; practical knowledge; general awareness. This framework is devoted to business analysis and, therefore, the skills are defined at a more granular level than those within SFIA.

Organisational skills frameworks

Most organisations use standard frameworks, such as SFIA or the IIBA Business Analysis Competency model, to provide information and a basis for discussion, but then develop their own tailored skills frameworks. One way of doing this is to use the BA Service Framework as a basis, augmented by the business analysis T-shape. The next section in this chapter explains the development of an organisational skills framework.

SERVICE VIEW OF SKILLS DEVELOPMENT

The business analyst role is complex and wide-ranging. Business analysts work on a variety of assignments and projects that may be at a portfolio, programme or project level. The outcomes from business analysis also vary. While requirements definition is typically at the heart of business analysis, there may also be a need for business analysts to conduct activities relating to other areas such as feasibility assessment and business process improvement. The BA service portfolio should be the starting point for developing the performance and skills of the business analysts. This portfolio identifies the services to be offered and should drive the identification of the skills required to deliver the services.

Developing the skills framework

The process to develop a skills framework for a BA Service is shown in Figure 4.5.

Figure 4.5 Process to develop a skills framework

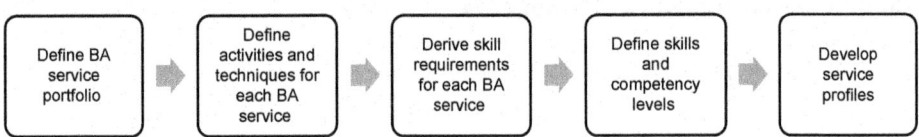

Essentially, the activities within this process are as follows:

- **Define BA service portfolio.** This may be based upon the BA Service Framework defined in Chapter 2, which should be customised in line with the organisation's approach to business analysis.

- **Define activities and techniques for each of the business analysis services.** This may also be based upon the BA Service Framework but will need to be customised for the domain or organisation.

- **Derive skill requirements for each BA service.** The skills required to offer each service in the portfolio and to perform the related activities should be identified. The T-shaped business analyst discussed earlier in this chapter provides an initial view of the skill requirements.

- **Define skills and competency levels.** Each skill should be described in overview and at different levels of competency. It is helpful to apply a standard framework when defining the competency levels. SFIA provides a seven-level framework and the IIBA Business Analysis Competency model uses five levels, as described earlier. However, in practice, this may be considered to be too complex. Many organisations apply a three-level framework and a good example is the Aware, Proficient, Expert framework. This framework is defined in Table 4.4.

- **Develop service profiles.** Identify the skills and the required level of competency required to provide each service. If a service is conducted by business analysts at different grades, it may be necessary to provide different profiles for each grade.

Table 4.4 Framework for competency definition

Competency level	Definition
Aware	Knows about the skill and has a general idea of how and when it might be used. Needs training (formal and informal) before applying the skill, and guidance when applying the skill
Proficient	Is able to apply the skill without guidance; can explain how to apply the skill and can help others to apply the skill. Personal development may be required to keep up to date with good practice and to extend the ability to apply the skill
Expert	Has comprehensive knowledge of all aspects of the skill. Is both highly trained and highly experienced. Is respected and acknowledged as a source of definitive guidance. Is able to confidently provide advice on the use of the skill to address complex problems

Example skill framework components

An example skill description is shown in Table 4.5. This is for a business process improvement skill, which is described in overview and at three levels of competency.

Table 4.5 Business process improvement skill description

Skill title	Business process improvement
Skill description	Use methods and techniques to construct views of business processes at different levels of the process hierarchy, from value stream/value chain to individual task. Analyse documented business processes to identify opportunities for improvement. Evaluate the impact of business process improvements upon capability dimensions such as information systems, people skills, roles and responsibilities, and management structure
Competency level	Competency level description
Aware	• Explain the relevance to the BA Service of business process improvement • Describe a variety of methods that may be used to model, analyse and improve business processes • Explain the 'Lean' philosophy and principles • Describe the relationship between the elements that are relevant to a holistic analysis: process, organisation, people, information and technology • Support business process improvement for straightforward business change initiatives

(Continued)

Table 4.5 (Continued)

Skill title	Business process improvement
Proficient	• Conduct business process improvement for complex change initiatives
	• Create and maintain business process models at different levels of the process hierarchy
	• Apply BA Service standards and techniques for business process improvement
	• Apply the 'Lean' philosophy and principles when conducting business process improvement
Expert	• Determine standards for business process improvement
	• Develop the skills and knowledge required to conduct business process improvement across the BA Service
	• Develop business process improvement plans for highly complex business change initiatives and facilitate the execution of the plans
	• Collaborate with senior stakeholders from a range of different disciplines to support ongoing business process management

An example service definition is shown in Table 4.6.

Table 4.6 Example of service definition

Service name	Service proposition (describes the value proposition that is offered to the customer of the service)	What is delivered (what will be delivered by the service)	How the service is delivered (the activities performed to conduct the service)
Requirements definition	Requirements are elicited, analysed, modelled and recorded	Requirements definitions	Elicit requirements using a range of techniques as appropriate for each situation Analyse requirements and record clear, organised and prioritised requirements

(Continued)

99

Table 4.6 (Continued)

	Develop requirements models when appropriate to represent the solution and clarify business rules
	Build prototypes to represent the interface requirements
	Define business acceptance criteria for requirements
	Apply validation processes and work with stakeholders to ensure acceptance of requirements
	Manage the requirements throughout the project, ensuring traceability of requirements

An example service/skills profile is shown in Tables 4.7–4.9. Each table covers a skill area as follows:

- Table 4.7: professional skills for the requirements definition service;
- Table 4.8: personal skills for the requirements definition service;
- Table 4.9: business skills for the requirements definition service.

Table 4.7 Professional skills for the requirements definition service

Skill name	Skill description	Competence level/description
Process modelling	Use methods and techniques to construct views of business processes at different levels of the process hierarchy, from value stream/value chain to individual task. Analyse documented business processes to identify opportunities for improvement. Evaluate the impact of business process improvements upon capability dimensions such as information systems, people skills, roles and responsibilities, and management structure	Aware: • Explain the relevance to the BA Service of business process improvement • Describe a variety of methods that may be used to model, analyse and improve business processes • Explain the 'Lean' philosophy and principles • Describe the relationship between the elements that are relevant to a holistic analysis: process, organisation, people information and technology • Support business process improvement for straightforward business change projects

(Continued)

Table 4.7 (Continued)

Skill name	Skill description	Competence level/description
Investigation	Elicit information to record requirements. Select and apply techniques as appropriate to the business context and the project requirements	Proficient: • Apply a range of elicitation techniques • Record information for complex situations and change projects • Apply BA Service standards when eliciting information • Apply investigation approaches relevant to stakeholders • Define and execute stakeholder communication plans
Requirements engineering	Analyse, model, record, validate and manage business and solution requirements to provide an effective foundation for an information system development or procurement	Proficient: • Plan requirements engineering activities • Undertake requirements engineering activities for complex situations and change projects • Apply requirements engineering techniques relevant to complex situations and change projects • Apply requirements quality standards • Negotiate requirement priorities and conflicts
Stakeholder management	Establish and maintain relationships with stakeholders from a variety of backgrounds and disciplines. Identify, analyse and manage relationships with and between stakeholders	Proficient: • Apply a variety of techniques to conduct stakeholder relationship management • Identify and analyse the stakeholders for a change project • Determine communication and management strategies for working with stakeholders

Table 4.8 Personal skills for the requirements definition service

Skill name	Skill description	Competence level/description
Facilitation	Moderate discussions between stakeholders to enable participants to share views, information and ideas, and achieve defined objectives. Ensure that all participants contribute to discussions and are able to express differing points of view	Proficient: • Explain the facilitation process and key techniques • Prepare for and design facilitated discussions with groups of stakeholders • Facilitate meetings and workshops attended by groups of stakeholders • Ensure follow-up actions are documented and allocated to participants
Negotiation/ conflict resolution	Identify business situations where negotiation is required to address conflicts and disagreements regarding requirements. Select and apply techniques to negotiate and resolve conflicts between stakeholders	Proficient: • Identify requirements conflicts • Describe and apply a range of negotiation approaches and techniques • Resolve straightforward negotiation situations
Assertiveness	Express ideas and opinions, and challenge stakeholder views, with confidence and mutual respect	Aware: • Explain the difference between assertive and aggressive behaviours • Demonstrate personal assertiveness when dealing with challenging situations • Explain techniques used in order to be assertive when working with stakeholders
Communication	Listen actively to elicit tacit and explicit information accurately Produce written communications that are clearly expressed and grammatically correct	Proficient: • Apply active listening techniques • Select appropriate media for delivering verbal and written communications • Apply the rules of grammar, spelling and punctuation correctly in line with BA Service standards

(Continued)

Table 4.8 (Continued)

Skill name	Skill description	Competence level/description
	Create engaging presentations and written communications that convey information in a clear and succinct way Deliver presentations and written communications that align with the needs of specific audiences	• Produce clear and effective presentations and written communications • Ensure that communication style meets the needs of different audiences

Table 4.9 Business skills for the requirements definition service

Skill name	Skill description	Competence level/description
Business domain understanding	Understand the relevant business domain in order to perform a particular business analyst role effectively. The domain knowledge may concern the enterprise and/or closely associated organisations, such as customers, suppliers, partners and competitors	Aware: • Explain the importance of having a working knowledge of the business domain in which the organisation operates • Describe the main dimensions of the business domain – its rationale, values, drivers and constraints • Identify the customers, suppliers, partners and competitors in the business domain • Recognise that there are regulatory differences between operating regions and explain the impact this has upon requirements
Generic business understanding	The required level of understanding of the market drivers and customer segments that a product or service sits within, the business purpose of the product/service and the features and capabilities offered by it. Articulate the needs of different customer personas within the market	Aware: • Explain the relevance of market and product knowledge to a business analyst • Identify the main products/services offered by the organisation • Identify the customers served by the organisation

Role profiling

Once the skill and service profiles have been developed, it is possible to develop a profile for each business analyst role within the BA Service. This involves defining the role in terms of the services offered and the skill/competency requirements for the delivery of the services. The role profile may be visualised using a 'heat map' approach, showing the skills required to conduct the role and the levels of competency required. An example of a role profile is shown in Figure 4.6.

Figure 4.6 Example of a business analyst role profile

Professional skills	
Process modelling	Proficient
Investigation	Proficient
Requirements engineering	Expert
Stakeholder management	Proficient
Personal skills	
Facilitation	Proficient
Negotiation/conflict resolution	Proficient
Assertiveness	Aware
Communication	Proficient
Business Skills	
Business domain understanding	Proficient
Generic business understanding	Aware

A role profile sets out the skill requirements for anyone performing a particular role and, therefore, provides a benchmark against which performance may be assessed and monitored. It also helps managers to recruit staff, set performance objectives, determine training needs and identify candidates for promotion.

THE BA SERVICE AS A LEARNING ORGANISATION

Acquiring and maintaining the required skills is important for anyone working in a professional discipline. Where that discipline has a technological and business focus, as is the case for business analysis, ongoing skill development is critical to meet the needs of a constantly changing business environment.

For example:

- **Government policy or legal regulation changes** have an impact upon how organisations work. Business analysts have to keep up to date with such changes in order to support their organisations in ensuring compliance.

- **Socio-cultural changes** often result in new or extended customer requirements. Business analysts need to be tuned in to different ways in which customers want services to be delivered and the experience they expect them to have when dealing with the organisation.

- **Technological changes** are frequent and can change the way in which organisations operate and the services they can offer. Business analysts have to conduct their work within a digital context, and this requires them to be knowledgeable about new developments and the potential that they can offer.

Given the frequency of change and the nature of the business analyst role, the acquisition of new knowledge and skills – and the enhancement of existing knowledge and skills – is important for both BA leaders and individual business analysts.

Peter Senge wrote that the following characterises a learning organisation:

> Where people continually expand their capacity to create the results they truly desire, where new and expansive patterns of thinking are nurtured, where collective aspiration is set free, and where people are continually learning how to learn together.
>
> Senge, 2006

Senge's description is highly aspirational and offers a vision for business analysts and leaders when building and developing the BA Service. While BA leaders are responsible for developing a learning focus and embedding a culture of learning within the BA Service, the business analysts have a shared responsibility for executing the vision of the learning BA Service:

- Each individual needs to be aware of the skill requirements for the role they perform. Beyond having an awareness, the individual also needs to embrace learning and adopt several mechanisms to ensure the required skills are developed, maintained and enhanced as necessary.

- Each BA leader has to offer their staff support for their personal skills development. This support has several facets: provision of learning opportunities, learning resources and a clear direction for learning. There has to be coherence and consistency amongst these three elements. For example, a BA leader who emphasises the importance of skills development yet offers limited support – whether through training or other resources – will undermine the message and fail to embed a learning culture within the team.

Skills development process

The process for personal skills development is represented in Figure 4.7.

Figure 4.7 Skills development process

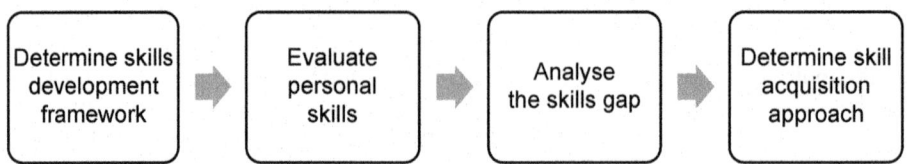

This is a standard gap analysis process that should be familiar to most business analysts. The process depicts how the skills development framework may be used to support BA leaders when developing the business analysts within their team. The individual stages in this process are as follows:

- **Determine skills development framework.** As discussed earlier in this chapter, the skills development framework consists of service, skill and role profiles that set out what an individual business analyst needs to know and to be able to do. This framework offers the 'to be', or 'target', state.

- **Evaluate personal skills.** Each individual business analyst can be assessed, or may assess themselves, against the relevant role profile within the skills framework. The framework also offers the potential for individuals to assess themselves against other role profiles when they wish to move into a different business analyst role or gain promotion. This assessment provides the 'as is', or 'current', state.

- **Analyse the skills gap.** The gaps are identified by comparing the desired target state with the current state. This evaluation will identify the skills or knowledge that the individual does not hold at the required levels of competency.

- **Determine skill acquisition approach.** The competency gaps should be considered in the light of the resources provided within the BA Service. Relevant approaches to address any gaps should be identified and adopted. Skills acquisition is an ongoing process that should be reviewed regularly. Ideally, business analysts should be responsible for monitoring their individual skill sets and identifying where a need for development has arisen.

Triple Loop learning

The BA Service can increase the effectiveness of its learning and decision making by understanding the feedback mechanisms, or loops, which are applied after an action has led to an outcome. The Triple Loop learning concept (Argyris and Schon, 1974), represented in Figure 4.8, shows how business analysts may learn from both challenges and successes. This concept prompts consideration of the quality of business analysis, the standards by which quality is evaluated, and the ways in which those standards are defined in the first place.

Figure 4.8 Triple Loop learning (adapted from Swieringa, Wierdsma and Swieringa,1992)

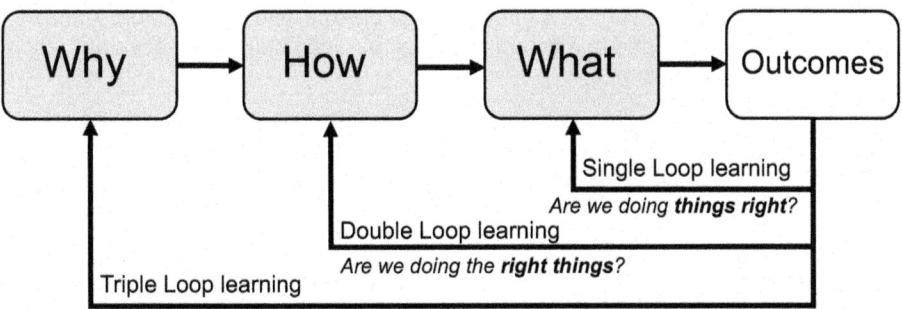

- **Single Loop:** Doing things right. Policies, procedures, standards and quality criteria (in other words 'the rules') are all applied successfully by business analysts. Business analysis techniques are used correctly and in line with the standards defined by the BA Service (see Chapter 6).

- **Double Loop:** Doing the right things. Business analysts provide services defined in the BA service portfolio and reflect on whether the procedures, rules and standards should be changed or updated (see Chapter 12). New business analysis techniques are adopted as appropriate and BA leaders review and update the BA service portfolio when required (see Chapter 2).

- **Triple Loop:** Defining what is right. The direction and approach of the BA Service may need revision or transformation in response to changes in organisation strategy, internal context, external influences and industry practices. BA leaders may need to review and update the vision for the BA Service (see Chapter 8) and BA Service Charter (see Chapter 11).

Learning approaches

A variety of learning approaches exist and may be made available to business analysts. Again, it is not just the responsibility of the BA leaders to determine the learning resources – all of the business analysts within the team should share responsibility for identifying these resources.

Different individuals learn in different ways and this, plus the continuing nature of learning, requires different learning resources to be made available (see also Appendix 4). The possible resources are described in Table 4.10.

Table 4.10 Learning and development approaches

Learning approach	Description
Formal training course (face to face)	Formal training courses provide an efficient means of learning new techniques and gaining new skills. It is also the case that a training course enables the exchange of experience and insights, and, if provided to a group of colleagues, can help in the development of a BA Service
	Formal training courses are usually based on established good practice and provide a means of standardising the approach taken to business analysis work across the BA Service. For example, the adoption of UML techniques such as use case and class diagrams
Formal training course (online)	Online formal training courses should also be based on established good practice. However, it is important to evaluate the quality of such products. They can also provide a means of standardising how the business analysis work is conducted
	Online learning is typically a form of personal study, so does not generate the advantages that may accrue from group discussions and sharing of experiences. These products have greater flexibility, though, as they can be accommodated within time constraints at work
Personal study using other resources	Skills development requires individuals to engage with the development process and to spend their own time on this, even if also attending formal training. The resources that are available to support personal development are extensive, easily accessible and varied
	Business analysts should be encouraged and motivated to look for available online instruction (videos, articles, online learning) and published material (books, magazines, articles)
Informal learning event	Many organisations run informal business analysis team events such as lunchtime presentations or discussions. These may focus on a specific topic and last for a limited time (such as an hour). They offer an opportunity to share skills and knowledge and are often tailored to the organisation. An ongoing programme of informal events helps to foster a culture of learning, which allows benefits from investment in formal training to be realised
Conference	Business analysis conferences have increased in number over the last few years. While they charge for admittance, they can offer a way of gaining additional skills, knowledge and insights in a short space of time. The nature of such conferences is that the range of topics tends to be extensive, so they can offer a significant development opportunity

(Continued)

Table 4.10 (Continued)

Learning approach	Description
Seminar	Professional bodies such as BCS or IIBA run meetings and seminars on a regular basis. Each event tends to focus on a set theme and there is typically at least one speaker and time for discussion. These events also offer an opportunity to meet and network with fellow business analysts
	The BAMF runs seminars twice a year for BA leaders and managers. These seminars also offer an opportunity for discussion, sharing experiences and networking
Internal learning resources	Many business analysis teams have a shared repository where individual business analysts may share information. The repository also presents an opportunity for the organisation to share standards, policies and other forms of guidance. Such repositories can be a valuable resource for personal development
Voluntary work	Business analysts may work on a voluntary basis to support organisations such as charities or small businesses. This provides opportunities to gain experiences in environments that are outside the normal workplace

Learning as a community

Benefits of a Community of Practice

The business analysis profession places particular emphasis on the benefits of engaging with the professional community across organisations and sectors. This enables business analysts to learn from their peers and to share ideas and insights. The CoP concept may be applied internally to a BA Service, as discussed in Chapter 1, as this helps to provide business analysts with a sense of identity and common purpose within the organisation. This sense of identify and purpose may be fostered through face-to-face or virtual events, and the provision of collaboration spaces and tools (see Chapter 7).

The benefits from a CoP are defined as follows:

> The *community* creates the social fabric of learning. A strong community fosters interactions and relationships based on mutual respect and trust. It encourages a willingness to share ideas, expose one's ignorance, ask difficult questions and listen carefully.
>
> Wenger, McDermott and Snyder, 2002

Therefore, a CoP will form a strong basis for the BA Service, as it will engender the sense of a sharing, learning community.

Wenger, McDermott and Snyder also commented on the nature of 'practice':

> The *practice* is a set of frameworks, ideas, tools, information styles, languages, stories and documents that the community members share.

This requires a CoP to be supported by a wide-ranging repository that exists to share information amongst practitioners about the work conducted by their profession. Within a BA Service, this repository would help to define 'how' business analysis is conducted and would provide business analysts with access to the collective wisdom of their internal community.

Developing a sense of community is essential if the aims of identity, focus, collective wisdom and sharing are to be achieved. This requires business analysts, particularly BA leaders, to arrange regular community events in order to foster a culture of common understanding and shared values (discussed in Chapter 11). While this may involve a significant investment of time, effort and funding (see Appendix 9), there are significant benefits to be gained from such events, including:

- an environment for professional development;
- a source of inspiration and motivation;
- a professional support mechanism;
- a professional network;
- a sense of professional identity;
- an opportunity to strengthen relationships;
- an opportunity to learn as a group;
- an opportunity to share knowledge;
- a means of identifying dependencies and associating related work;
- a way to establish consistent ways of working;
- a mechanism to improve ways of working.

The CoP concept can be particularly beneficial if a BA Service is large or geographically distributed. The sense of shared purpose can help to encourage communication with colleagues in different locations or domains; the central repository can provide a basis for communication and sharing across geographical boundaries. A CoP can also offer a means of structuring the community through 'local' events, based around physical location or business area, that can generate contributions to the learning resources.

Reasons Communities of Practice fail

Inevitably, there will be innovators and early adopters who welcome the creation of a CoP enthusiastically; there will be others who defer adoption until they can see the benefits clearly; and there will be those who resist or avoid engaging with a CoP until forced to do so (Rogers, 2003). Given this mix of perspectives, and the pressures of everyday business analysis work, both new and established CoPs can run into issues.

Table 4.11 sets out some key reasons why CoPs fail to prosper.

Table 4.11 Reasons why Communities of Practice fail

Reason	Detail	Options
All talk no action	Agreements made or learning received is not put into practice Actions taken are not followed up or are continually deferred	Be realistic about what can be achieved, but try to hold people to account. Remind people of previous actions in advance of meetings. Only allocate key actions; capture other ideas and suggestions on a backlog and prioritise them
Detail over value	Standards are discussed and debated in extensive detail, and peripheral or theoretical issues are given too much focus The CoP loses sight of the real needs of the community and how business analysis may offer value to customers	Set up sub-groups to look at detail if needed Create agendas that engage the widest number of members
Exclusivity/ cliques	A core group dominates the CoP, leaving others unable or unwilling to contribute	Create term-limits on roles; invite different chairs; invite different members to contribute rather than waiting for volunteers
Inward looking	The CoP does not engage with other professions or communities and does not try to learn from outside its own membership	Invite external speakers and engage with other similar internal groups or professions. Enable business analysts to attend related CoPs to learn from their approach
Lack of support	Where engagement with the CoP is voluntary for business analysts and the projects or organisation do not provide support to the CoP, the business analysts may report that they are too busy, not able or not allowed to attend	Focus on promoting the benefits of engaging and attending; plan well in advance and seek support from senior managers

(Continued)

Table 4.11 (Continued)

Reason	Detail	Options
	Attendance and frequency of meetings decline	Use surveys, seek feedback from members and act on feedback received
	Lack of support at an organisation level may also translate to a lack of funding	Make the business case for appropriate funding for the CoP
Reliance on one person or a small group	Individuals or small groups run out of ideas or feel unappreciated. The CoP takes up a large amount of their time. If key people leave or are unavailable, the CoP is at risk	Create term-limits on roles; invite different people to take on the chairperson role; invite different members to contribute rather than waiting for volunteers; engage a wider number of people
		Ensure that key volunteers are thanked and appreciated
		Ensure that knowledge management practices concerning the logistics of the CoP are in place so that others can pick up the roles more easily
Too top-down	The community feels that it is being told what to do, or 'told-off' rather than being engaged and contributing to both the agenda of the CoP and the development of standards	Aim to create an agenda from the community rather than from management
	The CoP is used as a channel for cascading corporate messages	Carefully consider what topics are relevant to the CoP and avoid general organisation updates

Some key, generic actions that can help to address this variety of issues that can arise are as follows:

- Encourage everyone to be honest about issues.
- Focus on building relationships as a core activity.
- Continue to seek senior support and sponsorship.
- Create or revisit regularly the terms of reference or purpose for the CoP.

A learning community can offer an additional means of ensuring that business analysts develop their knowledge and skills. Taking time to foster this community can reap significant rewards both for the BA Service and the organisation.

Professional business analysis certifications

Training courses may be accredited or endorsed by professional bodies. An accreditation is typically based upon a professional certification that has a defined syllabus setting out the topics to be included in the course. Where this is the case, course attendees are able to sit an examination leading to the particular certification.

The major professional bodies that offer certifications in business analysis are as follows:

- BCS, the Chartered Institute for IT:[1] BCS offers certifications that support the business analyst career path from entry/apprentice level to expert. The BCS International Diploma in Business Analysis is widely adopted by organisations wishing to ensure that their business analysts have professional certifications. This certification has also been adopted as a means of ensuring standardisation and consistency of approach to business analysis work.

- IIBA[2] offers a range of certifications, including the Entry Certificate in Business Analysis, Certificate of Competence in Business Analysis and Certified Business Analysis Professional. These certifications are based upon the IIBA Guide to the Business Analysis Body of Knowledge (BABOK®), which has been adopted as a standard by many organisations.

- BAMF:[3] the BAMF offers the Expert BA Award (which is endorsed by BCS) and has also contributed to the development of the BCS Advanced Diploma in Business Analysis.

- International Requirements Engineering Board (IREB)[4] offers certifications that are concerned with Requirements Engineering.

- Project management awarding bodies, such as Project Management Institute (PMI)[5] or the Association for Project Management Group (APMG),[6] also offer business analysis certifications.

Business analysis certifications have been available since the mid-1990s, when BCS introduced a certification in Business Activity Modelling. This was followed by the BCS Diploma in Business Analysis, which was launched in 1999. Since this time, certifications have grown in importance within the business analysis community. The advantages offered by certification are as follows:

- Certifications confirm that an individual has achieved a level of competence in a topic. For example, a business analyst holding the BCS International Diploma in Business Analysis has been tested for knowledge, understanding, application and the ability to analyse and synthesise information within a business analysis context.

---

1 See www2.bcs.org/certifications/ba

2 See www.iiba.org/certification/core-business-analysis-certifications

3 See www.bamanagerforum.org/the-expert-ba-award

4 See www.ireb.org/en

5 See www.pmi.org/certifications/types/business-analysis-pba

6 See www.apmg-international.com

- Certifications usually require significant effort from examination candidates, so they also confirm that they are prepared to apply themselves to learning and personal development.

- From an organisational perspective, certifications signal that the organisation is prepared to invest in their staff. From a business analysis perspective, they also provide evidence to the rest of the organisation of the professionalism of the BA Service.

- Where certification examinations are taken within the context of a formal training course (whether in class or online), course participants tend to devote more time and attention to study and, therefore, tend to gain more from the experience than when attending courses where there is not a certification.

- Certification provides common language and baseline understanding of core concepts for all members of the BA Service.

The BCS publication, *Business Analyst* (Reed, 2018), offers further information on business analysis certifications.

CONCLUSION

BA leaders have a broad range of staff development responsibilities. Fulfilling these responsibilities can be time-consuming and difficult, and an approach that incorporates the use of skills development frameworks and role profiles can be extremely helpful. Given that business analysts work within business environments that are subject to frequent change across many different areas, there is a pressing need for ongoing personal development.

There are a variety of learning approaches available to business analysts, some formal and some less so. Formal learning approaches, such as training courses, are often based upon professional certifications like those offered by BCS.

A CoP offers a basis for building a sense of a common purpose and identity amongst business analysts. This helps to develop a shared responsibility for learning, where everyone within the team contributes to learning and development. A willingness to share information, knowledge and experiences, and the provision of resources to support sharing, is key to the success of a community learning initiative.

The provision of a skills development framework and an internal information sharing repository is the responsibility of the BA leader. However, participating in learning activities and contributing to the learning resources are the responsibility of everyone in the BA Service. It is only when both leaders and practitioners engage in the learning process, and the principles and philosophy of a learning organisation are embraced, that a learning culture will be embedded within the BA Service.

CASE STUDY 2: GREEN-FIELD BA SERVICE

Michael Greenhalgh, British Council

When Michael Greenhalgh joined the British Council, he found a green-field site for business analysis. There were several BAs based at sites across the UK and in Europe, but there had been little opportunity to clarify the role or share best practice. Therefore, there were no standards, templates or shared ways of working across the business analysis team.

The situation was in contrast to the business analysis approach at Michael's previous organisation. He moved to the British Council from a financial services institution where there was a mature BA practice, having taken for granted all the components that make the delivery of a BA Service successful. Michael commented: 'I realised everything had always been in place; building it was daunting but also a great chance to review what was important.'

The first task that Michael decided upon was to listen to the existing BAs and their customers. There was mixed understanding of the BA role, even amongst those who had the job title 'business analyst'. Keen to use industry standards and best practice where possible, Michael looked to BCS and IIBA resources, and developed a clear definition of the BA role within the British Council.

There was a sense of urgency within the organisation to adopt business analysis tools and templates. However, Michael felt it was important to concentrate first on the people within the business analysis team, focusing on the development of key business analysis skills. He was keen to build trust within the team and enable more senior BAs to mentor their less experienced colleagues.

Michael carried out a maturity assessment of the British Council's BA community and used the results of this assessment to set targets and create a shared improvement plan to which all the BAs would contribute. He wanted to create a sense of a highly professional community, so set up monthly meetings (a mixture of face to face and virtual) as well as encouraging the establishment of business analysis working groups. These groups were tasked with developing specific initiatives and reporting progress to the main BA community meeting. Guest speakers from other roles were invited to present to the BA community, providing a basis for the BAs to learn from others and avoiding an insular focus. The British Council encourages professional development and is highly supportive of learning from external sources.

Reflecting on the initial period when he was creating the BA community, Michael said: 'I was conscious of the opportunity and the responsibility. I wanted to get it right, and there was a lot of information available to support us; I read lot of books! We needed to find our space within the organisation, to build good relationships and trust with other roles, particularly project managers, architects and business partners.'

The BAs at the British Council are still striving for continuous improvement and, having established many changes, Michael's role has changed over time. He commented: 'My role is to support BAs day to day to do their job better, more effectively, and to try to clear blockers. I also communicate with colleagues outside the BA community and sell the benefits of the BA role.'

5 ENABLING A HIGH-PERFORMANCE BA SERVICE

INTRODUCTION

The BA Service has a broad portfolio, as discussed in Chapter 2, so requires business analysts to be proficient in using a wide range of business analysis frameworks and techniques. This demanding context presents performance challenges for practising business analysts and managerial challenges for BA leaders as they endeavour to support business analysts to perform their role successfully.

The staff responsibilities landscape was introduced in Chapter 4, which covered the development of business analysts. This landscape is shown again in Figure 5.1.

Figure 5.1 Staff responsibilities landscape

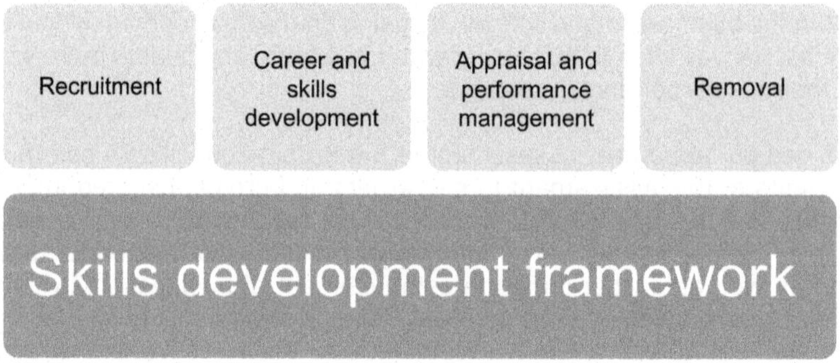

This chapter covers the following topics related to the final two elements of the staff responsibilities landscape:

- appraisal and performance management;
- mentoring and coaching to facilitate improved performance;
- providing performance feedback;
- removal from the BA Service or the organisation.

APPRAISAL AND PERFORMANCE MANAGEMENT

The terms 'appraisal' and 'performance management' can sometimes have negative connotations, implying a formal intervention or process that has the aim of identifying or addressing perceived problems with an individual's performance. However, it is possible to reframe appraisal and performance management to encompass the activities needed to ensure that a team, and the individual members within that team, are meeting the predefined performance objectives and are conducting their work in an effective and efficient way.

While appraisals and performance reviews inevitably identify where an individual's performance is not of the required standard and improvement is needed, a more positive view of appraisal and performance management may be developed if the process is used to do the following:

- guide performance;
- enhance and extend individual competence;
- identify factors that are hindering performance but are outside the individual's control;
- recognise people for their performance;
- provide reassurance that objectives are being met;
- celebrate milestones and achievements;
- design team building activities;
- provide supportive challenges for team members;
- inform reward and recognition of individuals and the team.

Benefits of performance management

Annual performance appraisals can seem like an overhead, a distraction or a tick-box exercise. They are often perceived to be onerous tasks that distract employees from delivering service. However, good quality, continuous performance management offers many benefits to organisations, teams and individuals. Adopting an ongoing approach to performance management can ensure that any issues are resolved quickly and can prevent the development of isolated incidents into poor performance habits.

Within a BA Service, effective performance management can help realise the following benefits:

- identify anyone who is overloaded, overwhelmed, not working effectively or failing to contribute;
- allow evidence-based decision making for new assignments, additional support and progression opportunities. BA leaders often 'know' who their best and worst performing business analysts are but can't pinpoint why or provide tangible evidence;
- clarify objectives, responsibilities and expectations;
- establish who likes to do what, who is good at certain tasks and where development needs exist (which may or may not be recognised by the individual business analyst);

- increase overall accountability and productivity. Many business analysts need a level of pressure (both time frame and appropriate attention) to be able to do their best work. Some are demotivated when there is no visibility or recognition for the work they do;

- form part of an ongoing commitment to seek and act on feedback;

- provide an opportunity to identify exemplar pieces of work and inform best practice that may be shared with other business analysts;

- improve transparency. By sharing appropriate detail and aggregate information from the process, everyone can see who is assigned to what and where team strengths and development areas lie. This can foster collaborative working and sharing of work;

- answer questions such as: 'Are we improving?' and 'Are we meeting our objectives?'

Managing the performance of the BA Service requires a focus on the particular needs of the business analyst role. It requires BA leaders to recognise the skills, behaviours and attitudes required to deliver an effective BA Service and to manage the business analyst's performance accordingly. This work may be supported in part by a comprehensive skills development framework, as it will provide a basis for identifying where required skills are lacking or needing enhancement. Well-defined competency levels for each skill will also help to identify which aspects need further work. Approaches such as the GROW model, described later in this chapter, can help BA leaders to manage and improve their team's performance.

Some people are keen to improve their performance, while others seem to avoid this at all costs. This avoidance sometimes results from a belief that the current level of performance is adequate and does not need further improvement, although this is likely to be a misplaced belief. Other reasons for avoidance are that the business analyst does not see a need to achieve certain performance targets or possibly does not understand why certain skills are required. Ultimately, some business analysts may shy away from striving for better performance because of a fear of failure. BA leaders have to address all of these reasons if individuals are to understand what is expected of them and the BA Service is to achieve the level of performance required to support the organisation effectively. It is also vital that performance management is applied consistently to the business analysts, irrespective of grade, seniority or contractual basis. Contracted business analysts should be evaluated in the same way, and against the same benchmarks, as those employed by the organisation.

Behaviours of business analysts

While it would be reassuring to assume that all business analysts are dedicated professionals who are determined to develop their skills on an ongoing basis, unfortunately, in the real world, this is not always the case. Anecdotal stories about business analysts who do not perform at the required level abound within the business analyst community – in particular, during discussions amongst senior or managerial business analysts. Empirical research undertaken in 2018 (Paul 2018), uncovered criticism by senior business analysts about some of their colleagues. The following comments were made:

- There are good BAs and there are bad BAs.
- Some BAs are happy to just take the notes.
- Some BAs are not competent.
- I can do this work, but others just can't.

A more detailed view of unhelpful behaviours that have been observed or commented upon by senior business analysts is shown in Table 5.1.

Table 5.1 Unhelpful behaviours demonstrated by business analysts

Behaviour name	Behaviour description
Self-limiting	Use of limited range of business analysis skills such as process modelling and facilitation
BA in name only	Job title is business analyst, but the individual does not reflect the business analyst role or the required skills and experience
Subject matter expert	Conducts work through application of specific business or application knowledge rather than through the use of the business analysis skill set
'I know the business'	Entered business analysis via a business route, so makes assumptions, doesn't ask questions, has out-of-date business knowledge
Pedantic	Inappropriate focus on less relevant detail, leading to inability to meet deadlines; focuses on finding mistakes
Maverick	Will not conform to defined standards, templates and ways of working. Does not contribute to the development of the business analysis service. Thinks they 'know better'
'Told you so'	Unable to move on, accept current situation/chosen option. Enjoys issues materialising
Just a BA	Unable to influence and does not try to analyse; happy to just take notes or document what is said
Negative	Wants to say no; everything has been tried, nothing will work
	Us and Them; causes or contributes to divisions
Stepping stone	Not invested in business analysis but sees it as a move towards a role perceived to have more seniority or authority
Superior	Does not display empathy for other roles and regards other roles with disdain

The impact of poor business analysis on the perception of the entire BA Service – or even the business analyst role itself – was discussed in Chapter 1. Table 5.1 highlights behaviours for which BA leaders should be vigilant, as they have the potential to diminish the performance of business analysts and result in a poor perception of the BA Service.

Growth mindset for business analysts

The key differentiator between a good business analyst and a great business analyst often derives from the attitude towards personal and professional development. The Growth Mindset theory, developed by Professor Carol Dweck (2017), identified that people who believed their intelligence and abilities could be developed (a growth mindset) outperformed those who believed their intelligence and abilities were fixed (a fixed mindset). Table 5.2 shows the impact of a growth or fixed mindset on different areas of the BA Service.

Table 5.2 Impacts of fixed and growth mindsets

Area	Fixed mindset	Growth mindset
Learning and development	I already know how to do my job	There is always more to learn to help me be a better business analyst
Tools and techniques	I will stick with what I know	I want to learn more and expand my business analysis toolkit
Quality	That's as good as I can get it	It can be improved through personal effort and working with others
Relationships	My working relationships are fine	Working relationships can be developed and investing time in this is part of the business analyst role
	Success of others is threatening	Success of others is inspiring
Feedback	Is critical and personal	Is constructive and useful
Change	I've always done it this way	Innovation and experimentation will help me, the BA Service and the organisation to develop
	Change is distracting and disruptive	
BA deliverables	Customers will be given the deliverables I have to produce	Deliverables can be tailored to meet customer needs and expectations
Standards and templates	Are set in stone and hard to change	Can be improved through my experience and contribution
Challenge	I give up easily	Embrace challenge, it provides the opportunity to learn and develop
	Challenging work and situations should be avoided	I like to try different approaches/ strategies

These examples show how a growth mindset helps people to move forward. BAs with a fixed mindset may plateau in their career, whereas those with a growth mindset are more likely to be able to continue to develop and reach their potential. Understanding the differences between a fixed and a growth mindset can be invaluable when managing performance as it helps to identify where a fixed mindset is preventing individuals, and by extension the BA Service, from achieving performance objects. This is a key aspect of enabling effective performance, as mindset can have a significant impact on performance improvement.

If a problem with a fixed mindset has been identified, the BA leader should aim to encourage a growth mindset. There are several ways to do this, including conducting the following actions:

- Instigate a discussion about the concept and implications of the growth mindset.
- Provide internal learning and development opportunities.
- Provide opportunities to try new skills in a safe-to-fail environment.
- Champion training and professional certification.
- Build a culture of sharing work and peer review.
- Provide supportive challenge of fixed-mindset behaviours.
- Offer a role model for personal and professional development.
- Protect time for development activities.
- Discuss limiting beliefs and share success stories.

Each of these actions can help the BA leader to encourage individual business analysts to adopt a growth mindset. In turn, this can help to address some of the unhelpful behaviours listed in Table 5.1 and support business analysts with their professional development.

Evaluating the business analysts

It is important to consider the entire range of required skills across the personal, business and professional dimensions when evaluating business analysts. It is also important to identify where unhelpful behaviours are evident, analyse the root causes of the behaviours and decide how they may be addressed.

The performance management matrix shown in Figure 5.2 can help with the performance evaluation of business analysts. It considers performance in the light of two axes: technical performance and behavioural performance.

The four quadrants of the performance management matrix help BA leaders to evaluate the performance achieved by individual business analysts and offer high-level strategies to improve their work. Table 5.3 describes the quadrants within the performance management matrix and the related strategies.

APPROACHES TO FACILITATE PERFORMANCE MANAGEMENT

The performance issues that emerge from using the performance management matrix are likely to require action. These actions may require the creation of development plans for individual business analysts, which may prescribe training or other formal development approaches. However, it is often helpful to consider supplementing formal development with other approaches such as mentoring, coaching or buddying.

Figure 5.2 The performance management matrix (reproduced with permission from Maura Shields, Human Edge Consulting)

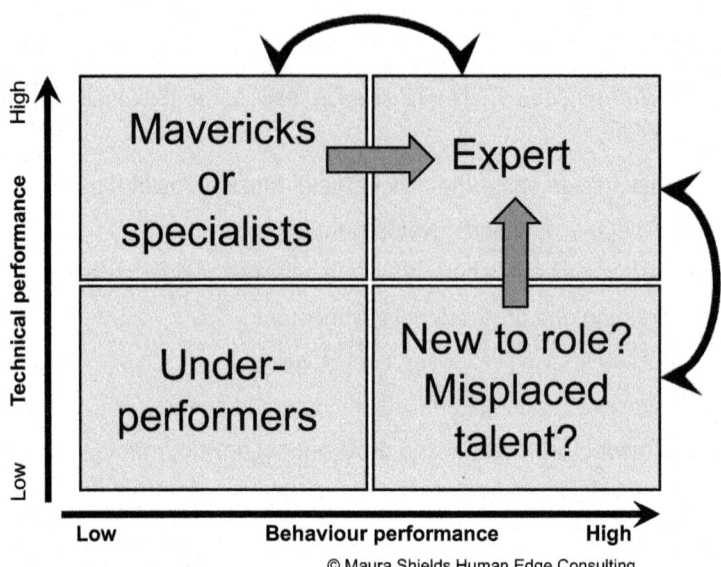

© Maura Shields Human Edge Consulting

Table 5.3 The performance management matrix strategies

Quadrant	Description
High technical performance, high behaviour performance	**The expert:** the business analysts who possess the required skills across all three categories. These are the role models who may be able to support or motivate those who are not performing at this level. They may be able to mentor less experienced colleagues or encourage improved behaviour from the maverick business analysts
	The business analysts within this group should be deployed as ambassadors for the team and as mentors and role models
Low technical performance, high behaviour performance	**The new business analyst or misplaced talent:** the business analysts who demonstrate the required ability to engage with stakeholders and a desire to learn
	Where new to the role, these business analysts need to develop the required technical skills. This may be achieved through the development approaches discussed earlier, coupled with the allocation of a mentor (from within the expert category)

(Continued)

Table 5.3 (Continued)

Quadrant	Description
	However, some business analysts in this category may not have the innate ability to develop the technical skills. While it is wise to deploy development strategies and mentoring, ultimately this may prove ineffective. BA leaders need to recognise where this is the case and decide on the best outcome, both for the team and the individual. It is possible that a more limited area of business analysis might be helpful. However, a move to another role may be more beneficial both for the individual and the organisation
High technical performance, low behaviour performance	**The maverick or specialist:** the business analysts who have excellent technical business analysis skills but fail to work well with stakeholders and colleagues. This can be a serious failing for a business analyst, given the need to work effectively with stakeholders in often challenging situations. A business analyst who has low behavioural performance may cause problems for the entire BA Service despite the accuracy of their technical work
	Expert business analysts may be able to support development work for maverick or specialist business analysts. They may be able to uncover the reasons for poor behavioural performance and achieve improvements through demonstrating their proficiency. An expert business analyst role model or mentor may be able to move a maverick or specialist towards the expert quadrant
	However, for some individuals, behavioural issues may be deep-seated, and improvement may be limited, short-lived or impossible. In these situations, the options are to either accept the behavioural issues and limit the assignments to which an individual is allocated, or to facilitate a move to another role where technical excellence is required but there is less emphasis on behavioural performance
Low technical performance, low behaviour performance	**The under-performer:** these business analysts are sometimes the most difficult people to manage. While some genuinely may have difficulty in performing the business analyst role, the lack of behavioural skills indicates that they may lack interest in business analysis or may be content to perform at a lower level than that required
	BA leaders need to explore the reasons for poor performance with these business analysts and decide if a development strategy is appropriate. It may be that the under-performer business analyst does not have an affinity for business analysis so does not wish to improve, or it may be that there is a genuine misunderstanding about the needs of the business analyst role (which is an easier problem to address). However, it may be that there are other problems – perhaps of a personal nature – that are affecting performance

(Continued)

Table 5.3 (Continued)

Quadrant	Description
	Ultimately, BA leaders have the responsibility for addressing performance issues. In the case of the under-performer, a development strategy may address the problems, although low behavioural performance suggests that this is unlikely to be sufficient. Where there are external issues, this may require a longer-term approach, perhaps involving colleagues from HR. Where a business analyst is disaffected and content to perform poorly, it may be necessary to consider disciplinary action and removal

Mentoring and coaching: differences

The terms 'mentoring' and 'coaching' are often used interchangeably. While similar, they have a different focus and intent and the method adopted will depend upon whether a person is being mentored or coached.

Mentoring has been defined as enabling:

> an individual to follow in the path of an older and wiser colleague who can pass on knowledge, experience and open doors to otherwise out-of-reach opportunities.
> Thomas, Paul and Cadle, 2012

The purpose of mentoring is to provide access to knowledge and experience within a supportive professional relationship. A mentor is usually at a more advanced career stage than the person to be mentored, but this does not mean that anyone mentoring a business analyst has to be a senior business analyst and possess business analysis skills. The role of a mentor is to help an individual understand their development needs and performance challenges, but this does not necessitate that the mentor has expertise within the particular discipline.

The mentor should enable the mentee to define the actions needed to develop and may set goals and milestones to monitor progress. A mentor has to be able to apply active listening in order to support the mentee and should be professional and non-judgemental during discussions.

Coaching is often conducted by the manager of the individual whose development is to be supported. The specific areas addressed by a 'coach' have been defined as follows:

> (A coach) deals with a person's tasks and responsibilities, has a specific agenda or development approach, has a focus on improving a person's job performance and will often be the person's line manager.
> Thomas, Paul and Cadle, 2012

Coaching should not be viewed as only a 'deficit' development activity for under-performing business analysts. Many organisations use coaching to enable performance improvement for high-performing individuals.

Mentoring is a relatively informal approach to personal development. It is typically additional to the professional development plan for business analysts, so a mentor would not be expected to provide feedback on progress or provide input into a performance review. This is not the case with coaching where there is likely to be a specific focus on meeting performance objectives, so a coach may provide input to a performance review. Whichever the case, it is helpful to agree the terms for the mentoring or coaching arrangement so that both parties are clear about the objectives to be achieved. Appendix 5 provides a template for a coaching or mentoring agreement.

Mentoring and coaching: approaches

The GROW model
The GROW model (Whitmore, 2009) was developed originally in the 1970s and is one of the most popular approaches used to mentor or coach colleagues or staff. This model is represented in Figure 5.3.

Figure 5.3 The GROW model

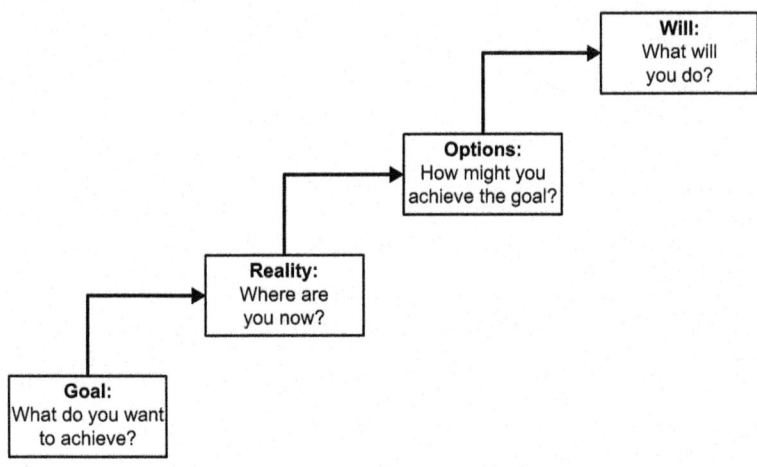

The four stages of the GROW model are applied as follows:

- **Goal:** define where the mentee or coachee wants or needs to be.
- **Reality:** define to what extent and in what way the mentee or coachee needs to develop to achieve the goal.
- **Options:** identify and develop ideas to achieve the goal.
- **Will:** define and commit to a plan.

The GROW model provides a basis for helping individual business analysts to improve their performance. It sets out a similar process to that often applied in business analysis whereby a target situation is defined, the current situation is understood, the gap is analysed and the actions to move towards the target are agreed.

This model remains one of the most popular and widely used performance development models. It provides a questioning framework for the mentor or coach to help the person set a goal (G), objectively consider the current reality (R), discuss potential options (O) then define what they will (W) actually do. In practice this is an iterative conversation, where new options emerge that refine the goal, or the reality of the situation becomes clearer, resulting in adjustments to the original goals set.

Mentoring and coaching requires active listening, insightful questioning and supportive challenging; three key skills for business analysts. Therefore, the GROW model should be straightforward to adopt within a business analysis setting and should equip business analysts to help staff or peers with their personal development.

When adopting the GROW model, BA leaders need to be open to supporting individuals through exploring their current skills and identifying their development needs. An example usage of the GROW model when supporting the development of a business analyst is as follows:

- **Goal:** where does the individual want to be as a business analyst? What career path is envisaged? Possibilities include becoming a highly skilled professional business analyst, a consultant specialising in business analysis or a BA leader.

- **Reality:** using a benchmark such as a profile of the desired role or the T-shaped business analyst definition, what business analysis skills does the individual need to develop? Is this possible and, if so, what would be the required time frame?

- **Objectives:** what are the specific business analysis development objectives? Identifying the 'skill gaps' to be addressed will provide a basis for defining the business analyst's development objectives.

- **Will:** when and how might the business analysis skills development be achieved? Possibilities include attendance at formal training events to enable learning about specific frameworks and techniques, achievement of certifications, and application of skills within practical contexts. This can then be defined within a plan of action; this plan will also provide a basis for monitoring the business analyst's progress towards achieving the objectives and the overarching goal.

The Johari window

The Johari window (Luft and Ingham, 1955) is another framework that may be used within a coaching or mentoring context. It provides a basis for exploring an individual's performance needs and identifying skills, attitude or knowledge gaps. The Johari window is shown in Figure 5.4.

The Johari window helps to explore what is known and recognised about an individual and what may not be known or recognised. The aim in using the Johari window is to encourage self-discovery by the individuals within the team. The possible combinations of 'known' and 'not known', represented in the four quadrants of Figure 5.4, support the discussions described in Table 5.4.

Figure 5.4 The Johari window

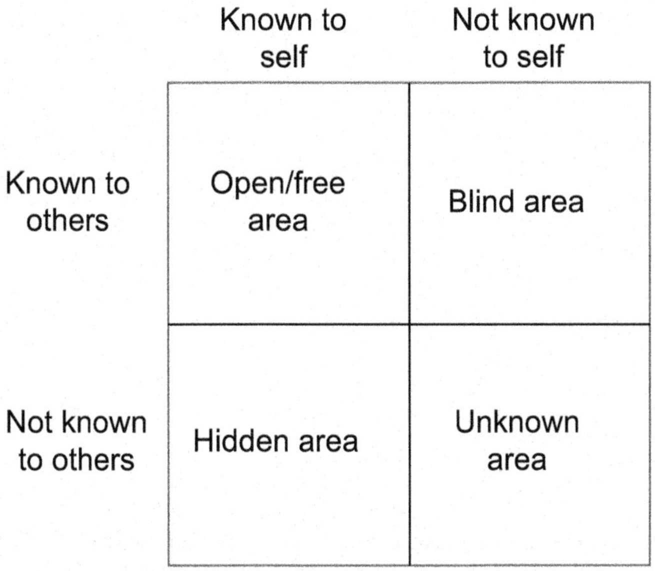

	Known to self	Not known to self
Known to others	Open/free area	Blind area
Not known to others	Hidden area	Unknown area

Table 5.4 The Johari window quadrants

Known to others; known to self	This is labelled the open/free area and is where an individual's skills, attitudes, knowledge, opinions and behaviours may be discussed. The aim is to develop this area so that the team members are able to discuss their performance openly and productively, with feedback being given and received in a constructive manner
Known to others; not known to self	This is the area where an individual may be unaware of their shortcomings to the extent that there is a blind spot. Their colleagues are aware of the lack of skills or knowledge, or problems with behaviour, views or attitudes, but may also identify hidden/unrecognised strengths. The aim is to foster a culture where feedback may be given sensitively so that the individual is able to accept it and consider how to improve. Mentors, coaches or team colleagues may need to help each individual achieve this level of acceptance and can facilitate this process by offering guidance and providing non-judgemental advice
Not known to others; known to self	This is the area where individuals may conceal areas where they feel they are not as skilled or knowledgeable as required. It is also possible that there may be hidden agendas or action plans. Mentors or coaches should foster an atmosphere of openness and constructive discussion in order to decrease the hidden area and increase the open area

(Continued)

Table 5.4 (Continued)

Not known to others; not known to self	This is the area where skills or other abilities are unknown or not recognised. This requires strategies that will help to discover an individual's potential or latent abilities and move them into the other areas. Depending upon the situation it may be that knowledge about ability may move into the hidden, blind or open area. Mentors or coaches may offer an individual the opportunity to work in a particular area in order to uncover unknown ability. Care needs to be taken in this area as some unknown abilities may be of a sensitive nature

The performance known/unknowns matrix

The performance known/unknowns matrix, shown in Figure 5.5, offers a similar approach to the Johari window. The matrix shows four combinations of 'known' and 'unknown' and helps to uncover where an individual's performance issues might lie and which actions may be helpful.

Figure 5.5 Known/unknowns matrix for personal development

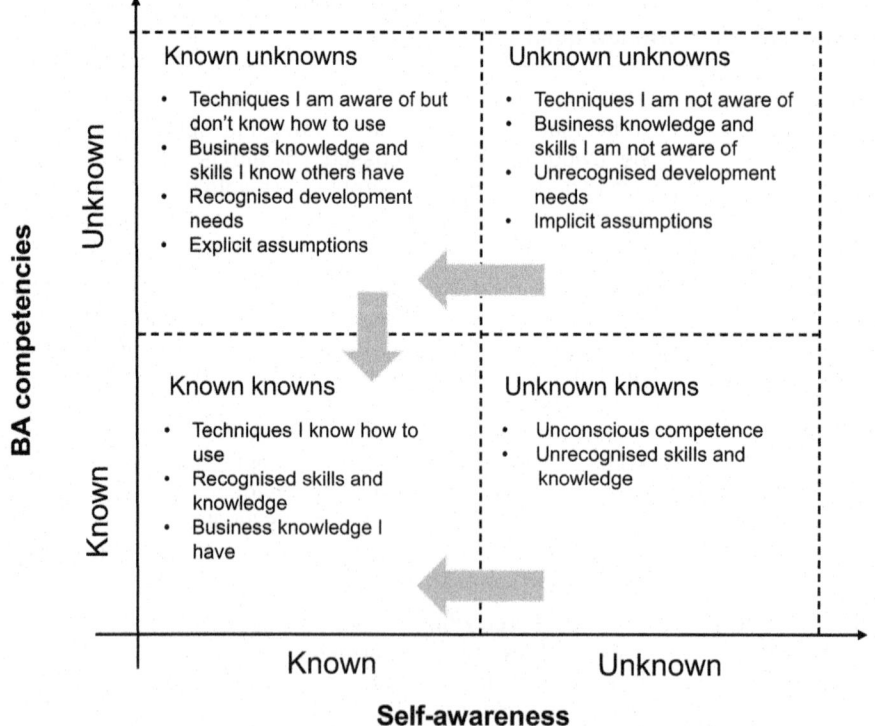

This matrix shows the desired development paths towards the 'known knowns' quadrant, from 'unknown knowns' to 'known knowns' or from 'unknown unknowns', to 'known unknowns' and then to 'known knowns'. These pathways may be traversed through applying many different learning approaches, which, for a business analyst, include the following:

- attending business analysis training courses and learning events;

- requesting and listening to feedback and reflecting on how business analysis skills may be improved or development objectives may be achieved;

- shadowing a colleague who is more experienced in a particular business analysis service;

- conducting independent research. For example, using online business analysis learning resources such as those available at www.assistkd.com/knowledge-hub;

- reading background information;

- receiving coaching from a BA leader or another colleague in a leadership or managerial role;

- being mentored by a senior business analyst, possibly from a different organisation; IIBA UK offer a business analyst mentoring scheme at www.iibauk.org/mentoring;

- participating in a buddy scheme (see next section).

It is often the case that having awareness of performance shortcomings can help development and improvement. The Johari window and the known/unknowns matrix offer a basis for exploring awareness and identifying where this is lacking.

Buddy schemes

The purpose of a buddy scheme is to create a supportive connection between individuals and does not necessarily relate to seniority or experience. Buddying can help with personal development and performance improvement in a less formal way than mentoring or coaching.

A buddy scheme can be used within a BA Service to:

- help new business analysts settle into the organisation;

- legitimise and encourage peer-to-peer relationships across the business analysis team;

- connect business analysts with different levels of experience and strengths so that they can learn from each other.

Levels of formality of a buddy scheme can vary. Some may offer little or no structure or guidance on the role of buddies and will allow people to define their own relationships; others may provide guidance on the role of a buddy and will make recommendations about areas such as the frequency of meetings, the content and focus of discussions, and the expectations regarding outcomes.

An effective buddy needs to be supportive and open to sharing knowledge. A buddy should also be willing to ask and answer questions, and should be able to prioritise sufficient time to work with the other person.

Randomised Coffee Trials (RCTs)

For a large BA Service, or one with dispersed locations, the concept of Randomised Coffee Trials, developed by Nesta[1] in the UK and popularised by the Red Cross, is another approach that may be used to create connections with colleagues. These connections can provide a basis for discussion, support and learning.

The idea is very simple to apply in practice. Individuals who do not know each other (or who have not worked together) are paired up randomly and encouraged to arrange a real or virtual coffee break. They discuss their roles, their work, previous experience, ideas and inspiration – anything they wish. The RCT allows people to expand their internal network, share ideas, identify and explore shared issues, and build the sense of a professional community. There is no expectation of an ongoing relationship, but connections are often maintained and used to ask questions or facilitate introductions at a later date.

RCTs can be beneficial when trying to establish a sense of community within the BA Service; the advantages associated with the community concept were discussed in Chapter 4. Some business analysts are able to build their internal network without a framework to help them, but the use of RCTs involves everyone, legitimises the time commitment and removes the awkwardness that may be associated with 'networking'.

UNDERSTANDING PERSONAL MOTIVATION

Business analysts have varying attitudes towards producing analysis deliverables and the desired level of quality. Some of the less desirable behaviours displayed by business analysts were described in Table 5.1. The underlying reasons for these unhelpful behaviours can be difficult to understand, as individuals have different attitudes and motivations. The examination of personal motivations can help to make sense of a business analyst's approach to the work and can assist BA leaders when they are managing the performance of the team.

Kahler's 5 drivers

Kahler's 5 drivers (Kahler, 1975), shown in Figure 5.6, provide a framework for understanding personal motivations and can be invaluable when considering the most appropriate way to support an individual business analyst.

Understanding the drivers that may motivate the behaviours demonstrated by business analysts can help to clarify the positive and negative impacts of that driver on the quality of the work. Listening to the language used by business analysts about their tasks, deliverables and workload, and how they feel about the work of their colleagues, provides clues about their drivers. It may be a useful exercise to consider the business analysis team in the light of the 5 drivers to analyse how the drivers may be affecting the quality of the work. Table 5.5 defines the performance management approach relevant to each driver when aiming to improve performance.

---

1   See www.nesta.org.uk/blog/institutionalising-serendipity-via-productive-coffee-breaks

Figure 5.6 Kahler's 5 drivers

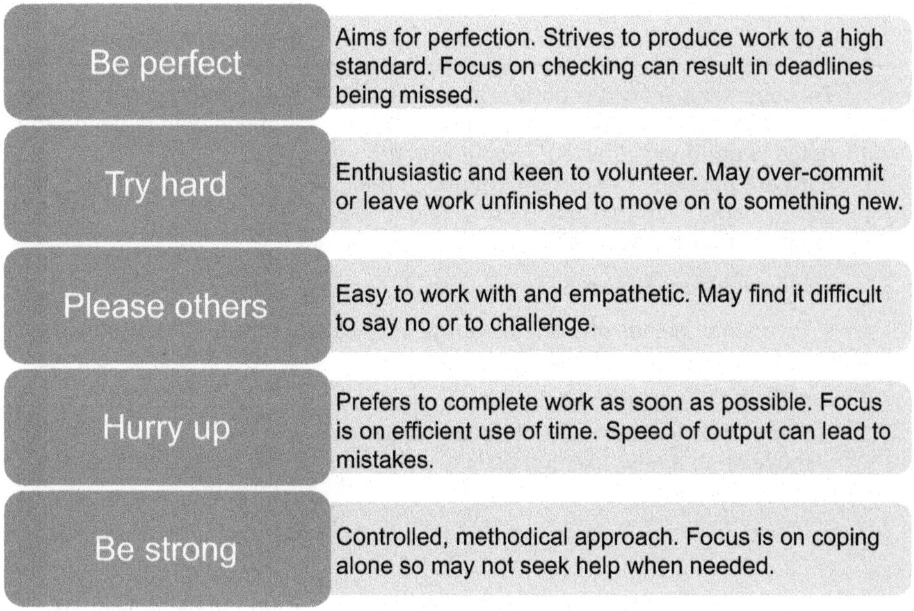

Be perfect	Aims for perfection. Strives to produce work to a high standard. Focus on checking can result in deadlines being missed.
Try hard	Enthusiastic and keen to volunteer. May over-commit or leave work unfinished to move on to something new.
Please others	Easy to work with and empathetic. May find it difficult to say no or to challenge.
Hurry up	Prefers to complete work as soon as possible. Focus is on efficient use of time. Speed of output can lead to mistakes.
Be strong	Controlled, methodical approach. Focus is on coping alone so may not seek help when needed.

Table 5.5 The impacts of Kahler's 5 drivers

Driver	Impact upon performance	Performance management approach
Be perfect	This business analyst aims to produce excellent work and is able to conduct a detailed review when accuracy is critical. However, this business analyst's approach can seem pedantic, focusing on attention to detail at the expense of meeting deadlines. This can cause project friction and downstream delay The business analyst may: • Seem overly critical when reviewing the work of others • Seem pedantic, having attention to detail at the expense of meeting deadlines • Cause project friction and downstream delay by missing deadlines • Be reluctant to share their own work • Be defensive when receiving feedback and unwilling to incorporate feedback	• Focus on defining appropriate quality expectations up front • Encourage sharing early drafts of work and agree interim review dates where progress will be shared • Be clear on deadlines and the impact of missing them • Praise delivery within time frame

(Continued)

Table 5.5 (Continued)

Driver	Impact upon performance	Performance management approach
Try hard	This business analyst is enthusiastic, gets involved in lots of different activities, and helps to get things started. People who try hard are popular with customers due to their positive approach to problem-solving and are happy to try new approaches The business analyst may: • Turn small pieces of work into large projects because they want to pursue all options • Become bored with detailed work, sometimes leaving work undone in order to move on to a new, exciting activity	• Assign to work that needs help to get off the ground • Encourage to be specific about commitments (move from 'I'll try' to 'I will') • Agree and monitor work and ensure a task is completed before moving to a new task • Help them set realistic targets • Prevent them from over-committing to work • Nominate individuals rather than relying on volunteers • Praise completion of work
Please others	This business analyst has good rapport with stakeholders, so may be popular The business analyst may: • Keep extending work to incorporate changes from customers resulting in uncontrolled change/scope creep • Fail to challenge, even if something is known to be wrong • Agree to help others or complete other work at the expense of finishing the current task or deliverable • Avoid making recommendations and sit 'on the fence'; seek approval or re-assurance • Take the blame and be overly apologetic	• Agree and monitor business analysis work package • Use product descriptions if necessary • Discuss the impact of change • Discuss strategies for staying focused on delivery, being assertive and challenging in a positive way • Provide reassurance after they have had to challenge or say no to a customer

(Continued)

Table 5.5 (Continued)

Driver	Impact upon performance	Performance management approach
Hurry up	This business analyst meets deadlines and is highly productive The business analyst may: • Move to solution-focused thinking too quickly, resulting in missed options or unrealised assumptions • Make mistakes, offer superficial analysis or lack attention to detail • Attempt to save time by taking shortcuts such as involving fewer stakeholders, not taking into account all perspectives, or not following the required process • Become frustrated with colleagues or the process	• Appreciate the volume of work they are getting though • Ensure that sufficient time is spent on problem definition and options analysis • Use quality checklists to get the business analyst to apply rigorous self-assessment • Agree lists of stakeholders to engage • Assign a peer reviewer who applies high level of attention to detail • Discuss the benefits of applying templates and following standard processes
Be strong	This business analyst is able to cope in a crisis, deal with difficult people and situations, and works methodically The business analyst may: • Prefer everything to be (or appear to be) under control • Seem to lack empathy and avoid emotion	• Agree a process for obtaining input, assistance and support so that this does not feel like a failure • Help to consider their own and other people's emotions • Praise tailoring their approach to different stakeholders

Impact-behaviour cycle (the Betari Box)

It can be tempting to discount how our own attitudes and behaviours contribute to the behaviours displayed by others. The Betari Box, shown in Figure 5.7, defines the cyclical relationship that happens during interactions and can help BA leaders to analyse and adjust their behaviours where necessary.

Figure 5.7 The Betari Box

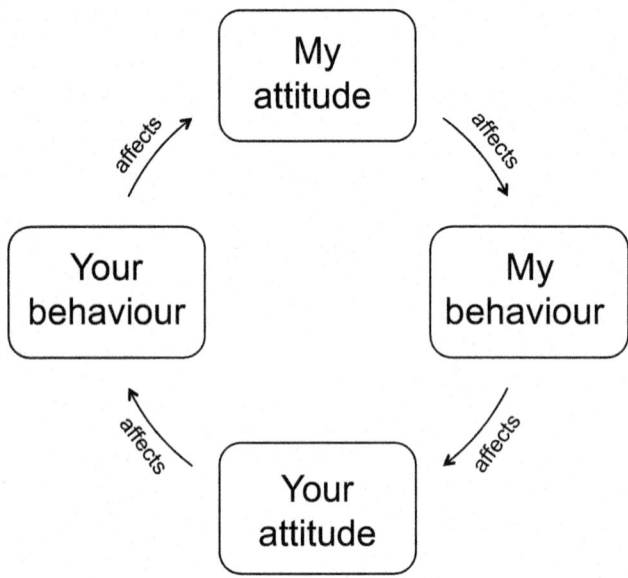

This model provides a useful representation of the cycle occurring within all communications. It shows the impact an individual's attitude and behaviour may have on the motivation and productivity of other team members, and on the customers of the BA Service.

The Betari Box may be used to analyse where the attitude or behaviour of a business analyst has affected another member of the team or a stakeholder. This model offers a basis for reflection about the behaviour displayed and the impact this has had. It can also support behavioural skills development; for example, when participating in high-emotion interactions such as engaging with a stakeholder who is perceived to be 'difficult'. The Betari Box can help business analysts as follows:

- to reflect on the beliefs and values that underpin their attitudes towards colleagues and stakeholders;
- to analyse how these attitudes can influence their behaviour and, in turn, affect the attitudes and behaviours of others.

PROVIDING FEEDBACK

In line with the phrase 'performance management', the term 'feedback' also has negative implications for many people. Given the implications of poor performance on a role set (discussed in Chapter 1), BA leaders need to be able to provide feedback and help individuals to take necessary actions in response.

Individuals need to believe that the motivation for providing feedback originates from a desire to see them succeed. Within the BA Service, this means helping them to be the best business analyst they can be. Where individuals accept, reflect and act on feedback, performance improvements should result, and their actions and behaviours should improve the perceptions of the role and the BA Service.

Feedback can be broadly categorised as appreciative, evaluative and coaching feedback (Stone and Heen, 2014):

- **Appreciative** feedback concerns providing specific praise and thanking the feedback recipient for their work and support.

- **Evaluative** feedback concerns reporting on how well or how poorly the work has been done.

- **Coaching** feedback concerns raising awareness of how actions or behaviours may be improved.

Good feedback does not necessarily equate to positive feedback. It is often the case that negative feedback is necessary to prevent the continuation of problems or difficulties arising in the future. For example, it may be important to provide feedback to an individual business analyst that may be perceived as negative because improvements are required. Without this feedback, though, the business analyst may continue to struggle with the role and may not achieve their performance or career objectives.

Constructive, specific feedback can be invaluable in helping an individual improve their performance and develop their career. Deciding not to give feedback can be relevant if this is warranted by the particular individual or circumstances, but this can reduce the opportunities available to the individual. If feedback is considered to be necessary, it needs to be direct, specific, timely and actionable.

Feedback frameworks

It can be challenging to request and to provide feedback, and there are a number of frameworks that can help both the person giving the feedback and the recipient. Table 5.6 shows a number of feedback models that can help to guide a feedback conversation or present written feedback.

Table 5.6 Frameworks used for performance feedback

Feedback model	Description	When to use
Situation Behaviour Impact (SBI)	Provides a structure for keeping feedback specific and fact-based. An explanation is provided of the following: • The context for the observation (the nature of the situation) • What was observed (the behaviour displayed, or performance demonstrated) • The impact this had on the situation or the individuals involved	When a helpful or unhelpful behaviour that needs to be highlighted has been observed

(Continued)

Table 5.6 (Continued)

Feedback model	Description	When to use
Good, even better if...	Applies a two-part structure comprising of what went well and what could be done better or differently in future	When stakeholders/ groups find it difficult to give developmental feedback; keeps the focus positive
Affirming and adjusting	Applies a two-part structure of appreciative feedback (affirming) and coaching feedback (adjusting). A more constructive version of 'positive and negative'	When asking for feedback; for example, to feed into a formal review process
Behaviour Effect Alternative Result (BEAR)	Provides a structure for keeping feedback specific and providing a logical sequence to derive a helpful level of detail. An explanation is provided of the following: • The behaviour that has been observed • The effect resulting from this behaviour • Alternative approaches or behaviours that may have been adopted • The result that may have been achieved from an alternative approach	When an individual needs to develop alternative approaches/ behaviours, as it helps highlight some of the options available. For example, how a similar situation could be approached differently in future and how the outcome might differ
Start Stop Continue	Provides a structure that explores: • What could I start doing that would make an improvement or help you? • What could I stop doing that is not helpful? • What should I continue doing that is working well?	When conducting a team-based feedback exercise 'Stop doing this' can feel quite confrontational if used for individual feedback
Feedback 321	Provides a flexible structure that may be adapted to a variety of situations. For example: • 3 things I do well • 2 areas to focus on in future • 1 piece of advice Or • 3 things you enjoyed • 2 things you would change next time • 1 question you still have	Useful when asking for feedback; for example, to feed into a formal review process or to evaluate interactions such as when facilitating a workshop

(Continued)

Table 5.6 (Continued)

Feedback model	Description	When to use
Succinct, Sincere, Specific (3S)	Provides a structure for keeping feedback short and to the point, so that people can understand and act on it	Useful for giving any category of feedback

Top tips for giving feedback:

- Depending on the relationship, offer the option of receiving the feedback.
- Think about time and place.
- Consider using a framework to help keep the feedback on track.
- Practise the words you are going to say in advance.

Top tips for receiving feedback:

- Try to appreciate the person is making time to try to help you.
- Don't try to defend yourself.
- Ask questions to clarify if you need to.
- Ask if they have advice or alternatives if none suggested.
- Spend time considering the appreciative feedback you receive. This may be a hidden strength or something you know you do well and could improve even further.

Emotional intelligence

Many aspects of personal and professional performance, and how people perceive and relate to each other, are influenced by emotional intelligence.

Emotional intelligence (EI) is defined as:

> the ability to monitor one's own and others' feelings and emotions, to discriminate among them and to use this information to guide one's thinking and actions.
> Salovey and Mayer, 1990

BA leaders require significant emotional intelligence when managing the performance of individual business analysts and the business analysis team.

Business analysis is at its core a profession about communication and relationships. The more an individual is able to develop their EI, the greater the chance they have to improve and succeed as a business analyst. In particular, the ability to empathise and see different perspectives are elements considered to be central to the role of a business analyst. Therefore, senior business analysts are likely to have developed a significant level of EI during their career, which should prove extremely helpful when providing feedback to the business analysts working within their teams. Individual business analysts are also likely to be more receptive to feedback because of the EI they have developed as part of their role.

The ability to give and receive feedback is closely linked to the Emotional Intelligence Competencies model defined by Goleman (2013), a version of which is shown in Figure 5.8. Through actively seeking feedback, and then reflecting upon this, business analysts can improve their self-awareness and gain a more accurate picture of their strengths and development needs.

Figure 5.8 Emotional Intelligence Competencies model (after Goleman, 2013)

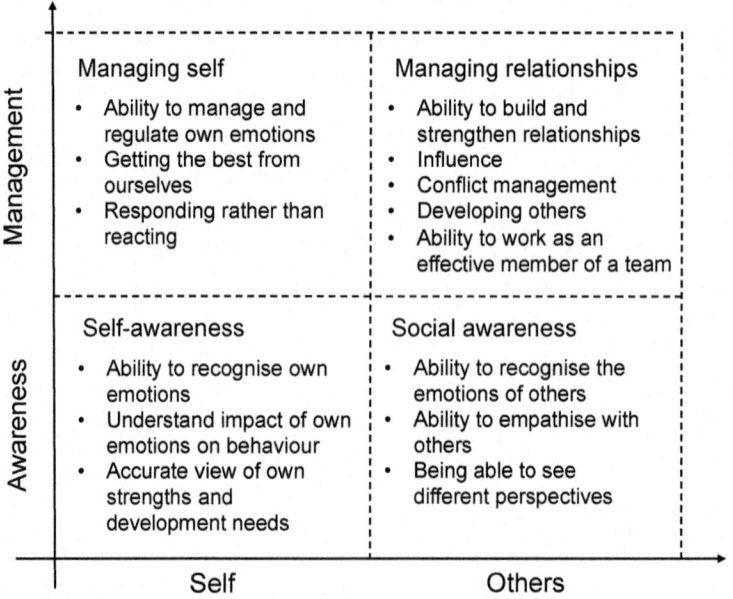

Recognising the need for change is often a key first step to increased emotional awareness and intelligence. Taking time to reflect on feedback can be instrumental in gaining self-awareness, accepting the need for improvement and then seeking ways of achieving this. BA leaders can support business analysts who need to improve their emotional intelligence through the following actions:

- highlighting the relevance of emotional intelligence, possibly through identifying situations where this has benefited the BA Service;

- ensuring that performance or behavioural feedback is provided in a supportive and constructive manner;
- explaining the process of receiving feedback, reflecting on the feedback and determining actions to address the feedback;
- offering support for actions to improve the business analyst's emotional intelligence;
- maintaining contact through regular discussions to review performance, identify further actions and celebrate successes.

Active listening

Active listening is a technique that aids effective communication and is a skill that business analysts need to possess. Business analysts need to develop this skill where they do not have a natural listening ability as it is a pre-requisite for effective communication – a vital component of the business analyst skill set.

Active listening helps to build trust and relationships, provides a framework for helping people to solve their problems, ensures understanding and enables conflict to be resolved. The technique also helps to avoid assumptions, misconceptions and misunderstandings.

Six key behaviours that are required when applying active listening are set out in Figure 5.9.

Figure 5.9 Active listening behaviours

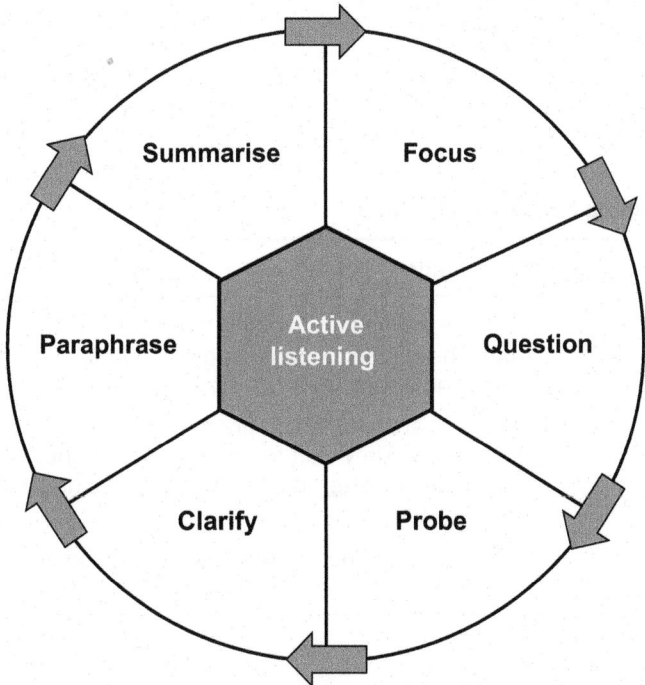

The behaviours shown in Figure 5.9 are described in more detail in Table 5.7.

Table 5.7 Description of active listening dimensions

Behaviour name	Behaviour description
Focus	Give the person your full attention. Consider all the aspects that feed into this: physical environment, distractions, technology, other people, eye-contact, body language
Question	Ask open-ended questions that follow on from what the other person has said
Probe	Ask for further detail, to help you and the person understand what they are really saying
Clarify	Request clarification on anything you feel is unclear or that potentially contradicts previous information or understanding. Be alert to anything you feel isn't being said and test out anything you have 'read between the lines'
Paraphrase	Play back what the other person has said, using your own words to validate and demonstrate understanding
Summarise	Provide a recap of key points of the conversation, check understanding and potentially move forward into further questioning or prompted problem-solving

Having awareness of the importance of active listening and then applying the behaviours defined in Table 5.7 can improve significantly an individual's ability to listen. This is particularly relevant when a BA leader is conducting a performance review discussion.

There are certain communication behaviours that should be avoided when applying active listening. These behaviours diminish the quality of the listening and are described in Table 5.8 below.

Table 5.8 Listening behaviours to avoid

Behaviour name	Description
Being right	Listeners only hear anything that confirms that they are right. They listen to identify anything that supports their views and disregard anything else
Comparing	Listeners are focused on presenting information about themselves. They wait to respond so that they can explain how they are better in some way or have had worse experiences
	They may also attempt to minimise or dismiss the concerns or experience of the speaker

(Continued)

Table 5.8 (Continued)

Behaviour name	Description
Derailing	Listeners are keen to eliminate their feelings of boredom, so interrupt the speaker by changing the subject or making a joke in order to derail them from what they are saying
Daydreaming	Listeners stop concentrating on what the speaker is saying and mentally drift into thinking about something else. This may also be done to alleviate boredom or anxiety
Filtering/advising	Listeners wish to ensure that their opinions are confirmed, so listen for evidence of this and then present their advice or quickly jump to suggesting solutions rather than listening
Mindreading	Listeners focus on working out what the speaker is really trying to say rather than what they are actually saying. They believe that they can uncover the meaning behind the words spoken. This behaviour manifests itself when people 'search for' words during pauses rather than letting the person think, or display a tendency to finish speaker's sentences
Rehearsing	Listeners are concerned with what they are going to say next instead of listening to the speaker
Impatience	Listeners want the speaker to 'get to the point', so give 'hurry-up' signals such as finishing the person's sentences, interrupting or circling hand gestures

Having awareness of these listening behaviours, and making attempts to avoid them, can be extremely helpful to business analysts.

Applying active listening, and being conscious of doing so, may cause some initial discomfort as it can require an unnatural conversation pattern. However, practising and maintaining active listening can help business analysts to achieve significant improvement in their ability to communicate with colleagues and stakeholders.

Active listening can turn a general conversation into an opportunity for a performance management conversation and can be beneficial for both parties. Gaining the ability to listen actively will help the BA leader to review performance and provide coaching or mentoring to staff. It is also a listening approach that has the potential to support many business analysis activities, including investigating business situations and eliciting requirements. Learning to apply active listening, and supporting business analysts to acquire this skill, can be highly beneficial for the BA Service.

Control, Influence, Accept model

Some aspects of performance may be genuinely outside the control of individual business analysts. For example, where an organisation dictates a particular approach or solution, even though it is apparent that an alternative would be more beneficial.

The Control, Influence, Accept (CIA) model can help with feedback discussions, as they enable individuals to recognise where they should best concentrate their efforts and how they might proceed.

Understanding the aspects that fall outside the control of an individual business analyst can be extremely helpful. This is an area that affects business analysts' performance regularly. Appreciating the limitations that are constraining a situation can ensure that the focus is on those areas where it is possible to exert influence.

___

Figure 5.10 The CIA model

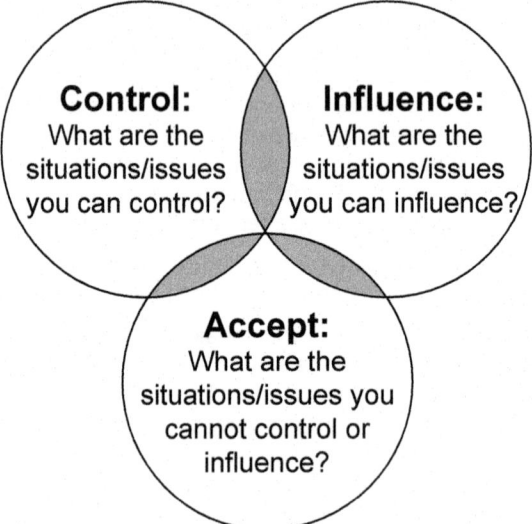

Business analysts are trained to analyse situations but can become preoccupied with potential threats, such as external or organisational level changes that could impact on the project or work to which they are assigned. It can be very difficult for business analysts to understand where the boundaries lie between these areas of concern and, as shown in Figure 5.10, the boundaries are sometimes unclear and there are 'grey areas' to be explored. Table 5.9 describes the CIA areas and the implications for the business analysts.

REMOVAL

Organisations may employ some business analysts who under-perform and do not make a positive contribution to the BA Service. It is important to face this difficult situation head on, through feedback and use of appropriate internal processes, as it is unlikely that the person wants to perform poorly and may not realise that they are not working effectively. BA leaders should explore different avenues to facilitate performance improvement; many possibilities have been discussed earlier in this chapter.

Table 5.9 CIA descriptions

Area of concern	Description	Implications for business analysts
Control	**Personal/task level** Areas for which the business analyst is able to set the approach, make decisions and take responsibility for delivery of work and any changes	Business analysts can feel that nothing is within their control and that they are not empowered. They may lose motivation and simply wait for instruction How to address: • Highlight the observed behaviour • Be clear on expectations and areas of responsibility • Identify areas where a business analyst can be proactive, perhaps being asked to take on responsibility for a BA Service improvement activity alongside project work In some cases, the business analyst can feel far more responsibility for a project than is truly necessary, believing that the full weight of the project is on their shoulders. How to address: • Revisit work allocation • Identify areas of responsibility clearly • Consider how other people could or should be supporting the business analyst
Influence	**Interpersonal/ team level** Areas for which the business analyst is able to suggest the approach, affect decisions and is consulted on changes	'Lack of influence' is a common complaint amongst business analysts How to address: • Support business analysts to improve interpersonal skills, including to develop influencing, relationship building and communication skills • Provide opportunities for understanding the key stakeholders better • Consider the use of a mentor or look for shadowing opportunities with those who are seen to 'have influence' There are five influencing styles that are helpful to use in a situation where the business analyst needs to be able to influence the approach or outcome. The styles are described using the acronym BRAIN (Bridging, Rationalising, Asserting, Inspiring and Negotiating) (Musselwhite and Plouffe, 2012):

(Continued)

143

Table 5.9 (Continued)

Area of concern	Description	Implications for business analysts
		• **B**ridging: using personal relationships to achieve agreement. Obtaining support, uniting people and building alliances to influence outcomes
		• **R**ationalising: using logic, facts and reasoning to evidence ideas and suggestions
		• **A**sserting: using personal confidence, seniority or authority to get agreement
		• **I**nspiring: using stories and metaphors to encourage a shared sense of purpose
		• **N**egotiating: using compromise, exchanges and concessions to reach agreement
Accept	**Organisational level** Areas for which the business analyst is told the approach, given the outcome of decisions and informed of changes	If business analysts are asked to implement a decision or course of action that they do not agree with, this may generate resistance and negativity Spending time and energy on an area that the business analyst needs to simply accept can have an impact on other areas of work How to address: • Highlight the observed behaviours • Acknowledge feelings and beliefs that may be driving the behaviours • Assist the development of influencing skills and suggest ways of providing positive challenge • Help the business analysts to understand that there may be other factors behind a decision that are not widely apparent • Discuss the fact that many decisions do not have permanent consequences – if more information is available or circumstances change, it may be possible to influence a decision in future that at present needs to be accepted

Ultimately, it is important to recognise where a business analyst is not able or willing to develop in order that they may perform at the required level. The presence of unhappy or under-performing business analysts can have an adverse effect on other members of the team. In extreme circumstances, this can even lead others to decide to move to another role or organisation. In this situation, there are two possible courses of action: enable movement to another role within the organisation or deploy an exit process.

The process to remove a business analyst (or any other member of staff) will be defined by the employing organisation. It is likely that his process will be controlled by the HR Department as it will need to take account of relevant employment law and it is important that this process is followed carefully to ensure that no contraventions occur. Typically, the process will include opportunities for performance review and the development of a personal improvement plan, which will ensure that the business analyst has clear guidance on the areas to improve and the timescale for review.

It is possible that during this process, the business analyst identifies, and is allocated, an alternative role within the organisation. However, where this is not the case and the performance improvement process has not succeeded, the organisation's removal process will need to be invoked.

CONCLUSION

This chapter has examined some of the issues associated with managing performance within a business analysis context. BA leaders have to consider many areas when developing business analysts in order to enable the successful performance of the BA Service. This may be helped through mentoring and coaching and by the use of tools such as the performance management matrix, the GROW model and the Johari window model. Sometimes, business analysts who are new to an organisation, or have grown used to a particular way of working, fail to appreciate the breadth and depth of the business analyst role and the extensive set of skills it requires. The use of the techniques and frameworks described in this chapter and in Chapter 4, can lead to interesting, unexpected and beneficial insights that should provide a strong basis for performance discussion and development.

CASE STUDY 3: MANAGING PERFORMANCE WITH EMPATHY AND UNDERSTANDING

Sandra Leek, Financial services

Sandra Leek has been a business analyst for over 18 years. She works within the financial services industry, where she has led several business analysis teams. She was the IIBA BA of the Year 2014 and is a member of the organising panel for the BA Conference Europe.

Sandra approaches managing the performance of business analysts from two perspectives: the formal – what should be done from an organisational perspective; and the informal – what works for the individual? She believes that the individual has to believe in the process for it to work.

There are two key aspects that Sandra feels are important:

1. **Regular reviews with each member of staff**. This should include formal review points and also informal reviews. The latter may be at frequent intervals, such as on a weekly basis, but it is each individual's decision as the informal reviews must work for them.

While the formal reviews will require forms to be completed, this is not the case for the regular informal reviews, which should be more focused on understanding and getting to know each member of staff. Sandra feels that it is important to understand what is important to each person, such as the pressures they are under outside – as well as inside – work, and where their priorities lie.

2. **Openness and transparency are paramount**. Nothing should come as a shock when discussing performance, and the team members should know that you are trying to do your best for them. Where discussions are difficult – and they often are – it is important to be constructive and focus on what needs to be addressed and how this might be done.

Sandra believes that managing performance is extremely important because it affects everyone and everything: the individual's input, the team's input and organisational performance. If performance management is not done well, there is a risk of a detrimental impact upon the organisation. Also, a people-focused, flexible approach to performance management is highly beneficial. For example, an hour away from work when needed often results in two hours of extra effort. Basically, performance management is key to successful company performance.

In Sandra's experience, barriers arise when formal performance management processes are put in place without any business analysis or understanding of the need for flexibility; every individual is different, so being flexible and adaptable is key. Trying to combine the use of formal objectives and processes while working within an Agile environment is also difficult. The limitations placed by formal processes on the performance assessment process can also be problematic. A typical issue concerns the use of quotas; for example, a quota for 'good' performers that limits accurate assessment and fails to focus on the desired outcomes for company success.

Sandra has found that it is often difficult to address formal process problems primarily due to a lack of understanding that performance management is not a black and white situation and there are likely to be shades of grey. Sandra tries to address challenges by working within the defined processes, while also attempting to be flexible where possible and adapting her approach to each individual's needs. This sometimes means that, as a manager, she has to challenge her senior manager, but she sees this as part of her role and her responsibility to her staff.

Sandra does not believe in micro-managing her team. Instead, she works with her team to understand them, meet their individual needs and ensure that they are given the leeway to perform.

Sandra's advice to anyone responsible for performance management concerns the need to understand the team and the individuals, asking what it is that they want that will help them to perform well. She believes that understanding each person's worldview, challenges and personal situation is vital. Sandra also feels that organisations should not only focus on performance at work but also support people where they are contributing more widely to their profession.

6 STANDARDISING THE BA SERVICE

INTRODUCTION

The role of the business analyst has been the subject of much discussion in this book. Clarification of the role is supported by adopting a service viewpoint, and this is enhanced by introducing standards and templates that provide a basis for consistency and efficiency. Consistency is important, as it helps to remove role ambiguity and ensures effective communication with stakeholders and colleagues. Efficiency is equally relevant given the time pressures upon business analysts (and many other roles) when working on business change and IT projects; business analysts are expected to be able to be productive immediately so 'reinventing the wheel' for each project is not acceptable. Therefore, the introduction and adoption of standards and templates is often one of the driving forces during the introduction of a BA Service, as shown in Figure 6.1.

Figure 6.1 The role of standards in driving the creation of a BA Service

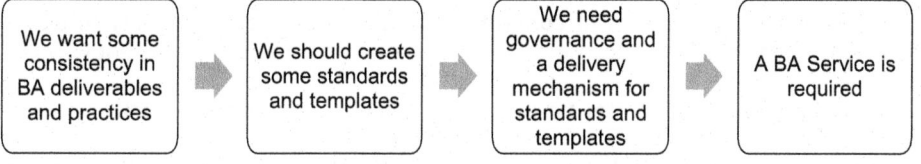

This chapter covers a range of topics related to consistency and standardisation including:

- re-use;
- selecting standards;
- modelling standards;
- creation and maintenance of templates;
- adoption of standards.

The BA Service must provide a framework of standards and templates to support the delivery of business analysis, as some business analysts don't know where to start and others don't know when to stop.

THE ROLE OF STANDARDS AND TEMPLATES

Standards refer to the rules, guidance and characteristics used during business analysis activities. They determine the methods, languages, techniques and life cycles that are applied and provide a basis for deciding upon the deliverables that are produced. Standard approaches to business analysis work typically offer clarity about the deliverables, enabling the identification of the required techniques and the development of templates. Examples of standards used by business analysts are as follows:

- **methods/languages:** UML, Dynamic Systems Development Method (DSDM), BPMN and Soft Systems Methodology (SSM);

- **techniques:** diagrams, business process models, data models, stakeholder perspective analysis (CATWOE) and RACI charts;

- **life cycles:** Iterative (Agile), Linear (Waterfall), Incremental.

Templates are re-usable business analysis deliverables that provide a starting point when performing a particular task or developing a particular document or model, so they can save time and effort. Templates provide the opportunity for re-use and avoid the need to develop a new format or structure each time a technique is used.

Templates should conform to the relevant standards, including formatting, branding, agreed content and notation. The alignment of templates with agreed standards helps business analysts to embed consistency and efficiency across business analysis work.

The nature of re-use

There are two main types of re-use: the re-use of **format**, which concerns the application of standards, and the re-use of **content**, which provides the opportunity to ensure consistency and avoids re-interpretation of the same information in different ways.

Examples of templates that may be re-used during business analysis work are:

- **format/structure templates:** document content headings; column headings, BA support tool configuration;

- **content templates:** introductory information; glossary entries; compliance statements; standard requirements such as those at business level or non-functional requirements that apply to different systems.

Specific examples of format, and the corresponding content, templates are provided in Table 6.1.

Knowledge may also be re-used through sharing information, insights and lessons learned (see Chapter 9).

Benefits of standards and templates

The BA Service should provide a consistent and efficient approach when working with customers if role clarity is to prevail. This is a key differentiator between a BA Service organisation and the use of a business analysis resource pool, where typically there is

Table 6.1 Examples of re-use templates and content

Re-use of format	Re-use of content
Document templates	A bank of business level and non-functional requirements
	Legislative or regulatory requirements such as data protection compliance requirements are a good example of template business level requirements; usability requirements are a good example of template non-functional requirements
Skeleton processes	Common functional use cases or user stories (such as 'system log-in' or 're-set password')
Generic screen prototype	Standard screen formats based on organisational style guide and preferred user interface (UI) elements
Analysis elements	Lists of typical stakeholders/actors, logical data entities, attribute definitions, domain definitions, terminology

only limited consistency in the business analysis work. The BA Service will offer a suite of services, enacted through a range of repeatable processes, where the activities and outputs are similar regardless of who has undertaken them.

The importance of standards is more likely to be recognised within a BA Service. The use of standards and templates offer organisations significant benefits including:

- **Reduced elapsed time/effort:** activities and templates for approaching the business analysis work and for developing deliverables are known at the outset.

- **Improved quality:** quality controls and best practice can be applied proactively from the outset.

- **Consistency of content and presentation:** customers and stakeholders know which tasks and behaviours to expect and how to use the deliverables provided.

- **Strengthened organisational identity:** the use of elements such as logos, branding, colour and tone of written 'voice' reflect a consistent organisational approach.

- **Improved compliance:** there is likely to be a common understanding of the requirements of legislative or regulatory compliance.

- **Improved risk management:** consistency of approach prevents information and processes from being missed or only included to a limited extent.

- **Increased learning:** the use of standards within an adaptive continual improvement culture with an outcome focus enables the development of a learning organisation.

These benefits, and the path towards their realisation, collectively support the establishment of a highly professional BA Service, whose members apply best practice approaches in an informed manner. The removal of the 'follow the book' approach to business analysis will require business analysts to learn, apply and adapt the standards, thus ensuring continual improvement.

The introduction of standards does not necessarily result in the realisation of the benefits listed above. There are several elements that will impact how much benefit can be gained from re-use:

- **The culture of the organisation and within the BA Service.** Are the business analysts willing to share information and enable re-use of their work?

- **The prevailing governance approach.** Are there mechanisms and the capacity to audit and mandate re-use?

- **The body of work available.** Are there sufficient templates and completed deliverables available?

- **The delivery mechanisms.** Are the tools in place that make information readily available and facilitate re-use?

All four elements need to be considered, and the required actions taken, if the benefits from re-use are to be achieved. It is often the case that a significant investment of time and money is made to consider, design and implement the support tools and technology. However, it is also often the case that insufficient effort is invested to establish the culture necessary to support and encourage re-use. Accordingly, the debate about re-use is often centred on selecting and procuring a relevant support tool with insufficient emphasis given to the management of the benefits and the environment required to realise them.

SELECTING THE STANDARDS

There are numerous standards available and they cover a wide range of categories. For example:

- **Methods and life cycles:** there are many methods and life cycles available to business analysts. Examples are Scrum or DSDM (Agile methods) and Waterfall/ Linear, Incremental or Iterative (life cycles).

- **Modelling standards:** these offer rules and notation sets for the development of models to represent specific views of the system under consideration. For example, data or process models.

- **Narrative standards:** these are documentation templates and may be for externally used reports produced by business analysts, such as a business requirements document or business case, or for internally used documents such as project initiation documents or meeting agendas. Often, templates developed by individual business analysts may be adapted for use across the BA Service. This is discussed below.

Standards may be applied on a project-by-project basis or across the organisation. For example, some projects may benefit from the use of an Agile method, while others may require a more linear approach resulting in the development of a detailed requirements definition.

There are a number of factors that will influence and constrain the standards and templates adopted by the BA Service. These factors are, to a greater or lesser extent, outside the control of the BA leaders who have to appreciate that any standards selected need to be adapted to take the different factors into account. The constraining factors are the methods used, the procurement processes, the outsourcing requirements, and the opportunities afforded and limitations imposed by the use of support tools.

Development methods and life cycles

Different methods may influence the types of business analysis deliverables required by the project team. A good example concerns the use of a requirements catalogue versus a solution or product backlog. Many organisations have different project life cycles and development methods in use simultaneously. This may be for a variety of reasons such as the existence of legacy systems, the nature of supplier contracts, the suitability of one method over another for a given situation, and the skills and knowledge of the business analysts and the stakeholders. Therefore, it is likely that the BA Service will need to adopt and maintain standards and templates that align to several different development methods and that the project team will need to select the standards that are appropriate to meet the needs of the project.

Procurement

Where there is limited competitive advantage to be gained, many organisations choose to buy rather than build information systems. Organisational and legal constraints surrounding procurement processes may place specific demands on the business analysis deliverables and may restrict engagement with potential suppliers. It is worth investigating how business analysis activities and deliverables need to comply with or conform to the procurement process when defining the standards and templates.

Outsourcing

Whether software is developed in-house or is outsourced to an external supplier may influence the use of analysis standards and templates. There may be agreements between the customer and supplier organisations on specific standards to be used. For example, the supplier may have specified that certain templates must be used, or new templates and approaches may have been created jointly.

It is a useful investment of time to talk about the format and content of expected deliverables with suppliers, and to determine who will use them and how. However, it can be very easy to sink a great deal of time 'up front' in negotiating the details of standards and templates to the detriment of delivering usable outputs.

Support tools

Automated tools may be used to support just requirements engineering activities or even the full software development life cycle (SDLC). The tool configuration may include 'templates' that determine the standards to be used. Sometimes, the templates may be configured to reflect the approach agreed upon by the project team and the stakeholders. This may determine the information that must be recorded and the format in which it is presented, so may impose customisation of the templates. For example, if a template had existed as a spreadsheet, business analysts may have been free to customise headings and add columns to meet specific needs. When using a tool, there may be constraints on how the templates are tailored, so it may not be possible to meet the required information needs.

MODELLING STANDARDS

The purpose of most business analysis outputs is to aid communication and enable the audience to come to a shared understanding. With this in mind, it seems appropriate to adopt standards and notation that will be familiar to the highest number of people and to remove ambiguity as far as possible, which will simplify rather than add complexity.

Business analysts may need to produce models at different levels of abstraction including:

- **conceptual:** may be either high level or a partial representation of a situation;
- **logical:** a representation that is independent of any specific implementation environment;
- **physical:** a representation that is specific to a particular implementation environment;
- **reality:** a representation of the physical world.

BA Service standards need to take into account the variety of situations that will require analysis – and the needs of different stakeholders – and agree standards relevant for different scenarios and audiences.

An obvious contender for standardisation within a BA Service, and one that causes much debate, is the area of modelling and notation. The decision between using UML or BPMN is only a relevant question for the area of modelling processes, and there may be a reasonable argument to use both in certain circumstances. For example, business process modelling (at a specified level of detail) may need to conform to BPMN, but where a use case description is articulated as a process, a UML activity diagram may be used. These approaches are described in further detail below.

Unified Modelling Language (UML)

UML is maintained by the Object Management Group® (OMG®), an international, not-for-profit technology standards consortium, founded in 1989. OMG® standards are driven by vendors, end users, academic institutions and government agencies, and membership is open to all. UML aims to support consistency in systems modelling as defined in the UML standard:

> One of the primary goals of UML is to advance the state of the industry by enabling object visual modelling tool interoperability.
>
> UML Standard[1]

UML[2] provides a suite of modelling techniques that may be used during the business modelling, analysis, design and specification of business and IT systems. It provides a robust and precise set of standards that define for each technique the modelling notation, terminology, rules and syntax. Key modelling techniques provided by UML are described in Table 6.2.

---

1   UML Standard Version 2.5.1. Available from: www.omg.org/spec/UML/About-UML

2   See www.omg.org/spec/UML/About-UML

Table 6.2 Key UML models

Model name	Purpose
Activity diagram	Sometimes known as the UML flowchart. It provides a diagrammatic representation of business processes, use cases, tasks, system processes and test scenarios. It supports elicitation and analysis of scenarios and business rules
	This is a straightforward notation set, so it is accessible to business staff. It is an excellent technique for use when eliciting and recording both tacit and explicit information during interviews, meetings and workshops
Use case diagram	This provides a diagrammatic overview of a system, whether a business system or IT system. It shows the scope of a system, the functionality within the system boundary and the actors who interact with the system
	It has a straightforward notation set, so is accessible to business staff. This is a useful technique to facilitate discussion, particularly during meetings and workshops. Provides a basis for the functional design of the software
Class diagram	This provides a diagrammatic representation of the data recorded within an IT system. It shows the classes of data and their attributes, the operations enacted within each class and the nature of the relationships between the classes
	It has a straightforward notation set but some concepts are complex, so requires the analyst to support business staff in understanding the diagram. It can be useful to elicit information during meetings about data and the business rules applied to the data. It provides a basis for database design
State machine diagram	This provides a representation of a particular class and the events to which objects within that class may be subjected. It shows the sequence of the possible events. It supports the definition of test scenarios
	It has a simple notation set that is very similar to the activity diagram notation. It models concepts that can appear complex without sufficient explanation, so requires care when using with business staff
Sequence diagram	Provides a representation of a use case realisation, including the classes that collaborate to enact the use case, the operations performed as part of this realisation and the communications between the classes
	It has a higher level of complexity than the other key models, so is less accessible to business staff. However, the concepts included may be described to business staff in order to validate the processing components required to realise a use case

Business Process Model and Notation (BPMN)

The OMG® has also developed a standard for business process modelling known as Business Process Model and Notation (BPMN[3]). This international standard represents the combination of best practices within the business modelling community to provide a standard approach to business process models and notation. It provides a consistent approach to communicating process information between all those interested in business process implementation, improvement and automation.

> The primary goal of BPMN is to provide a notation that is readily understandable by all business users, from the business analysts that create the initial drafts of the processes, to the technical developers responsible for implementing the technology that will perform those processes, and finally, to the business people who will manage and monitor those processes.
>
> BPMN Standard[4]

The BPMN notation set is significantly more complex than the UML activity diagram technique, which is also used for modelling processing. However, the extent of the BPMN provides a basis for modelling processing where the rules to be applied are represented in a rigorous and specific way. This can provide a basis for automatic generation of software to deploy the process; for example, within workflow software.

Decision Model and Notation (DMN™)

This standard, published by the OMG®, has been developed to support the specification of business decisions and business rules, separately from the processes that use the decisions. Attempting to model business decisions as part of a process can lead to large and complex process models that are difficult for stakeholders to engage with and for business analysts to maintain. For complicated business logic, it may be preferable to model the decision independently of the process, showing only the decision outcomes on the corresponding process diagram.

> The primary goal of DMN™ is to provide a common notation that is readily understandable by all business users, from the business analysts needing to create initial decision requirements and then more detailed decision models, to the technical developers responsible for automating the decisions in processes, and finally, to the business people who will manage and monitor those decisions.
>
> DMN™ Standard[5]

Other modelling standards

Other options exist that provide notation sets for use during business analysis. There are a range of 'structured' approaches – which essentially means that they are not part of the object-oriented set. These approaches may be found in methods such as Structured

---

3   See www.omg.org/spec/BPMN/2.0

4   BPMN Standard Version 2.0.2. Available from: www.omg.org/spec/BPMN/2.0

5   DMN™ Standard Version 1.2. Available from: www.omg.org/spec/DMN/About-DMN

Systems Analysis and Design Methodology (SSADM) and Information Engineering. Typical modelling techniques within such approaches are shown in Table 6.3.

Table 6.3 Alternative models available to business analysts

Model name	Purpose
Entity relationship diagram (ERD)	Provides a diagrammatic representation of the data recorded within an IT system. Shows the data groups (entities) and the nature of the relationships between them. The notation set is relatively straightforward to understand at an overview level but some concepts, such as optionality and recursion, are often found to be more difficult. This technique can be used to elicit information about data and the business rules applied to the data during meetings with business staff, but the business analysts will need to support them in understanding the diagram. A completed ERD provides a basis for database design
Data flow diagram (DFD)	Provides a diagrammatic representation of the processing conducted within a current or required information system. A DFD also shows the external entities (the actors or roles) that interact with the system and the data that is received, stored and output by the system. A hierarchy of DFDs tends to be built at increasing levels of granularity. The notation set looks off-putting to business staff so requires explanation. It is a useful technique to facilitate discussion, particularly during meetings and workshops. It provides a basis for the process design of the software
State chart/state transition diagram	These are alternative names given to the state machine diagram from UML. They use a very similar notation set and purpose
Create, Read, Update, Delete (CRUD) chart	A matrix that provides a means for modelling the effect of an event on the entities from the data model. The resultant matrix may be read in two ways: each row shows the impact of an event occurring, i.e. all of the entities and the effects on each of them; each column shows each entity and the effects on it that result from certain events occurring. This technique may also be used to map use cases against classes or events against classes. It is extremely useful for more granular analysis and often exposes gaps in the analysis work. It is not part of UML but is often used in conjunction with UML models, as it supports the creation of the state machines and sequence diagrams

When a standard notation has been adopted, it is often necessary to adapt its notation set and application. This may be due to the particular constraints or factors present within the organisation or project environment.

Many business analysts feel comfortable with modelling processes but are less confident in the analysis and modelling of data. However, analysing and modelling data are as integral as process modelling to the success of business improvement initiatives. The drive towards a more digital mindset necessitates an understanding of data amongst the business analyst community.

Business analysts may also need awareness of notation and standards used by other related professionals, not necessarily to create but to review and consume these artefacts. Relevant standards will differ across organisations, but examples could include Gantt charts, created to visualise planning and scheduling, capability maps to represent the business capabilities, TOGAF® and ArchiMate® standards developed by The Open Group[6] to underpin architecture definition, and XML for storing and sharing data.

BA leaders need to consider the techniques and types of models that may be helpful when working on business change and IT projects within their organisation. The appropriate set of models for an individual organisation will depend on a number of factors, including:

- the BA Service offering;
- the nature of projects and problems requiring analysis attention;
- the experience, skills and preferences of customers and stakeholders.

BA leaders should also ensure that business analysts have the skills and confidence to apply the selected techniques effectively. This is likely to require development activities to be introduced, as described in Chapter 4.

CREATION AND MAINTENANCE OF TEMPLATES

Most business analysts have a collection of templates that they may use for a range of deliverables. However, these may or may not adhere to the business analysis standards in place within the organisation. This can cause many versions of similar products to be in use simultaneously within an organisation and contrasts with the need for consistency and efficiency.

Template gap analysis

It is helpful to apply the gap analysis technique when creating a set of standard templates that will support the BA Service Framework. This is reflected in Figure 6.2.

The gap analysis approach is applied to template creation as follows:

1. **Look at what exists.** Hold a 'template amnesty' to uncover all business analysis deliverables and guidance documentation in use. For a single product this may generate examples in different formats (e.g. spreadsheet, document, presentation, specific tool).

---

6   See www.opengroup.org/togaf

Figure 6.2 Template creation using gap analysis

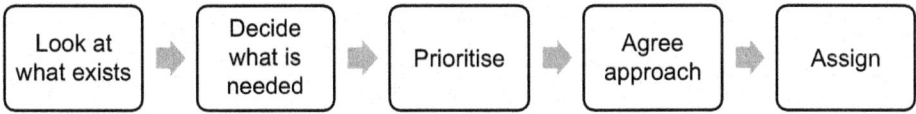

2. **Decide what is needed.** The BASF in Chapter 2 sets out the portfolio of services to be offered by the BA Service, the activities to be conducted and the techniques that may be used; this provides a basis for identifying where templates may be of use. Business analysts are usually able to quickly describe what 'good' looks like for a given situation. Techniques such as mind mapping or a product breakdown structure could be used to structure the conversation. It may be appropriate to include customers and other stakeholders in these conversations to prevent the BA Service from being too inward looking.

3. **Prioritise.** Consider what is most likely to be needed in the near future and what offers most value to the BA Service and its customers.

4. **Agree approach.** To generate a consistent set of products, some ground rules must be established, such as file formats, use of branding, naming conventions.

5. **Assign.** The largest possible number of business analysts should be engaged in the creation of the standards and templates, as this helps to promote the sense of ownership and community responsibility. Where possible, template creation should be developed when creating a specific deliverable for a project or piece of work, rather than a theoretical prediction of what might be needed in future.

It is helpful to create a repository of templates, guidance materials and worked examples that business analysts may access as and when required. The ongoing maintenance of the standards and templates must be undertaken by the business analysis community. If a business analyst needs to augment or amend a template for a particular purpose, there may be a gap that could be reflected in a new version of a template or a new template.

The analysis deliverables that are most likely to be of use within the BA Service should be prioritised when creating standards, templates, guidance and worked examples. Building these standards as a group enables the BA leaders to share ownership, the agreement of priorities and the commitment to the agreed priorities. The action priority matrix shown in Figure 6.3 reflects a means of prioritising this work.

When establishing a BA Service, this model helps to identify where to prioritise the initial efforts (the 'quick wins') and where longer-term, more complex activities may be needed (the 'major projects').

- **Quick wins:** can be accomplished rapidly and will be used regularly. These are often not as quick or simple to achieve as it first appears, so it is important to be realistic and not put too many items into this category. Business analysts often find it possible to fit these in around project commitments.

Figure 6.3 Action priority matrix

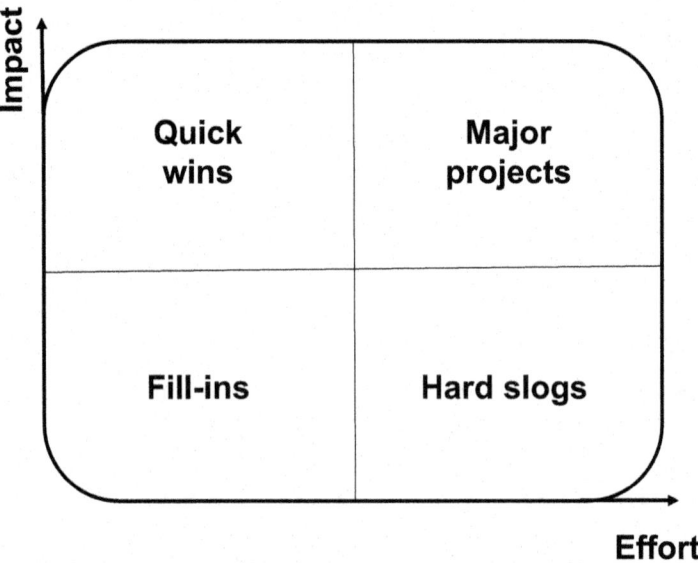

- **Major projects:** may require dedicated BA resource, or the coordinated effort of several business analysts over a long period. The benefits of the major projects to the BA Service and customers should be well understood, and these projects should appear on the BA Service Road Map or Service Improvement Plan (see Chapter 12).

- **Fill-ins:** may be considered as 'nice-to-have' and present a good opportunity for less experienced business analysts to contribute to the ongoing improvement of the BA Service.

- **Hard slogs:** the BA Service should be vigilant about undertaking any 'hard slogs'. These may present as 'pet projects' by a business analyst or to address the wants (rather than needs) of an individual customer or project. A 'major project' can turn into a 'hard slog' if it takes significantly longer than imagined, or the potential impact of delivering is reduced for some reason.

This model also shows that the full set of standards desired for use by the business analysts may take a considerable amount of time and effort to produce and that prioritisation can help to make this work achievable.

Linking standards and templates to services

Different standards and templates apply to the different services provided. It is useful to describe the typical deliverables produced for each service, as this enables customers to understand what will be produced and why. Table 6.4 shows the relationship between the business analysis services, the standards that support them and the templates that may be used. This links to the discussion in Chapter 2 of the techniques which are applicable to each service.

Table 6.4 Business analysis service portfolio with relevant standards and templates

BA Service	Example standards	Example templates
Situation investigation and problem analysis	Governance standards such as gateway reviews, project management methodologies	Business analysis process and activities, business analysis work-package, problem statement, (Vision) Mission, Objectives, Strategy, Tactics ((V)MOST) analysis, inception deck, context diagram
Feasibility assessment and business case development	Investment appraisal methods, the Green Book (for public sector investment appraisal)	Business case, options analysis, SWOT analysis, cost/benefit analysis, force-field analysis, risk analysis
Business process improvement	BPMN, decision modelling and notation	Business process hierarchy, value chain, process inventory, suppliers, inputs, processes, outputs, customers (SIPOC)
Requirements definition	Prioritisation approach (e.g. must have, should have, could have, want to have but won't have this time (MoSCoW), Kano model, weighted shortest job first (WSJF)), definition of ready, data modelling notation, UML models, review checklist	Requirements document, requirements catalogue entry, traceability matrix, solution/product backlog, user story, use case description, report specification, data model, feature tree
Business acceptance testing	Definition of done, acceptance criteria	Test script, test scenario, test plan
Business change deployment	Change management framework (for example, CPPOLDAT)	Post-implementation review, benefits review, training needs analysis, training material
Stakeholders engagement (auxiliary service)	Interviewing, facilitation, sampling, survey, organisational commitments such as agreement to engage with regulators or unions	Stakeholder wheel, power/interest grid, communication plan, RACI, empathy map, persona, CATWOE, agenda, survey structure and technology, customer journey

ADOPTION OF STANDARDS

The creation and initial adoption of a set of appropriate standards and templates is the first step on an ongoing journey of making additions and improvements and ensuring compliance. BA leaders must ensure that all business analysts:

- are aware of the standards;
- know how to use and apply them;
- understand when standards can be tailored and adapted.

The BA Service will require a governance mechanism to review and improve the set of standards. A number of BA Service processes will need to be aligned to the standards and templates including new business analyst induction (see Chapter 3), peer review (see Chapter 12) and BA planning (see Chapter 9).

Communication of standards

With a wide range of applicable standards to choose from, it is necessary for each organisation to determine and then communicate exactly which business analysis standards will be applied.

Documentation and communication of the selected standards does not have to be onerous; it could be as simple as a list on a poster or whiteboard, a presentation, a set of documents or web pages. Considerations for the communication of standards include:

- Are they **available** to those who need to access them?
- Are they **understandable** to those that need to apply them?
- Are they **maintainable** as the standards evolve over time?

The aim of communicating the agreed standards is to have mutual understanding, both within the BA Service and by its customers, about the analysis approach that will be taken and what the outputs will be measured against.

The BA Service also has a responsibility to support others in the organisation who are outside the service and who may need to utilise or apply business analysis techniques. For example, process modelling, or SWOT analysis are often in widespread use within an organisation, so the BA Service has three options:

1. attempt to discourage or limit the application of business analysis techniques by those outside the BA Service;
2. try to deploy business analysts to meet all possible demand and thereby maintain full control of the use of the business analysis techniques;
3. enable and support others to use the tools and techniques accurately, successfully and consistently.

Option 3 is the one realistic and sustainable approach, though business analysts and BA leaders may only come to this conclusion after attempting the first two. There are often situations where business analysis approaches and techniques will be very useful to the business, but this does not necessarily mean that a business analyst must be involved. For example, stakeholder analysis and management techniques used by business analysts may be equally useful to other internal services such as finance, marketing and HR for them to better understand their stakeholders.

Applying the standards

Converting to or complying with standards should not be done by the business analyst in isolation once the analysis process has been completed. Successful business analysis involves co-creating analysis deliverables that have a clear purpose and audience and ensuring that all customers understand how to utilise them.

For example, one approach to data analysis may involve the business analyst holding interviews, analysing forms, systems and spreadsheets, and building a fully formed data model that is then shared with stakeholders. However, this approach is likely to generate confusion and a reluctance amongst the stakeholders to engage with or validate the model.

A more successful approach is to generate models collaboratively, developing them alongside stakeholders and using simple notation that conforms to standards and business language that is accessible by stakeholders. The resultant models can then be cross-checked against other sources of information and, potentially, discussed with the wider stakeholder community.

Business analysts need to appreciate the rationale for applying standards and the benefits that the use of standards can deliver so that they can communicate this to colleagues and customers. This will enable the widest application of standards and will support improvements in business analysis practice.

Adapting the standards

Some business analysts (and those performing other IS professional roles on projects) are reluctant to adopt standards, as they are seen to constrain and restrict their work. Therefore, it is important to adopt an approach that is **tailorable, scalable** and embraces **continual improvement** in the development and maintenance of standards and templates.

Business analysis projects are varied, as illustrated in the BA Service Framework in Chapter 2. Business analysts may be required to work to establish a change project, to support the development of the change solution or to enable the successful acceptance and deployment of business changes. Part of the skill of the business analyst concerns the ability to apply relevant approaches as appropriate, and to adapt them as necessary to the needs of the particular situation. Tailorable standards offer a basis for this adaptation and ensure that the business analyst does not expend valuable time working on irrelevant and unhelpful deliverables.

Less experienced business analysts may need support and guidance when working with standards, as there can be a tendency to 'follow the method' or 'fill in the form'. A 'one-size-fits-all' approach to analysis that fails to recognise that projects have particular differences and concerns is rarely successful, so standards should be applied in an informed manner and with an outcome focus. Business analysts have to ensure that the work they do, and the standards they apply, contribute to achieving the desired outcomes. Where this is not the case, they need to question the relevance of all or part of a particular standard and adapt it accordingly.

Ensuring that business analysts and stakeholders are aware that standards and templates can be tailored, and communicating the benefits of adaptation, can help to overcome initial resistance to standards. Claims such as 'this project is different', 'that won't work here' and 'we don't need these deliverables' can be overcome through the use of an adaptive approach. Both standards and templates should be 'shrink-to-fit', and the relevance of any activities, diagrams, information items or documents that do not support the achievement of the required outcome should be questioned. This may result in the reduction, replacement or removal of all or part of the standards, which should ensure that they are applied effectively within a particular context. Templates can be designed to explore of a wide range of areas to guide the analysis and prompt discussion. Anything that is not relevant or not needed for the given situation can be removed or revisited later.

The adoption of a tailorable approach to the use of standards contributes to the continual development and improvement of the BA Service and individual business analysts. It encourages everyone to apply standards in an informed way and to think about how they might be improved so that they better support the business analysis work. This approach also helps to develop professionalism amongst business analysts. Rather than accepting a standard as a 'rule', business analysts are encouraged to consider whether the standard will benefit the project and whether there is a better alternative. This extends their understanding of the standards and improves their analytical thinking skills.

Examples of effective adaption of standards are as follows:

- Selecting relevant techniques to analyse and represent conceptual aspects of business situations. Possibilities include capability maps, value streams and business use case diagrams. Business analysts are required to understand the different techniques and have the ability to evaluate and apply them.
- Identifying where a central repository of information that supplements other requirements artefacts would improve communication and understanding. Possibilities include creating a scoping model, such as a use case diagram; developing a glossary of terms that incorporates definitions, synonyms and antonyms; building a central repository of business rules.

A standards-based approach, combined with the ability to adapt where relevant, balances the need for flexibility on projects with the drive for re-use and the benefits this offers. This balancing act is reflected in Figure 6.4.

Providing examples

To aid the adoption of templates and the compliance with standards amongst business analysts, it is incredibly helpful to provide completed examples. Examples provide business analysts with good insight into the appropriate level of detail. Initially, it may be necessary to apply new standards retrospectively to some existing business analysis deliverables, but over time all business analysts should be encouraged to share examples to show how the standards can be adapted to meet different business needs and analysis goals.

The emphasis is on these being 'previous examples' rather than 'best practice', as this reduces the pressure on the creator, lessens the tendency of business analysts towards perfectionism and re-enforces the message that business analysis deliverables may be tailored to meet the situation. Ensuring that examples are shared within the BA Service fosters both efficiency of approach and potential for collaboration.

Figure 6.4 Balancing the need for standardisation

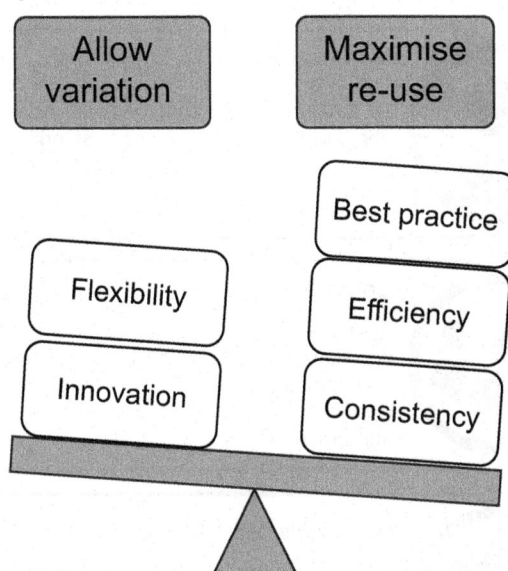

Governance

Governance of standards is needed to ensure that there is a mechanism for the standards to evolve in a controlled way. The level of formality of the governance approach will be influenced by a number of factors, including the size and maturity of the BA Service and the prevailing organisational and sector culture.

There are three main governance models for standards (shown in Figure 6.5) and, depending on the needs and approach of the BA Service, there may be multiple governance levels. For example:

- A large BA Service may encourage a community approach where anyone is able to suggest updates to standards and templates. These may be considered periodically and consolidated by a steering committee or change board, and, if sufficient information and justification is provided, these changes may be put forward to be ratified and accepted by the whole community.

- In a small or highly integrated BA Service, individuals may be empowered to make sensible changes that will be immediately accepted by all.

A committee approach can work well if obtaining input from those who use business analysis deliverables is practised. For example, testers, developers and business representatives can suggest improvements and also advise on the potential impact of changes.

A SIPOC analysis (shown in Figure 6.6) may be used to determine an appropriate level of governance and associated processes. If the customers of the standards are many and varied, this may point to a committee-led approach. If suppliers and customers are largely overlapping and confined to a small number of people, a community approach will be suitable.

Figure 6.5 Governance models for business analysis standards

Individually led

BA leader makes autonomous decisions about updates and changes to standards.

Committee led

A standards steering group or other decision-making body discuss and agree updates and changes to standards. Requires either consensus or majority agreement.

Community led

Business analysts, either individually or collectively, are empowered to make or propose updates and changes to standards.

Figure 6.6 SIPOC analysis for business analysis standards and templates

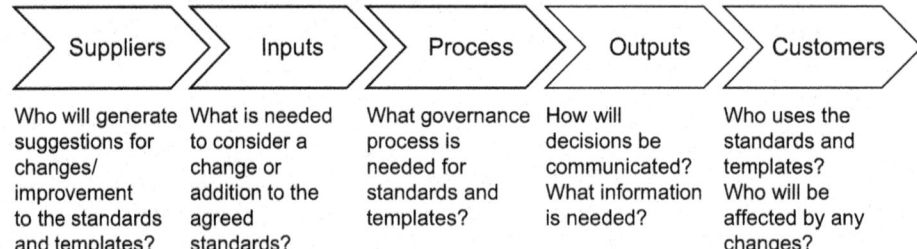

Suppliers	Inputs	Process	Outputs	Customers
Who will generate suggestions for changes/ improvement to the standards and templates?	What is needed to consider a change or addition to the agreed standards?	What governance process is needed for standards and templates?	How will decisions be communicated? What information is needed?	Who uses the standards and templates? Who will be affected by any changes?

The process used to provide governance of standards requires a careful balancing act for the following reasons:

- Not everyone has the same level of interest in standards.
- People can become frustrated if over- or under-consulted.
- Very detailed debate about topics that affect only a small number of people can alienate members of the community.
- If the process is too laborious or slow, it can stifle innovation and improvement.

- Without governance, the standards and templates may not be fit for purpose for the BA Service.

Reasons standards and templates fail

Despite the benefits that may be achieved from adopting standards, the creation, review maintenance and version control required to ensure that standards are relevant and in use can be seen as an overhead. Even when standards are in use, there are several issues that can arise. Table 6.5 shows a number of typical issues that arise from the use of standards and possible ways to address them when they occur.

Table 6.5 Issues with standards and templates

Issue	Why this issue occurs	Ways to address
No standards or templates available	No one is allocated responsibility; there isn't a sponsor/driver for standards and templates; standards and templates are not seen to be a priority **Typical comments:** 'too busy' 'just find one online'	Highlight benefits; find a sponsor; allocate responsibility/ownership; define an approach to selection of standards or creation of templates (just enough/just in time/right people involved); re-use existing standards and templates that have been applied successfully on previous projects An online resource may be a great starting point but does not reflect internal requirements, lessons learned on previous projects, organisational culture, terminology, style guide and priorities Best practice can mean different things to different people, so this needs to be agreed and communicated
Many template variations in use	Individuals/projects have complete freedom; personal preference is allowed; no version control mechanisms exist; lack of leadership **Typical comments:** 'we are all professionals' 'the good thing about standards in our organisation is that there is so many to choose from'	Introduce quality-checking mechanisms, set targets and individual objectives, agree version control and dissemination mechanisms The Service as a whole is more professional if it is consistent

(Continued)

Table 6.5 (Continued)

Issue	Why this issue occurs	Ways to address
Templates not used	Information about templates is not communicated; there is no dissemination mechanism; no buy-in to using the templates; not considered fit for purpose; too generic, so perceived to be irrelevant or requiring too much effort to adapt; too specific, so can't be tailored; out of date in terms of content or branding; senior stakeholder wants something different; no checking or enforcement **Typical comments:** 'I can't find them' 'I didn't know' 'We had no input'	Review which templates are used or are not used and why; involve the right people in establishing templates; communicate regularly; engage wider stakeholder group; implement quality assurance and control mechanisms; agree storage location; set targets and individual objectives based on the application of templates Commitment to continual improvement combined with the toolkit approach ensures that this is not a one-off activity
Standards not followed	No leadership, so limited or no buy-in; standards not defined within governance approach; not communicated; no dissemination mechanism; belief that the standard is not fit for purpose; differing views amongst senior stakeholders; no review or enforcement **Typical comments:** 'This is an exception' 'There are no consequences of not doing it'	Introduce quality-checking mechanisms; set targets and individual objectives; agree version control and dissemination mechanisms; communicate regularly; engage wider stakeholders Every project believes it's an exception. Focus on benefits, build valid exception criteria into the standards
Too much change	New standards being constantly added; so many standards now exist that business analysts don't know how to apply them, or which ones have the highest priority **Typical comments:** 'I don't know where to start' 'The standards have changed since I started this'	Consider how a 'release cycle' for new standards could be adopted; define the rules for compliance for deliverables already in production Find a balance between continual improvement and allowing business analysts to meet reasonable standards

The specific reasons business analysts suggest for the lack of adoption of standards and templates provides a basis for identifying the root causes of problems and defining the specific actions required to address them. When creating, selecting and adopting standards and templates, it is important to keep in mind the main objective, which is to produce clear, concise and complete analysis deliverables that aid communication and meet the needs and expectations of stakeholders. This goal may have to overrule the need for compliance with the most recent version of a template or slight divergence from standards.

CONCLUSION

The use of standards and templates within the BA Service can be highly beneficial, providing a starting point for the work to deliver each service in the BASF, avoiding the need to 'reinvent the wheel' on every project, and removing the temptation for every business analyst to develop and apply their own personal 'standards'.

Numerous industry standards and templates exist, and these can provide BA leaders with a basis for improving the consistency of the business analysis work. The selection process needs to take into account the availability of standards plus factors such as organisational policies, processes, culture and values.

While a single person can be the driving force behind standardisation, if that individual leaves or moves on, a gap is created. Even if the particular individual remains with the organisation, it can be a lonely place if you are trying to establish standards in the face of apathy or disagreement. Therefore, an individual bearing all of the responsibility can become disillusioned and this can result in the usage of standards coming to a halt and the objectives of consistency and efficiency failing to be met.

A 'champion' for the standards approach can be highly beneficial for the organisation and the BA Service, but this is not sufficient to ensure that they are adopted successfully in a sustained way. Instead, the BA leaders need to offer clear support for the initiative and should allocate different areas of responsibility across the members of the BA Service; ownership and responsibility for creation, review and maintenance should be shared by all.

Where the benefits are genuinely understood and appreciated by the whole community, there is a far greater chance that the standards and templates will be adopted. Where there are consequences if standards are not applied, this will also increase the chance of adoption.

CASE STUDY 4: PROVIDING CONSISTENT BUSINESS ANALYSIS

Matt Eastwood, Care Quality Commission (CQC)

Like many organisations, the Care Quality Commission has recognised the need for a consistent and repeatable approach for delivering projects for many years. There was a PMO (Project Management Office) in place, with a remit to establish and maintain standards, create templates, embed project management good practice, and offer advice and mentoring. CQC identified the value that coordinated business analysis could have and created a new Lead BA role who would define and lead the BA team. As a Lead BA, Matt was contributing to projects at the same time as developing the BA Service.

'One of the first things we did was create a BA Service Catalogue; this defined the services we offered to our internal customers. The main aim was to help other people in our organisation understand what we do and how we do it.' By using language that customers could understand, the BAs were able to engage and guide stakeholders to consider how business analysis could be used to best effect on their project.

Matt wanted to introduce standardisation in two main areas, (1) competency of BAs and (2) business analysis outputs. To address the first area, he researched professional standards for business analysis and was inspired to create a four-level capability framework specific to CQC. The model made it really clear to BAs what was expected of them, and they were supported to address any gaps.

To ensure consistency of the outputs produced by BAs they created a set of standards, templates, definitions and completed examples. They believed it was really important to have examples of 'what good looks like' to help BAs achieve the required levels of detail and quality. They already had a number of strong examples produced by the team, but these were updated to align to the new agreed standards. 'I was trying to ensure a good level of quality across the whole team, so no matter who was allocated, standard outputs would be delivered.'

CQC has been using BPMN for many years, and had a lot of good examples, not just of stand-alone models, but models of different levels and how they interrelate. There is consistent application of the notation across different BAs, underpinned by the use of templates in MS Visio.

On the whole, both BAs and their customers were very happy with the move towards standardisation. One slight pocket of resistance was from individual contract BAs, who had been brought in for their expertise, were used to a high level of freedom and had their own ways of working. Matt was able to ensure that their concerns and experience from elsewhere were taken into account and reflected within the organisational standards.

Considering the benefits of standardisation, Matt said: 'It improves and standardises quality and provides assurance to projects that the right things are being produced in the right ways. For BAs it helped remove ambiguity and they had access to good examples to work towards. In terms of personal objectives and performance management conversations, they can provide evidence of work that they have done that meets the quality standards.'

Following an internal re-structure, Matt has progressed to BA Practice Manager, and is leading a single BA practice that now provides BA support across the whole change framework to transformational programmes, business change projects, digital projects and improvement initiatives, so the benefits of standardisation have the potential to be even wider. Matt knows that the new remit of the team brings a new dimension to standards: 'As the range of work is so varied, standardisation must not be overly prescriptive. I want to ensure that our new BA function has the flexibility to use the right tool for the job.'

7 APPLYING SOFTWARE TOOLS TO SUPPORT THE BA SERVICE

INTRODUCTION

Almost every area of our work and personal lives is now supported by software tools, and business analysis is no exception. The key question is: **'To what extent are business analysis activities and outputs improved and supported by the tools available?'** The answer to this varies greatly across different organisations and even across business analysts in a single organisation.

There is a significant variation in tools in use to support both the delivery of business analysis and the management of the BA Service. This chapter considers the use of support tools and covers the following areas:

- types of tools that can support business analysis;
- levels of maturity in using support tools;
- the need for a support tool strategy;
- reasons why tools may fail to realise expected benefits and how to address common issues.

SUPPORT TOOL CATEGORIES

Support tools will be used on a daily basis by business analysts during the performance of the services, and also by senior business analysts in the management and operation of the BA Service. The software tools required by the BA Service must be considered in terms of the features needed to support this work.

Although it is very difficult to find any consistency in support tool use, it is possible to understand the types of tools that may be used to support different elements of business analysis. There are six main categories of tools, shown in Figure 7.1, which business analysts use on a regular basis to successfully carry out the role (BA Manager Forum 2016).

Further details of the capabilities associated with each type of tool, and a description of how the tools support business analysts, are shown in Table 7.1.

Figure 7.1 Categories of support tool used when conducting business analysis

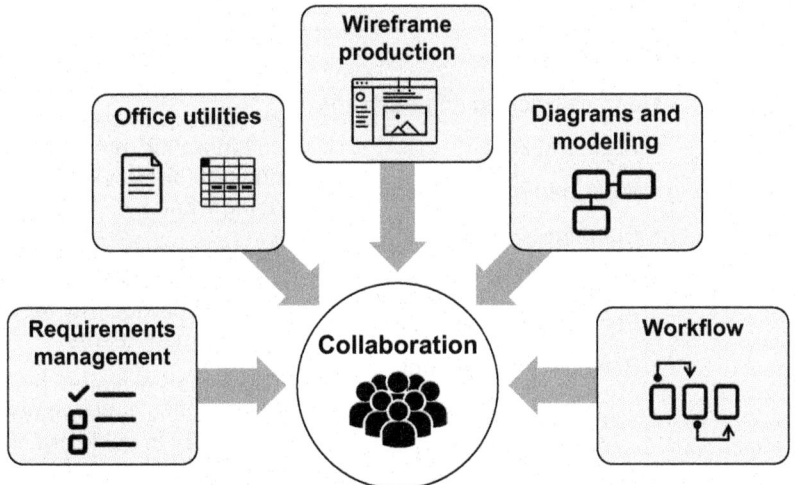

Table 7.1 Software tools and capabilities

Category of tool	Functionality	Description
Collaboration	• Information/document storage • File sharing • Email • Instant messaging • Virtual/online meetings • Announcements/broadcast lists • Community forums • Alerts/notifications	These tools are central to any type of business. There are two types of collaboration and communication to consider: 1. business analysis work with project teams, business stakeholders and customers 2. within and across the BA Service
Diagrams and modelling	• Visual representation • Efficient creation and editing of diagrams and models • Re-use • Conformance with standards and notation consistency • Generation of associations and dependencies between diagrams and models	To be able to use an appropriate range of business analysis techniques, business analysts need access to tools that offer diagram editing features that extend beyond the capabilities of standard office utilities

(Continued)

Table 7.1 (Continued)

Category of tool	Functionality	Description
Task and workflow management	• Task allocation • Status tracking and reporting • Issue tracking • Workload management • Planning • Prioritisation • Escalation and approvals • Backlog management	Task and workflow management software may also provide a framework for team collaboration, providing clarity on team priorities and who is doing what Workflow tools are often integral to successful project delivery, particularly for system development teams These tools are often highly configurable, and it may be necessary to guide or constrain how the tool is used
Office utilities	• Word processing and document creation • Presentation creation • Spreadsheets • Databases	Even where business analysts have access to specialised tools, it is likely that analysis outputs produced by business analysts will need to feed into documentation such as business cases, option appraisals or presentations to stakeholders. Over 90% of business analysts surveyed in 2015 (IIBA UK 2015) use standard office utilities to produce business analysis deliverables, in addition to tools that offer specific features
Requirements management	• Traceability • Requirements linkages and dependencies • Version control • Guided process • Shared repository • Search • Re-use • Status tracking and reporting • Acceptance criteria and linkage to testing processes	Specialist tools to facilitate consistency and efficiency in managing the activities and outputs of the requirements engineering framework (elicit, analyse, validate, document, manage) Some tools provide full systems development life cycle support, from requirements through to design, build, test and deploy

(Continued)

Table 7.1 (Continued)

Category of tool	Functionality	Description
Wireframe production	• Screen mock-up • Screen design • Navigation design • Report mock-up	Tools to support the development of outline prototypes, wireframes and mock-ups. Wireframes help stakeholders to visualise systems and screens, act as a focal point for collaboration and can significantly reduce the reliance on translating textual requirements into reality

Software tools can offer the opportunity to develop the sense of community across business analysts as they enable them to share information and work collaboratively to deliver their services.

Where more extensive tools are not available, it is still important to enable this sharing and collaboration. As a minimum this will require:

• an email distribution list for all business analysts working in the organisation;

• a shared area where standards, templates and guidance may be stored and accessed.

Requirements engineering and management

Requirements engineering, including requirements management, is a core competency of the BA Service, so this needs to be an area of tool support that is given specific consideration. Using office utilities (primarily documents and spreadsheets) for requirements is manageable up to a point, but for a large or complex area of work, ensuring that a vast number of interrelated requirements are captured and controlled becomes a challenging task.

A complex system development project requires specialist software to ensure that all relevant stakeholders are working with the current version of the requirements. Requirements engineering and requirements management software are not always popular with business analysts or other stakeholders, but do offer significant potential benefits to several stakeholder groups, as described in Table 7.2.

Requirements engineering and requirements management tools can overlap with Computer Aided Software Engineering (CASE) tools and configuration management tools. The level of resource overhead, on the part of the business analyst and others, to keep requirements tools up to date can be considerable. To realise the benefits of a tool, it must become an integral part of the analysis and development process and be seen as an enabler of the project or development team work.

173

Table 7.2 Benefits of requirements management tools

Stakeholder group	Benefits of requirements management tools
Project manager	Metrics can be provided on numbers of requirements and progress. Tool can enable the impact of change to be understood
Development team members	Single source of the current version of the requirements enables collaboration, ease of access and immediate availability
Business staff, including end users and other stakeholders	Provides confidence that all requirements are recorded, the current version of the requirements will be used by all project team members, and no requirements will be overlooked or mislaid
Business analyst	Enables version control, audit tracking, status tracking
	Helps to answer traceability questions about the requirements such as:
	• Why was requirement X rejected?
	• Who agreed that requirement Y could be left out of the solution?
	Reduces manual processing of requirements

Management tools

A range of tools are required to support the management of the BA Service. Depending on the size and business analysis maturity of the organisation, some of the functionality may be provided by enterprise-wide tools. However, in smaller or less mature organisations, local software solutions may need to be established by the BA Service. The functionality offered by these tools and the rationale for their use are described in Table 7.3.

The entire delivery portfolio offered by the BA Service is likely to encompass a mixture of corporate processes and systems (e.g. HR and Finance), and local systems, processes, documentation and spreadsheets. It may be a worthwhile exercise to use the functionality provided by support tools to define the systems in use, the relationships between systems and processes, and the flows of data between the systems. This should be augmented by information about the responsibilities of the BA Service regarding the systems and processes. This will provide the holistic picture of how the BA Service operates and interacts across the organisation and will offer opportunities to identify possible business improvements.

The features offered by support tools enable efficient business analysis activity. Therefore, the procurement and use of relevant support tools is key to the efficient operation of the BA Service.

Table 7.3 Management tools

Category of tool	Functionality	Rationale
Management information	• Spreadsheets • Performance or progress dashboard • Business analytics	The BA Service needs to be able to answer questions and make informed decisions through the use of timely management information
Resource/ demand management	• Resource management • Tracking business analysis demand and requests • Forecasting • Recording assignments/ allocations • Tracking actual time (timesheets)	The BA Service will need a way to track demand, availability and deployment of business analysts; this is likely to be more complex as the number of business analysts increases
Knowledge management	• Shared repository • Searching and indexing • Linking information • Retention/life cycle	Storing, disseminating and re-using information is vital to achieve service consistency and efficiency. There may be multiple tools or systems available within a single organisation, and the BA Service needs to determine the most relevant approach
Planning	• Visual planning • Dependencies • Estimates and actuals	Planning capabilities are closely linked with management information. Effective planning at a BA Service level will inform many other processes such as resource management, recruitment and service improvement
HR	• Recruitment • Advertising • Staff records • Absence management • Performance management • Learning and development	The BA Service needs to understand corporate and local processes and systems to establish where boundaries in responsibilities lie The quality and reliability of business analysis information in 'HR systems' is only as good as the flow of information from the BA Service

(Continued)

Table 7.3 (Continued)

Category of tool	Functionality	Rationale
Finance	• Budgeting • Expenses • Purchasing • Payroll	The capabilities and systems are likely to be enterprise wide. The BA Service needs to understand how to engage with these processes and systems

SUPPORT TOOL MATURITY ASSESSMENT

The level of maturity a BA Service has reached regarding support tools is informed by the answers to these key questions:

• Do business analysts have access to the support tools that will help them to produce the required analysis outputs?

• Do business analysts know which support tools are available, and how and when to use them?

Figure 7.2 shows a 5-Level Maturity model analogous to the CMMI model discussed in more detail in Chapter 12.

Figure 7.2 BA Service support tool maturity levels

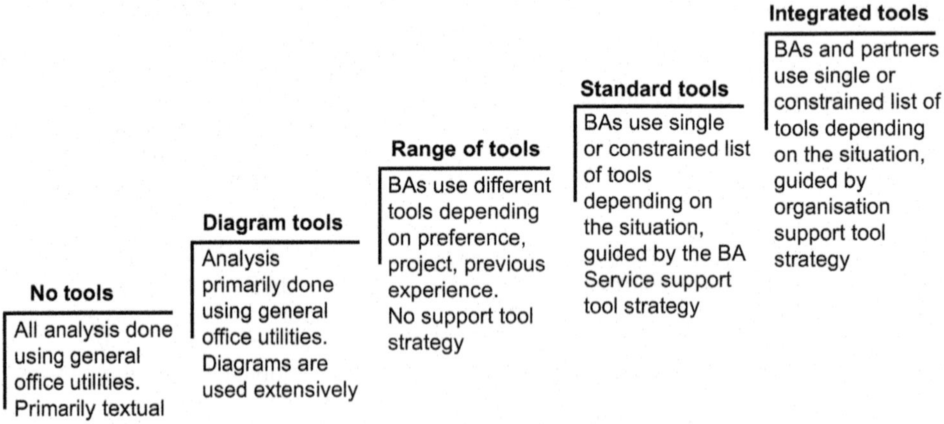

Integrated tools

BAs and partners use single or constrained list of tools depending on the situation, guided by organisation support tool strategy

Standard tools

BAs use single or constrained list of tools depending on the situation, guided by the BA Service support tool strategy

Range of tools

BAs use different tools depending on preference, project, previous experience. No support tool strategy

Diagram tools

Analysis primarily done using general office utilities. Diagrams are used extensively

No tools

All analysis done using general office utilities. Primarily textual

Increasing levels of maturity show that there is consistency in the use of support tools; this is guided by a strategy for deploying and using support tools, and the tools available meet the needs of the BA Service and its customers. The maturity levels relevant to the use of business analysis support tools are described in Table 7.4.

Table 7.4 BA Service support tool maturity levels

Maturity stage	Description	How to move forward
No support tools	Tool support is limited to basic office utilities software. Analysis is recorded and presented in documents and spreadsheets	Articulate the benefits of diagrams and models and support business analysts to increase confidence and capability. Select diagram tools that support this
Diagram tools	Tool support includes software to produce diagrams. Analysis is presented in documents and spreadsheets and is supported by appropriate diagrams and models	Agree standards such as range of diagrams in use, notation sets and presentation. Provide ways for business analysts to store and re-use diagrams or elements of diagrams
	Diagrams are typically 'stand-alone' and there is no integration of diagrams	
Range of tools	Analysis is presented in a range of different ways and is recorded using a range of support tools. This can differ between projects depending on preferences of business analysts and stakeholders. The number of tools expands in an ad hoc way, as no strategy exists to guide or constrain the use of tools	Review existing tool set and select the most relevant, acceptable and beneficial tools Engage with business analysts and customers on the rationale for selecting and using specific support tools
Standard tools	BA Service develops a support tool strategy which defines the tools that should be used and the rationale for their use within given circumstances. Business analysts are supported to use the constrained list of tools and other tools are discouraged or added to the strategy as appropriate	Communicate with stakeholders about their support tool needs and approaches. Look for opportunities to collaborate or rationalise tool set
	Tools provide opportunity to achieve re-use and traceability	

(Continued)

177

Table 7.4 (Continued)

Maturity stage	Description	How to move forward
Integrated tools	Organisation applies an integrated support tools strategy that covers all of the BA Service The entire portfolio of business analysis services should be underpinned by the strategic tool set. All project colleagues should have access to the tools they require to undertake their work and to share information. Business analysis artefacts should be held within an integrated tool set that should provide required management information and progress tracking	Establish commitment to continual improvement in the strategic use of support tools. Influence updates of organisational support tools strategy, assess new tools as they become relevant, continue to ensure that changes in staff do not lead to loss of support tool knowledge

The aim of the support tool strategy is to set out the goals and objectives of the BA Service and show where these are, or could be, supported by appropriate tools and technology. It should consider the current business analysis capabilities that are enabled by support tools, and those that could be enhanced or enabled by tools in future. It will also contain any support tool policies or requirements that have been agreed at an organisational or enterprise architecture level. The strategy should also outline the approach to procure and deploy support tools. Over time, the strategy should be updated to reflect which tools have been selected for which purposes (see Appendix 6).

As new tools and technology emerge on a frequent basis, there must be a mechanism to assess new support tool options against the strategy and make updates when necessary.

SELECTING BUSINESS ANALYSIS SUPPORT TOOLS

It is important to consider providing support tools to business analysts beyond the standard office utilities and basic corporate software suite if they are to provide an efficient and effective BA Service. The high-level requirements to be delivered by business analysis support tools include the ability to:

- improve the consistency of business analysis deliverables;
- facilitate collaboration;

- ensure that outputs meet quality expectations and are usable by the intended audience;
- enable mechanisms for traceability;
- provide an efficient approach to creating deliverables;
- store and organise analysis artefacts;
- provide mechanisms for efficient re-use of artefacts;
- provide security, audit history and change control;
- generate information for tracking progress and quality measurement.

When considering the requirements for business analysis support tools, there is often an initial focus on the functionality, as demonstrated by the list above. However, it is also important to consider and define appropriate non-functional requirements, in particular regarding the following areas:

- security and access;
- usability;
- accessibility;
- availability;
- resilience;
- performance;
- capacity and scalability;
- backup and recovery;
- archiving and deletion.

The platform on which the tools will be run, and any other technical infrastructure requirements, will also need to be considered. Essentially, deciding on a support tool for the BA Service requires business analysts to undertake several of the services within the BASF to assess feasibility and relevance (see Chapter 2). This is further discussed later in the chapter.

Free versus commercial software

There are many software suppliers that provide free online tools or free (reduced functionality) versions of software that support some business analysis activities. The functionality provided by these versions may include support for mind mapping, process mapping, wireframes development, analytics, document sharing and collaboration. The use of these tools may help a small or developing BA Service to understand the value they offer.

There are advantages and disadvantages to free and commercially available support tools. These are discussed in Table 7.5.

Table 7.5 Advantages and disadvantages of free and paid-for tools

Type	Advantages	Disadvantages
Free	Allows users to evaluate this type of tool Build knowledge and confidence of the functionality amongst business analysts Have access to analysis features without financial commitment	Tool can be withdrawn without notice Security, availability and resilience unknown Limits of the functionality available may require upgrade to paid-for version May result in dependency on a tool that has not undergone a formal evaluation process Free is never entirely free because there is a cost of time spent learning and configuring the tool and supporting other users Lack of formal procurement process may result in several different support tools used across the BA Service
Commercially available	Breadth of functionality Support available Quality of outputs Consistency of process supported	May be expensive to purchase the support tool, and pay for licences and maintenance Complex tools will require training for business analysts Business analysts and customers may be resistant May enforce unwanted standards

With both free and commercially available software, it is usually possible to try the tool before a final decision is made. In the case of a significant investment (of both time and money) it may be possible to do a 'site-visit', to see an organisation that uses the tool extensively and discover what the business analysts believe are the benefits and constraints of the tool.

Deploying support tools

Once a product has been selected, which should include testing the software for 'fit' with the business analysis requirements, it may also be necessary to undertake the business change deployment service. Therefore, procuring a support tool for the BA Service requires as much analysis as any other project. Many organisations have invested large amounts on purchasing tools for use within their business change and IT disciplines and these have not always been wise investments. Applying good business analysis and project management approaches to these purchases offers a much greater likelihood of success.

Using specific analysis software rather than generic office utilities software may require the BA Service to assume greater responsibility for the business analysis deliverables. Given that they are information assets of the organisation and projects, it is important to protect them to ensure that they don't become unavailable, corrupted or compromised. This requires the business analysts to consider how this may be prevented, the impact if issues arise and who would be responsible for rectifying the issue.

Where a decision is taken to implement business analysis support tools, the specialist nature of the tools also places the responsibility on the business analysts to consider the following questions:

- How will software upgrades be managed?
- How will licences be managed?
- How will new business analysts be trained in the use of the tools?
- How will new business analysts gain access to the tools?
- How will staff departures be managed?

These questions need to be considered as part of the evaluation and deployment of the support tools.

Applying the business analysis process

Understanding the tools and technology needed to support the BA Service provides the perfect opportunity for business analysts to demonstrate good practice. Debates on which tool to use can be lengthy and applying a business analysis approach is likely to be beneficial. The following business analysis services will help to ensure that the desired outcome from adopting a support tool is achieved.

- **Situation investigation and problem analysis:** to determine why a support tool is needed, identify any issues that would need to be considered and analyse the stakeholder views regarding a proposal for a support tool.
- **Feasibility assessment and business case development:** to evaluate the feasibility of different products and define the costs, benefits, impacts and risks associated with each of them.
- **Requirements definition:** to elicit and analyse the requirements to be provided by a support tool, including both functional and non-functional requirements, as discussed above.

Therefore, before making a major investment of time and money, it is helpful to apply the relevant business analysis services. The business analysis process model (Paul, Cadle and Yeates, 2014) shown in Figure 7.3 offers a similar view, in this case with specific reference to the consideration of stakeholder perspectives.

Figure 7.3 Business analysis process model

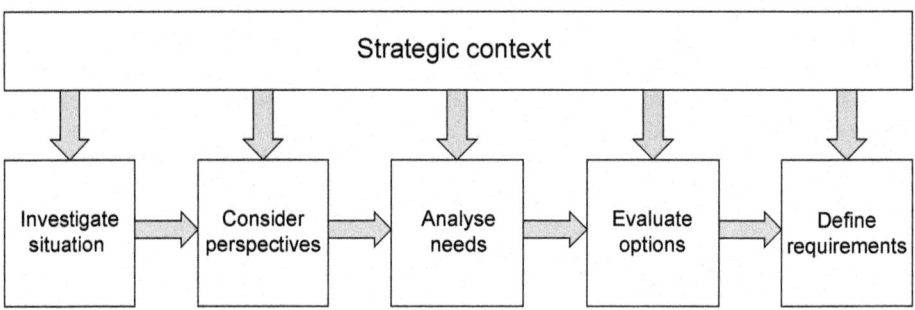

Without the discipline of this approach, the BA Service runs the risk of making an unwise investment due to the following:

- viewing technology as the answer to all issues;
- progressing quickly without understanding the context or problem to be addressed;
- listening to whoever speaks loudest;
- believing that a support tool that worked in another area or organisation is a valid solution;
- buying something that seems to meet the need without understanding the business requirements;
- failing to consider ongoing costs;
- relying on implementation by osmosis;
- failing to realise the predicted benefits.

Adopting 'free' software also runs the risk of falling foul of hidden costs that may prove expensive in the longer term.

Table 7.6 shows a number of questions that need to be addressed at each stage of the business analysis process; the route to addressing each question may require one or more analysis techniques to be applied.

Two further business analysis services are likely to be required to ensure a successful adoption of a support tool:

- **Business process improvement:** to review the business analysis activities and identify where they might change following the adoption of a support tool.
- **Business change deployment:** to plan the transition towards the adoption of the new tool and revised processes.

Table 7.6 Business analysis stages applied to tool selection

Stage	Objective	Questions
Investigate situation	Define the problem to be solved and the BA Service objectives to be achieved	• What are we aiming to achieve? • Why is a support tool required? • What will it enable the BA Service to do? • What organisational constraints are relevant?
Consider perspectives	Understand who the stakeholders are and the nature of their worldviews regarding the business analysis support tools	• Whose processes and deliverables will be impacted? • What are the issues? • To what extent will a support tool address the issues? • Who will use the support tool? • Who will use the outputs? • What are the expectations and preferences of different groups?
Analyse needs	Explore and evaluate the differences between the current and desired situations	• Where are we now? • Where do we want to be? • What activities are needed to address the gap?
Evaluate options	Identify options and assess them from business, technical and financial standpoints	• What level of support do we have from stakeholders? • Which options best meet our objectives? • What does the cost/benefit analysis tell us? • What are the impacts and risk of the options?
Define requirements	Elicit, analyse and validate detailed requirements for support tools required by the BA Service	• What are the requirements? • Who has raised the requirements and why? • What are the priorities? • How will processes look in future?

This work requires a holistic approach that takes into account all of the POPIT™ model elements. Questions to be considered during the delivery of the new support tool are as follows:

- Who will lead the delivery of the change?

- What is the process to purchase, deploy, build and configure the software?

- What training will be required for business analysts and others affected by the use of the support tool?

- How will current business analysis work be impacted?

- What documentation needs to be created or updated to support the use of the tool?

- How will usage be encouraged and embedded?

- How will benefits be tracked and realised?

- Who will have ongoing maintenance responsibility?

REASONS TOOLS CAN FAIL

Despite the benefits that may be achieved from investing time and money into implementing a standard support tool set, there are several issues that can arise. Table 7.7 shows a number of typical issues and possible ways to address them.

Table 7.7 Issues with use of support tools

Issue	Why this issue occurs	Ways to address the issue
Tools not used	No one is encouraging or mandating the use of the tools or they are not seen to be a priority	Highlight the benefits of using the tools to business analysts and stakeholders; find a sponsor; identify internal 'champions'; provide training when needed; invest in the required number of licences
	Typical comments:	
	'too busy'	
	'I wasn't given training'	Online help, guidance and other resources are often a good starting point, but may require additions or adaptions setting out how to use the support tool given the context of the organisation
	'it's too complex for what I need'	
	'stakeholders don't like it'	
	'we only have a limited number of licences'	

(Continued)

Table 7.7 (Continued)

Issue	Why this issue occurs	Ways to address the issue
Competing tools	Individuals and projects have complete freedom; personal preferences are permitted; senior stakeholder wants something different; no support tool strategy exists; lack of leadership **Typical comments:** 'I prefer X tool' 'I have always just used Y tool for this' 'the senior stakeholder has said we must use Z tool instead'	Develop a support tool strategy and engage widely with the business analysts and other potential users of the tools (see Appendix 6) Focus on the benefits offered by the tools; consider if there are valid reasons why different tools may be used for similar purposes; communicate rationale for the tools selected Promote the need for the BA Service to standardise on specific support tools in order to be more efficient and demonstrate professionalism
Tools used in limited way	Entire functionality set offered by the tool not understood; limited training and support; no checking or enforcement **Typical comments:** 'I only use it for...' 'I cut and paste into...' 'I don't know how to...' 'It takes too long to...'	Review which functionality is used or not used and why; involve the right people in establishing training and guidance materials; implement quality assurance and control mechanisms; set targets and individual objectives based on the use of tools
Compatibility issues	Uncontrolled configurations and upgrades; use of range of hardware. **Typical comments:** 'It doesn't work on my machine' 'Our supplier doesn't use it/ have access' 'Team X won't use it' 'We're all on different versions'	Move to controlled or centralised upgrade process; investigate hardware compatibility; communicate with infrastructure architects; collaborate with suppliers and partners to agree an approach

The specific reasons business analysts suggest for the lack of adoption of tools provides a basis for identifying the root causes of problems and defining the specific actions required to address them.

When selecting and implementing support tools, it is important to keep in mind the main objective, which is to support the efficiency and effectiveness of the BA Service. This involves ensuring that the business analysis deliverables aid communication and meet the needs and expectations of stakeholders. It may be necessary in some situations to prioritise good working relationships and effective collaboration over the use of a specific support tool.

CONCLUSION

Business analysis cannot be conducted in isolation. The results from business analysis need to be recorded so that they can be communicated to stakeholders and reviewed for consistency. Support tools offer a range of features that can help business analysts to perform their roles effectively.

The tools used to support the delivery of business analysis services must align with the needs of the different customer categories, as well as the business analysts, and should provide features that are relevant to particular situations and services.

Support tools offer the opportunity to increase efficiency, bring clarity and enable collaboration. However, effort, planning and commitment are required to adopt and embed support tools successfully. Failure to ensure that sufficient time and resources are available when deploying tools risks undermining the investment and may limit the extent to which any benefits are realised.

CASE STUDY 5: REALISING BENEFITS FROM INVESTMENT IN SUPPORT TOOLS

Terri Lydiard, Teal Business Solutions

Having worked with a large number of organisations across a range of sectors, including finance and global consultancy, Terri Lydiard has had the opportunity to see a range of tools in use to support business analysis. Some organisations have had real success, and realised the benefits of their investment, others have wasted a huge amount of money.

The instances where requirements engineering and management tools work well are where there is a stable team of business analysts, ongoing training and an emphasis on knowledge sharing and collaboration. Where tools are also used by other disciplines, such as architecture, development and testing, this increases the usefulness of the tool and the potential benefits for the organisation. Terri has seen that some organisations spend a lot of time trying to get information out of tools, into documents, spreadsheets and reports for different audiences. Business stakeholders can be reluctant to change their processes (such as accessing information directly in the tool), or to accept information in new formats.

There can also be challenges from the business analysts; some seem to do everything possible to avoid using a tool. Tracking and workflow management tools are often more readily accepted by BAs, as they are typically easy to learn, have intuitive interfaces and don't constrain the analysis approach. With a more complex tool there will be a significant training overhead, and if the BA workforce is subject to a lot of change, for example, through the use of large numbers of contractors, there is an ongoing need to train new members. For some BAs the training need may be twofold, learning how to use the tool, and how to use any standards or notation the tool supports, such as UML.

There may also be a level of internal politics surrounding the adoption or replacement of tools, in relation to which teams or senior stakeholders advocate for which tools, and this will influence decision making.

Reflecting on how organisations may successfully adopt support tools, Terri said: 'Think about how the tool will be implemented, and don't necessarily mandate it for every project; sometimes it's not worth it. Create a set of criteria such as size, length and complexity of the project and number of people involved; only projects that meet the criteria are likely to get the benefits from the investment in tooling.'

The culture of the organisation has a huge impact on the effectiveness of any tools adopted. 'The key to the success of a tool is the people; you have to show them it's worth it. Make sure the tool is stable, that there are core people who are proficient, and make others want to use it!'

8   LEADING THE BA SERVICE

INTRODUCTION

Leading a business area such as a BA Service is similar to running a small business and, as a result, many of the same issues need to be considered. BA leaders have extensive responsibilities ranging across areas such as promoting business analysis work, developing business analysts and, particularly given the issues discussed in Chapter 1 concerning recognition and authority, clarifying the service offering. BA leaders also have to combine the day-to-day management of the team with providing leadership that will guide and motivate the members of the BA Service. Chapter 9 examines this from a managerial perspective. This chapter examines leadership concerns and responsibilities. The leadership topics covered are:

- the role of the BA leader and techniques that help to analyse the BA Service;
- the vision and values required for effective leadership;
- standard leadership frameworks;
- challenges facing BA leaders.

WHAT IS A LEADER?

Much research has been devoted to the topic of 'leadership' and the characteristics of 'leaders', and this has resulted in numerous definitions of leadership. A common theme is that leadership is the ability to guide and motivate a team towards achieving a vision and goal. This provides a good definition to work with.

Leadership differs from management, as it is concerned with moving forward, inspiring and setting aspirations rather than focusing on operational efficiency. This means that leaders have to be clear about their vision for their organisation and must ensure that everyone moves in the direction required to achieve the vision.

Translating this to business analysis, the BA leader has to develop the vision for what the BA Service should be and what it should achieve. Further, the BA leader should motivate business analysts to work towards the vision and achieve the defined goals. When defined in a couple of sentences, this can sound straightforward. In practice, this can be a significant undertaking that requires many skills. The BA leader also has responsibility for an organisation that is involved in business change programmes, which requires skills that can support innovation. These skills include the ability to:

- define the BA Service strategy that aligns to the organisational strategy;
- put in place the tactics and operational processes that enable strategy execution;
- engage with business representatives and partners;
- ensure that the BA Service develops and retains relevancy within the organisation;
- focus on outcomes;
- foster ideas and accommodate risk-taking;
- encourage collaboration;
- build and develop a team;
- challenge assumptions;
- communicate clearly and appropriately (adapted from Portnova and Peiseniece, 2017).

This list of skills reflects the need for anyone leading a BA Service to be focused on results and able to influence the team to achieve what is required.

ROLE OF THE BA LEADER

The leader needs to set the scene for the BA Service, helping to clarify the answers to questions such as:

- Why does the BA Service exist?
- Who benefits from business analysis work?
- How can these benefits be achieved?

BA leaders are those at the forefront, ensuring that business analysts are afforded respect for their work and have the resources to conduct the work in line with the organisational needs.

It can be helpful to use a model or framework to think about the BA Service from a leadership perspective. Examples of relevant techniques and how they might be applied are shown in Table 8.1.

Table 8.1 Techniques used to consider the BA Service

Technique	Purpose	Application to a BA Service
CATWOE	A means of exploring the values and beliefs held about a business system, plus related aspects such as the customers who benefit and the actors who perform the work	May be used to consider different perspectives and viewpoints held by interested parties or stakeholders about the BA Service

(Continued)

189

Table 8.1 (Continued)

Technique	Purpose	Application to a BA Service
Business model canvas	A framework for analysing different elements of a business model, including the value proposition, key activities and revenue streams	May be used to identify, analyse and review the operational components that make up the BA Service
Business use case diagram	A modelling technique used to represent the key actors involved with a business system of interest and the functions to be offered by that system	May be used to visualise the scope of the BA Service, in particular the services to be offered and the beneficiaries of those services
Value chain analysis	A modelling technique used to represent the key areas of activity that together provide the means of offering a value proposition	May be used to represent the key activities required to provide a business analysis service and offer a value proposition

CATWOE and the BA Service

The CATWOE technique was developed by Peter Checkland (1999) and is part of the Soft Systems Methodology. This technique incorporates at its core the concept of *Weltanschauung*, which is often translated as 'worldview'. This concept offers a means of stating the values, beliefs and priorities held by an individual or a group about a particular area or system of interest. The other elements of the CATWOE are then considered, using the worldview as a base.

A possible CATWOE for the BA Service is shown in Table 8.2.

Table 8.2 CATWOE for the BA Service

Customer	All levels of organisational management and staff; external customers of the organisation
Actor	Business analysts
Transformation	Investigate business situation, analyse needs, evaluate options, define requirements
Worldview	The BA Service exists to ensure that all proposed business changes address a stated need, are evaluated against alternatives and offer a holistic solution
Owner	Director of business transformation
Environment	Organisational standards, budget and resources. Relevant legislation affecting areas such as data protection, accessibility, regulatory compliance

Creating a CATWOE for a BA Service can help both BA leaders and practising business analysts. The starting point for using the technique is to consider the worldview held by anyone who might have an involvement with the BA Service. This involves asking for views on why the BA Service is in place. This can result in the identification of different worldviews amongst the business analysts and the wider business community and provides an opportunity to consider where these views are sympathetic or in conflict with each other.

Uncovering differences at an early stage can help to identify real and potential conflicts and ensure that they are managed before problems emerge. This can also help to build awareness of where there is limited recognition of the BA Service and alert BA leaders to the need for positive action to address this issue. The case study at the end of this chapter sets out an approach adopted to improve recognition of the BA Service. This approach included the development of a Service Catalogue; an example Service Catalogue is provided in Appendix 1.

Ultimately, the discussion that results from considering the CATWOE for the BA Service, or any other group, helps to clarify areas such as the underlying focus of the work system, the activities and actors required to achieve this focus and the types of customer who are to benefit from the outcomes and deliverables. Understanding these aspects helps BA leaders to ensure that the vision and values of the BA Service are clearly defined and provides a basis for building consensus and common understanding.

Business model canvas

The business model canvas was developed by Osterwalder and Pigneur (2010) and offers a framework consisting of nine elements. Exploring and analysing these elements can help a leader to review beliefs, understanding and assumptions about the BA Service. It can also help to clarify the positioning of the BA Service, consider whether or not the business model is appropriate and improve effectiveness by identifying practice inconsistencies or areas where changes are needed.

A possible business model canvas for the BA Service is shown in Table 8.3.

Table 8.3 Business model canvas for a BA Service

Value proposition	Ensure wise investments in business and IT change
Key activities	Shape business change projects, evaluate feasibility of options, improve business processes, define requirements, support transition to new business system
Key partners	Business managers and staff; software developers and testers; business change managers
Cost structure	BA salaries, support tools, learning and development costs
Revenue streams	Internal cost centre – limited revenue
	Internal profit centre – fees paid by internal customers based on assignment charges

(Continued)

191

Table 8.3 (Continued)

Value proposition	Ensure wise investments in business and IT change
Channels	Route to internal customers via business change and programme/project management professionals
Customer segments	Major segments: business owners, business managers, business staff, external customers, project customers
Customer relationships	Translating, interpreting, questioning, communicating, influencing, negotiating
Resources	Business domain knowledge, professional business analysis skills, interpersonal skills, facilities, tools

Business use case diagram

Use case modelling is a technique from the UML that is used to represent and describe business and IT systems. Each use case diagram shows the actors who require a use case to be completed and their associations with the use cases. The technique offers many benefits to anyone wishing to provide an overview of the features offered by a system and may be used to represent a BA Service and its service offering.

Figure 8.1 shows an example business use case diagram for the BA Service, based upon the BASF described in Chapter 2.

Figure 8.1 Business use case diagram for the BA Service

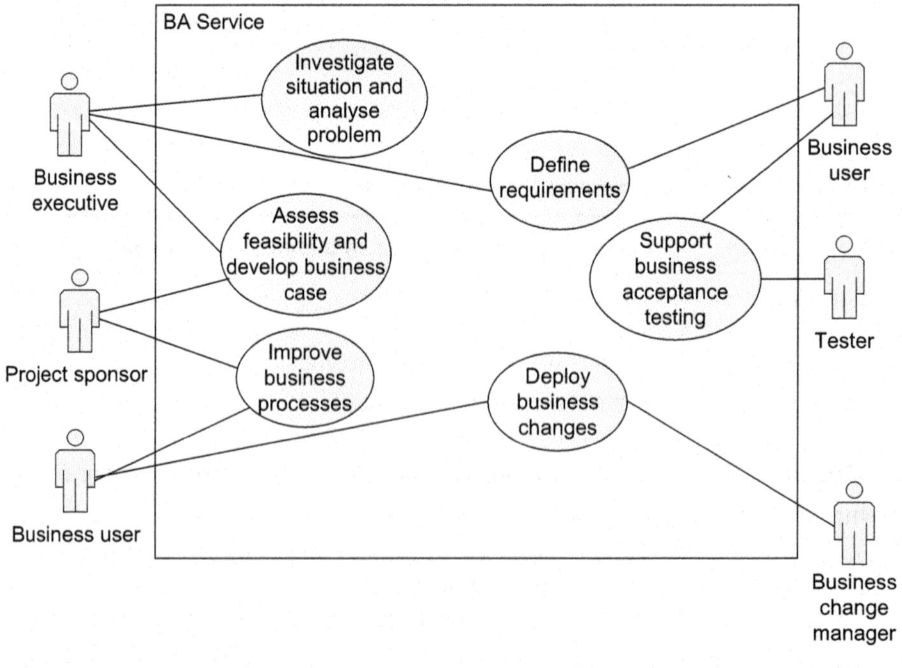

A business use case diagram can help communicate to stakeholders an overview of what the BA Service offers. It facilitates further exploration of the different services provided, which may be documented further in a Service Catalogue, such as that provided in Appendix 1.

Value chain analysis

The value chain was originally defined by Michael Porter in 1985. It offers a means of viewing the activities required to be performed by an organisation in order to offer a value proposition (goods or services) to customers. The identification of the activities provides a basis for analysing the costs associated with this proposition and, through the addition of a profit margin, the price that should be charged.

Given the length of time that has elapsed since the creation of the value chain concept, this technique is often considered to be out of step with the needs of organisations in today's business world. Also, the original value chain focused on manufacturing organisations rather than the dominant service focus that exists currently.

However, the structure offered by the value chain can be very helpful to identify the primary and support activities required to offer the business analysis value proposition. An example of a business analysis value chain is shown in Figure 8.2.

Figure 8.2 BA Service value chain

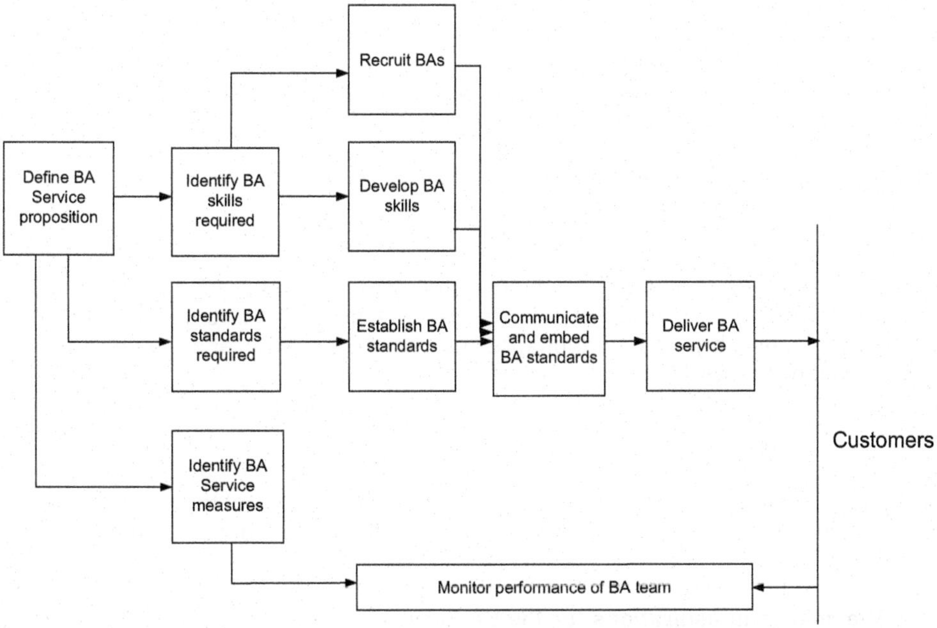

The value chain diagram provides a target state for the BA Service and offers a basis for analysing the gaps that exist within the current state. This helps to identify where changes are needed to move the BA Service towards the target state. The value chain also provides a means of structuring the changes and understanding where dependencies between different activities lie.

Given that there are six services defined in Chapter 2, each of which has an associated value proposition, set of activities and proposed techniques, it may be desirable to define a separate value chain for each service.

EFFECTIVE LEADERSHIP

Effective leadership requires a number of factors to be defined and/or established for the BA Service:

- vision for the BA Service;
- VMOST for the BA Service;
- values and ethics of the BA Service;
- knowledge-sharing culture.

Vision for the BA Service

All leaders have to define the vision for the organisation that they lead, whether that vision is to offer products at the cheapest price, with limited post-sales service, or to be the highest-quality service provider within a particular domain. The nature of the vision doesn't really matter if there is a market to which it appeals, but lack of a vision is a key weakness in an organisation.

The vision for an organisation or business area has been defined as:

> a concise statement that defines the mid- to long-term (three- to ten-year) goals of an organization. The vision should be external and market-oriented and should express—preferably in aspirational terms—how the organization wants to be perceived by the world.
>
> (Kaplan and Norton, 2008)

BA leaders are responsible for the definition and communication of the vision for the BA Service. Given Kaplan and Norton's definition, this vision should include the following aspects:

- **The goals and aspirations for the BA Service:** the leader should ask questions such as 'What do I believe this team should achieve?' and 'Where do I want the BA Service to be in 3/4/5 years' time?'

- **How the leader wants the BA Service to be perceived:** this requires consideration of questions such as 'How do I want the business analysts to perceive the reputation of the BA Service and the work undertaken?' and 'How do I want the stakeholders within the organisation to feel about the BA Service?' and 'What do I want our customers to say about the BA Service?'

Organisations should have a vision to guide work activities and decision making. Without a vision, the BA Service has a fundamental weakness, and can be compared to a car being driven when the destination is unknown and the windscreen is iced over. The general purpose of the activity may be known but the actual route travelled is a blur. Attempting to lead any team without a vision would be difficult and would result in poor performance and failure. The BA Service is no exception.

Simon Sinek (2011) offers a vision of leadership that begins with answering the question 'Why?' Sinek emphasises that it is vital to ask 'Why?' as a first step in formulating a vision for an organisation or team. This is reflected in his statement:

> Very few people or companies can clearly articulate WHY they do WHAT they do. By WHY I mean your purpose, cause or belief – WHY does your company exist? WHY do you get out of bed every morning? And WHY should anyone care?
>
> (Sinek, 2011)

Sinek's proposition is that success begins with answering these questions, which are then explored further through considering how the desired position is achieved and what the outcomes would be. Sinek represents this in his 'golden circle' model, which has been adapted for the BA Service in Figure 8.3.

Figure 8.3 Simon Sinek's golden circle adapted for the BA Service

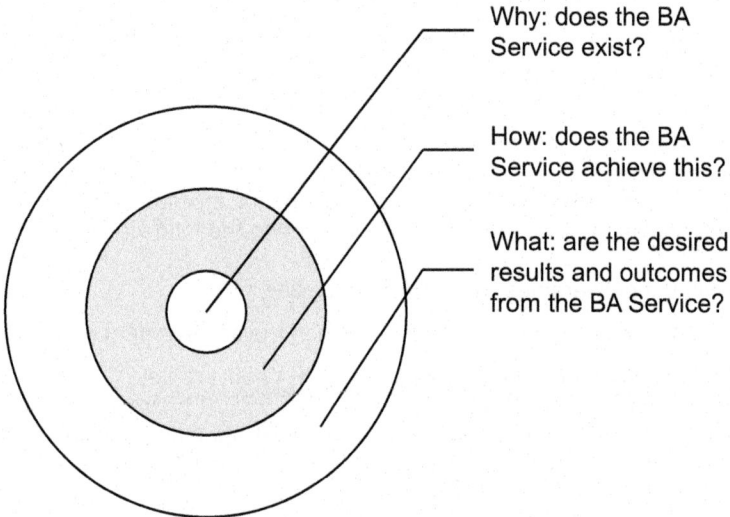

Why: does the BA Service exist?

How: does the BA Service achieve this?

What: are the desired results and outcomes from the BA Service?

This model, and the 'start with why' concept, may appear to be relatively straightforward but it is often evident that a leader does not understand the underlying rationale for their organisation or team. This results in confusion amongst staff members, which is manifested by a lack of clear focus, a propensity to prioritise internal requirements rather than customer needs, and, ultimately, a failure to deliver what is needed for the organisation to succeed.

If considered within the BA Service context, Sinek's golden circle emphasises the need for BA leaders to clarify their vision, to link vision to action and to ensure that this leads to the desired results. A Vision Development model offers a way of exploring a vision and determining a route to achieve the vision. This model extends the three levels provided in the Sinek model. Figure 8.4 offers a Vision Development model that explores how a vision for the BA Service might be developed using a 'why, who, what, how' structure.

Figure 8.4 Example Vision Development model

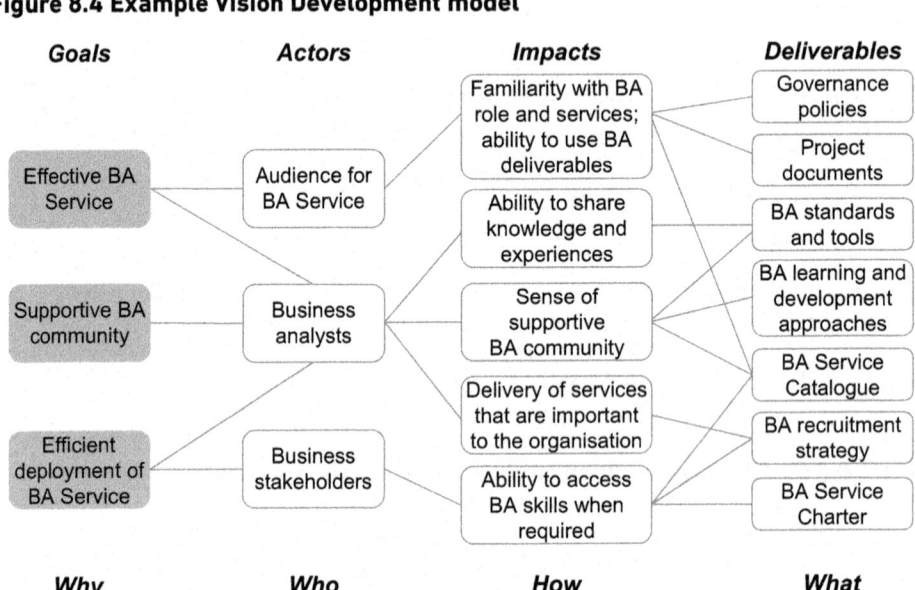

The example shown in Figure 8.4 identifies three goals that underpin the vision for the BA Service. These goals concern the establishment of an effective BA Service, developing a supportive BA community and ensuring the efficient deployment of the BA Service. Each goal is then achieved through traversing the following levels:

- What will the deliverables of the BA Service be?

- How will deliverables be used to impact upon the achievement of the goals?

- Who will be the actors that benefit from the BA deliverables?

Applying Sinek's 'start with why' concept and then extrapolating a Vision Development model will help the BA leader to establish a vision for the BA Service and a means of achieving that vision.

VMOST for the BA Service

VMOST is a technique known to the majority of business analysts; the acronym stands for Vision, Mission, Objectives, Strategy and Tactics. The VMOST for an organisation sets out the overall aim, the means of achieving that aim and the measures by which achievement will be assessed.

Developing a VMOST helps anyone in a leadership position to crystallise their thoughts and beliefs about the organisation they lead. The existence of a VMOST helps the members of a team to understand the overall direction for the organisation and the means by which the defined goals will be achieved. It is a helpful approach for leaders and team members within any organisation, including a BA Service.

A suggested VMOST for the BA Service is shown in Figure 8.5.

Figure 8.5 Example VMOST for the BA Service

BA Service VMOST analysis

Vision	A highly skilled service-oriented team of professional business analysts that helps the organisation to make informed decisions about IT-enabled change initiatives and to realise the predicted benefits.
Why does the BA Service exist?	
Mission	To provide effective and consistent business analysis services that enable the co-creation of value with colleagues and stakeholders.
What is the direction for the BA Service?	
Objectives	Increase awareness and understanding of the BA Service offering. (Monitor number of requests for business analysis support over 6 month period.) Achieve Net Promoter Score >X. Achieve business analysis satisfaction levels >Y. Ensure >Z% of business analysts hold professional certification within 12 months.
What does the BA Service aim to achieve? (Measurable)	
Strategy	Define BA service portfolio and catalogue. Conduct BA Service maturity assessment and create improvement plan. Implement pipeline recruitment strategy within 6 months to increase number of business analysts from xx to yy within 12 months. Develop and deploy knowledge repository.
How will goals be achieved? Medium to long-term actions.	
Tactics	Implement BA Service Improvement Plan (SIP). Establish BA standards and tools. Monitor BA Service performance. Attend industry events for business analysis and related disciplines. Introduce buddy scheme and make peer review part of BA objectives. Organise interesting and engaging CoP events.
How will goals be achieved? Short-term plans and actions.	

A VMOST may be produced by a BA leader, but it is often helpful to have input from business analysts when doing this. The business analysts may have additional ideas, which can improve the VMOST, and they are more likely to engage with the content of the VMOST if they have been involved in its development. Discussing the VMOST with other stakeholders can also help them to understand what they require of the BA Service.

The completed VMOST is a good communication tool that can be used in conjunction with the BA Service Catalogue to improve role clarity and improve recognition of the benefits offered by business analysis.

Values and ethics

Every leader should have a value system that informs the way in which they lead their organisation. BA leaders should think about the values and beliefs that they hold with regard to aspects such as:

- their beliefs about how to engage with people and understand their concerns;
- their priorities in the work context;
- their ethical and behavioural standards.

Essentially, a leader's values explain why they view the organisation as they do and should align with the concept of worldview (in CATWOE) and Sinek's 'start with why' approach. They should also be in alignment with the values of the wider organisation if conflicts with colleagues are to be avoided. Understanding the values that prevail within an organisation, and aligning with them where possible, is vital to avoid conflicts and confusion.

A statement of the values for an organisation, such as a BA Service, can be extremely powerful as it will guide the behaviour and activities of the team members. For example, a leader of a BA Service might hold the following values:

- Business analysis work is of a high standard.
- Business analysts operate in an ethical and professional manner and are highly skilled and motivated.
- The BA Service supports and enables organisational change such that benefits are realised for the organisation.

Communicating the values will also help to empower business analysts when undertaking their work and improve the consistency of decision making.

LEADERSHIP FRAMEWORKS AND STYLES

A leadership framework provides guidance on the areas to be considered when in a leadership position and the options for approaching leadership situations. Three helpful frameworks are John Adair's Three Circles model, the Challenge and Support model and the 8Ps structure. Each of these frameworks takes a different view of team leadership and thereby offers different insights. It is often the case that consideration of several frameworks is useful, but it may be that a particular model is more suitable for certain organisations or situations.

BA leaders need to be aware of different approaches, as this will ensure areas aren't missed and they are in a good position when making leadership decisions.

Adair's Three Circles model

John Adair's work on leadership led him to define the Three Circles model (Adair, 2009). This model reflects the three key areas of concern of a leader:

- **The team:** the leader should be concerned to generate a team culture, whereby individuals support each other and work for the good of the team.
- **The individual:** the leader should be concerned to develop and mentor individuals so that they are able to achieve their potential within the team and the role.
- **The task:** the leader should be concerned to clarify the nature of the task and the activities to be conducted.

Anyone leading a team needs to focus on these three areas and ensure that they are kept in the correct balance. For example, where a leader is concerned primarily with the work performed by the team and fails to consider the team and individual dimensions, issues may be missed resulting in a failure to complete the task successfully. Similarly, where the focus is on building the team, the needs of individuals may be overlooked and there may be insufficient effort allocated to the task completion. Keeping all three areas in mind and in balance is extremely useful when leading a team.

An adapted version of Adair's Three Circles model that is specific to a BA Service context is shown in Figure 8.6.

Figure 8.6 Three Circles model for the BA Service (adapted from Adair, 2009)

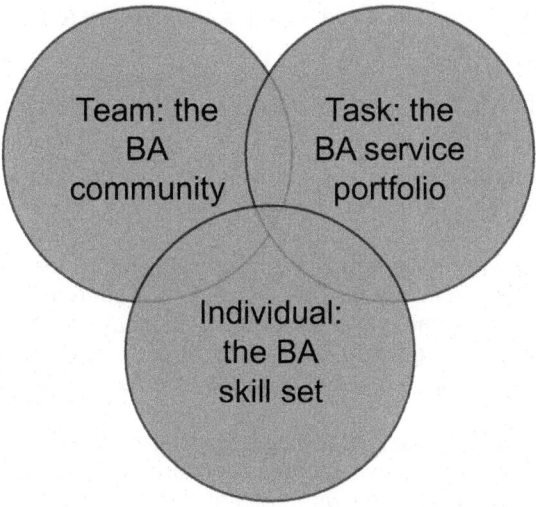

This adaptation shows that BA leaders should focus on the following with regard to the BA Service:

- **The BA community:** generating a sense of enthusiasm and commitment to business analysis and a community-based culture.

- **The BA service portfolio:** it is useful to define the business analysis tasks with some clarity (as discussed in Chapter 1). The application of a service view can be extremely useful to define the business analysis work and the value proposition offered.

- **The BA skill set:** BA leaders need to be aware of the skills required to work effectively as a business analyst. Chapter 4 defines the skills development framework approach; this can be extremely beneficial when considering the individual dimension of team leadership.

Again, benefits may be gained from using this model when BA leaders ensure that all three dimensions are considered and are kept in the required balance. Building a supportive community of business analysts is highly laudable, but business colleagues and stakeholders are unlikely to be happy with the BA Service if the individuals within the community lack some essential skills and are unclear about the work they need to carry out.

Challenge and Support model

The Challenge and Support model was originally developed by Nevitt Sanford (1966) and may offer insights for BA leaders. An adapted version of this model is shown in Figure 8.7.

The Challenge and Support model sets out alternative approaches to managing staff members and identifies the risks or benefits associated with each approach. Each of the quadrants offers advantages and disadvantages and they are most useful when applied to a relevant context. For example:

- A **'comfort zone'** approach can be beneficial should a staff member encounter a difficult, personal issue such as health or family problems.

- A **'pressure zone'** approach can be beneficial to ensure that a staff member who lacks focus is given clear direction to complete a task.

Problems can occur where there is a mismatch between a leader's preferred style and the values of the organisation. For example, a leader may have a preference for a directive, 'pressure zone' style, while the organisation has a culture based on empowerment and encouragement. It is important to recognise where there is a mismatch in leadership style in order to tailor the approach taken where possible.

The Challenge and Support model helps the leader to assess their leadership preference and to identify where an alternative approach is likely to be more helpful. It also helps to ensure that the risks associated with each of the approaches are considered and avoided.

Figure 8.7 Challenge and Support model (adapted from Sanford, 1966)

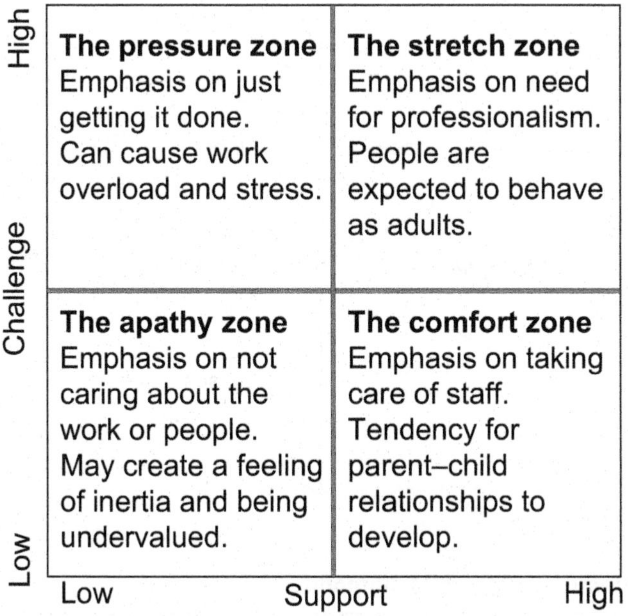

High	**The pressure zone** Emphasis on just getting it done. Can cause work overload and stress.	**The stretch zone** Emphasis on need for professionalism. People are expected to behave as adults.
Challenge	**The apathy zone** Emphasis on not caring about the work or people. May create a feeling of inertia and being undervalued.	**The comfort zone** Emphasis on taking care of staff. Tendency for parent–child relationships to develop.
Low	Low	Support High

The 8Ps diamond

When leading a community of business analysts, it is necessary to consider the range of aspects that contribute to the delivery of an effective BA Service. The 8Ps diamond extends traditional frameworks such as the 4Ps marketing mix (Place, Price, Promotion, Product) by identifying eight areas that BA leaders need to consider when taking a holistic view of the BA Service and the services offered.

This framework consists of a range of elements as shown in Figure 8.8.

The individual elements of the 8Ps diamond are described in Table 8.4.

Each element may be considered in turn to identify the following:

- where work is needed to improve an element. For example, the processes to engage with the BA Service may be ill-defined or unclear;
- where there are opportunities to extend the BA Service offering. For example, partners that could enable additional innovations for customers or provide a basis for new services;
- where there is a need within the organisation for additional business analysts or new business analysis skills.

Figure 8.8 8Ps diamond (reproduced with permission from AssistKD)

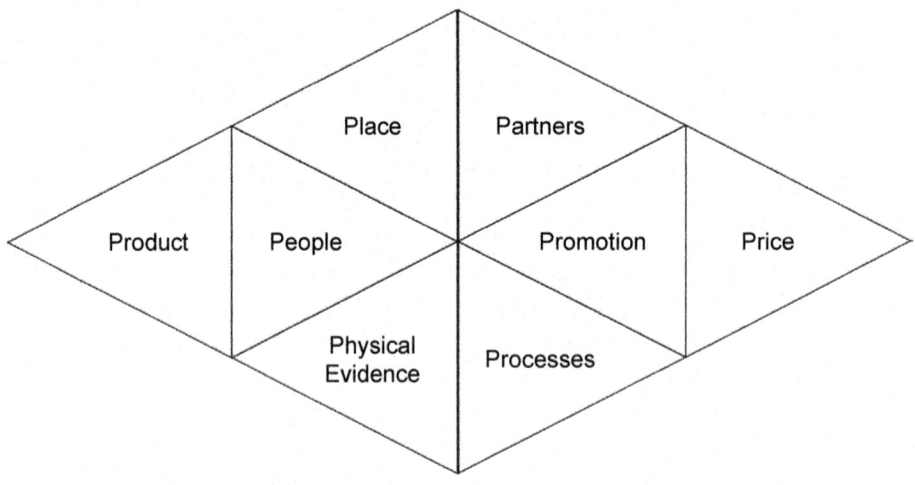

Table 8.4 The elements of the 8Ps diamond

8Ps element	Description
Product	A Service Catalogue is extremely helpful in setting out what the business analysts can offer to the organisation. This forms a team charter for the BA Service, helping to clarify the different services offered and the activities and techniques applied in the delivery of the services. This element aligns with the task dimension of Adair's Three Circles model
People	The characteristics and skills of the business analysts employed in the BA Service should be decided by the team leader. This element identifies the need to consider the people within the team and their development needs. It aligns with the individual dimension of Adair's Three Circles model
Place	This is an interesting aspect of team leadership when applied to business analysis. It is often the case that where a team is located can have significant impacts or repercussions. There has been much debate over where a BA Service should sit within an organisation (as discussed in Chapter 1). The leader needs to be part of the discussion regarding the place of the BA Service and the management structure that is applied
Physical evidence	The artefacts produced by professional business analysts are the physical items that stakeholders read, review and use. They leave a permanent record of the work that has been done and the quality of that work

(Continued)

Table 8.4 (Continued)

8Ps element	Description
Partners	One of the key elements of business analysis work concerns how interactions with key stakeholders and internal customers operate. Understanding the nature of the interactions and the boundaries between different teams can be critical. This can be assisted by a clear definition of the service portfolio, extended to incorporate a definition of deliverables and outcomes
Processes	While the BA Service Framework sets out the services that may be offered and identifies the relevant activities to undertake these services, the specific processes will need to be determined for each organisation. This involves BA leaders establishing the standards, such as for modelling activities, the templates and the support tools to be used. These areas are discussed in Chapters 6 and 7
Promotion	BA leaders have to be advocates for the BA Service and the community of professional business analysts. Sometimes they also have to ensure that the service offering is understood, given the issues with role clarity discussed in Chapter 1. Promotional activities include: • Engaging with senior executives to explain the services and value propositions of business analysis • Highlighting contributions made to projects by the BA Service and the link to successful outcomes via internal communications • Organising forums and informal events that increase the profile of the BA Service
Price	The nature of charging for business analysis services is often related to where the BA Service is situated within an organisation. However, a key factor is also whether or not the BA Service is subject to a cost, break-even or profit centre budgeting model. Cross-charging for business analysts is discussed in Chapter 9

This model helps BA leaders to ensure that all elements and the interdependencies between them are considered when developing or improving the BA Service.

CHALLENGES FACING BA LEADERS

In many organisations, questions continue to be raised about whether or not business analysis is needed and, even if business analysis is recognised as an essential discipline, whether or not a BA Service should be established. BA leaders face many challenges that they need to overcome if they are to justify the continued survival of the BA Service.

The BA leader's personal challenge

To succeed as a leader, it is not sufficient to manage the team and the work. A leader also has to demonstrate excellence by example. The 'do as I say, not as I do' approach is never successful. This means that the leader has to live by their stated (and hopefully, shared) values. For example:

- **Possession, development and maintenance of skills.** It is not enough to admit to once having had the skills – if you want team members to strive for excellence, you have to be able to offer excellence yourself.

- **Going above and beyond.** Expecting others to 'put in the hours' when needed but not being willing to do so yourself will result in resentment and demoralisation.

- **Remembering to engage and lead at a human level.** Leaders are people who fulfil a leadership role, so they should demonstrate empathy and understanding towards colleagues.

The first area of challenge is for BA leaders to review their personal skills and qualities, and ensure that they align with what is required of a leader.

The BA Service SWOT analysis

A SWOT analysis provides an effective way of summarising any organisation, including a BA Service. This technique has the potential to offer insights into the organisational and industry context for business analysis and to identify where challenges exist and how they might be addressed by the BA leader.

Table 8.5 sets out a possible BA Service SWOT analysis. This summarises opportunities where the BA Service might support organisations, the threats that need to be overcome, and the capability and limitations of the BA Service (strengths and weaknesses) that could aid or prevent successful outcomes.

Table 8.5 SWOT analysis for a BA Service

Strengths	Weaknesses
• Skilled individual analysts	• Role ambiguity/lack of clarity
• Defined business analysis standards	• Variable reputation
• Consolidated knowledge	• Proliferation of standards
• Professional certifications	• Limited leadership
Opportunities	**Threats**
• Significant change in all PESTLE areas; for example, global political changes, economic issues, rise of artificial intelligence (AI) and robotics, increasing drive for sustainability	• Lack of recognition
	• Lack of awareness
	• Land grab by other disciplines
• Continuing awareness of IS project failures/challenges	• Dismissal of business analysis by emerging roles and approaches within IT and change

This SWOT analysis highlights that there are many opportunities for change within organisations, and change initiatives may be supported by a professional BA Service. However, the threats facing the BA Service may undermine this support. While threats are usually outside the control of a group such as a BA Service, recognising them will help to ensure that they are not overlooked and are analysed to determine how they may be addressed.

The weaknesses inherent within business analysis may contribute to the continuation of the threats. Overcoming these weaknesses presents a significant challenge for BA leaders. The issues resulting from a lack of role clarity were discussed in Chapter 1 and an approach to overcoming this challenge, the adoption of a BA Service Framework, was described in Chapter 2. If the lack of clarity weakness is not addressed, ongoing ambiguity regarding the business analyst role will increase the likelihood of colleagues and customers failing to recognise when business analysis is relevant (if not essential). In extreme circumstances, this could result in organisations discontinuing the BA Service on the basis that it does not contribute to the success of IS and change projects.

The capability challenge

A further challenge is to ensure that the BA Service has the capability to deliver the service portfolio. A capability map is an excellent technique that would help to define the capability requirements for an effective BA Service. This 'desired' capability view would provide a basis for conducting a gap analysis and identifying where there are missing or partial capabilities. A capability map typically considers three 'strata': Strategic, Customer-facing and Support strata. Suggestions for capabilities within each of these strata are shown in Figure 8.9.

Figure 8.9 Example capabilities for the BA Service

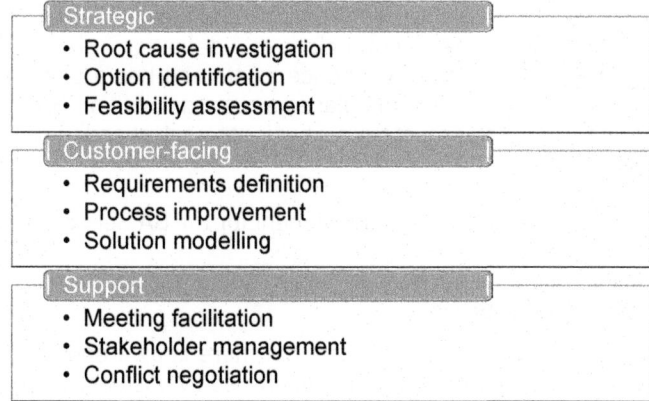

It is often the case that 'capability' is equated with 'skill', but this is not a one-to-one relationship and capability is not established solely by the acquisition of specific skills. If a BA Service is to possess a genuine capability, it will need to have the ability to do something in order to offer a service. All of the POPIT™ model elements will need to be in place if the BA Service is to have the ability to do something. Figure 8.10 shows a suggested set of elements required to establish a capability.

Figure 8.10 Elements required to establish capability

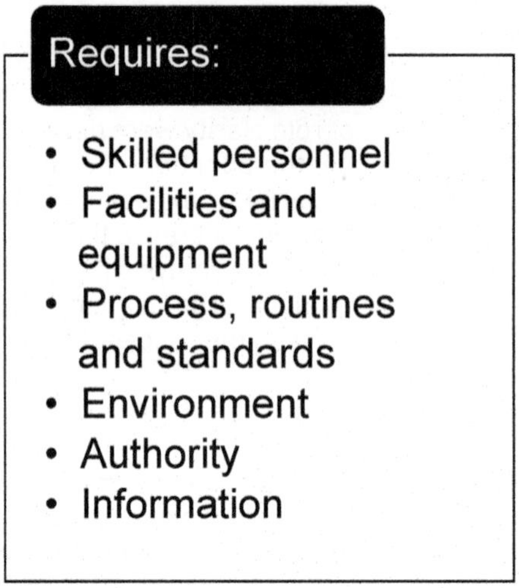

Requires:

- Skilled personnel
- Facilities and equipment
- Process, routines and standards
- Environment
- Authority
- Information

BA leaders need to review all of the elements shown in Figure 8.10 to ensure that they exist and that capability is established.

Positive reputation

Establishing a positive reputation for the BA Service is a major challenge for BA leaders. Chapter 1 discussed the issues regarding the business analyst role and the ambiguity that exists when there is not a clear role definition. It is essential that the organisation understands why the BA Service exists and has a positive view of the business analysis services offered. This places a responsibility on BA leaders to help customers understand what to expect from a business analyst and to ensure that these expectations are met or even exceeded.

Factors that can support expectation management for the BA Service are:

- provision of clear definitions of the services and the associated value propositions to be offered by the BA Service;
- engagement at senior levels to ensure that there is awareness of the business analysis services offered and the benefits offered by business analysis;
- support for business analysis skills development and information sharing amongst business analysts;
- establishment of a continual improvement culture that encompasses performance measurement and feedback.

It could be argued that all organisations or business areas need to share knowledge and engage in continuous learning and development. However, this is particularly the case for the BA Service because of the breadth and variety of business analysis work. Research into the project experiences of 20 business analysis specialists (Paul 2018) identified the following different types of project:

- business transformation;
- competency improvement;
- feasibility study;
- integration of business systems;
- software development;
- knowledge management;
- data migration;
- organisational design;
- process improvement;
- regulatory and government policy change.

This range of project experience illustrates how widely business analysis skills are applied within organisations and the breadth of skills business analysts need to possess. A culture where business analysts are encouraged to share experiences, expertise and knowledge helps to build the skills held within the team and contributes to the development of BA Service capability. This prevents constant reinvention and encourages re-use of artefacts and information (see Chapter 9).

The culture in a BA Service emerges from the BA leader. A culture that values learning and knowledge-sharing needs to be fostered through supportive actions. These may include provision of the following components:

- a knowledge repository providing storage and access to examples, standards and templates;
- informal knowledge-sharing events, such as lunchtime discussions or presentations;
- formal knowledge-sharing events, such as BA Service seminars or conferences.

BA leaders face many challenges, not least of which concern establishing a positive reputation. The frameworks, techniques and principles described in this chapter can provide insights to help BA leaders address these challenges and build a highly skilled and well-regarded BA Service.

CONCLUSION

One of the key challenges that can face any leader, and is particularly relevant to business analysis, is neatly summed up by the Abilene paradox (Harvey, 1988). The paradox is as follows: a group will sometimes agree to take an action that none of the group believes in because they each assume that everyone else agrees with the proposal, so do not want to state that they disagree. The example provided by Harvey concerns a family group who embark on a trip to Abilene, experience an unpleasant journey and meal, and only realise that none of them really wanted to do this once they have returned. When a suggestion is made to make the trip, everyone 'nods along', resulting in the entire group doing something that none of them wants to do.

This paradox may be encountered in many different business situations. It is particularly applicable to business analysis, where conventional wisdoms can often prevail despite poor previous experiences and widely held concerns. One of the challenges facing BA leaders is to ensure that the BA Service does not fall foul of the Abilene paradox. This requires BA leaders to do the following:

- set a clear vision for the BA Service and communicate this vision to the business analysts;
- provide clarity about the values of the BA Service and exhibit those values at all times;
- use the BA Service Framework and techniques such as SWOT analysis, the business model canvas and the 8Ps, to define a strategic direction for the BA Service;
- apply leadership frameworks, such as Adair's Three Circles model, to ensure a holistic leadership approach;
- ensure that empathy and understanding of business analysts' personal situations is a key element of the leadership style.

CASE STUDY 6: LEADING A BA SERVICE TRANSFORMATION

Kim Bray, Nationwide

Kim Bray has worked within business analysis for over 25 years in a number of different organisations. She developed and led the business analysis practice for Nationwide Building Society for six years. Kim is also a keynote speaker at business analysis conferences.

Kim's approach to leading and developing a BA Service is based upon the following steps:

1. Understand the business need for business analysis.
2. Understand the current position.
3. Understand what 'good' would look like. At the start, it is important not to aim for 'great', as this is likely to be a step too far.
4. Build a vision of what 'great' would look like at a point in the future.
5. Put together a plan of action to take the BA practice from the current position to the 'good' state.

6. Don't try to 'boil the ocean' straight away. It is important to get the practising BAs and the stakeholders to work together on the journey.

7. Demonstrate the difference as quickly as possible to get buy-in from the practising BAs and stakeholders.

8. Assess the stakeholders to identify who would be advocates and then work closely with them.

9. Assess the practising BAs – where is their strong capability? These BAs can ensure that stakeholders are on board to achieve the vision and can build momentum to take the rest of the BAs with them.

10. Define a road map on one page, showing everything that there is to do. Carry this road map to every meeting or discussion with stakeholders and practising BAs. Use it to track progress – where are we and who is doing what?

When developing the BA practice, Kim identified that many of the BAs were very capable but there was a sense that the business analysis service offered was not valued within the organisation. Therefore, it was important to convince stakeholders about the importance of business analysis and demonstrate how valuable it could be if used. Kim wanted to promote business analysis to ensure that the BAs were not just doing what they were asked to do but were also able to challenge, such as by asking questions about the business need and the desired outcomes. Good project managers began to recognise the value of business analysis and they then communicated this to stakeholders.

Kim encountered many challenges, in particular:

1. Architects were a barrier, as they felt that business analysis encroached on their area. Kim and her colleagues had to analyse how the business analysts and architects could complement each other and work together. They also had to prove that the business analysts had the required capability.

2. Testing was also an area that proved a barrier. The BAs were conducting the testing alongside the testers rather than helping to identify what to test and how to test this. As a result, the BAs weren't being recognised for the support they were providing. Kim and her team defined the BA service so that it was clearer and everyone understood what the BAs should do in the testing area. This was well-accepted by everyone and the frustrations went away.

3. Some of the BAs were not positive about the changes and wanted to stay with their fixed ways of working. Some BAs had been designated as requirements analysts and spent most of their time writing requirements. Once they were given the autonomy and tools – and were empowered to use them – they were able to understand the potential and extent of the BA role. Kim also engaged with industry bodies to demonstrate the wider BA context. She brought BCS and AssistKD into the organisation. She showed the BAs that business analysis can be a career and she benchmarked business analysis work with the wider marketplace.

One of the key initiatives Kim instigated was defining a Service Catalogue for the BA practice. This set out the services the BAs could offer and also defined what the BAs should be doing to deliver the services in terms of the outputs, templates and techniques. This Service Catalogue could be used in many different situations. Kim felt that this was an important step.

Kim's key lesson is 'build your management team' – you can't do this on your own. There should be strong support for the leader, at the level below, if the change is to be made with pace. During the change, Kim brought in external consultant BAs and found this helpful as it offered a means of building on different experience and ways of working.

Finally, Kim believes that repeatedly and continually communicating the key messages about business analysis is vital.

9 OPERATING THE BA SERVICE

INTRODUCTION

A number of operational and management activities are required if the benefits of a coordinated business analysis effort are to be realised by the organisation. This chapter discusses the key processes that underpin the operation of the BA Service. These are:

- consultancy management;
- demand management;
- planning and estimating;
- process management, including knowledge management, risk and issue management and financial management.

Many of these processes are not unique to business analysis, and there may be opportunities to align them to corporate approaches or to apply common standards in some organisations. However, the specific context of the BA Service, and the corresponding challenges that may arise when applying these processes within that context, need to be considered.

GAP ANALYSIS OF THE MANAGEMENT PROCESSES

When effective management is in place, it is not always evident to team members what managers actually do! This same conundrum often applies to the discipline of business analysis as a whole, where practitioners often struggle to articulate the benefits of business analysis, but the impacts of poor or no analysis are readily apparent.

It is helpful to use defined frameworks to identify potential gaps in management processes, capacity and capability. Two possible approaches are:

1. **The project 'Triple Constraint' model** of time, cost and quality (TCQ) sets out the major aspects to be managed to enable successful delivery. This can be applied to the BA Service to ensure that these aspects receive appropriate attention and there is clarity of responsibility and accountability.
2. **The POPIT™ model** provides a further level of detail to consider whether appropriate management processes and controls have been defined and are consistently applied.

These frameworks are discussed in the light of the BA Service context in Table 9.1.

Table 9.1 Management gap analysis

Management process category	BA Service management responsibilities
Time	Planning and estimating business analysis activities and deliverables; comparing planned with actuals and providing evidence; refining planning and estimating processes
Cost	Providing clarity on ownership and management of the budget for the BA Service; demonstrating cost-effectiveness and efficiencies; identifying appropriate non-staff costs to develop the Service (including training and events, recruitment costs, materials, software); developing a charging model for the Service; tracking and forecasting budgets
Quality	Overseeing business analysis activities and deliverables; assuring quality of approach, completeness and accuracy; defining and assuring the use of standards and templates
People	Providing clarity on who provides support for people and their professional development, including coaching, mentoring and management; having responsibility for recruitment and retention of staff, and resource/demand management; ensuring adherence to relevant HR procedures and policies; creating and maintaining appropriate networks and relationships for the Service
Organisation	Having responsibility for BA Service structures and career paths; defining job roles; defining and monitoring relevant metrics, including critical success factors (CSFs) and key performance indicators (KPIs) (see Chapter 13); designing how the BA Service interfaces and operates with other related functions within the organisation
Processes	Deciding who defines and owns the processes used to deliver the BA Service, and the interfaces and relationships with other processes
Information	Having responsibility for information about the BA Service, in particular information used by those delivering the Service, knowledge management, information sharing and skill transfer, and re-use of information and deliverables
Technology	Having responsibility for determining, implementing and supporting technology required to provide the BA Service

BUSINESS ANALYSIS CONSULTANCY MANAGEMENT

Business analysts are often referred to as 'internal consultants', able to act in an objective way, see things from a new perspective and bring relevant experience, knowledge and expertise. They provide a service, hand over the results of their work, and then move on to their next assignment. Many business analysts act as internal consultants; those who do this most successfully have an understanding of the consulting cycle. The BA Consulting Cycle is shown in Figure 9.1. The cycle is comprised of two halves that cover the following aspects:

- **Doing business analysis:** delivering business analysis services (see Chapter 2 for the Business Analysis Service Framework). The practice of business analysis, including the activities, tasks and techniques.

- **Enabling business analysis:** delivering business analysis as a service. This means starting and ending each piece of work or project in a way that sets up the business analyst for success, builds the relationship with the customer and enhances the reputation of the BA Service.

An individual BA may be able to perform both halves of this cycle effectively (and for external 'contract' business analysts, their business model depends on it) but, for larger BA Services, BA leaders may be responsible for undertaking all or part of the enabling phases.

Figure 9.1 The BA Consulting Cycle

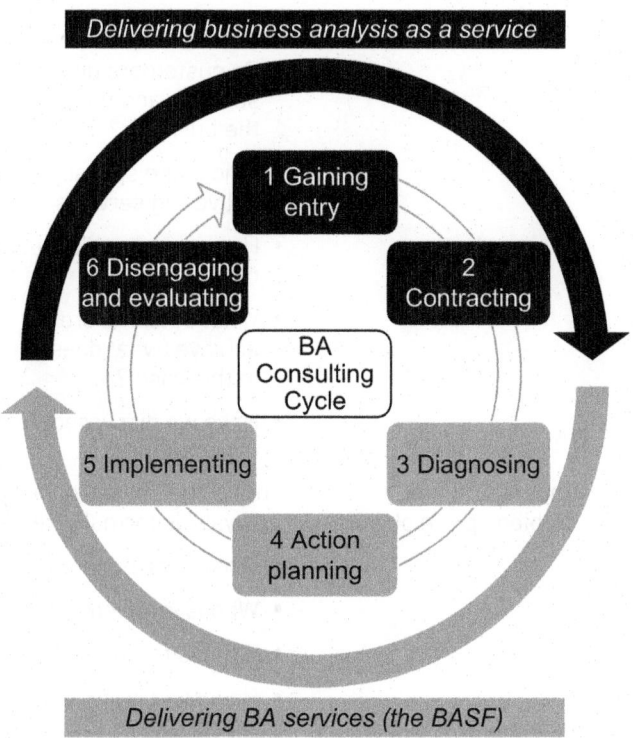

Table 9.2 shows each of the phases of the BA Consulting Cycle in more detail.

Table 9.2 Phases of the BA Consulting Cycle

Consulting phase	Goal	Implications for business analysis
Gaining entry	Consultant is invited or selected to carry out a piece of work	This phase is critical for the ongoing existence of the BA Service • How do we gain entry if not invited? • Who needs to be aware of the BA Service? • What networks do BA leaders need to be part of? • How is the pipeline of BA work managed?
Contracting	Agreement between consultant and customer	This is phase is critical for the successful delivery of BA services and for the services to be valued by the customer • Are we clear on our service offering? • Do customers understand the services and the value we offer to the business? • Who is the sponsor, to whom we are delivering services? • How can we build trust in the relationship? • What outcome are we trying to achieve (what does success look like in this case)? • Have we discussed and agreed expectations?
Diagnosing	Understand the problem/piece of work	This is the phase when 'business analysis' is formally begun • What information is needed? • Who is involved? • What is the scope? • How can clarity or agreement be reached? There is a specific BA service that is focused on diagnosis: situation investigation and problem analysis

(Continued)

Table 9.2 (Continued)

Consulting phase	Goal	Implications for business analysis
Action planning	Define options for carrying out the engagement and agree plans	For any piece of work there will be multiple ways that the outcomes can be achieved. This is the phase when various options for the assignment are identified and offered to the customer • Which BA services, techniques and deliverables are most relevant? • What are the options? • What can be achieved in the time frame/in budget/other constraints? Related BA services: feasibility assessment and business case development
Implementing	Deliver the agreed plan of consultancy activities and deliverables	This phase does not necessarily relate to the implementation of a solution, but the delivery of the agreed BA consultancy. Put simply – doing the BA work that has been agreed Related BA services: all (see Chapter 2)
Disengaging and evaluating	Handover, reflect, review and exit	This phase is needed to allow the business analyst to move to new work, and to allow the customer to move to a new 'business as usual state' • What knowledge transfer and handover needs to happen? • Who will be asked for feedback? • How did the assignment go from the business analyst's point of view?

If business analysts within the organisation are only concerned with 'doing business analysis', and the enabling phases are missed, the BA Service will be operating at a low level of maturity. There are a number of issues that can occur when there is limited understanding of the consulting cycle, or when phases are not adequately addressed – these are shown in Table 9.3.

These issues can occur on both short-term pieces of work and longer-term assignments; for example, where the business analyst is embedded in a development or product team. Both situations can still be considered internal consultancy services.

Table 9.3 Common issues arising throughout the BA Consulting Cycle

Consulting phase	Common BA issue	Ways to address
Gaining entry	Not engaged early enough in the work/project	Ensure senior stakeholders are aware of the BA Service and the catalogue of services it offers
		BA leaders should invest time in building relationships, highlight successful case studies of business analysis involvement in initiatives and provide a clear process or contact point for new work
Contracting	Customer has unclear or unrealistic expectations of business analysts	Use the Service Catalogue (including value propositions) and work packages to aid discussion of what is on offer from the BA Service and to define what is needed by the customer before any work begins. Work to build trust and relationships
Diagnosing	Given solutions to implement rather than problems to analyse	Showcase the techniques and deliverables business analysts can produce to investigate and analyse a problem
		Produce simple and relevant analysis artefacts to demonstrate what could be achieved
		Use testimonials or internal references from successful engagements
Action planning	Customer dictates BA deliverables and ways of working	Revisit contracting phase
	Priorities, activities and deliverables keep changing	
Implementing	Business analysis deliverables not fit for purpose/take too long/insufficient depth/too detailed/do not aid decision making	Revisit contracting phase

(Continued)

Table 9.3 (Continued)

Consulting phase	Common BA issue	Ways to address
Disengaging and evaluating	Business analysts become SMEs Difficult to disengage	Use work packages, review points to discuss progress and have defined end dates wherever possible. Create transition and handover plans Request feedback from customers (see Chapter 12)

BUSINESS ANALYSIS DEMAND MANAGEMENT

Allocating business analysts to requests for business analysis support is a core component of operating the BA Service. Receiving, assessing, prioritising and addressing requests for business analysis support are processes that must take account of many factors. There is often a belief within organisations that resource management can be achieved through use of a tool or spreadsheet. These can support the process, but the number and complexity of human factors at play mean this is never a fully automated process.

Fluctuating demand

Managing fluctuating demand for business analysis support can be time-consuming and complex but it is unusual to have completely level and predictable demand within an organisation. So, the need to manage fluctuating demand for business analysts is a key issue for anyone managing a BA Service.

Demand for business analysis will be influenced by the:

- level of understanding and awareness of business analysis within the organisation;
- mix and stages of portfolio of projects/programmes/business as usual (BAU) within the organisation;
- perceived complexity of change initiatives;
- level of stability of the organisation and the need for change;
- speed of mobilisation;
- level of maturity of the BA Service;
- reputation of the BA Service;
- ease or likelihood of obtaining a business analyst;
- other roles in use across the organisation;
- access to business analysis skills via other routes.

Depending on the mix of factors at work, BA leaders may be faced with various demand issues. The key situations that arise, and may need close management, are as follows:

- **Insufficient demand**, which occurs where there is not sufficient work for the business analysts. Options to address this situation include raising the profile of the BA Service, targeting potential internal customers and, in the short term, using the time to focus on continual service improvement of the BA Service. If demand does not increase, allowing people to use transferable skills or develop new skills so that they can support areas of skills shortage elsewhere in the organisation, or reducing the size of the BA Service, may be longer-term options.

- **Demand equal to supply**, which occurs where all of the business analysts are occupied, future demand is planned and small deviations from these plans can be accommodated by the Service.

- **Excess demand**, which occurs where the BA Service cannot meet all the requests for business analysis support. In this situation, the BA Service will have to either increase the supply by hiring additional business analysts on a permanent or contract basis (depending on the longer-term need) or limit the demand by applying a prioritisation approach. Ensuring that business analysts are doing appropriate work and not plugging resource gaps for other roles may be another way of 'freeing up' additional BA Service capacity.

Prioritising demand

The relative priority of two projects or work assignments is often difficult to evaluate. Many organisations do not have a single view of priorities, with each department or business area having its own set of prioritised initiatives. Some organisations have established mechanisms for prioritising all work within their change portfolio. However, even where a clear ranking for projects or assignments is known, the high-level priority does not necessarily translate to the most appropriate deployment for the business analysts. Table 9.4 sets out an example comparison of project requests.

BA leaders must understand and apply multiple criteria to inform business analysis resource decisions, including the factors shown in Table 9.5. The number of factors mean that, inevitably, leaders will at times have to make resourcing decisions that are unpopular with business analysts or with customers. Having the ability to justify the resourcing decisions made and demonstrating an empathetic and customer-focused attitude, will help to build up trust in the decisions made.

Resourcing models

The BA Service can deploy business analysts using various deployment models. Within the BA Service, several of these models are likely to be evident as different models are required to respond to different situations. For example, the approach may depend upon:

- the size and complexity of different projects/assignments;
- the experience of the business analysts and the levels of support required;
- the need for increased responsibility for more senior business analyst roles.

Table 9.4 Example comparison of business analyst resource requests

Project A	Project B	Outcome
This project is a lower priority to the organisation than Project B but has a clearly defined business analysis work package to help address an issue that has arisen during testing The project is two months from completion. When it completes it will release eight people from different roles who are scheduled to start work on a number of projects	Project B is higher priority within the organisation than Project A. However, the business analysis work is not clearly defined, and there is already a business analyst assigned to the project who has little clarity or support	In this scenario, if both projects are competing for a single available business analyst, it may offer more overall benefit to the organisation to support Project A, despite the higher priority of Project B Adding an additional business analyst to Project B is unlikely to bring benefit in the short term. Focus on Project B to clarify the analysis work needed while the immediate issue on Project A is addressed

Table 9.5 Criteria impacting business analyst resourcing decisions

Criteria	Key questions
Priority	Is this an organisational priority?
	How do we know the level of priority?
Risk/impact	What would be the impact of not supporting the request?
	Is this a high-risk project or assignment?
Relationships	Who is the customer?
	What would be the impact on stakeholder relationships of not supporting the request?
	Is the request likely to be escalated?
	Does this request present a new area or new opportunity for the BA Service?
Clarity	Is the request clear?
	Is the business analyst role understood?
	Is this within the scope of the BA service portfolio?
	Does the requester know what is needed?
	Does the BA Service have the opportunity to influence?

(Continued)

Table 9.5 (Continued)

Criteria	Key questions
Lateral thinking	Who else could do the work required?
	Are there options to fulfil the request in a different way?
	What alternatives or compromises could be suggested?
Business knowledge	Is it appropriate to assign a business analyst with existing knowledge and experience of this area?
	Do any of the business analysts need to build knowledge in this area?
Development needs and preferences	What skills and knowledge are required? (Business knowledge or business analysis skill set?)
	Do any of the business analysts need to develop skills in this area?
	Do any business analysts have a preference or aptitude for working in this area?

Four possible models for business analyst deployment are shown in Figure 9.2. The concept of a 'project' is used to illustrate any piece of business analysis work, which includes projects, assignments, programmes, teams, business areas or work packages.

Model D is most likely to occur where there are specialist skills or knowledge within the BA Service that need to be shared across multiple assignments, or where there is a hierarchy of business analysts where more junior business analysts are dedicated to the project and a more experienced business analyst provides leadership or oversight across multiple projects.

There is also the possibility of a many-to-many model where a group of business analysts work on multiple projects simultaneously. This is far less common because a sufficiently large or complex project will require the input of multiple business analysts and it is usually preferable that most, if not all of them, will be dedicated to that work. The many-to-many model may be applicable in a consultancy setting where a team of business analysts work together across several projects.

Table 9.6 provides an explanation of the advantages and disadvantages of the models within Figure 9.2.

Model C probably requires the most planning and ongoing management, as it is important to consider how different areas of responsibility can be divided across the assigned business analysts. For example, where there is a large project or programme of work, it is usually possible to allocate individual business analysts to different business areas, work streams, releases or areas of functionality. The use of work packages (see Appendix 7) is critical to establish accountability and avoid the disadvantages of this model.

Figure 9.2 Business analysis resourcing models

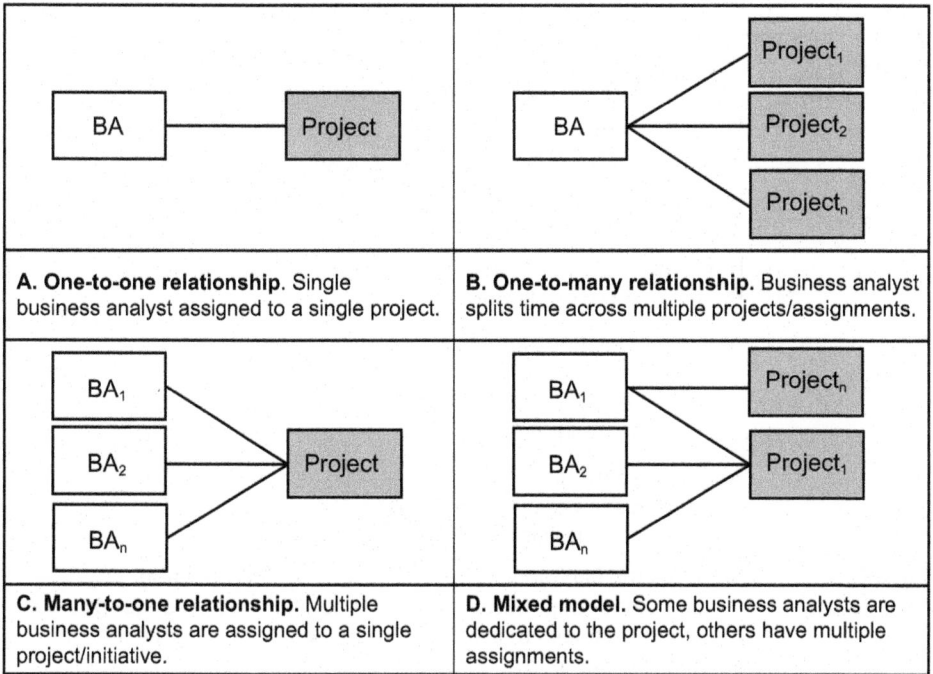

A. One-to-one relationship. Single business analyst assigned to a single project.	**B. One-to-many relationship.** Business analyst splits time across multiple projects/assignments.
C. Many-to-one relationship. Multiple business analysts are assigned to a single project/initiative.	**D. Mixed model.** Some business analysts are dedicated to the project, others have multiple assignments.

Table 9.6 Advantages and disadvantages of business analysis resourcing models

Model	Advantages	Disadvantages
Model A: one-to-one	'Dedicated resource' approach often popular with customers Business analysts often enjoy being part of a dedicated project or delivery team Business analyst is able to build up knowledge and relationships quickly Some level of autonomy and independence for the business analyst	Increases likelihood of business analyst doing non-BA work or grey area work Increases likelihood of under-utilisation and waiting time Business analysts may lack direction or ability to share ideas (therefore experience professional isolation) Business analysts may have limited opportunity to use different skills or acquire different knowledge (work becomes repetitive/unchallenging) There is a single point of dependency for the work

(Continued)

Table 9.6 (Continued)

Model	Advantages	Disadvantages
Model B: one-to-many	Increases likelihood of business analyst focusing on business analysis work Ability to balance work in response to project peaks and troughs of activity Business analysts often enjoy the variety and challenge Ability for business analysts to gain experience of different types of work and use different tools and techniques Ability to share learning across different pieces of work and identify dependencies	Business analyst may become overloaded Customers may be frustrated that the business analyst is not always immediately available Single point of dependency for multiple areas of work
Model C: many-to-one	Reduces the likelihood of a single point of dependency for the work (business analysts can provide some level of cover for each other) Business analysts often enjoy working together and providing professional support for each other Multiple business analysis skill sets and perspectives may be valuable to the work	Confusion of roles and responsibilities amongst business analysts, plus possible lack of accountability Duplication of business analysis effort Possible inefficiency due to need for agreement and decision by committee Potential for power struggle or conflicting approaches to business analysis Increased likelihood of inequity of workload; some business analysts contribute, others do not Possibility that some business analysts are not given equal opportunity to contribute due to how customers engage with business analysts

(Continued)

Table 9.6 (Continued)

Model	Advantages	Disadvantages
Model D: mixed	Ability for senior oversight, business analysis leadership and direction setting Specialist knowledge or skills can be used effectively across multiple projects	Senior business analyst can become a bottleneck for review or allocation of business analysis work Business analysts with multiple assignments can become left behind and may need to catch up. This may require time and effort from other business analysts Customers may be confused or dissatisfied about who is available

Additional resources

Adding more business analysts is not necessarily the answer to the perceived need for additional business analysis resource. Supplementing the business analyst team without identifying or quantifying individual effort can lead to 'social loafing' (Karau and Williams, 1997), explained as follows:

> Individuals often engage in social loafing, exerting less effort on collective rather than individual tasks.
>
> (Karau and Williams, 1997)

To avoid this situation, it is important to have defined areas of responsibility, so that the contribution of an individual is visible to the team. Too many analysts operating in the same space can also lead to reduced efficiency due to duplication of effort and analysis by committee.

It is important to understand at the outset whether the existing business analyst(s) are focused on delivering business analysis services or whether they are involved in other types of work. Consideration is then required to determine if the business analysts could be reallocated or working more efficiently.

Providing additional business analysts increases the relationship complexity of the work. If only two people are engaged in delivering a piece of work, there is only one relationship to build and maintain. If there are three people, there are three relationships. However, for five people, there are ten relationships, and, where there are as many as nine people, there will be 36 individual relationships!

To determine the number of one-to-one relationships relative to the number of individuals in the group (n), the following calculation may be used:

$$\text{Relationships } (r) = (n \times (n-1)) / 2$$

For example, for a group of 12 people, $n = 12$.

$$r = (12 \times 11) / 2 = (132/2) = 66$$

This calculation shows the additional communication and relationship management overhead required as the number of people, and relationships, increases. This is likely to impact significantly upon the overall time available for the group to deliver the work.

Hoarding resources

Customers of the BA Service, such as project managers, product owners and delivery managers, sometimes act in the best interests of their business area, at the expense of wider organisational priorities. This is an example of the 'just-in-case' mindset, with statements such as:

- 'If we release the business analyst, we might not get them back.'
- 'We are not busy now, but what if something comes up?'
- 'The analysis activities are complete, but there are lots of other things the business analyst could get involved in.'

These statements are indicators of 'resource hoarding' behaviour. It does not benefit the organisation as a whole to have skilled business analysts underutilised or inappropriately engaged. BA leaders and individual business analysts may have a role to play in negotiating project priorities versus needs of the organisation.

Top tips for addressing business analysis resource hoarding:

- Invest time in relationships with those likely to engage in this behaviour; try to understand the different perspectives of the situation. Discuss organisational priorities and business analyst development needs.
- Discuss the impacts of this behaviour with all parties involved. A common response from business analysts affected by this resource hoarding is to look to leave the organisation.
- Ensure end dates or review dates are in place for all BA assignments to projects or development teams.
- Give business analysts visibility of upcoming work so they are motivated to move on.

Assignment process

Creating a structured process for customers to be able to request business analysis support is a BA Service imperative. The process must be consistent and repeatable in order to maintain good relationships with customers. An example process is shown in Figure 9.3.

The level of formality and documentation can vary significantly. For example, the whole process could be managed as a series of conversations, so, in this case, steps 1–3 of the process in Figure 9.3 would be covered by a single phone call. At the other end of the scale, a 'request' may be required using a structured template that is submitted via a workflow management system with various checks and approvals.

The assignment may be on a time frame of days, months or even years, so the process must accommodate a wide range of situations. Before an assignment can be made, a recruitment may have to occur, so the process may experience significant waiting periods. Ensuring customer communication is maintained through the process is critical whatever the timespan of the process.

Figure 9.3 Business analyst assignment process

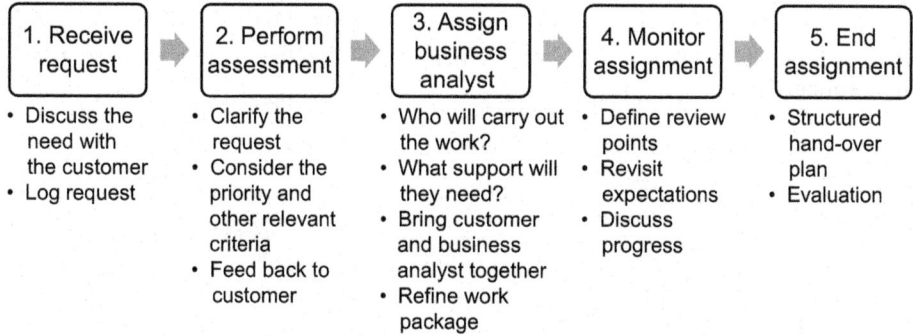

This process assumes that all business analysis resource requests progress to assignment. In reality, requests may be withdrawn, refused or fulfilled differently.

Ensuring that a planned end date is in place is helpful for customers, the business analyst and BA Service planning. Validating the end date, planning any handover and seeking feedback are important activities towards the end of the assignment.

Assignment issues

Many assignments end as planned at the expected time but often this is not the case. There are several common resourcing scenarios which may arise that the BA Service will need to address. Where possible, both business analysts and customers should be encouraged to try to address the issue directly before involving others. Often, this is not felt to be possible and a more senior representative of the BA Service may need to be involved. Some of the most typical scenarios are described in Table 9.7.

Table 9.7 Common business analyst resource management scenarios

Scenario	Description	BA Service approach/ considerations
Customer raises concerns	Common concerns include: • business analyst performance • unmet expectations • relationship issues	Listen to business analyst's perspective Seek other feedback Check: • Is there a performance issue? • Were expectations discussed? • Has a work package been agreed? • Can the relationship be repaired? It may be necessary to create or update a work package, set new targets and clarify expectations, or consider removing or replacing the business analyst
Business analyst raises concerns	Common concerns include: • being underutilised • being overstretched • not doing business analysis work • wanting a new challenge • wanting wider experience • relationship issues	Listen to customer perspective Seek other input Check: • Were expectations discussed? • Has a work package been agreed? • What is the target end date or end point? • Can the relationship be repaired? It may be necessary to create or update a work package, set new targets and clarify expectations, or consider removing or replacing the business analyst

(Continued)

Table 9.7 (Continued)

Scenario	Description	BA Service approach/ considerations
Customer requests extension to assignment	Often due to: • project delays/extension • additional analysis work identified • desire to retain knowledge	Check: • What will be the impact of extension? • Is this actually business analysis work? • Has the business analyst become an SME? • How can knowledge be transferred?
Assignment paused or ended early	Often due to: • project delays/closure • budget issues	Check: • Is any handover required? • Is there an underlying or undisclosed issue? Evaluate assignment Plan new assignment

Assignment basis: input versus output

A typical BA Service will provide business analysts on an input basis, usually a number of hours per week or a percentage of a whole-time equivalent (WTE). This is because it is easier to plan and re-charge on this basis.

It may be useful to agree with customers and business analysts that a '100 per cent allocation' to an assignment is likely to include time required for other responsibilities, such as personal development, BA Service improvement commitments, line management responsibilities or peer reviewing. It may be necessary to convey some of the two-way benefits gained from these activities (such as efficiency, quality, re-use, knowledge sharing and identifying dependencies), or else to agree that the assignment equates to 100 per cent of their delivery hours; for example, these may be 80 per cent of a working week. The need for 'service overhead time' may need to be considered as part of the charging model.

Customers are more accepting of business analysts being assigned to service improvement activities or multiple areas of work if the agreement is based on the business analysis outputs to be completed within a pre-determined time frame, rather than being based on the time worked. This requires a level of trust that the business analyst will be able to balance competing demands and produce the agreed deliverables by the required deadline.

BUSINESS ANALYSIS PLANNING

Ensuring that appropriate analysis activities can be carried out within timescales needed by customers may feel like competing concepts to business analysts, as analysis can often be improved or provide more information if given more time. Therefore, anyone in a leadership role for the BA Service needs to champion business analysis planning and assist this process as far as possible.

Estimation and planning

Estimates for business analysis activities often emerge by working backwards from a hard deadline in order to develop a plan. A more realistic approach is to break down business analysis deliverables and activities and build up an estimate by making informed assumptions. It is common that the causes of overdue business analysis products include the fact that the plan was never realistic, or the business analyst has not agreed with the delivery timescale.

Where the BA Service is good at delivering business analysis but poor at planning, this will impact:

- the reputation of the BA Service;
- the level of customer satisfaction;
- the timely delivery of the work;
- the business analysts' morale and motivation;
- the level of pressure business analysts experience.

Therefore, planning is vitally important to the delivery of an effective BA Service. Figure 9.4 shows the key steps in the estimating and planning process. This cycle shows the need to tailor business analysis activities and deliverables to meet the situation, deliver within constraints and learn from the process.

It is very difficult to be entirely certain about a business analysis approach before analysis has started. New information comes to light, stakeholders emerge and priorities change. Business analysts with responsibility for planning and estimating need to build and constantly refine a bank of activity estimates. These should reflect what was planned, plus details of the conditions that have affected actual delivery time.

Indicative timelines for business analysis services can be communicated to stakeholders using a 'plus or minus' tolerance (for example, 10 days effort, ± 2 days). Estimates and timescales may be explained using evidence-based statements such as the following:

- 'The last three times we have produced X for a project, the average time had been Y.'
- 'We have never delivered Z in less than three weeks, although this does not include sign-off timescales.'

Figure 9.4 Business analysis estimating and planning process

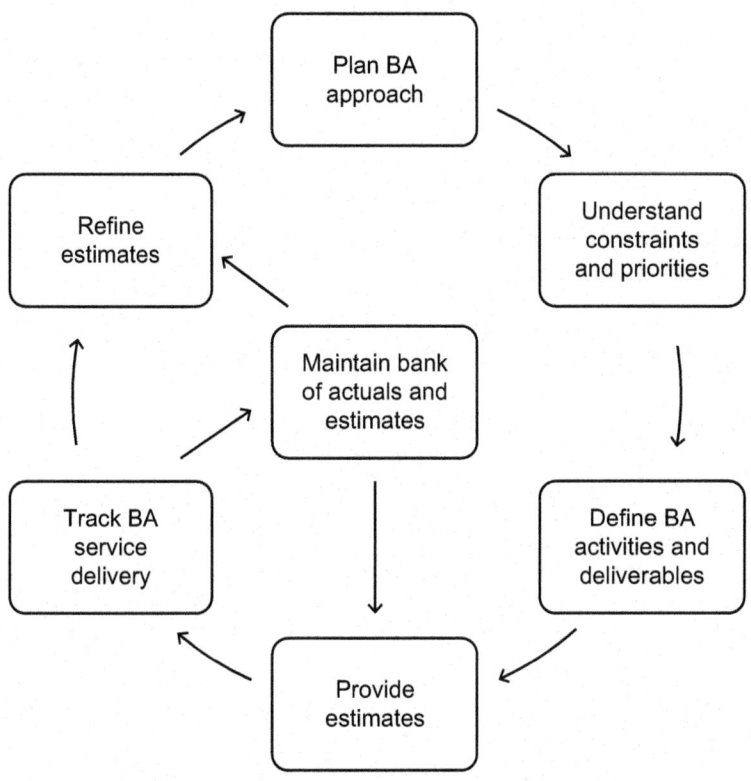

Evidence-based approaches help to build confidence and provide a starting point for a constructive negotiation with customers regarding the delivery of business analysis outputs. This also helps to manage customer expectations.

Where a business analyst has no visibility or understanding of the impact of failing to meet a deadline, they will be unlikely to achieve it. Good professional practice dictates the need for business analysts to highlight a risk that a deadline will not be met. However, a sense that a deadline is 'moveable' may cause business analysts to question if this may be overlooked in order to ensure that the required level of quality is achieved. In essence, they may be more concerned with producing a detailed and accurate document than one that is fit for purpose and delivered within the required time frame. It is extremely important for timescales and quality to be agreed between business analysts and customers at the earliest opportunity (see Appendix 7).

The process step of 'Understand constraints and priorities' must consider several viewpoints and requires a level of negotiation between different stakeholders. Potential viewpoints are shown in Table 9.8.

Table 9.8 Business analysis planning constraints and priorities

Viewpoint	Constraints and priorities
Customer	Urgent issues, areas to focus analysis effort, external commitments, budget, timescales, expectations, level of clarity on business analysis work packages needed
BA Service	BA service portfolio, standards, customer relationship, reputation, avoiding over-commitment
Business analyst	Skills and experience, development needs, capacity (other assigned work and commitments)

BA planning profiles

When projects over-run in terms of time or cost, there are two areas that require scrutiny: the way the work is being delivered and the planning of the work. In some situations, the work may be progressing at an appropriate speed, but it is the plans that are unrealistic.

The business analysis delivery process typically comes under more scrutiny than the business analysis planning process. Figure 9.5 shows a number of different planning profiles for how business analysis effort is assigned to projects and pieces of analysis work.

Many organisations take a simple approach to planning, agreeing start date, end date and WTE. This is often difficult to implement in practice, as a piece of work may take a while to get started, other stakeholders may not be readily available and prior pieces of work may be ongoing and taking up the business analysts' time.

Even where organisations believe they are using a block planning approach (see profile A in Figure 9.5), it is often the case that profile C is actually occurring. Business analysts may feel they are in a difficult position if their 'new' project does not fully occupy their time and their previous project or team still requires their input, even though it is 'supposed' to have finished. Profile D provides a useful solution that can be discussed and shared with all customers. The business analyst draws an existing assignment to a close ('roll-off'), in a controlled handover, and embarks on new work ('ramp-up'), leaving a 'gap' so that there is sufficient capacity to contribute to BA Service improvement activities and engage in personal development opportunities.

Table 9.9 provides an explanation of the advantages and disadvantages of the profiles within Figure 9.5.

Figure 9.5 Business analysis resource profiles

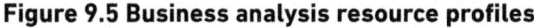

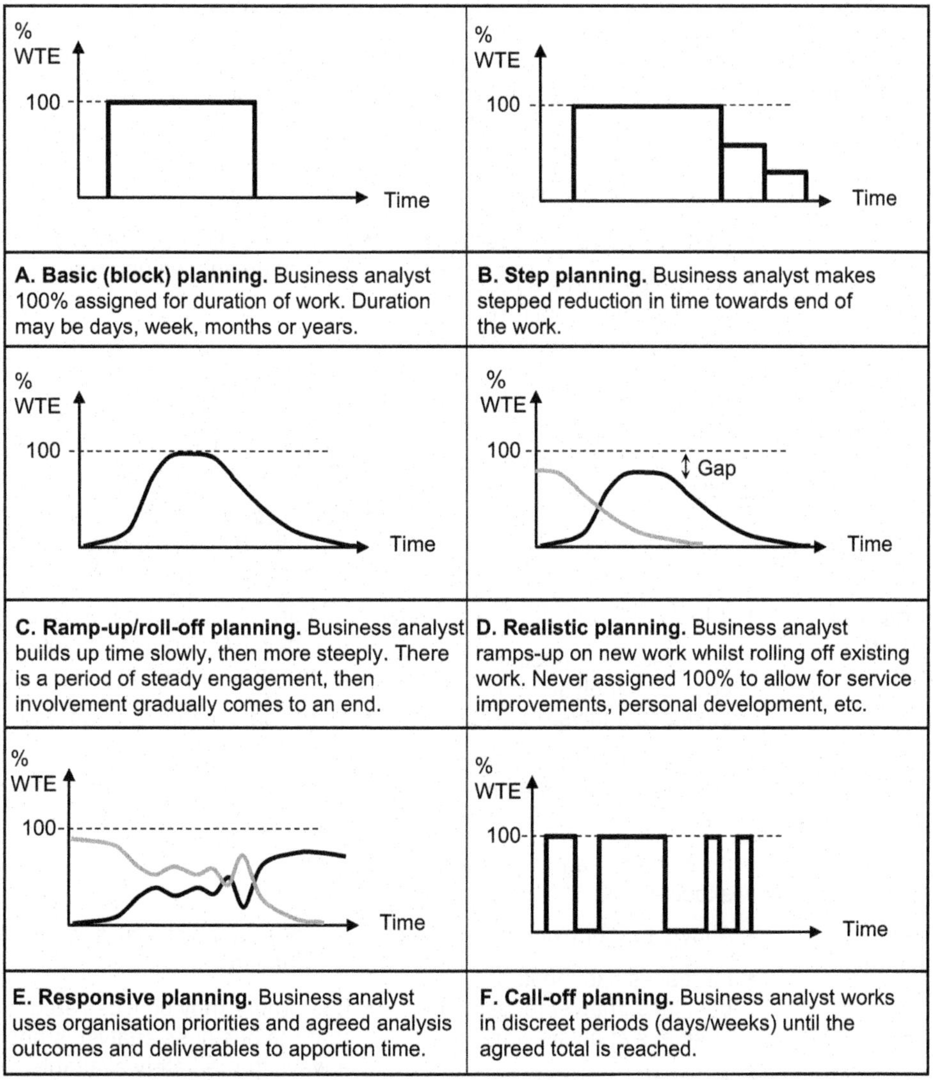
% WTE
100
Time
A. Basic (block) planning. Business analyst 100% assigned for duration of work. Duration may be days, week, months or years.
% WTE
100
Time
B. Step planning. Business analyst makes stepped reduction in time towards end of the work.
% WTE
100
Time
C. Ramp-up/roll-off planning. Business analyst builds up time slowly, then more steeply. There is a period of steady engagement, then involvement gradually comes to an end.
% WTE
100
Gap
Time
D. Realistic planning. Business analyst ramps-up on new work whilst rolling off existing work. Never assigned 100% to allow for service improvements, personal development, etc.
% WTE
100
Time
E. Responsive planning. Business analyst uses organisation priorities and agreed analysis outcomes and deliverables to apportion time.
% WTE
100
Time
F. Call-off planning. Business analyst works in discreet periods (days/weeks) until the agreed total is reached.

Business analysts and BA leaders should use these different resource profiles to initiate conversations with customers about the best planning approach to adopt for each business analysis assignment.

Table 9.9 Advantages and disadvantages of different BA resource profiles

Planning profile	Advantages	Disadvantages
Basic (block) planning	• Start date and end date are only variables to be considered and tracked • Simple to understand • Easy to budget for/charge for • Useful to enforce a hard end date (e.g. when no further funding available)	• Rarely reflects reality • Increases likelihood of business analyst doing non-BA work or grey area work • Increases likelihood of under-utilisation and waiting time
Step planning	• Allows for controlled handover • Builds business confidence that business analyst can step away	• Customer more likely to accept 'stepped disengagement' at the end, than 'stepped engagement' at the beginning • Requires coordination to ensure that new BA work is available and manage expectations
Ramp-up/ roll-off planning	• Allows for controlled handover • Increases likelihood of business analyst focusing on business analysis work • Makes visible to all parties what is often happening anyway • Helps to manage customer expectations	• Requires coordination to ensure that new BA work is available and manage expectations • More complicated to budget for/ charge for
Realistic planning	• Allows for controlled handover • Increases likelihood of business analyst focusing on business analysis work • Ability to balance work in response to project peaks and troughs of activity • Business analysts often enjoy the variety and challenge • Makes visible to all parties what is often happening anyway	• Business analyst may become overloaded • Customers may be frustrated that the business analyst is not always immediately available • Requires coordination to ensure new BA work available and manage expectations • More complicated to budget for/ charge for

(Continued)

Table 9.9 (Continued)

Planning profile	Advantages	Disadvantages
	• Helps to manage customer expectations	
	• Provides capacity for the business analyst to contribute to continual service improvement activities and engage in personal development opportunities	
Responsive planning	• Increases likelihood of business analyst focusing on business analysis work	• Requires high level of trust in business analysts to make decisions to balance business priorities
	• Ability to balance work in response to project peaks and troughs of activity	• Requires organisation to be focused on outputs and outcomes rather than inputs
	• Business analysts committed on basis of outputs (deliverables) rather than input (time)	• Business analyst may become overloaded
		• Customers may be frustrated that the business analyst is not always immediately available
		• Can appear as if no planning is taking place
Call-off planning	• Useful for providing specific knowledge or expertise at defined times	• Requires coordination across different areas if 'internal consultants'
	• Useful for making best use of 'external consultants'	• Requires mature planning culture
	• Useful for follow-up after an initial piece of work	

Defining business analysis activities and deliverables

There are often multiple valid ways that analysis for any given situation could be approached. The BA Service must provide a framework for analysis that can be tailored and scaled to provide consistency and repeatability. It is this framework that marks the step change from a number of business analysis practitioners deployed independently and using business analysis techniques as they deem appropriate, to a coherent and coordinated BA Service. This is discussed in more detail in Chapter 6.

For large, lengthy or complex business analysis assignments, it is useful to set out the approach that will be taken. This could take the format of a document, diagram, presentation, plan or structured conversation. An example is provided in Appendix 8.

Figure 9.4 offers a generic life cycle that is applicable to any of the business analysis services, including improving business processes, supporting change or defining requirements. The process does not change depending on the development methodology in use, although the mechanisms to carry out the process and the outputs of the process may be different.

In a Linear (or Waterfall) development environment, the process may result in, or contribute to, documented plans. Where the BA Service is being delivered within an Agile development environment, the process may become the structure of a conversation repeated on a daily or weekly basis and fed into sprint or release planning. In this setting it is still important to track actual versus estimates to be able to provide more accurate estimates in future.

The high-level requirements dilemma

A common issue that arises at an early stage of a project is the difference and overlap between 'scoping' and 'high-level requirements'. The impact of this can be highly detrimental to the progress of the project in the following ways:

- **No clear scope agreed.** There are different interpretations of what the project needs to achieve.

- **Limited engagement from senior stakeholders.** Occurs where requirements engineering is seen as a more detailed task involving lower levels of business stakeholder.

- **Lack of direction** for those involved in the project.

- **Unclear responsibilities** for bringing clarity and facilitating consensus.

- **Circular conversations** between business analysts and other stakeholders. For example, stakeholders asking, 'when will high-level requirements be ready?', and business analysts requiring an agreed scope as the boundary of analysis, responding, 'it depends when we can agree the scope...'.

Scoping and determining high-level requirements are not synonymous activities. Scoping may be considered primarily a planning activity, while defining the high-level requirements is an analysis activity. Neither can be done in isolation and each informs the other. It is impossible to provide a definition of 'high-level requirements' that is applicable in all contexts. The level of requirements must be informed by the purpose for creating them.

Requirements engineering is a route to understanding, agreeing and documenting business needs. The level of granularity needed will be influenced by a wide range of factors, most significantly the context, the objective of the project and the audience of the output.

This issue of 'analysis versus planning' can be demonstrated by considering a simple example.

Example: digging a hole

A group decides that a hole in the ground is needed. Each person can clearly picture the hole. This seems a simple proposition, and a couple of people are given responsibility to 'make it happen'. Progress towards digging the hole will not be perceived until soil is moving.

Table 9.10 Analysis and planning example

Analysis	Intersection of analysis and planning	Planning
• Why is the hole needed? • What problem are we trying to address? • Who is impacted by the problem? • What else could solve the problem? • Who will use the hole? • What do they think?	• What is the size, shape and depth of the hole? • Where will the hole be?	• What equipment is needed? • What equipment is available? • Who will dig it? • How long will it take? • How much will it cost? • What could go wrong? • When is it needed by? • What will we do with the removed soil?

In the time taken to ask and answer the questions shown in Table 9.10, the original group is starting to think 'It's only a hole, why is it taking so long? Work has not even started. I could have dug it myself by now.' However, without answers to these analysis and planning questions, a hole of the wrong size will be dug in the wrong place (or perhaps a hole is not even needed!).

In this example, planning concerns resources, timescales, risks and costs; analysis focuses on drivers, purpose, options and stakeholders. The intersection of the two processes describes the features of the hole itself. When stakeholders ask for 'high-level requirements', they typically mean this intersection of planning and analysis and do not fully understand that both processes must be undertaken and iterated to have confidence in the answers given.

The BA Service must be clear with customers about the services it offers in relation to scoping and high-level analysis (see Chapter 2). Within the BA Service, it may be useful to define various levels of analysis that can be referred to consistently across projects and develop a bank of examples that can be used to 'calibrate' the level of detail. This allows a learning feedback loop to be applied such as: 'this level of requirements was created for the purpose of X [gaining stakeholder approval/invitation to tender/ specifying a system...] and these are the types of issues we have had feedback about...'.

To address the 'high-level requirements dilemma', keep scoping conversations focused on business outcomes. Appropriate techniques such as a business use case model or an inception deck can act as a helpful starting point for scoping discussions.

The 'grey area' of project work

While there are deliverables and activities that fall clearly within the category of 'business analysis work', that is, within the BA Service Framework (see Chapter 2), there are some that fall outside the typical BA Service remit. For example, project management, system testing or code generation. However, there may be activities that fall into a 'grey area', shown in Figure 9.6, where there is uncertainty about whether or not the work falls within the business analysts' area of responsibility.

What constitutes the grey area will depend on the level of detail specified in the portfolio offered by a particular BA Service (which may be an adaptation of the BA Service Framework) and, to some extent, on the other specialised roles that exist within the organisation, such as business architect, business change manager, user researcher, user acceptance tester, product owner and data analyst. Where these roles do not exist, some of the work that they might undertake may become the responsibility of the business analysts.

Figure 9.6 The BA Service grey area

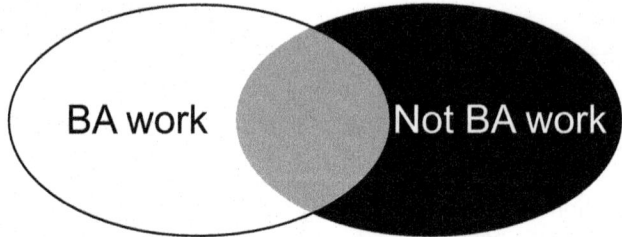

There may be valid reasons for an individual business analyst to undertake non-standard business analysis work (grey area work). For example, it may offer the opportunity to develop new skills, to enhance existing skills or knowledge or to support the achievement of the project objectives. This needs to be a conscious decision taken by the BA Service, the business analyst and the customer (e.g. project or business stakeholders). Where this is done unconsciously, or without the agreement of all parties, a number of issues can arise, including the following:

- a lack of clarity regarding the business analyst role;
- a failure to meet expectations on all sides;

- the business analyst feeling or becoming de-skilled;
- the business analyst feeling uncertain and ill-equipped to meet the demand;
- business analysis activities that are needed do not happen;
- skill and capacity gaps are hidden;
- business analysis skills shortage may occur elsewhere.

It is important that BA leaders identify when grey area tasks are requested of the BA Service and make informed decisions about whether or not to permit these tasks to be conducted by the business analysts. The BA Service should be focused on conducting business analysis work, but a known quantity of grey area or non-BA work may be performed as long as it is recognised as such and agreed and accepted by all those involved.

Sustained demand for certain grey area work may mean that a new service should be added to the BASF or that a specialist role is now required by the organisation.

BUSINESS ANALYSIS PROCESS MANAGEMENT

Operating business analysis as a service means delivering a coherent and coordinated business analysis function. Effective management of the BA Service requires the definition and delivery of some key processes that are used to support and deliver business analysis within the organisation. The level of complexity and formality of each of these processes may vary for different organisations depending on factors such as size of the BA Service and organisation, and culture and level of maturity of the BA Service.

To ensure consistency (if applied by more than one person, or by one person infrequently) these processes need to be documented in some form. Where only one person is carrying out the process for the whole BA Service, consistency is not necessarily the key driver – knowledge management and succession planning may be more relevant. The maturity of the BA Service would experience a significant setback if the owners for the BA Service processes were to move to another organisation or function and these processes were not documented sufficiently.

Continual service improvement is difficult to achieve or evidence if a baseline process is not available. Equally, improved ways of working do not 'stick' unless practitioners are able to refer to records setting out what should be done. This does not mean that business analysts have to undertake weeks or months of mapping the processes that underpin the BA Service. A pragmatic approach should be taken, which could include the steps shown in Figure 9.7.

Defining a lower level of detail for the more complex or contentious processes could involve documenting the process in a number of different ways, such as business process models, task descriptions and SIPOC models. The creation of these models would provide several benefits for the BA Service by providing:

- the opportunity to standardise and agree processes within the BA Service;

- a basis for training and future reference for new business analysts;

- a backlog of service improvement work that can be undertaken during periods when there are business analysis resources available;

- the opportunity for business analysts to practice creating unfamiliar models in a low-risk context;

- the opportunity for business analysts to be subject matter experts for a process modelling assignment and thereby gain insight into the customer perspective.

Figure 9.7 Business analysis process inventory approach

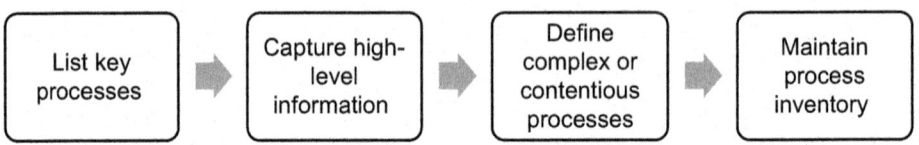

A process inventory for the BA Service will also help to identify where the processes need enhancement or refinement, providing a basis for continual improvement of the BA Service (see Chapter 12).

Knowledge management for the BA Service

Knowledge management (KM) is not simply a repository of information, it also requires the creation of opportunities, forums and networks that will allow knowledge to be shared and discussed. It necessitates the development of a culture that encourages knowledge sharing, re-use and the adoption of new knowledge. BA leaders are responsible for the following actions:

- encourage an environment and culture where knowledge sharing is valued;

- establish and encourage events, networks and forums that allow knowledge to be shared;

- provide the necessary mechanisms to underpin knowledge management.

Support or guidance is required for knowledge to be captured, shared and used by others. Business analysts need access to knowledge relating to business analysis, their specific area of work and their organisation/sector. Therefore, a variety of different networks, forums and KM systems may be required to provide the necessary infrastructure.

The business analysis KM cycle is shown in Figure 9.8. This cycle emphasises the continuous nature of knowledge management and the stages that are necessary for the BA Service to obtain benefit from the knowledge.

Figure 9.8 Business analysis knowledge management cycle

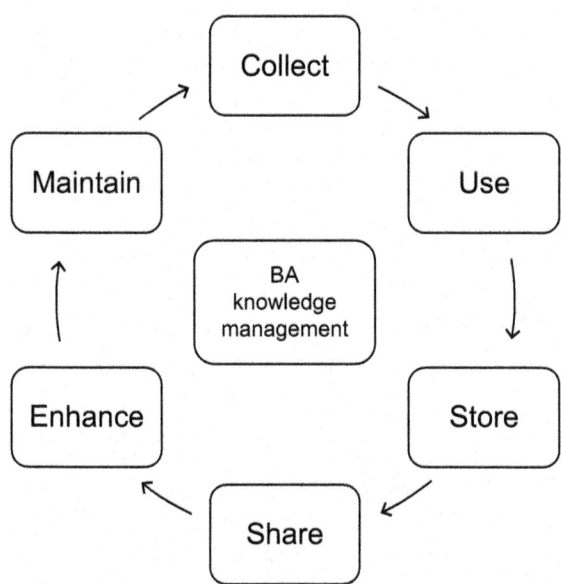

The purpose of the business analysis knowledge management cycle is to:

- avoid business analysts and stakeholders wasting time re-discovering things that are already known;
- reduce the risk of loss of knowledge from the BA Service and organisation;
- promote the generation of new information and knowledge to provide organisational efficiency, innovation and competitive advantage;
- reduce unintended consequences of change;
- ensure that information can be appropriately accessed in a timely way;
- reduce the risk of business analysts becoming SMEs and not being able to move away from an assignment.

The stages of the business analysis knowledge management cycle are described in Table 9.11.

Risk and issue management

All services face risks and must manage issues. The BA Service should take a structured but proportionate approach to identifying and assessing service risks. Some organisations have a corporate approach to risk management across services and change initiatives, where risks are aggregated, reported on and managed at several levels within the organisation. Where a wider corporate approach is not available, the BA Service must consider, document and manage key risks that could impact the delivery of the BA Service and then take appropriate action (see Appendix 13).

Table 9.11 Business analysis knowledge management cycle stages

Cycle stage	Stage description
Collect	Research and obtain information from different sources
	Assess, analyse and transform the information
Use	Apply the information to the BA Service activities; this is the primary purpose for which the information has been collected
Store	Apply clear organising principles to ensure effective storage and the ability to search for information quickly
	Business analysts should be encouraged to use the KM store as the starting point, then add to and enhance as necessary
Share	Disseminate, present and guide others on the use of the information in order to genuinely share knowledge
Enhance	Add, extend, enhance and refine the existing information
Maintain	Keep KM assets up to date. This can be challenging, so triage the KM assets by applying three categories: 1. A small sub-set of the knowledge assets that will be actively updated 2. The assets that will be reviewed at suitable time intervals 3. The assets that should be verified before use, as they will not be actively maintained BA Service knowledge assets that should be actively maintained (so are in category 1) include glossaries and lists of acronyms, organisational charts, project summary information, business rules and key contacts

There are several reasons for creating and maintaining a BA Service risk assessment. This document:

- provides the opportunity to consider both challenges and opportunities;
- allows the BA Service to be proactive rather than reactive;
- ensures that a plan exists to provide a quicker response to risks that materialise;
- supports the case for additional BA Service funding.

The POPIT™ model provides a framework for a holistic assessment of risks. Many of the potential risks faced by the BA Service will relate to the 'People' element, including loss of key members of staff, lack of progression opportunity or significant changes in demand for business analysts.

Simply identifying and logging risks serves no real purpose. For risk management to be of benefit to the BA Service, actions must be taken to evaluate each risk, identify counter-measures that will address the risk and to create a plan setting out actions to take if the risk becomes an issue. In a large BA Service, there may also be complex or persisting issues, which would point to the need for structured documentation and management of issues in a similar way. For a small BA Service, issues are often managed less formally than risks.

Financial management for the BA Service

The BA Service provides a service portfolio that is delivered through the skills held by people. While the major part of the BA Service budget will relate to staff costs, the total budget needed to deliver the BA Service will need to cover more than the aggregated salaries of those delivering business analysis. Areas that the budget should encompass are:

- ongoing overheads such as management and administration costs;
- irregular but ongoing costs such as recruitment;
- training and development;
- travel and expenses;
- internal event costs;
- equipment such as laptops, phones and tablets, as business analysts may be more mobile than other business areas;
- specialist software, including licences;
- materials, as business analysts may require a larger range and volume of stationery than other areas of the business.

Anyone in a leading role within a BA Service needs to have financial management skills such as budgetary forecasting, tracking, baselining and reporting. A key financial management area concerns the charging model applied for the BA Service, which concerns the costs of delivering the BA Service. Organisations often have multiple charging models in place. For example, an HR department may be 'top-sliced', so that all departments pay for an element of the HR service operating costs based on the number of employees in each department; a business change function may be project-funded, and will only work on projects or initiatives that provide specific and agreed funding for the staff. Table 9.12 discusses the various charging models used when delivering the BA Service.

Where the costs of business analysts are split over a number of budgets (for example, across different areas of the business or different projects), it is still necessary to understand the full cost of delivering the Service and ensure that the non-salary costs are quantified. The ability of the Service to develop and provide the maximum benefit to the organisation will be significantly hampered if it constantly runs up against costs that have fallen through the gaps in budget planning.

The BA Service operates as an internal consultancy to the other areas of the business within some organisations. In these situations, re-charge mechanisms need to be clearly defined and understood, or the cost of the Service must be 'top-sliced' as a centrally

Table 9.12 Common charging models

Charging model	Description
Re-charge	The BA Service must (at least) cover its own costs by charging customers for the Service
	This model may use hourly rate, daily rate or fixed pricing. This may require a mechanism to track time allocated so that it may be invoiced or re-charged accordingly
Top-slice	All potential (internal) customers of the Service share the cost of the BA Service; this may be based on the relative size of the customer divisions or teams
Centrally funded	The BA Service is provided as a central function, costs are met by the organisation or a sub-function, and no re-charging occurs
	This approach may require a clear prioritisation mechanism, as there is no concept of 'having the budget' to access business analyst resources, which would typically limit the usage
Project-funded	Business analysts are recruited or assigned to specific projects or business areas, each of which meets all of the attendant costs
	This approach can leave a gap relating to overheads and non-salary costs, unless they are factored into the project costs
Mixed models	There are various ways of operating mixed models:
	1. Certain internal customers have access to business analysis services, others will be re-charged
	2. Certain business analysis services are provided from central funds, additional services will be re-charged
	3. Individual business analysts are directly funded by projects/business areas, but management and service overheads are centrally funded

provided capability. It is also possible to run a mixed model, where some customers can access the service for 'free' and others explicitly pay for the service. In this model the approach to how work will be allocated and prioritised must be clearly defined, particularly if there is a shortage of business analyst availability.

CONCLUSION

The BA Service may be considered an internal consultancy service that operates within an organisation. This perspective requires the BA Service to apply a professional consultancy life cycle when engaging with the organisation. The consultancy life cycle includes the phases of service delivery but also recognises the need for the BA Service to 'gain entry' to business change initiatives and to disengage from assignments.

This chapter has identified a number of key processes that need to be in place to ensure that the BA Service is run in an effective and efficient way. These processes concern the management of the demand for business analysis services, the approaches to planning and estimating the delivery of these services, and the processes for managing BA Service knowledge sharing, service delivery risks and finances. Each of these processes must be defined, applied consistently and subject to continual improvement. These key processes do not stand alone, but are interrelated, and the BA leader has the responsibility for managing any overlaps and dependencies.

Fulfilling the operational responsibilities of the BA Service can be time-consuming and requires generic management skills. However, business analysis principles and techniques are invaluable to BA leaders as they offer novel ways to consider how best to manage and operate the BA Service.

CASE STUDY 7: OPERATING A LARGE-SCALE BA SERVICE

Jamie Toyne, Department of Work and Pensions (DWP)

With over 300 BAs across the organisation, the DWP has focused on building a shared understanding of business analysis and demonstrating the value the role can offer. There are six hubs spread across the UK, so building a sense of both professional identity and local community has been extremely important. Jamie Toyne is the Head of Role for Business Analysis within DWP and works alongside a number of lead and senior business analysts to deliver an effective BA Service for a wide range of digital services being developed for use by UK citizens.

With a large number of people and activities to keep track of, tools are used to understand what BAs are doing and the dates they may become available for future work. Jamie noted, 'We do use tools to support us, but conversations are much better for really getting information, identifying development opportunities and understanding what is happening for a particular development team. The tools are a way of recording conversations, not driving them.' It is useful to get the perspectives from both the business analyst and service or product lead, as there are sometimes different views on what business analysis work is still needed and these conversations provide the opportunity to bring clarity and gain agreement.

A key part of operating the service is negotiating with stakeholders about the business analysis activities that are required, what proportion of a business analyst's time is needed, opportunities and development needs and whether it is even a business analyst role at all! BA leaders must be advocates for the profession – as Jamie put it: 'promoting what BAs are (and what they aren't!)'. Building relationships with stakeholders and business analysts is critical, making sure that BA leaders don't hide behind their inboxes, but regularly speak to people, listen to ideas and hear concerns first hand. Operating at scale means a single leader cannot know every individual well. Jamie said:

'Make sure you have the right structure around you, you can't know everyone, and have all the conversations yourself.'

Not every business analyst is a good fit for every piece of work. Some of the services being developed require specialist skills, or a higher level of experience. Some require only a sub-set of BA skills and techniques, which for some BAs provides a great opportunity to practice those techniques; for others, this might be too repetitive and might not give them the chance to develop. Some development teams are very supportive of rotating BAs, giving people the opportunity to use their professional BA toolkit and to avoid becoming SMEs on a particular product or service.

The DWP uses local BA Communities of Practice to share and develop best practice. They have found that when launching a new community or initiative, it pays to practice what they preach: 'Be iterative – fail fast and learn fast, apply the same techniques we use as a BA to our own areas, such as building the community.'

10 DELIVERING A CUSTOMER-ORIENTED BA SERVICE

INTRODUCTION

Building relationships with stakeholders is fundamental to business analysis. It isn't something that is a by-product or a necessary pre-requisite, it is at the heart of what business analysts do. While it may be said that this is true of all service providers, the range of stakeholders, the various perspectives held and the different needs that they have, contribute to the complexity of business analysis work.

BA leaders have to ensure that business analysts within the business analysis team understand the importance of identifying their stakeholders and working effectively with them to ensure that their perspectives are understood and, where possible, their needs are met. In some situations, it may not be possible to meet all stakeholder needs but effective engagement with stakeholders should at least ensure that their expectations are understood, and any shortfalls or disappointments are managed.

In most business analysis contexts, there are all manner of stakeholders to be considered and techniques such as the stakeholder wheel, shown in Figure 10.1, can help to identify the stakeholders for a particular situation or project. Figure 10.1 reflects that stakeholders may come from many different groups, organisations and communities.

Some of these stakeholders may be deemed to be business analysis 'customers' and should be considered as such when working to deliver a customer-oriented BA service.

If a customer-oriented service is to be delivered by business analysts, the essential first step is to identify the customers who are recipients of the BA service. Business analysts often talk about their 'customers', but to deliver a service that is customer-focused requires understanding of the variety of individuals and groups that fall within this broad category, and ongoing, focused efforts.

One aspect of working well with customers is to understand that while we may use a generic term, such as 'customer', or, more broadly, 'stakeholder', within each category are individual people. Individuals possess values, priorities, concerns and beliefs. They have personal agendas, and needs, and are likely to have expectations that must be managed. A personalised approach that considers people with a range of needs is more likely to be successful when delivering a service. Viewing a stakeholder or customer as an individual is more likely to ensure that the focus is on the person rather than the role they perform. Techniques such as personas can be very useful in this context, as they help to uncover the factors of importance to individual customers.

Figure 10.1 Stakeholder wheel (adapted from Paul, Cadle and Yeates, 2014)

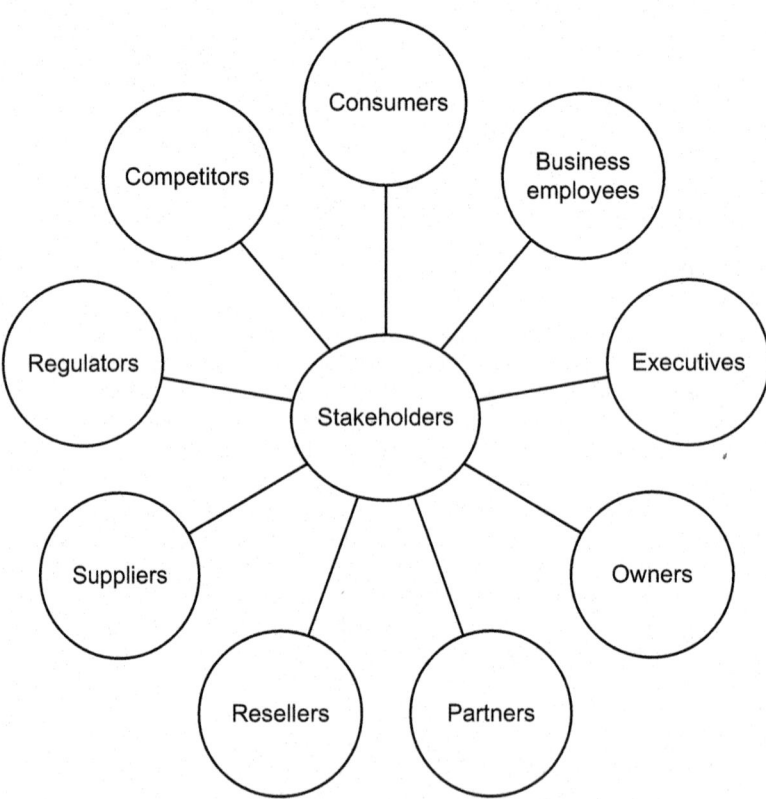

Effective customer engagement may be enabled by developing the personal skills that form part of the business analyst T-shape, as discussed in Chapter 4. However, business analysts with excellent personal skills may still struggle to work effectively with their customers if they lack the business knowledge and understanding and the professional skills that are relevant to the particular context.

This chapter explores the following topics:

- customer categories for the BA Service;
- working effectively with customers;
- techniques for analysing customers.

IDENTIFYING THE 'CUSTOMER'

The term 'customer' is used with an increasing frequency in all manner of business situations and often seems to be applied with an unwarranted level of confidence when discussing the nature of the customer and their requirements. However, when challenged, it is often the case that many individuals and organisations do not have a clear view of the 'customer' but instead are using the term in a broad sense, often making sweeping assumptions about what customers actually need.

A customer may be defined as:

> someone who purchases or consumes a product or service provided by an organisation or individual.

However, when we consider the term 'customer' within a business analysis context we might extend this definition as follows:

> someone who purchases, consumes or is able to co-create value from a product or service provided by a business analysis team or individual business analyst.

Given this definition, many of the stakeholder groups shown in Figure 10.1 are in fact different categories of customer so should be offered the level of customer service that meets or exceeds their expectations and requirements. The exceptions are suppliers, regulators and competitors, where the nature of the stakeholder relationship is different to that of a customer-oriented service relationship.

CATEGORIES OF CUSTOMER

It is worthwhile exploring three different categories of customer: business customers, governance customers and development project customers. Each category may be decomposed to identify specific types of customer and their different priorities and requirements. The key roles are shown in in Figure 10.2.

Business customers

Business customers are those who are the recipients or beneficiaries of the outputs from the projects. Working with these customers has become increasingly important for business analysts over the last few decades, as the importance of taking a holistic view of business changes has attracted greater recognition.

Business analysts represent the needs of the business customers to those responsible for designing and developing new systems and processes. They work collaboratively with business customers to co-create value through discussing and analysing requirements in order to clarify what is required from the new systems and processes. Chapter 2 explored the nature of 'value' and the need for co-creation of value.

Figure 10.2 Customer categories and roles

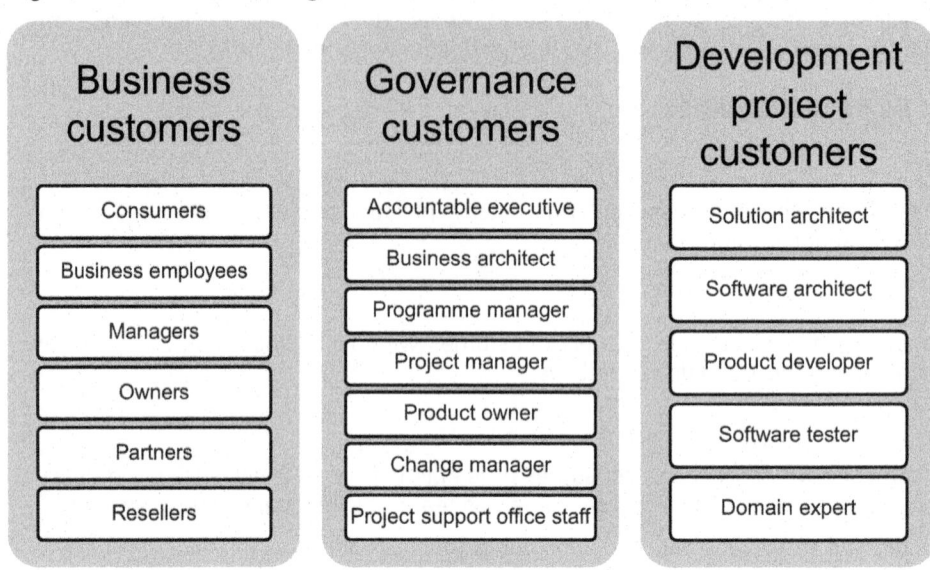

Understanding the specific needs of business customers has increased in complexity over the years as different categories of customer have become more established. As a result, the broad term 'customer' is often insufficient to reflect the differing issues, problems and requirements of the different customer groups.

A structure that identifies different business customer categories is shown in Figure 10.3.

Figure 10.3 Categories of business customer

Consumer	Business employee	Manager	Owner	Partner	Reseller
A beneficiary or recipient of the product or service.	A member of staff who interacts with the system and operates the processes.	A senior member of staff within the business area.	A senior executive or shareholder for the organisation.	A representative of an organisation that works in partnership with the organisation.	A representative of an organisation that sells the organisation's products or services.

The nature of business analysis work is such that it may involve direct or indirect relationships with different categories of customer. For example:

- Business analysts typically interact directly with business employees. However, where there is a large team of business staff, the business analyst may interact with only a representative sub-set of this team.

- A consumer of the product or service provided by the business analyst's organisation is likely to interact with the business employees rather than directly with the business analysts.

Table 10.1 discusses the types of relationships that business analysts may have with the different categories of customer.

Table 10.1 Business customers and their relationships with the BA Service

Customer role	Business analyst relationship
Consumer	Consumers of the organisation's products or services
	These customers may not have direct contact with business analysts. However, the BA team has to understand their needs in order to support the success of the organisation. Techniques such as the Kano model and value network analysis may be particularly relevant when considering consumer needs. These techniques are discussed later in this chapter
Business employee	Business employees are typically the frontline staff who operate the business processes and systems, and interact with the consumers of the organisation's products or services
	These are the people who are responsible for defining what is required of the product or service, so business analyst engagement with them is likely to be considerable
Manager	The BA Service in some organisations has been recognised as having the capability to work with senior executives on strategy analysis and the strategic execution portfolio. However, even where business analysts work primarily with operational staff, there is a need to understand the executive managers and their perspectives on the business analysis work
	In some organisations, business analysis is not well understood or is perceived to have a limited scope. It may be that the business analysts are seen as the team who 'write down the requirements'. The BA leaders are those people who are likely to have the greatest opportunity to interact with senior executives and champion the BA Service and the value offered by business analysis
	Even where the business analysts are not working at an executive level, they need to consider the views of the executives with regard to any business analysis projects or assignments. Failure to do this could result in a project being derailed at a late stage or delivering a solution that does not address identified issues or problems

(Continued)

Table 10.1 (Continued)

Customer role	Business analyst relationship
Owner	The business owners are those ultimately responsible for the health of the business. For example, they may be shareholders or charitable trustees. These customers may be remote from the business analysts and any interactions may be indirect, via the business managers who are responsible for ensuring the delivery of the owners' requirements
	However, in some organisations, such as small private limited companies, it is the owners who have the overall vision for the organisation. Accordingly, they may be involved in change projects at an overview level and may identify the general business requirements to be delivered
Partner	Many organisations work with partner companies to deliver their products and services. This results in business analysts needing to work with partner organisations in a variety of situations. For example, the partner organisations may be responsible for running internal functions such as human resources or finance, or they may provide the operational service for the organisation's systems
	Engagement with partner customers is essential on some projects if the delivered solution is to be successful
Reseller	Resellers are intermediary organisations who resell products or services to consumers. Resellers are often the 'sales force' for the organisation, so may provide frontline services to the consumers in a similar vein to the business employees. Therefore, business analysts may need to engage with reseller customers to determine the requirements of the consumers as well as their own requirements

Given these different categories, building stakeholder relationships with customers can be time-consuming and complex, requiring due consideration if it is to be successful. BA leaders have to support business analysts in doing this and ensure that the nature of the relationships is understood.

Given these different categories, the relationships that business analysts have with the 'customer' can be varied and are often indirect. One way of representing these relationships is to think about the interactions that business analysts have with customers as relationship streams that show the extent to which a direct relationship may exist.

Examples of different relationship streams are shown in Figure 10.4.

Figure 10.4 Example customer relationship streams for business analysts

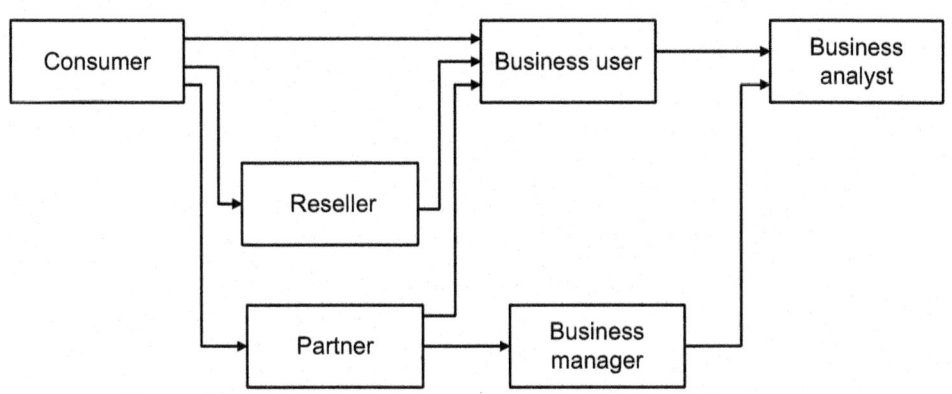

Understanding who the direct and indirect customers are is important if the business analyst is to represent the customer when working on change projects. The information that can be obtained from each customer needs to be clearly understood, as this is often constrained as follows:

- A particular customer role may provide only a limited view of the system of interest; for example, a business employee working in a sales team may only understand the sales viewpoint and may be unaware of the issues relevant to the service delivery team.

- An individual may have some strongly held views that do not represent the views of other stakeholders; for example, senior stakeholders that focus on meeting their targets and objectives.

- Some customers may have deep insights into a business sector or industry domain but very little knowledge of other areas; for example, a domain expert with knowledge of an industry domain but little understanding of how a particular organisation works.

Governance customers

Business analysis customers may also be found within the change programmes and projects; business analysts have to collaborate with their fellow change and IT professionals. One of the key elements of a BA leader role is to ensure that business analysts understand the roles performed by their fellow change professionals. It is sometimes the case that other roles are misunderstood, leading to overlaps, duplication and conflict. There is sometimes a sense that one role is of greater importance than another. However, all change professionals should be attempting to achieve the same thing – delivering business changes successfully in order to achieve the desired business benefits.

There are several business change roles that need to interact with business analysts and are reliant on the information, support and deliverables offered by the business analysis team.

A structure that identifies different governance customer categories is shown in Figure 10.5.

Figure 10.5 Categories of governance customer

Accountable executive	Business architect	Programme manager	Project manager	Product owner	Change manager	Project support office staff
The individual accountable to the business for the change outcomes.	The individual who is responsible for creating and maintaining the business architecture artefacts.	A senior member of staff who is responsible for delivering a change programme.	The individual responsible for delivering the project objectives.	The individual responsible for the management of the product backlog.	The individual who oversees the deployment of the business changes.	The staff members who ensure adherence to the organisation's standards for business change.

The governance customer roles are described in Table 10.2.

Table 10.2 Governance customers and their relationships with the BA Service

Customer role	Business analyst relationship
Accountable executive (project sponsor)	Accountable to the business executives for the outcomes from the change programme
	The BA Service supports various aspects of the change initiative and the achievement of the objectives for which the accountable executive is responsible. Depending upon the nature and size of the change initiative, the business analysts may work closely with this person
Business architect	Responsible for creation, maintenance oversight and the business architecture artefacts
	Works with business analysts to identify the impacts of proposed changes and where existing capability, processes or data may be leveraged to enable the implementation of the changes
Programme manager	Responsible for delivering the objectives of a change programme
	The business analysts ensure that a holistic view of the business changes is adopted, so may work very closely with the programme manager to ensure that project interdependencies are understood and managed
Project manager	Responsible for delivering the objectives of an individual change or development project
	The BA Service delivers services specific to a project, such as defining requirements or improving business processes (see Chapter 2). Therefore, business analysts work very closely with project managers
Product owner	Responsible for the management of the product backlog
	A business analyst may hold the product owner role on some projects or in some organisations. If this is not the case, the product owner will require support from the business analysts in prioritising and managing the requirements or work items for the project
Change manager	Oversees the deployment of changes and ensures that all necessary actions are taken to enable deployment
	This work is supported and, where appropriate, enacted by business analysts. For example, the definition and delivery of training in the application of new processes or systems

(Continued)

Table 10.2 (Continued)

Customer role	Business analyst relationship
Project support office staff	Ensure adherence to the organisation's standards for business change initiatives
	Business analysts need to be cognisant of the project support office standards and apply them as necessary. They may also provide input into decisions made regarding standards and templates (see Chapter 6)

Development project customers

Product development customers are those who work directly with business analysts to develop the deliverables of projects. The actors within the development team work closely with the business employees and managers who have specific responsibilities to enact on behalf of the organisation.

A structure that identifies different product development customer categories is shown in Figure 10.6.

Figure 10.6 Categories of product development customer

Solution architect	Software architect	Product developer	Software tester	Domain expert
An individual responsible for the overall design of the product.	An individual responsible for the design of a software product.	An individual responsible for the creation of all or part of the product.	An individual responsible for ensuring a software product has been tested sufficiently.	An individual who provides information about the business domain within which the organisation operates.

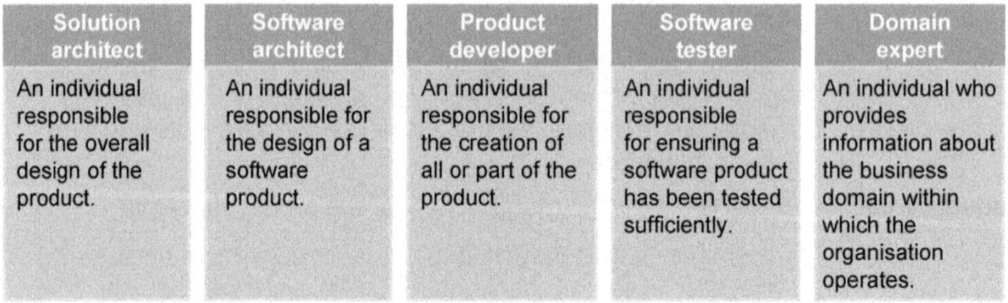

The product development customer roles are described in Table 10.3.

Table 10.3 Product development customers and their relationships with the BA Service

Customer role	Business analyst relationship
Solution architect	Responsible for the overall design of the product
	Works closely with business analysts to ensure a holistic view is adopted and all aspects of the solution are defined in order to meet the needs of business customers
Software architect	Responsible for the design of the software product
	Works closely with business analysts to ensure that the needs of the business customers are met
Product developer	Responsible for the creation of the product. Works closely with business analysts and the business staff to ensure that requirements are fulfilled accurately and any ambiguities are resolved
Software tester	Responsible for ensuring that the product has been tested sufficiently to identify and manage any software problems
	Works closely with business analysts, particularly during business acceptance testing
Domain expert	Provides information about the business domain within which the organisation operates. For example, domain experts may be specialists in areas such as the financial services or transport industries. Domain experts may be employees of the organisation or external consultants
	Business analysts work with domain experts when in-depth knowledge of the business domain is required to support the product development process

WORKING WITH CUSTOMERS

The majority of customers for the BA Service are internal to the organisation. Even where external customers will be affected by the changes, business analysts are likely to work with business representatives rather than the end consumer themselves. While these individuals may be viewed as colleagues, they should still be considered as customers and the service delivered should address their needs and expectations.

The need for professional respect between the various disciplines has never been greater. With so many calls upon the limited change resources, and increasing economic and competitive pressures, organisations have to change to keep up. If change professionals are able and disposed to collaborate, they have the potential to provide the support that their organisations need. If change professionals engage in 'land grab', whereby they fail to recognise the value of specialist expertise and attempt to take on the work of their colleagues from other specialisms, this will undermine collaboration opportunities and has the potential to result in poor-quality work that may risk the success of projects and organisations. Research (Parasuraman, Berry and Zeithaml, 1991) has shown that there are five service dimensions used by customers to evaluate a service provider. While these dimensions were identified with regard to the consumer customer rather than the internal customer, they are highly applicable to business analysts.

The five dimensions are described in Table 10.4.

Table 10.4 Five business analysis customer service dimensions (adapted from Parasuraman, Berry and Zeithaml, 1991)

Service dimension	Description
Reliability	The capability of the BA Service to perform the services that are offered at the required level of quality
Assurance	The credibility and professionalism displayed by the BA Service. This generates a sense of confidence and trust in individual business analysts
Tangibles	The physical evidence provided when performing the services. The BA Service may deliver documents, run workshops or meetings, and communicate using different mechanisms – all provide tangible evidence of the quality of the service provided
Empathy	The care and attention offered to the customers by business analysts, including treating them as individuals with their own needs and requirements
Responsiveness	The attitude demonstrated when working with customers. Business analysts need to show that they are willing to help and support customers in a timely fashion

These dimensions are helpful when establishing a BA Service because they support the delivery of a service that is valued by customers. They also highlight that while customers want to be able to rely on the deliverables or outcomes from a service (reliability and tangibles), they also want to have a good customer experience (responsiveness, assurance and empathy).

Understanding customer expectations

In evaluating the quality of the BA Service, customers consider the gap between what was expected and their perceptions of what was delivered. Therefore, it is critical that the customers' expectations with regard to the business analyst role and the services delivered are understood. Chapters 1 and 2 discuss the importance of expectations with regard to the business analyst role and how role ambiguity can lead to misconceptions and lack of recognition. The development of a service portfolio for the business analyst role helps to overcome role ambiguity and will help to build relationships with internal colleagues. However, problems can arise even when the BA Service is clearly defined, and customers know what to expect, if the delivery of a service fails to meet customer expectations in line with the five dimensions described in Table 10.4.

Customer expectations are not the same as customer requirements. Discussing expectations of the BA Service with current or potential customers will reveal interesting insights: 'What do you need from the BA Service?' is quite a different conversation to 'What do you expect from the BA Service?' (see Appendix 11). When something goes wrong and relationships break down, expectations (whether unmet or uncommunicated) are generally a contributing factor. Expectations are usually considered so implicit to both parties that 'they don't even need saying', and the word 'expectation' is not used until after a product or service has been delivered and the phrase 'that's not what I was expecting' makes an appearance.

The Kano model was developed by Professor Noriaki Kano and his colleagues from Tokyo University in 1984 and sets out a model for analysing customer satisfaction (Kano et al., 1984). The model (see Figure 10.7) distinguishes between three types of feature required by customers: basic or essential, performance and delighter.

Figure 10.7 The Kano model (adapted from Berger et al., 1993)

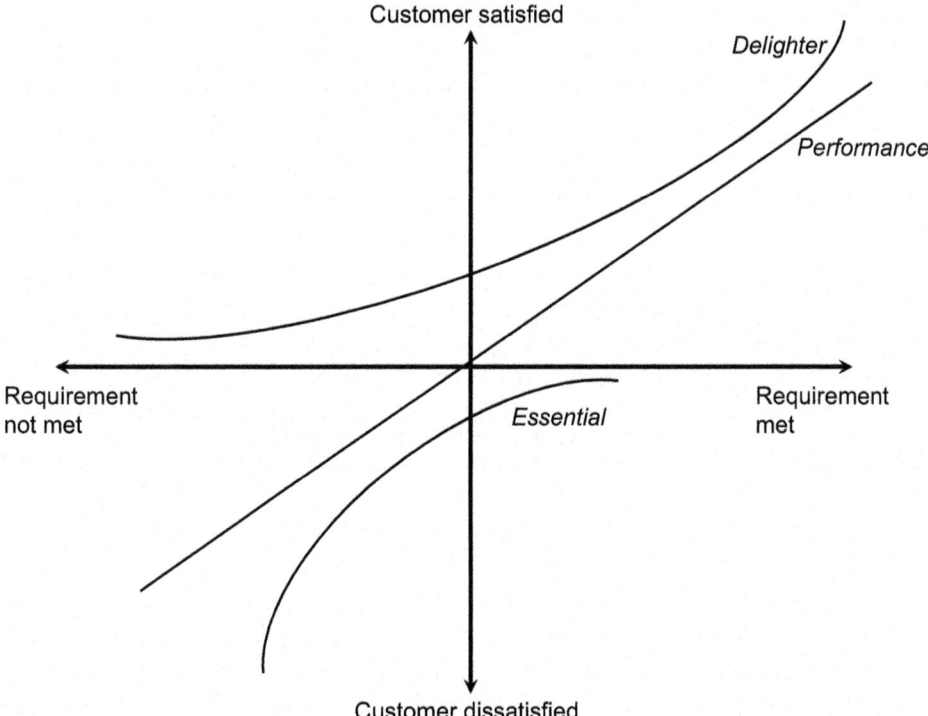

1. **Essential:** the requirements that are expected to be delivered by the product or system. In other words, these features comprise the minimal set that offer the basic functionality in the view of customers. Such requirements may not be requested specifically, as they are often assumed to be available. They are taken for granted when delivered by a product or service, so do not increase the customer's level of

satisfaction. However, customers are dissatisfied if these features are not provided and the requirements are not fulfilled. For example, customers expect that a car will have basic features such as central locking and air conditioning. They would be dissatisfied if the car locking feature did not work centrally as expected, but customer satisfaction would not increase if this was provided.

While the essential features do not contribute to customer satisfaction it is still the case that service providers need to know what they are so that they can be delivered.

2. **Performance:** the attributes of the product that a customer may request as additional options. For example, there may be a request for a car to have heated seats. Such requirements are typically expressed by customers and, if fully provided, can increase customer satisfaction to a great degree. However, if required performance features are not provided, customer dissatisfaction may result. Performance features may increase the amount charged for a product or service.

3. **Delighter:** the product or service features that are likely to delight the customer and hence offer the potential to deliver the highest degree of satisfaction. These features are those where a service provider can gain significant goodwill and loyalty from customers because the customer may not even be aware that they are available or desirable. Requirements regarding delighter features may be uncovered through considering and eliciting tacit knowledge or through service providers thinking innovatively about customer issues and finding ways to address them. A good example of this is the provision of heated front windscreens in cars.

A key milestone for a BA Service is establishing a shared understanding of the essential attributes with all customers. As many people have had different experiences of business analysis in other settings or organisations, expectations can vary significantly. Dissatisfaction with this BA Service may be down to an expectation set by working with business analysts elsewhere or possibly by ambiguity regarding the role (as discussed in Chapter 1). This may be reflected in expectation statements such as: 'I would expect the BA to cover when the project manager is on holiday' or 'I expect BAs to have SQL skills.'

The Kano model feature types and their implications for the BA Service are described in Table 10.5.

The 'best service' from a customer point of view would have all the essential attributes; it would also maximise the performance attributes, minimise the indifferent attributes and provide as many delighter attributes as possible for a price that the customer is willing to pay.

The Kano model and the BA Service Framework

It is helpful to consider the BA Service Framework (explained in Chapter 2) with regard to the levels within the Kano model. Each service within the framework may have different levels of requirement. Relevant examples are shown in Table 10.6.

Table 10.5 Kano feature types and the implications for the BA Service

Feature type	Description	Implications for BA Service
Essential	These are expected by customers and therefore are the 'musts' of a product or service. The absence or poor performance of these attributes would cause significant dissatisfaction	This can be an area of mismatch of expectations when a customer has had a different experience of business analysis in another setting or organisation, or where there are gaps (in skills/knowledge/capacity) that the customer wants business analysts to fill Consider 'minimum viable analysis' and where business analysis above this threshold will offer most value to customers
Performance	Aspects of the Service that are not absolutely necessary, but the provision of these will increase customer satisfaction When a customer is choosing between two products or services that meet the threshold, it is typically the performance attributes that act as differentiators	These are often activities carried out and behaviours displayed by the most successful business analysts without having to be told to do them. Examine positive feedback for possible sources of customer satisfaction that could be made consistent across the BA Service This can be an area of expectation mismatch when a customer believes a performance attribute is actually a threshold attribute
Delighter	Things that are generally not expressed by the customer explicitly and are not necessarily expected by the customer. The presence of these attributes delights the customer and results in high satisfaction. The absence of these attributes does not typically cause dissatisfaction	Is there an understanding of what would delight customers and exceed their expectations? If not, initiate a conversation to find out. It may be that some relatively minor adjustments to the BA Service could have a major impact on satisfaction

The Kano model reflects that customer expectations change over time and, accordingly, the value associated with a feature is likely to diminish. While a feature may be at the performance or delighter level initially, at a later stage customers may expect the feature to be provided and will disappointed if this is not the case. For example, an in-built satellite navigation system in a new car was originally seen as a 'delighter' but is now likely to be deemed a 'performance' feature. Eventually, it is likely to be considered 'essential' by customers of new cars. This is likely to be the same for the BA Service. The work business analysts conduct, for example, to determine the requirements to automate a business process, are now expected, and delighting customers is more likely to result from adopting a digital innovation approach whereby new process features are offered that customers had not anticipated.

Table 10.6 Features offered by the BA Service at the three Kano levels

Service name	Basic	Performance	Delighter
Situation investigation and problem analysis	Holistic investigation conducted into situation and root cause of problem identified	Problem statement definition provided	Innovative options to meet additional needs identified
Feasibility assessment and business case development	Options evaluated from business, technical and financial perspectives	Holistic impact analysis of options conducted and associated costs defined	Potential additional benefits identified and quantified where possible
Business process improvement	Swimlane diagrams created and incremental changes identified	Problematic tasks analysed in detail and improvements identified	Process architecture created
Requirements definition	Workshops facilitated Requirements identified and documented using organisational standards	Requirements modelled to identify inconsistencies and gaps	Requirements challenged and additional possible requirements identified that will address external customer needs
Business acceptance testing	Test cases and test scripts defined	Business staff supported when conducting acceptance tests and implications of incidents discussed	Non-functional requirements evaluated during acceptance testing
Business change and IT deployment	Training and help guidance provided	Ongoing personal support to address questions and issues provided	Emotional support provided during the transition process

Customers and conflict resolution

The nature of providing a service, particularly one in which we are attempting to co-create value with customers, will inevitably lead to situations where conflict can arise. Customer expectations is an area where conflict can arise when there is a lack of communication about what is expected, or when the expectations are known but are not met.

Conflict is not necessarily an issue in itself. The nature of business and IT change means that there are often different stakeholder perspectives to consider, which can result in requirements that are inconsistent or even opposing. Problems tend to arise when conflicts are ignored or when one party attempts to impose solutions or ideas without taking account of other views.

The Thomas-Kilmann Conflict MODE Instrument[1] (see Figure 10.8) assesses behavioural responses to conflict situations. The different responses are based upon two behaviour dimensions:

- **assertiveness:** the extent to which a party attempts to satisfy their own concerns;

- **cooperativeness:** the extent to which a party attempts to satisfy the other person's concerns.

Figure 10.8 The Thomas-Kilmann conflict styles

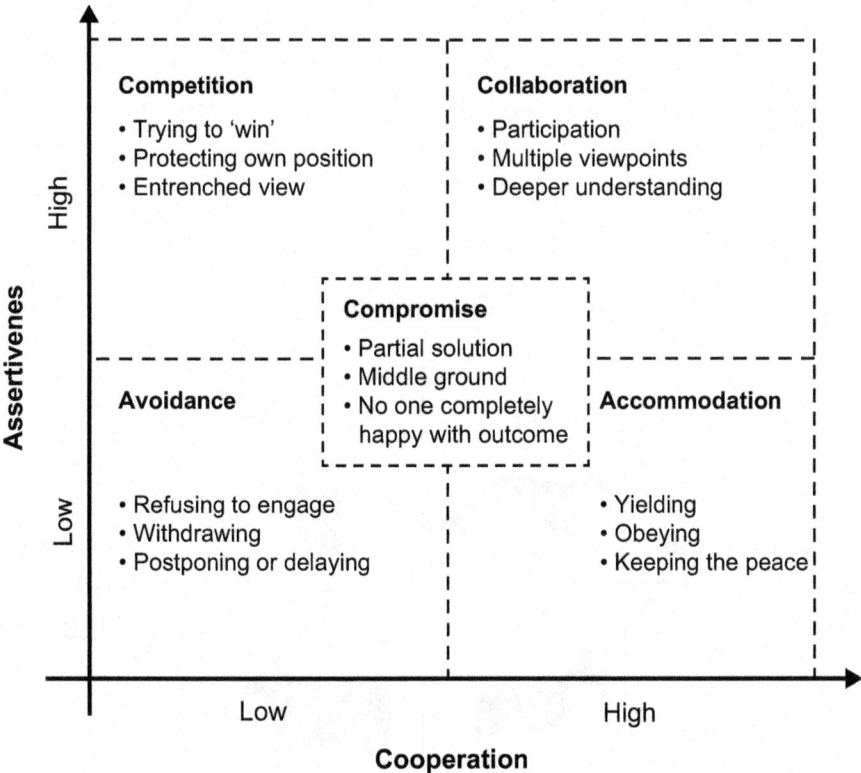

1   See www.kilmanndiagnostics.com/overview-thomas-kilmann-conflict-mode-instrument-tki

Individuals are capable of using all the conflict resolution modes shown in the model, but may have a preferred or default style for approaching conflict situations. At first glance the Compromise mode may seem most attractive, but this can lead to an outcome where no one is completely happy. The only route to a 'win–win' resolution is through collaboration. However, this doesn't mean that all situations require or even have the potential for a collaborative outcome. In some circumstances, a speedy decision is required, and a competing stance may be the best approach. In other situations, the conflict is best ignored as it is likely to be short-lived and attempting to move towards a compromise or collaborative result may inflame the situation.

Raising awareness within the BA Service of the different conflict resolution modes and encouraging a collaborative approach wherever possible, enables the BA Service to work with customers to find solutions that fully satisfy all concerns. This requires exploring issues in depth and using active listening to understand what is needed. Effective collaboration may take the form of a constructive disagreement to understand each person's perspective and to find a creative solution to a problem.

Political awareness

One of the factors that often needs to be considered when working with stakeholders is the incidence and level of internal politics and the impact this can have on working relationships. The Baddeley and James model, shown in Figure 10.9, offers insights into workplace behaviours.

Figure 10.9 Political awareness model (adapted from Baddeley and James, 1987)

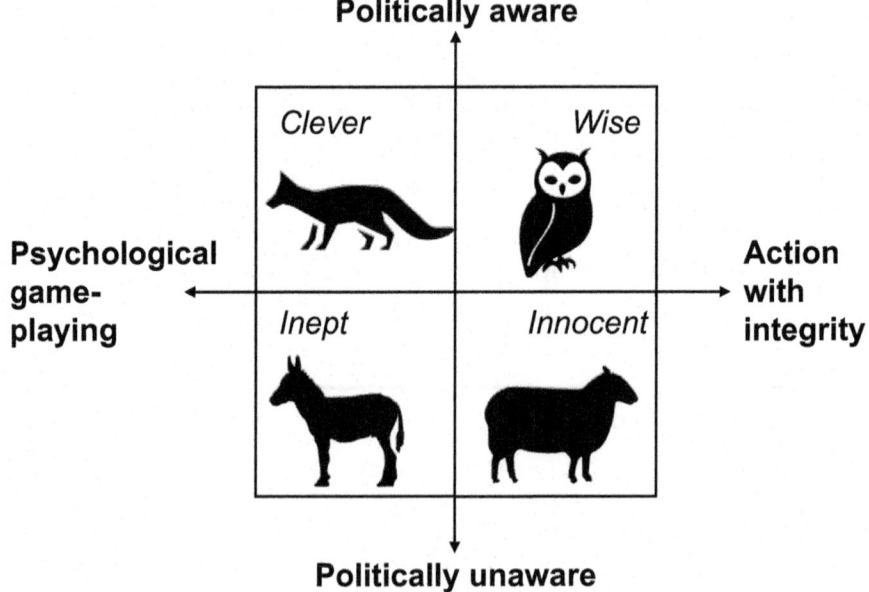

This model identifies four behavioural types:

1. **Inept** behaviour (the donkey) is displayed by those who do not have awareness of the internal politics, and often fail to understand why others behave as they do. They are focused on protecting their own feelings and egos. The resultant behaviour is obviously self-serving and may be detrimental to both the situation and the individual.

2. **Clever** behaviour (the fox) is displayed by those who are highly aware of internal politics and are also keen to serve their own agendas. The resultant behaviour is likely to be manipulative and reflect attempts to exercise control of situations.

3. **Wise** behaviour (the owl) is displayed by those who understand the internal politics and have sufficient self-awareness to act in a way that is beneficial to each situation.

4. **Innocent** behaviour (the sheep) is displayed by those who do not have an awareness of the internal politics and lack self-awareness. This results in behaviour that is well-intentioned but may result in individuals being exploited or ignored.

Unhelpful political behaviour needs to be identified and understood so that a strategy to work with the individuals concerned can be formulated. These four categories can help to identify the nature of the behaviour demonstrated by individuals and may provide a means of understanding underlying motivations. Recognising and managing political behaviour is often difficult but can be supported by the use of techniques to analyse and influence customers. These techniques are discussed later in this chapter.

Value network analysis

Value network analysis examines an organisation or business area from the perspective of the roles engaged in the value network and the value exchanges between these roles. The value exchanges may be tangible or intangible.

The value network analysis technique was developed by Verna Allee (2002) and shows the 'touchpoints' between roles associated with the work of the business system. These touchpoints are where interactions take place between the BA Service and its customers, in other words, where customer service happens. They provide the opportunity for the BA Service to meet or exceed customer expectations.

Value network analysis is a useful technique to understand the relationships between stakeholders and the BA Service by highlighting the touchpoints where stakeholders have contacts with the BA Service, and their expectations with regard to the value exchanges.

Value network analysis diagrams will vary between organisations and even teams within organisations. The roles defined will depend upon various factors, including the terminology, standards and approaches adopted by an organisation. An example value network analysis for a BA Service is shown in Figure 10.10.

Figure 10.10 Partial value network analysis for a BA Service

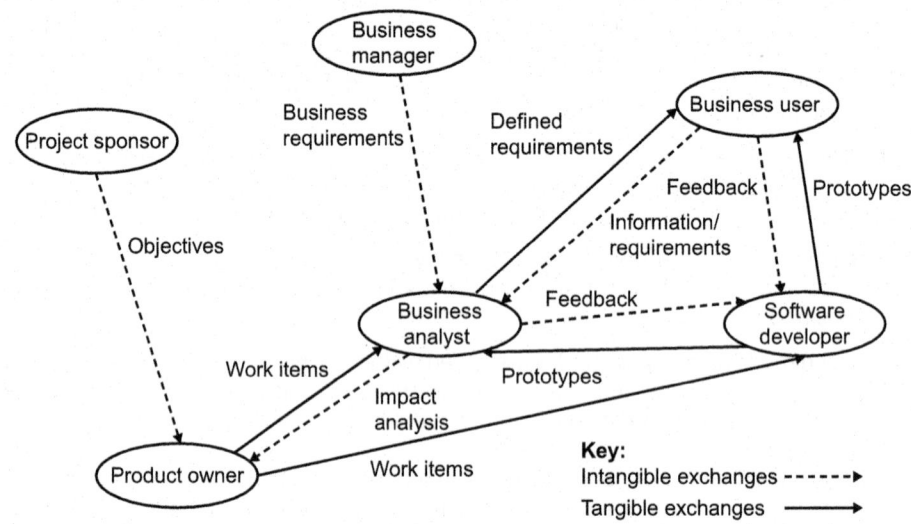

This diagram shows interactions between various roles. The dotted lines represent intangible exchanges of value proposing items and the solid lines represent tangible exchanges. In this diagram, the following exchanges are shown:

- **business user to business analyst:** intangible exchange of requirements information;
- **business analyst to business user:** tangible exchange of requirements documentation;
- **software developer to business user and business analyst:** tangible exchange of prototyped requirements;
- **business user and business analyst to software developer:** intangible exchange of feedback on prototypes.

The nature of these value exchanges, for example, how the exchange takes place and the way in which communication is facilitated, creates opportunities to build relationships with stakeholders and customers.

Building stakeholder relationships

Good stakeholder relationships are essential for the success of a BA Service. Chapter 1 discussed the need for role clarity in gaining recognition of business analysis work, but stakeholder relationships are a further key element in ensuring that the organisation involves business analysts when relevant.

Effective stakeholder relationship building requires a number of factors to be defined for the BA Service:

- an overarching vision;
- values and ethics;
- a knowledge-sharing culture.

The vision and values for the BA Service were discussed in Chapter 1; the culture of a BA Service and the development and importance of a knowledge-sharing culture are discussed in Chapter 11.

Active-Constructive Response model

Building better relationships with individuals and other teams is an important goal of the BA Service, but it may be difficult to identify practical steps to enable this to be achieved. One way to improve relationships is to consider the communication options available, in terms of levels of energy and tone, when responding to information or news.

Sharing positive information and experiences will amplify the positive impact for the individual. When an active-constructive response (Gable et al., 2004) is received, they experience even more positive emotions and the exchange helps to strengthen and build the relationship. Figure 10.11 illustrates the response options available to the business analyst.

For example, in the situation where a colleague shares the news, 'I have had some really positive feedback from my project team', different responses (adapted from Reivich, Seligman and McBride, 2011) can be mapped to different parts of the model, as shown in Table 10.7.

The only response option that builds the relationship is the active-constructive response. Responding in any other way, due to lack of time, energy or interest, means an opportunity has been missed to invest in improving the relationship.

Table 10.7 Example of Active-Constructive Response model

Response	Examples
Active/constructive	'That's great.'; 'What did they say?'; 'Who was it?'
Active/destructive	'That makes a change.'; 'They are probably going to ask for a favour.'
Passive/constructive	'That's nice.'
Passive/destructive	'I just got some feedback too.... .'

ANALYSING CUSTOMERS

Given the range and volume of customers who will work with business analysts, it is usually necessary to determine the level of priority each customer attracts. Some

Figure 10.11 Active-Constructive Response model for business analysts

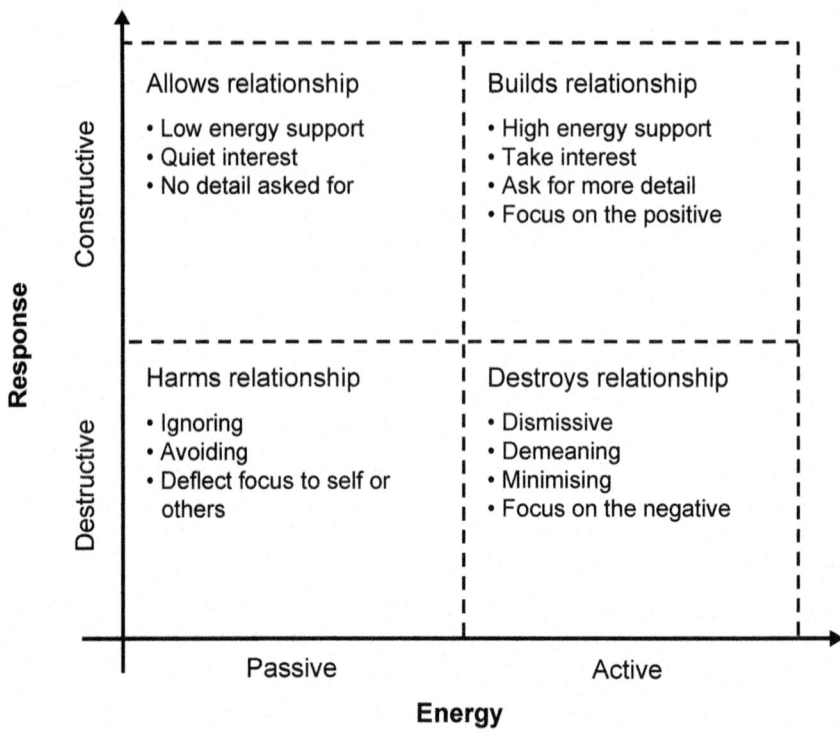

customers' views need to be taken into account when deciding on business changes, whereas other customers' views are not given such prominence. In some situations, there may be customers whose views are not considered at all.

The BA leaders may be required to clarify which customers are of the highest priority. There are several models that may be helpful when doing this:

- the power/interest grid;
- the Stakeholder Salience model;
- the responsibility assignment matrix (RACI).

The power/interest grid

The power/interest grid is essentially a matrix whereby customers and other stakeholders are mapped according to their level of power and their level of interest with regard to a particular situation. There are various versions of the matrix, including a 2 x 2 matrix, 3 x 3 matrix and a 2 x 3 matrix. The essence of the matrix (irrespective of version) is to allow business analysts to consider where a stakeholder, or stakeholder group, should be located on the matrix and then to use the position occupied to determine the amount of effort required to work with the stakeholder and the associated management strategy. A 3 x 3 version of the power/interest grid is shown in Figure 10.12.

Figure 10.12 3 x 3 power/interest grid (Paul, Cadle and Yeates, 2014)

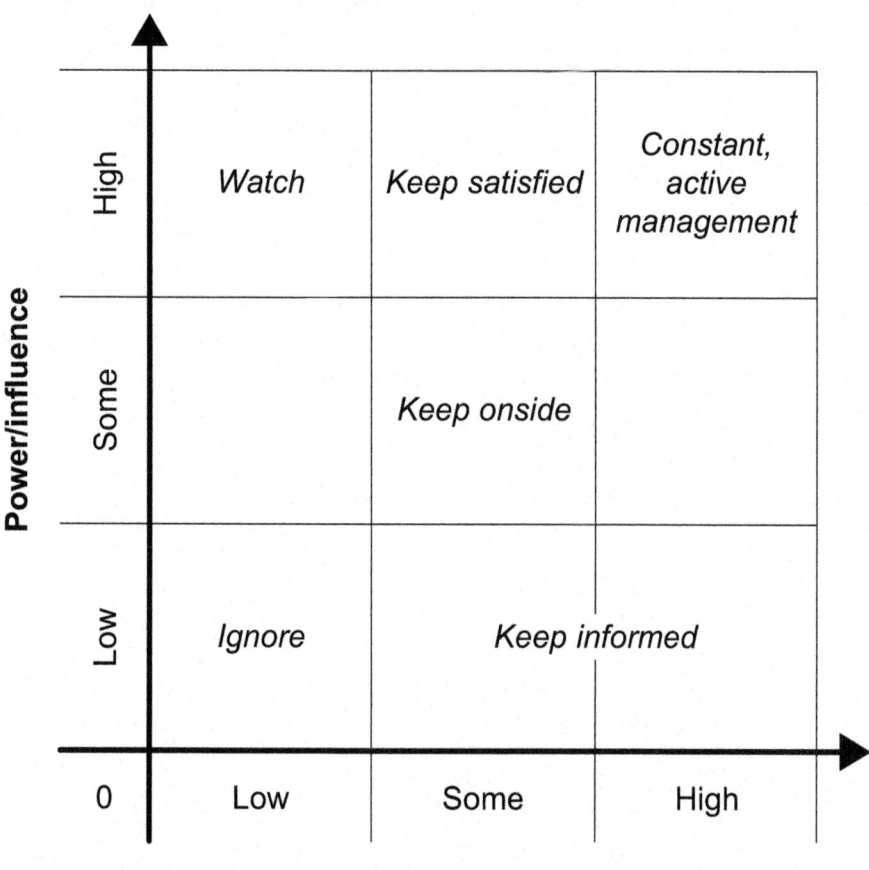

The position occupied by a particular customer will differ depending upon the circumstances. For example, at the outset of a project, the finance director for an organisation may not have a high level of interest although they may be extremely powerful. In this situation, it may be necessary to adopt a 'keep satisfied' management strategy. However, if the project begins to run into difficulties and there is a risk that the budget will need to be extended, the finance director may become very interested and may need to be actively managed as a key player.

Stakeholder categories
Alongside the power/interest grid, it is useful to consider if stakeholders are generally in favour or against the aims of the planned change, project or service. Table 10.8

shows different categories[2] of stakeholder (based upon the attitudes held) and how each category may be engaged to support a change.

Table 10.8 Stakeholder categories

Category	Detail	Engagement approach
Advocates	This group is driving the change or project and is clear on the intended benefits and enthusiastic to see the change delivered	• Use as internal champions and sponsorship • Input to key milestones and decisions • Active communication; keep regularly involved • Use for internal promotion of objectives and benefits
Followers	This group have a low understanding of project aims and objectives but tend to support the project and 'go with the flow'	• Keep informed and positive • Aim to increase understanding for closer engagement or future benefit
Indifferent	These are individuals or groups yet to take a definitive position on the project, due to lack of knowledge or perceived lack of impact upon them	• Continue to provide opportunities to engage/build knowledge • Seek views on key issues • Identify gaps in knowledge and seek to address if necessary
Blockers	This group shows resistance to the project or its aims. This may be due to having a low understanding or low agreement. This can be driven by: • A lack of communication • Perceived or actual loss from the project • Detailed knowledge that recognises errors in project assumptions or approach • Perceived lack of priority or different priorities	• Proactive communication; use interviews and listen to perspectives and knowledge • Consider if sense of loss is real or perceived. If real, explain drivers and wider benefits; if perceived, then evidence using data • Use conflict management techniques • Engage and seek views once understanding starts to develop • Discuss perspectives on priorities/competing demands or initiatives

(Continued)

---

2   Developed from categories defined by Civil Service Learning – Stakeholder Assessment. Available from: civilservicelearning.civilservice.gov.uk/sites/default/files/resources/ManagingBusinessPerformance_WLA_StakeholderIdentification_V2_140512.pdf

Table 10.8 (Continued)

Category	Detail	Engagement approach
Opponents	These are individuals or groups who have high understanding but low agreement towards the project. They will potentially lose out or be negatively impacted by the project	• Initiate discussions and understand reasons for low acceptance • Consider if sense of loss is real or perceived. If real, explain drivers and wider benefits; if perceived, then evidence using data • Look for opportunities to compromise, consider ways to mitigate adverse impacts • Consider the impact for the project of ongoing opposition

Using the information gained from both the power/interest grid, and the stakeholder categories shown in Table 10.8, it is possible to understand the following:

- the current level of engagement of each group;
- the target level of engagement required from each group to successfully deliver the change initiative or project;
- the actions that can be taken to achieve the required level of engagement.

Table 10.9 provides an example stakeholder engagement analysis based upon a typical project scenario. In this example, the owner is too busy, business employees see potential negative impacts of the proposed changes and partners have competing priorities to accommodate.

It would be a useful exercise to consider the different stakeholders of the BA Service, analyse the categories and determine the current and required level of engagement. This will inform the creation of a BA Service Communications Strategy (see Appendix 10).

Customer salience

Mitchell, Agle and Wood (1997) proposed a model for analysing stakeholder salience. Their research considered the relationship between an organisation and different stakeholders. The relationship was analysed in terms of three dimensions: power, legitimacy and urgency.

This model can be extremely helpful to anyone engaged within a BA Service, given that it can be applied successfully to analyse customers (as a sub-group of stakeholders)

Table 10.9 Example stakeholder engagement analysis

Stakeholder	Power	Interest	Category	AIH	LIH	HIH	MIH	Concerns	Actions
Owner	H	M	Advocate			○	●	Thinks project team can drive the change. Limited time available for this initiative.	Discuss and agree priorities, look at opportunities for representation or delegated authority.
Business employee	M	H	Opponent	○		●		Perceives negative implications and impacts of this change initiative.	Hold briefing sessions, meet with key managers and ask for involvement to be encouraged, invite to workshops, hold interviews, listen, discuss concerns.
Partner	M	L	Indifferent		○	●		Other priorities	Discuss levels of engagement, develop terms of reference, revisit contracts.

● = Target engagement   ○ = Current engagement

AIH = Against it happening, LIH = Let it happen, HIH = Help it happen, MIH = Make it happen when conducting business analysis. Therefore, the three dimensions may be applied to the BA Service as follows:

1. The power of the customer within the context of the project. Does the customer have the power to influence requirements, options and outcomes?

2. The legitimacy of the customer. Are the customer's actions and requirements desirable and appropriate within the business context? Does the customer have a legitimate right to exercise the power held?

3. The urgency of the customer's needs according to timing and criticality. Does action need to be taken in the immediate future or short term, to address the customer's requirements? Is the customer a key partner with regard to the project?

The assessment of these three attributes helps to identify the salience of the stakeholder or customer. This then determines the level of priority that should be assigned to each customer's requirements.

The extent of stakeholder salience is not fixed, but may vary over time and is only relevant within the context of the situation. Again, this is a relevant consideration when working with customers. For example, a customer who exercises significant power on one project may have only limited power in another context.

Combining these three dimensions results in the identification of seven different classes of customer. This is represented in the model shown in Figure 10.13, which has been adapted from the original Stakeholder Salience model and shows the relevant management strategies from the power/interest grid in Figure 10.12.

Figure 10.13 Customer salience model (adapted from Mitchell et al., 1997)

Power	Power	Power			Power	
	Legitimacy	Legitimacy	Legitimacy			Legitimacy
		Urgency	Urgency	Urgency	Urgency	

| Dormant: watch | Dominant: keep satisfied | Definitive: constant, active management | Dependent: keep onside | Demanding: keep informed | Dangerous: watch | Discretionary: ignore |

These classes of customer can be extremely useful within the BA Service, when analysing priorities and deciding on courses of action. The classes are described within the BA Service context in Table 10.10.

Table 10.10 Customer salience and the BA Service

Customer class	BA Service description
Dormant	**Power:** customers who hold positions of influence but are not engaged or interested in the situation or project. For example, senior executives from other areas of the business. It is important that BAs are aware of them but they may not need to manage them actively. However, it is important to recognise when their involvement would not be helpful and ensure that they do not become engaged, particularly as they do not have legitimacy. Alternatively, it is also important to recognise when their involvement would be helpful and try to gain their engagement and increase their legitimacy
Definitive	**Power/Legitimacy/Urgency:** these are the customers with whom the business analysts should work closely in order to ensure that the project will align with their values and needs. For example, the project sponsor is a definitive customer
Dependent	**Legitimacy/Urgency:** these customers are likely to be those who are impacted by the project but have little power to influence the outcomes. For example, the business staff who will need to carry out the new processes and use the new systems. It is important to engage with these customers because they may be able to gain power and thereby frustrate or resist the changes
Demanding	**Urgency:** these are people who are likely to be outside the project but make demands regarding the work and the outcomes. Again, it is questionable whether they fall into the category of customer (or stakeholder) but they may believe they have a right to be heard. These individuals can take up a lot of time and energy, but it is always important to be aware that they may be able to gain legitimacy (perhaps through alliances with other customers)
Dominant	**Power/Legitimacy:** customers who hold positions of influence, are not engaged or interested in the situation or project but have a legitimate interest in or influence on the outcomes. For example, senior executives from related areas of the business. It may be helpful to engage their interest and raise their sense of urgency in some situations
Dangerous	**Power/Urgency:** these are people who have power and want their needs to be met but don't have any legitimacy in the situation. It is questionable whether they should be categorised as customers (or even stakeholders). For example, this may be an executive who wishes to influence a project (possibly to meet a personal agenda) but doesn't have the legitimate right to do this. These people may be customers in the broadest sense, but may have very limited influence within the context of a change project. However, their power may enable them to disrupt the project or inhibit the desired outcomes

(Continued)

Table 10.10 (Continued)

Customer class	BA Service description
Discretionary	**Legitimacy:** these customers do not hold positions of influence, although it is perceived that they have a legitimate interest in the project. However, they do not have a sense of urgency with regard to the actions underway

The RACI matrix

The RACI technique is widely used in business analysis as an approach for analysing and defining levels of responsibility for particular tasks.

The RACI categories represent the areas shown in Table 10.11.

Table 10.11 Categories within the RACI matrix

Category	Description
Responsible	The role or individual responsible for taking ownership of the work to complete a task and deliver any associated deliverables
Accountable	The role or individual accountable to the organisation for the success or failure of a task and associated deliverables. There is only one accountable role or individual for each task or deliverable
Consulted	A role or individual who may be consulted so that they can provide additional skills, information or guidance to support the completion of the task or production of the associated deliverables
Informed	A role or individual who should be advised of any key aspects related to the task such as decisions or outcomes

Business analysts need to understand the various customer motivations and desired outcomes if they are to work successfully with different project customers. Examples of customers with RACI responsibilities are summarised in Table 10.12.

Table 10.12 RACI responsibilities of project customers

Role	Motivation/outcome/RACI categorisation
Project sponsor	Accountable for the realisation of the business case
Domain expert	Consulted regarding domain information
End user	Consulted regarding usage and organisational information

(Continued)

Table 10.12 (Continued)

Role	Motivation/outcome/RACI categorisation
Project manager	Accountable for delivery of the project objectives
Software developer	Responsible for developing the software element of the solution
Software tester	Responsible for testing the software element of the solution
Solution architect	Responsible for defining and designing the holistic solution

Top tips for creating an RACI matrix:

It is possible to engage many stakeholders simultaneously in the creation of an RACI matrix by playing RACI Poker.

- Create simple cards the size of playing cards for: **R** (I own it), **A** (I do it), **C** (I input to it), **I** (I know about it), plus: '**?**' (I don't know) and '**-**' (I'm not involved).
- Create a list of activities or deliverables where responsibilities need to be clarified and agreed.
- Gather stakeholders together; give everyone a set of cards.
- For each item on the list, stakeholders select and reveal their involvement.
- Capture agreement, discuss and resolve conflicts and gaps (such as multiple people who see themselves as responsible or no one is responsible), explore areas of ambiguity (use of the '?' card) and provide professional challenge.

This exercise aids role clarity for each person, helps to reveal expectations and builds trust and shared understanding across the group.

Influencing techniques

The BA Service occupies a central role in most business change and IT projects. While the project manager has to coordinate the activities undertaken and monitor progress towards the project goals, the business analysts have to ensure that the outcomes desired by customers stay at the forefront and that a holistic view is taken of what is needed to achieve the business objectives. Achieving this can be extremely difficult as it requires the business analysts to work collaboratively with a variety of customers and stakeholders, as discussed earlier in this chapter.

The difficulties in defining the role of the business analyst were described in Chapter 1. However, the BASF (see Chapter 2) requires business analysts to work closely with their customers, irrespective of which service is conducted. This is not always straightforward, as business analysts regularly encounter a broad variety of roles, individuals, priorities and values, all of which have to be considered. This situation is further complicated by the different authority levels of the customers. Some individuals may have greater authority and seniority than the business analysts, some may be peers, and some may have limited authority, typically occupying more junior roles. Figure 10.14 represents some of the BA Service customers and identifies where they fit within this 180° influencing schema.

Figure 10.14 BA Service customers within a 180° influencing schema

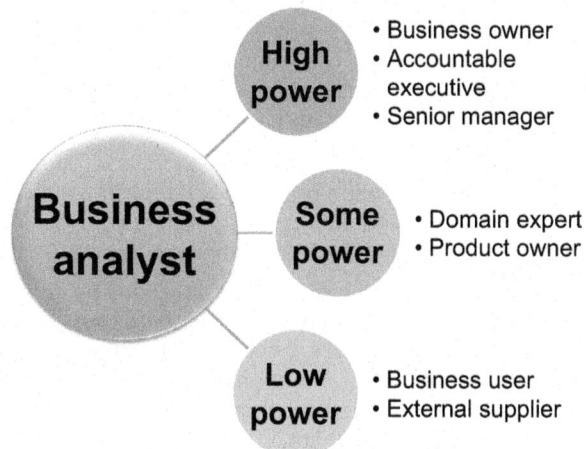

Within the customer community, there may be many different perspectives and varying opinions on the desired outcomes. Ultimately though, business analysts need to focus on the desired outcomes from the change project and have to engage with the personalities, views and values amongst their customers to ensure these outcomes are achieved.

Influencing approaches, such as Cialdini's six principles of influence (Cialdini 2007) and the Outcome Frame, can help business analysts to influence customers and work successfully with them.

Six principles of influence
Cialdini defined six principles that underpin why people are influenced to make certain decisions or act in a particular way. These six principles can help business analysts working within a BA Service to work effectively with their customers, particularly where they need to influence them to support the project in a particular way. The principles are summarised in Table 10.13.

The Outcome Frame
An outcome focus is essential when working as a business analyst. The service viewpoint is concerned to deliver a service that has the potential to offer value to customers. For example, the essence of the BA Service – 'situation investigation and problem analysis' – is the need to understand why a project is needed by asking 'What is the problem to be solved?' and to determine what might be done to address the root causes of the problem. The Outcome Frame identifies six questions that help to ensure that there is a focus on achieving the desired outcome, which helps to influence customers to work

Table 10.13 Cialdini's six principles of influence and the BA Service

Cialdini principle	Description
Reciprocation	People in all societies will try to repay a gift or favour in some way, even when the original gift was not wanted or considered to be of value. Reciprocity occurs because of the sense of obligation placed upon the recipient – people tend to dislike having a sense of obligation, so will act to repay a perceived debt. The reciprocation principle can also apply when one party has conceded something to a second party. The sense of concession can result in the second party feeling obliged to support another proposal
	The reciprocation principle can offer business analysts a basis for negotiating with customers. For example, when trying to resolve conflicts in views or requirements
Consistency	People like to be consistent once they have made a commitment to follow a particular path, so it can be difficult to influence them in a different direction. This is due to a desire to keep to – if not justify – a decision once it has been made and can cause people to behave in ways that may not be beneficial to them. Cialdini also highlights that where an individual has written down a statement, whether it is exactly what they believe or want or not, they have a strong tendency to commit to what they have written and to act accordingly
	Understanding the consistency principle can help business analysts to appreciate why customers may be so keen to adhere to particular ideas or requirements. Addressing these situations may be helped by considering the other influencing principles. For example, reciprocity may provide a basis for achieving a compromise
Social proof	People behave in a way that aligns with others. They tend to define 'correct' behaviour as that demonstrated by others because this demonstrates social acceptance or desirability. Where people are observed acting in a particular way, the actions are deemed to be appropriate
	Using this principle, the business analyst may be able to influence customers by highlighting where other colleagues have behaved or acted in a particular way

(Continued)

Table 10.13 (Continued)

Cialdini principle	Description
Liking	People prefer to agree with or be influenced by those that they like or find they relate to. If approached by a friend, most people will tend to agree to a proposal. However, it is also the case that people tend to engage with anyone who they feel is similar to them in terms of their backgrounds, views, values, etc.
	This principle emphasises the importance of interpersonal skills for anyone working with customers and, therefore, is highly applicable to business analysts. It is the responsibility of the business analyst to engage with their colleagues and stakeholders and positive engagement will improve the chances of influencing
Authority	People tend to accept and follow information provided by someone with authority or where there is reference to an accepted authority. Personal authority can originate from various sources, such as a designated role or acknowledged expertise. The use of information that is based on analytics or research can also help to bestow authority
	This principle is well established with change projects as a hierarchy of authority often exists and business analysts are able to exert influence by referring to the project authority. For example, a conflict in requirements that cannot be resolved through discussion and negotiation is likely to be escalated to the project sponsor
Scarcity	This principle relates to a person's desire to gain, access or participate in something if the opportunity to do so is limited. People often make decisions, or may be motivated by, the sense that there is a potential loss if the opportunity is not seized
	Understanding this principle can help a business analyst to influence customers where a decision is needed. For example, the business analyst may be able to identify the potential impact of delay when discussing a proposed solution

towards this. Thomas, Paul and Cadle (2012) provided an Outcome Frame consisting of the following six questions:

1. What is the outcome you want?

2. Where, when and with whom do you want it?

3. What will you see, hear and feel when you have achieved the outcome?

4. What will having this outcome do for you (what are your motivators)?

5. What stops you from having your desired outcome already?

6. What resources do you need to achieve your outcome?

Maintaining an outcome focus is vital when working within a business change project. Without this, it is too easy to be diverted away from what is needed and to waste effort on areas that will not have the desired impact or deliver the required benefits. Keeping in mind the questions provided by the Outcome Frame will help to maintain an outcome focus. For example, thinking about a customer's motivators and what is preventing them from accepting an outcome will help to identify what might be done to influence the customer towards achieving the desired outcomes.

The collaboration continuum

Business analysts must collaborate with many other professionals to deliver the portfolio of business analysis services and co-create business value. However, while there is often discussion about the need to collaborate and sometimes assumptions are made that this has occurred, true collaboration can be difficult to achieve and sustain.

'Collaborating' is often used as a catch-all term to encompass many levels of 'working together', but it is helpful to consider a more specific definition:

Collaborating is defined as exchanging information, altering activities, sharing resources, and enhancing the capacity of another for mutual benefit and to achieve a common purpose.

(Himmelman, 2002)

Collaboration has several characteristics (Patel, Pettitt and Wilson, 2011) as follows:

- high level of trust;
- shared objectives;
- significant investment of time;
- productive and open communication;
- compatible ways of working (including decision making).

If any of these characteristics are missing from a relationship, it is unlikely that true collaboration will occur and, accordingly, the benefits of collaboration will not be realised. The collaboration continuum shown in Figure 10.15 represents levels of trust and integration and shows the nature of the working relationship at the different levels.

At one end of the continuum, individuals or groups are in competition and are actively working against each other. At the other end, the boundaries between groups are completely removed and they converge to behave as a single integrated group.

Figure 10.15 The collaboration continuum (adapted from Himmelman, 2002; Mashek and Nan-fito, 2015)

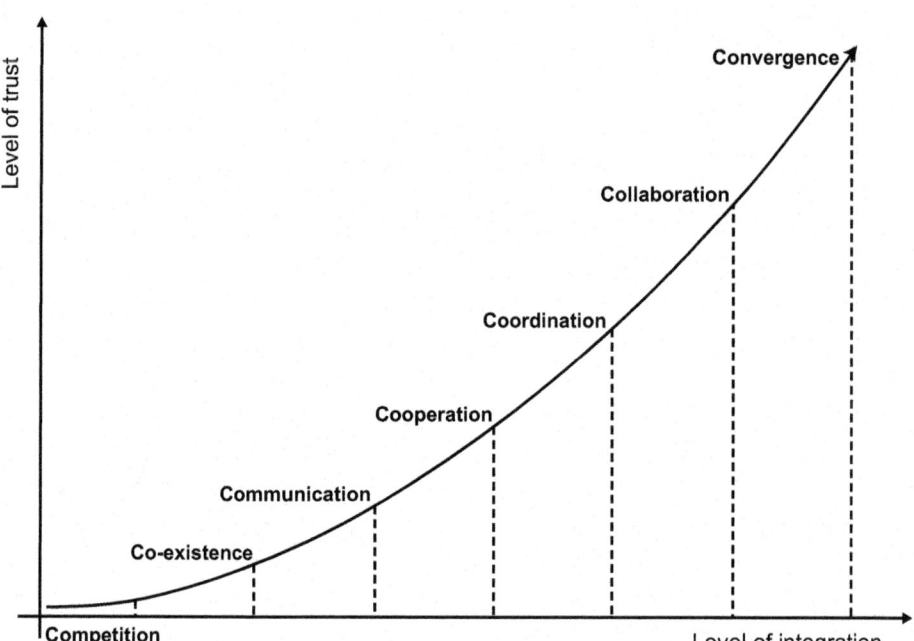

The model clarifies that collaboration is only possible where there is a high level of trust and of integration.

BA leaders must strive to create a climate (see Chapter 11) within the BA Service where people are encouraged and enabled to collaborate with customers and genuine collaboration is recognised and rewarded. Milestones along the journey to collaboration should be recognised and celebrated. However, it should also be accepted that merely stating 'we need to collaborate more' will not in itself increase trust and integration, so this should not be considered a solution to any problem!

The continuum can also be used to consider the different levels of integration that may exist across business analysis within an organisation. A Community of Practice approach (discussed in Chapter 1) may facilitate a level of integration in the communication/cooperation area of the spectrum. A BA Service approach provides the organisation with the ability to move into coordination and beyond.

CONCLUSION

The BA Service works closely with customers, so it is important that business analysis work is conducted with a customer-oriented focus. This requires business analysts to understand the different customer categories and characteristics, and to develop good working relationships with their customers.

Many techniques exist that can help business analysts manage relationships with customers. These techniques help business analysts to deal with customer concerns, influence customers and resolve conflicts. They can also provide insights that are extremely useful when dealing with difficult situations involving customers.

11 FOSTERING A BA SERVICE CULTURE

INTRODUCTION

Organisational culture may be defined as:

> the unwritten shared values and beliefs that drive the strategy of an organisation and influence the behaviours of its members.

Given that a 'service' is concerned with applying skills in order to offer benefit to customers, a service culture is present when the staff of an organisation share customer service values, contribute to the development of a service focus and are motivated to deliver an excellent service to customers.

Having awareness of cultural differences, and their impact, is essential for anyone whose work requires them to engage with stakeholders and understand stakeholder perspectives and requirements. Therefore, understanding the origins and characteristics of an organisational culture is essential for those delivering the BA Service. The breadth of the business analysis landscape is such that business analysts may work with stakeholders from many different organisations, such as external suppliers or regulators, and some of these stakeholders may be located in different countries. As a result, business analysts working with project stakeholders may have to take account of many different national and organisational cultures.

The impact of cultural differences can be extensive. For example, these differences may be apparent in the following scenarios:

- when eliciting requirements from stakeholders based in different countries;
- when defining requirements and business rules with business staff whose level of authority is limited by the organisation's hierarchical management style;
- when communicating with outsourced development staff; this may be further extended if they are working off-shore;
- when analysing product gaps with supplier organisations;
- when deploying a solution into customer organisations, both within the same country and internationally.

The nature of culture can be extremely subtle and understanding the cultural impact upon a project, team, requirements or solution may require considerable reflection and analysis. In some circumstances, despite careful planning, cultural differences may even threaten the success of a business change initiative.

Developing a service culture requires an understanding of two aspects: the customers and what they require from the organisation; and, the nature of organisational culture. The BA Service customers, and the various categories of customer, were discussed in Chapter 10. This chapter discusses the following areas:

- what is meant by 'culture';
- the frameworks that may be used to understand a prevailing culture and adapt behaviour accordingly;
- the difference between climate and culture;
- the existence of different 'nested' cultures within organisations.

THE ESSENCE OF CULTURE

The nature of organisational culture has been the subject of extensive research. Culture has been said to encompass 'taken-for-granted beliefs and values' (Johnson et al., 2017) and to consist of the 'unwritten rules of the social game' (Hofstede, Hofstede and Minkov, 2010) that drive feelings and actions. The various elements relating to culture were depicted by Edward T. Hall (1976) as an iceberg, as shown in Figure 11.1.

Figure 11.1 The Iceberg model of culture (adapted from Hall, 1976)

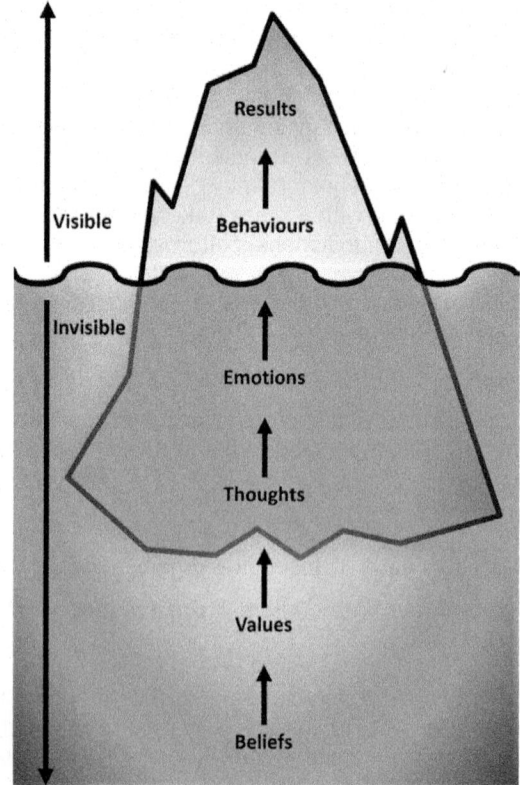

Business analysts regularly work with stakeholders who sometimes demonstrate behaviour that is challenging and perplexing. The need to engage with stakeholders as customers and, where possible, influence them towards achieving the desired project outcomes was discussed in Chapter 10. The Iceberg model reflects the way in which cultural behaviours are created by the invisible emotions, thoughts, values and beliefs that exist 'under the surface'. These may be felt and held very strongly by individuals; however, they may not be clearly expressed. The behaviours caused by such feelings will be evident though.

The Iceberg model offers a framework through which to understand and explore why stakeholders are behaving in a particular way. Where a stakeholder is being unhelpful or abrupt, it is helpful to think about what may be underlying this behaviour. In other words, what are the 'invisible' emotions, thoughts, values and beliefs that are leading to the behaviour. Unhelpful behaviour may result from a variety of personal or professional issues. For example, someone may be abrupt because they are trying to cope with a family problem and are distracted from the work in hand; alternatively, there may be a culture within the organisation that prioritises speed over attitude, imposes tight deadlines and leads to behaviour that may be deemed abrupt.

Understanding the source of the unhelpful behaviour can often provide insights into how this may be addressed. The Thomas-Kilmann conflict styles described in Chapter 10 offer five different ways to behave in a situation where there is an actual or potential conflict. For example:

- **Where the root cause for the behaviour appears to be cultural,** further analysis may be needed to determine how the issue should be addressed. The cultural frameworks described later in this chapter will help with this analysis. Unfortunately, some organisational cultures are so deep-rooted that resolving an issue may prove beyond the capabilities of the BA Service. In this situation, an accommodating style may prove most beneficial.

- **Where cultural behaviours are causing difficulties for the project,** it is probable that an early response will be required. In this situation, it may be necessary to adopt a competing style, possibly through leveraging support from a line manager.

- **Where the behaviour is out of character,** seems to relate to a personal issue and is unlikely to have an impact on the project, an avoiding approach may be the most appropriate short-term response.

A related technique that can also provide insights into a stakeholder's behaviour is Checkland's (1999) CATWOE; in particular, the 'W' element, which enables consideration of a stakeholder's worldview. This technique encourages analysts to consider what a stakeholder believes and values about a situation and helps to highlight their priorities. The organisational culture is likely to have an impact upon these beliefs, values and priorities.

Where there are several worldviews to accommodate, consideration of the other CATWOE elements can also provide insights to support positive engagement with the stakeholders. For example, as identified in Chapter 10, there are several different types of customer and CATWOE can help the business analyst to understand which customers are viewed as a priority by some stakeholders. Comparing the type of customer who would benefit from each stakeholder worldview will help to identify where customers may be overlooked (if a particular worldview is not accommodated) or where there are different levels of customer to consider (if each worldview targets a different customer and they are all potentially valid). Understanding the organisational culture can help to clarify why particular customers are prioritised and the underlying rationale for the worldview.

The CIA model discussed in Chapter 5 can help to determine if action is necessary or desirable to resolve a cultural issue. There may be some situations where it is possible to resolve a situation by taking control or where some influence may be exerted. However, in other situations a cultural issue may be deep-seated and acceptance may be the only way to move forward.

Schein levels of organisational culture

An accepted approach to viewing culture was developed originally by Schein (2016), whereby three levels of organisational culture were identified. These three levels are represented in Figure 11.2.

Figure 11.2 Levels of organisational culture (based upon Schein, 2016)

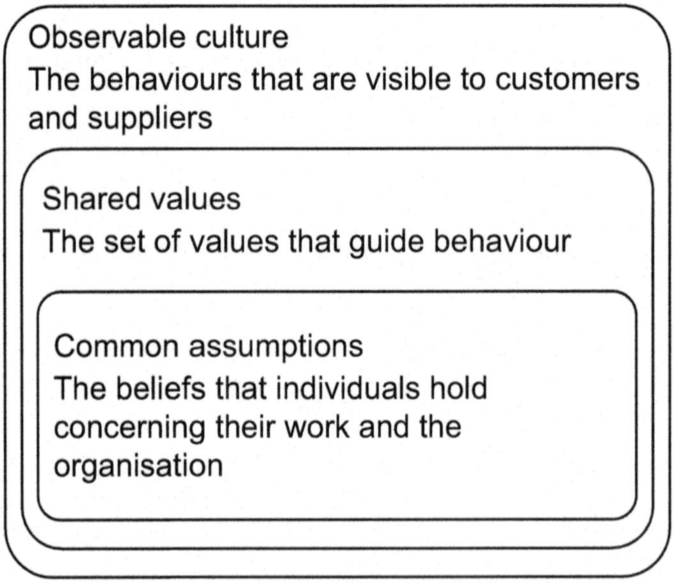

Observable culture
The behaviours that are visible to customers and suppliers

Shared values
The set of values that guide behaviour

Common assumptions
The beliefs that individuals hold concerning their work and the organisation

These three levels of a culture are described as:

1. **Common assumptions:** these are the deepest level of beliefs and assumptions held by the individuals within the organisation.

2. **Shared values:** this level derives from the aggregation of the shared values held by individuals within the organisation. These values guide how those within the group act in different situations.

3. **Observable culture:** this reflects anything that customers, suppliers or any other individuals or groups may observe with regard to the organisation. The observable level is a manifestation of the organisational culture and includes the documents, behaviours or symbols that represent the organisation. At this level, the deeper essence of the culture is reflected in how people act, what they say and how they respond to others.

When working with stakeholders, it is possible to identify the impact of shared cultural values on observable behaviour. If a stakeholder is uncooperative, or even rude, it is worthwhile analysing if the organisational culture, or its impact on individuals, is likely to result in the behaviour on display. This can improve understanding of the root cause of unacceptable behaviour.

Within a BA Service, it is possible to observe how individual business analysts behave, the artefacts that they create and the terminology they use when engaging with their customers or other stakeholders. The role of the BA leader when developing a service culture is to identify where the observable behaviours and artefacts are undesirable or are not aligned with the culture of the organisation, and understand the beliefs, assumptions and shared values that drive these behaviours. Through consideration of the levels identified by Schein, it is possible to uncover which beliefs and values held by individual business analysts should be challenged in order to assist cultural and behavioural change. It is also possible to uncover shared values amongst the team members that are not in line with the desired culture for the BA Service.

CULTURAL FRAMEWORKS

Several frameworks exist that enable business analysts to gain insights into organisational and national cultures and, accordingly, the behaviours and attitudes they observe. This cultural analysis can help analysts to understand the underlying values and beliefs that exist and may enable them to manage situations more effectively by:

- analysing cultural assumptions to ensure that a solution will gain acceptance;

- avoiding actions or terminology that will cause issues or even increase resistance;

- adopting approaches that demonstrate cultural sensitivity. These might include the use of phrases that align with the local culture.

The most popular frameworks for analysing and understanding culture are:

- the cultural web;

- Handy's model of organisation cultures;

- Hofstede's national culture dimensions.

These are discussed below, together with their application to a business analysis context.

285

The cultural web

The cultural web (Johnson et al., 2017) provides seven interlinked dimensions for analysing the culture within an organisation. Figure 11.3 shows the cultural web and the elements it encompasses.

Figure 11.3 The cultural web (Johnson et al., 2017)

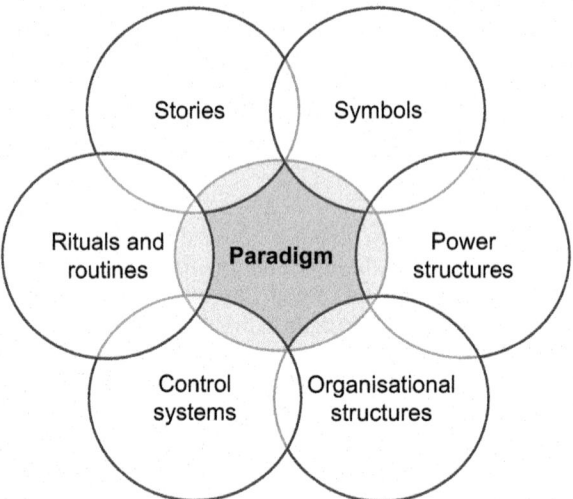

The paradigm is at the heart of this model and has been defined as:

> the set of assumptions held in common and taken for granted in an organisation.
> (Johnson et al., 2017)

The paradigm aligns with the shared values represented in Figure 11.2. It is based on the assumptions and experiences of those working within an organisation or a community (for example, a BA Service) and helps to guide how they act in response to business events and situations. The paradigm drives the other elements of the cultural web, including the behaviours of the employees within the team, the physical systems and the symbols applied. Where the shared values of a BA Service are concerned with delivering an effective customer-oriented service, this will drive the behaviours of the business analysts within the team and ensure that the required customer experience is achieved.

Establishing a cultural paradigm requires BA leaders to undertake the following approach:

- recognise and understand the values that are required to underlie the BA Service and the service culture;
- produce a statement of the values;

- communicate the values, the practices and the behaviours that must be adopted and demonstrated to ensure cultural alignment;

- foster a shared belief in the importance of these values to ensure that they are embedded and persist.

The six outer elements of the cultural web represent the practices that are the manifestations or observable behaviours resulting from the cultural paradigm. BA leaders can build and foster the service culture through ensuring that these elements align with the values that form the basis for the paradigm. The other elements are applied to the BA Service as follows:

- **Rituals and routines:** the ways in which things are done within the BA Service. These may be the routine processes and procedures, or the specific activities undertaken in particular circumstances. For example, a weekly meeting that follows a set agenda (routine) and always begins with coffee and cake (ritual).

- **Stories:** the tales told about people and events that have been part of the history of the BA Service and help to clarify the values and beliefs. For example, stories about behaviour demonstrated by stakeholders or business analysts that is deemed acceptable or unacceptable.

- **Symbols:** the items that exemplify or reflect meaning beyond the surface representation. For example, a large desk that denotes the importance of a particular stakeholder.

- **Power structures:** the ways in which authority, influence or control is invested in groups or individuals either within the BA Service or the customer community. For example, the automatic allocation of power to a designated role or job title.

- **Organisational structures:** the ways in which management and communication lines are organised and the extent to which decision-making authority is devolved to employees. For example, the application of hierarchical or delayered structures, and centralised or decentralised structures may result in a centralised BA Service that offers its services to the rest of the organisation. This could provide a strong basis for developing a service culture amongst the community of business analysts. The different ways in which a BA Service may be organised and structured are discussed in Chapter 1.

- **Control systems:** the metrics, measurements and reward systems applied within the BA Service. For example, the use of the Balanced Scorecard for each individual business analyst's performance review; the use of surveys to measure and monitor the performance of the BA Service. These are discussed in Chapters 5 and 13.

Figure 11.4 identifies questions to consider when exploring these cultural elements.

BA leaders need to consider these elements and ask themselves what they say about the culture within the BA Service. For example:

- Are there rituals that indicate a lack of engagement with stakeholders? How can these rituals be changed?

- Are the stories that are told representative of a prevailing attitude towards customers or colleagues? If this is critical or dismissive, why is this the case and what might be done to address this?

- Is there an immediate search for a culprit whenever an error occurs, or an issue arises? Alternatively, do the stories told reflect admiration for colleagues?

- Is there a focus on collaborative structures? If not, is this required and how might it be changed?

Figure 11.4 The cultural web applied to the BA Service (adapted from Johnson et al., 2017)

Rituals and routines	What are the routines or rituals of the BA Service? What are the assumptions that underlie the behaviour displayed by the business analysts?
Stories	What stories do the business analysts tell about their business analysis work experiences? Do the stories relate to business analysis failures or successes, conformity or maverick behaviour?
Symbols	Are there any visible symbols relating to the BA Service? Do they denote the status or grade of individual business analysts?
Power structures	Where does the power lie within the BA Service or within stakeholder groups? Where is the BA Service situated within the organisation?
Organisational structures	Is the structure for the BA Service flat or hierarchical? Are there specialist silos or structures that enable the business analysts to work collaboratively?
Control systems	What are the controls deployed within the BA Service? Where there are project issues or delays, is there a focus on blame or reward?

Consideration of these elements helps to uncover where the BA Service culture is out of alignment with the rest of the organisation or the BA leader's beliefs.

Handy's model of organisational cultures

Charles Handy (1993) developed a model setting out four cultures that may be seen within organisations. The key points of each of these cultures are shown in Figure 11.5.

These four cultures are further described in Table 11.1.

Figure 11.5 Summary of Handy's organisational cultures

The power culture	The task culture	The role culture	The person culture
• Central dominant individual • Little bureaucracy • Few rules so swift decisions	• Job or project oriented • Adaptable and flexible • Team work • Enthusiastic, committed individuals	• Roles clearly defined • Power related to position • Roles more important than individuals	• Emphasis on individuals who are 'key players' • Individual expertise is valued • Structure is minimal

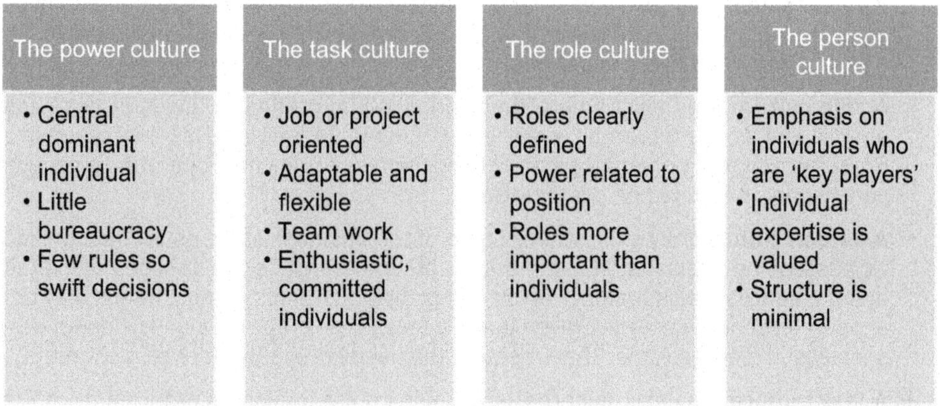

Table 11.1 Handy's organisational cultures

Type of culture	Characteristics
Power culture	• Power is held by a few key people • Power radiates from a central position • There are few absolute rules • Decision making tends to be speedy
Role culture	• Roles and responsibilities are clearly defined • Everyone knows their position within the organisational hierarchy • Rules exist to control behaviour • Decision making can be very slow
Person culture	• People have specialist expertise • The groups of people with the expertise have the power • The specialist groups are more important than the business itself
Task culture	• Teams are set up to solve problems and focus on the task • Each team may consist of different roles and people are expected to work together in order to achieve the task • Power sits with the expertise offered by individuals • Decision making is in line with task objectives

Each of these cultures may be found within a BA Service.

- **A power culture** may exist where the BA leader, and possibly some senior business analysts, hold the power within the BA Service and make decisions and set the rules to govern different situations.

- **A role culture** may exist where there are specific grades or levels of business analyst and a clear hierarchy is present within the BA Service. This may result in a BA Service that is more concerned with position and rules than operating a service culture that is focused on customers.

- **A person culture** may exist where some of the business analysts are recognised as possessing specialist skills and are able to determine the services delivered and the approaches adopted. However, this type of organisational culture may not support a service worldview, given that the focus is on empowering individuals with specialist expertise rather than meeting the needs of the BA Service customers.

- **A task culture** may exist where the focus is on the outcomes required from the task (for example, an iteration or project). This type of organisational culture may be highly relevant to a service culture where the emphasis is on utilising T-shaped skills to deliver a service with a stated value proposition.

To a large extent, how the BA Service operates, and the culture that is adopted, relies upon the values and beliefs of those in leadership positions within the organisation. In some situations, the BA leader may have sufficient authority to influence this; in other cases, there may be a clear organisational culture that imposes rules and drives behaviour. Within some organisations, it is possible for the BA Service to develop a localised climate or a distinct culture that determines how business analysts work with their stakeholders. The local climate and 'nested culture' concepts are discussed later in this chapter.

The definitions of Handy's organisational cultures may be used to analyse the BA Service. The definitions have the potential to offer insights into the way in which different organisational cultures work and the impact these cultures may have on business analysts and the delivery of business analysis services to customers. These insights may also support initiatives to develop a service culture within the BA Service and change behaviour that is unhelpful, inappropriate or unacceptable.

Hofstede's national culture dimensions

The work initially undertaken by Geert Hofstede, and later extended in collaboration with Gert Jan Hofstede and Michael Minkov (2010), has increasing significance for business analysts, as the need for project teams to work with international stakeholders continues to develop and grow. This may be the case whether working in large, medium-size or small organisations; even the smallest of organisations may offer services or products to overseas customers and partners.

The six dimensions identified by Hofstede et al. are:

1. Power distance;
2. Individualism vs. collectivism;

3. Masculinity vs. femininity;

4. Long-term vs. short-term orientation;

5. Uncertainty avoidance;

6. Indulgence vs. restraint.

Each of these dimensions helps the business analyst to better understand how to work with customers as they clarify the origins for behaviours and expectations. Hofstede's cultural dimensions and their application to business analysis are explained below.

- **Power distance:** the extent to which the less powerful members of society accept that power is distributed unequally. An acceptance that power resides in few hands may result in a reluctance to take decisions without deferring to those who hold the power. A high-power distance culture may also require business analysts to ensure that key stakeholders are engaged at all stages. Failing to take account of a power distance culture raises the risk that business analysts assume that ways forward have been agreed when this is not the case, as decisions have not been confirmed by a higher authority.

- **Individualism vs. collectivism:** the extent to which individuals either focus on looking after just themselves and their immediate family or believe that members of a society should look after each other. This is an interesting cultural dimension for business analysts. Within the IS industry, there are many roles and it sometimes seems that they are constantly trying to diminish, rather than support, each other. For example, this may be discerned when advocates of certain approaches or roles criticise their colleagues for using an alternative technique or varying a method. This can result in a culture where those within a particular group develop an internal focus, fail to recognise the broader picture and are more concerned with following a process than achieving the desired outcome.

- **Masculinity vs. femininity:** this dimension is concerned with the extent to which there is a focus on the aggressive pursuit of goals (masculinity) or a focus on consensus and quality of life (femininity). Organisations demonstrate more competitive behaviour at the masculinity end of this dimension and business analysts will need to understand that this behaviour reflects deeply held beliefs and collective values that prioritise the importance of goal achievement. In contrast, the femininity end of this dimension results from shared values that prioritise cooperation and caring.

- **Long-term (pragmatic) vs. short-term (normative) orientation:** the extent to which a society is concerned with long-term perseverance and a focus on the future, or on short-term tradition and norms where there are misgivings and concerns about change. Again, this is a cultural dimension that has implications for the BA Service. For example, a short-term-oriented culture may be reflected in some requirements that are concerned with short-term 'fixes', but may not support other requirements for a future-proofed solution. Business analysts may need to identify the potential implications of a short-term focus and clarify with stakeholders the extent to which this would cause difficulties for the organisation. Alternatively, requirements that are concerned with future business needs may not respect accepted ways of working and may result in resistance to proposed changes.

- **Uncertainty avoidance:** the extent to which members of a society prefer rules as a means of diminishing uncertainty and anxiety. This dimension can create significant issues for business analysts where uncertainty avoidance is the prevailing culture. The BASF (see Chapter 2) identifies early engagement services that focus on situation investigation, problem identification and feasibility assessment. These services often take place within a context where there is ambiguity and the approach to business analysis work relies on business analysts' ability to cope with uncertainty. A culture where rules pertain could also prove difficult when working within an Agile environment, as there may be a tendency to resist adapting the approach and allowing the solution to evolve.

- **Indulgence vs. restraint:** the extent to which a society is concerned with the ability to indulge oneself and have fun or is restrained by the norms and constraints imposed by the society. Indulgence may be perceived in organisations where a culture exists that promotes fun and enables creativity and innovation. The restraint perspective may be observed where there is a tendency to impose governance constraints upon activities and structures. The BA leader should consider how this dimension could apply within the BA Service and the extent to which indulgence and restraint may form part of the service culture.

While Hofstede et al.'s research regarding these six dimensions is concerned with national cultures, it is often the case that the dimensions apply within sectors and organisations. For example, in some industries a culture where there is a short-term orientation with a masculine focus on goals may prevail; in particular sectors, there may be a collectivist culture that has low power distance. These cultural dimensions may also apply at a project or team level. For example, a BA leader may have a perspective that aligns with uncertainty avoidance, even where this is not typical of the organisational culture. In this situation, the BA leader may impose this perspective on the team and expect behaviours that correspond to this view. An understanding of the cultural perspective may not result in a change to the perspective of the BA leader, but it will enable the business analysts to identify where this is likely to conflict with their work and attempt remedial action if possible.

THE BA SERVICE CULTURE

Any leader has to consider the culture that they wish to prevail within their sphere of authority, whether this is across an entire organisation or limited to a particular business area or support function. The frameworks described in this chapter clarify the characteristics that prevail within different cultures and offer insights to help BA leaders foster a service culture.

Applying the cultural frameworks

Figure 11.2 shows how a culture emerges from the beliefs and assumptions held in common by individuals that then lead to shared values held by the group. BA leaders wishing to foster a service culture can influence these shared values by considering the following:

- **The beliefs and values that they hold about the BA Service.** For example, why the BA Service exists, how the services should be delivered, how the business analysts should engage with stakeholders, which services the BA Service should offer.

- **The possible alignment of Handy's organisational cultures and Hofstede's national cultures with the BA leader's beliefs and values.** For example, are there any organisational cultures that would be detrimental to the BA Service? Which of the cultural dimensions defined by Hofstede et al. would support the values of the BA Service?

- **The ways in which the elements in the cultural web would be applied within the BA Service.** The questions shown in Figure 11.4 identify some aspects to be considered regarding the BA Service.

- **The strategies to foster a service culture and ensure that it is embedded within the BA Service.** For example, how the BA leader will communicate with business analysts and guide their behaviour; the ways in which business analysts will be able to contribute to the development of the service culture.

It is not sufficient for BA leaders to consider these aspects in isolation; they also need to demonstrate the values they espouse and adopt the behaviours they wish their business analysts to display. Ultimately, the development of a culture that is focused on understanding the customers and their service requirements is the responsibility of everyone within the BA Service. The aim should be to foster a service culture that is founded on the shared values of all members of the BA Service.

Nested cultures

Some business areas operate a 'culture within a culture' or a 'nested culture'. This occurs where there is an overriding culture within the organisation, but a senior manager has developed an alternative culture within a particular function or business area. Where this is the case, the interplay between the cultures can be a cause of confusion or even conflict.

Nested cultures may be particularly prevalent when working within a multi-national organisation. Where business analysts are working on projects that are to be implemented across several countries, an understanding of Hofstede's national cultures can help to highlight where cultural differences may exist and ensure that working practices are adapted as necessary.

A nested culture may also exist where more than one of Handy's cultures is found within an organisation. For example, Handy's task culture may apply within the change project teams even though they are operating within a broader organisation that has a role culture. The business analysts working within the project teams need to be aware that there are different cultures present to ensure that this doesn't cause difficulties when working with stakeholders.

Nested cultures should be considered when fostering a service culture. For example, the BA Service may operate within an organisation with a dominant culture that is at odds with a service perspective or there may be several cultures present across the organisation, all of which need to be understood. The ways in which the business analysis services are provided or stakeholders are managed may be determined by the prevailing culture. Where several cultures are present, the business analysts may be faced with complex situations and conflicting stakeholder behaviours. The cultural frameworks described earlier in this chapter offer information and insights that can help business analysts to better understand and manage these situations and behaviours.

Climate and culture

The culture of an organisation may have evolved and persisted over years or decades. There have been many cases where projects to 'change the culture' of an organisation have been instigated but these attempts often result in limited success or complete failure.

A more localised view of culture concerns the 'climate' for a team. The 'climate' concerns a team's working environment and making changes at this level may have a greater chance of success than trying to deliver wholescale cultural change.

The climate can have a huge impact on relationships, both within the team and with other stakeholders and, as a result, can improve overall performance. For example, improvements may be seen in how well team members relate and cooperate and how comfortable individuals feel about expressing themselves openly.

The following definition of 'climate' reflects this.

> Climate is the collective current impressions, expectations, and feelings that members of a local work unit have that, in turn, affect their relations with their boss, one another and with other units.
>
> (Michela and Burke, 2000)

The climate is linked to the organisational culture, but relates to a specific team so is 'closer to home'. Elements that effect the team climate include the following:

- perceptions of what is expected of the team;
- feelings about the manager and other team members;
- work standards;
- recognition;
- motivation;
- individual skills and abilities.

These elements are likely to be much easier for BA leaders and individual business analysts to influence and improve upon, while still ensuring that the climate within the BA Service is consistent with the organisational culture. Where the prospect of attempting to change the organisation's culture seems like an unsurmountable challenge, the more realistic aim of changing the climate of the BA Service can seem both empowering and achievable.

The BA Service Charter

A BA Service Charter can help to foster a service culture. This should be done in collaboration with business analysts and should encompass the following factors:

- vision and shared values of the BA Service;
- shared objectives of the business analysts, the BA Service and the organisation;
- how business analysts collaborate with each other and customers;
- what customers can expect from the BA Service;
- expected behaviours from the members of the BA Service;
- agreed ways of working.

Ideally, the BA Service Charter should be a single page and should include visual elements that provide an engaging representation. Figure 11.6 shows an example structure and layout for a BA Service Charter.

The BA Service Charter is a statement of the culture and values that underpin the work of the BA Service. It should be published so that customers and colleagues are aware of its contents. The aim should be for everyone within the BA Service to 'buy-in' to the charter and to demonstrate that this is the case when delivering the business analysis services.

Figure 11.6 Example of a layout for a BA Service Charter

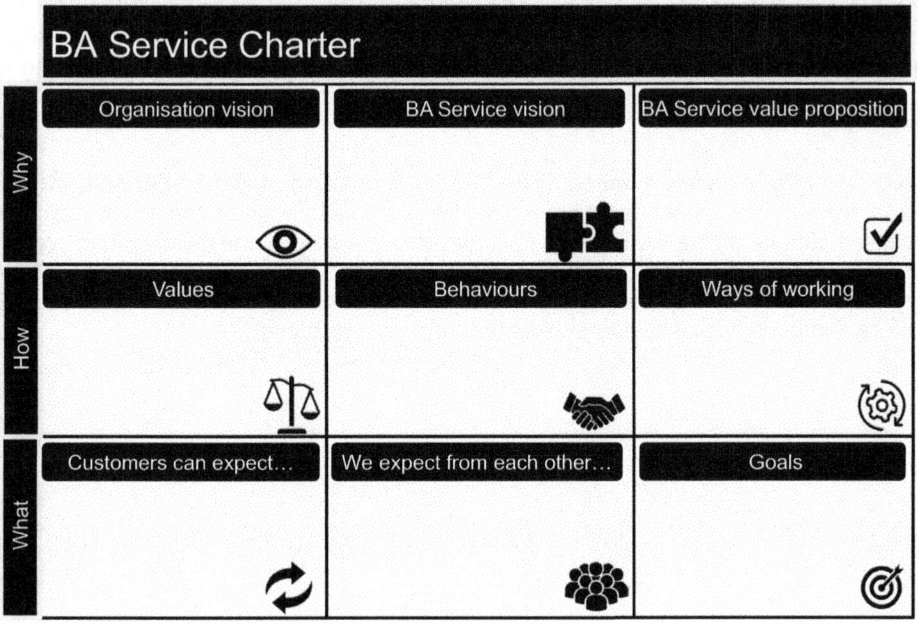

CONCLUSION

The existence of national, organisational, project or team cultures has been the subject of much research. This chapter has discussed several frameworks that describe the types of culture that may be found within organisations. Each of these cultures will have an impact upon performance and behaviour, and these impacts may be positive or detrimental.

The BA leader needs to understand the different types of culture that may exist within organisations and the impacts that emerge from different cultures. This understanding will help them to develop a service culture that is focused on co-creating value with stakeholders. The cultural frameworks also provide a basis for analysing the organisational culture within which a BA Service is required to work and will help to gain insights into the behaviours that result from different cultures.

Business analysts work with a wide variety of stakeholders and may encounter difficulties that originate from unhelpful cultural behaviours. However, there are situations where business analysts may recognise the source of the issues; for example, where there is an unhelpful or, in an extreme case, toxic, culture present, yet they may not have the authority or means to change this. There are often situations where it is not possible to change the organisational culture and attempts to do so can lead to disappointment and wasted efforts.

The CIA model (see Chapter 5) may be applied when evaluating such problematic cultural issues and will help when considering the options available to resolve them. Identifying where it is not possible to control or influence behaviour, and deciding to accept the situation, can be a more productive approach than trying to make changes and failing to do so.

While changing organisational culture is a daunting task that rarely succeeds without a transformational, longer-term approach, it is possible to analyse and adjust the more localised climate of the BA Service. This may prove a helpful measure to improve the attitudes and behaviours of the business analysts when delivering their services. A BA Service Charter may also prove beneficial to establish the characteristics of the desired culture and guide the behaviours expected from business analysts.

12 IMPROVING BA SERVICE QUALITY

INTRODUCTION

Delivering a high-quality BA Service for customers, and committing to continually strive for service improvement, should be high on the agenda for any BA leader. Quality must be considered in all aspects of the BA Service, from the delivery of the business analysis portfolio of services to the day-to-day management of the service. Figure 12.1 shows how different aspects of quality contribute to a high-quality service.

Figure 12.1 The journey towards service quality

This chapter discusses some key aspects of service quality in relation to business analysis. These are:

- a quality-focused culture;
- frameworks for enabling service improvement;
- quality assurance of business analysis outputs.

QUALITY AND IMPROVEMENT CULTURE

The culture of an organisation is often simplified to mean 'the way we do things around here'. Culture can vary hugely between different organisations, and even within a single organisation, but most organisations want to deliver to the best of their ability (a quality culture) and to enhance what they deliver over time (a continual improvement mindset).

Quality culture

The foundation of service improvement is a 'quality culture' amongst those delivering the service. The use of quality improvement methods and tools should become core to the delivery of the service. Quality needs to be core to every aspect of the BA Service, from recruitment through to standards, from production of analysis outputs to training and development, and must operate at both the individual and team level.

Research based on a study of over 60 multi-national corporations, published in the *Harvard Business Review* (Srinivasan and Kurey, 2014) showed that:

> A company with a highly developed culture of quality spends, on average, $350 million less annually fixing mistakes than a company with a poorly developed one.
> (Srinivasan and Kurey, 2014)

The research identified four key areas of action for organisations aiming to improve their quality culture:

- **Maintaining a leadership emphasis on quality:** leaders walk the walk on quality.
- **Ensuring message credibility:** communication about quality should match up with the activity and behaviour people observe.
- **Encouraging peer involvement:** quality is everyone's responsibility.
- **Increasing employee ownership and empowerment:** people can identify issues, suggest improvements and new ideas get implemented.

As business analysis is one of the first areas where mistakes can affect the direction of a project or piece of work, it is critical that quality should feature as a topic in key business analysis processes such as planning business analysis work, business analysis service delivery and lessons learned, and retrospectives.

A quality culture can be enabled by encouraging a 'continual improvement' mindset for the team, and a growth mindset for individual business analysts (see Chapter 5).

Continual improvement mindset

This approach to the BA Service means that all business analysts are encouraged and enabled to identify opportunities to improve the service and the quality of the work. This involves both large and small improvements, which should be subject to appropriate prioritisation and governance. This approach allows meaningful improvement of the BA Service in parallel with the delivery of projects and other commitments.

There are several areas to consider when aiming to achieve continual improvement:

- acceptance that there is always room for improvement; this can require individuals and the organisation to accept criticism, which may be difficult;

- appropriate attention to current ways of working so that improvements are set in context, are against a baseline and unintended consequences are minimised;

- recognition that all business analysts have the responsibility to identify areas for improvement;

- availability of mechanisms to raise, document/discuss and agree improvements;

- presence of appropriate controls to prevent the implementation of conflicting or diverging improvements.

It is important to focus improvement effort on those business analysis activities and outputs that offer the most value to customers and have the potential to eliminate waste, redundancy and errors. The Lean Six Sigma management approach encourages organisations to continually improve by reducing waste (Lean) and detecting and removing errors (Six Sigma). Lean methodology defines eight common types of waste that can exist in a service or process, highlighted by the acronym DOWN-TIME (**D**efects, **O**ver-production, **W**aiting, **N**on-used talent, **T**ransportation, **I**nventory, **M**otion, **E**xtra-processing). Table 12.1 describes the types of waste and how each can be considered in the context of the BA Service.

Table 12.1 The eight types of waste

Type of waste	Description	Considerations for avoiding waste in business analysis
Defects	Effort expanded for rework and to correct errors	• Engage the right stakeholders • Validate assumptions. Consider all options during feasibility analysis • Use appropriate reviews and checklists • Errors in business analysis deliverables can be eliminated much more easily and cheaply than errors that are allowed to persist into subsequent project or SDLC stages
Over-production	Producing more than is needed, or before it is needed	• Adopt a tailored business analysis approach that uses the principles of 'just enough' and 'just in time' • Encourage customers to want the analysis deliverables planned through use of work packages and product descriptions

(Continued)

Table 12.1 (Continued)

Type of waste	Description	Considerations for avoiding waste in business analysis
Waiting	Time wasted waiting for people to act or processes to complete	• Plan parallel business analysis activities during review and approval cycles where potential for waiting is increased • Understand the business analyst utilisation profile on projects and use troughs in project activity as an opportunity to do other work, such as BA Service improvement tasks, personal development, supporting other projects or management and peer reviews • Consider how change/system implementation is constrained by business dates (end of year processes, peak demand, change freeze periods, etc.) • Consider how late delivery of business analysis outputs may cause others to wait • Understand where analysis work has dependencies on other projects and other people
Non-used talent	Underutilising peoples' skills or knowledge	• Provide opportunities for business analysts to share knowledge and experience between projects and from other roles/ organisations (see also the learning BA Service in Chapter 4) • Use learning action plans to embed new learning • Ensure that the work allocation process includes opportunities to understand who has relevant skills and knowledge
Transportation	Unnecessary movement of products or deliverables	• This can be considered in terms of governance and approvals. Be clear on which decisions and deliverables need to be approved by which stakeholders/groups
Inventory	Having 'stock' that is not being used	• Ensure that business analysts are aware of templates, re-usable content (e.g. bank of non-functional requirements). Create templates on an as-needed basis; manage the volume of templates being produced and monitor usage • Provide opportunities to share work to avoid duplication of analysis effort

(Continued)

Table 12.1 (Continued)

Type of waste	Description	Considerations for avoiding waste in business analysis
Motion	Unnecessary movement of people	• Explore opportunities to co-locate business analysts with project or development teams • Ensure that meetings and workshops are attended only by the relevant people • Use collaboration tools and technology
Extra-processing	Over-processing or higher quality than is needed	• Ensure that all review effort is adding value, avoid gold-plating and work towards agreed quality criteria

CONTINUAL SERVICE IMPROVEMENT (CSI)

CSI is an approach to identifying and implementing opportunities to make services better, and to assess and measure the impacts of these improvements over time. The core concept of continual service improvement stems from research and models of quality devised by W. E. Deming. CSI for business analysis means understanding the baseline level of BA Service maturity, identifying improvements and devising a plan to carry out the improvements that have the most impact for customers. Suitable models and approaches for assessing and improving the BA Service are described in this section.

There are several models that can help to evaluate the maturity of the BA Service, two of which are the BA Maturity Model and the Capability Maturity Model Integration (extended by the business analysis version). We will start this section by examining these.

BA Maturity Model

The practice of business analysis and the role of the BA have developed over several decades; one of the earliest references to business analysis as a formal discipline was in 1986 (Jakob, 1986). Since then, it has been possible to track the development of business analysis from its original focus on system improvement to the wider and more holistic discipline defined in the BA Service Framework (see Chapter 2).

This trajectory is represented in the Business Analysis Maturity Model (BAMM), shown in Figure 12.2. The BAMM identifies three levels of business analysis work through consideration of two axes:

- **Scope:** the extent to which the scope of the assignment or project has been defined. This ranges from a narrow, well-defined and thus highly constrained scope to a broader but therefore more ambiguous, unclear scope.
- **Authority:** the extent to which a business analyst can challenge and recommend changes with regard to an assignment or project. This ranges from limited authority to extensive authority.

Figure 12.2 The Business Analysis Maturity Model (reproduced with permission of AssistKD)

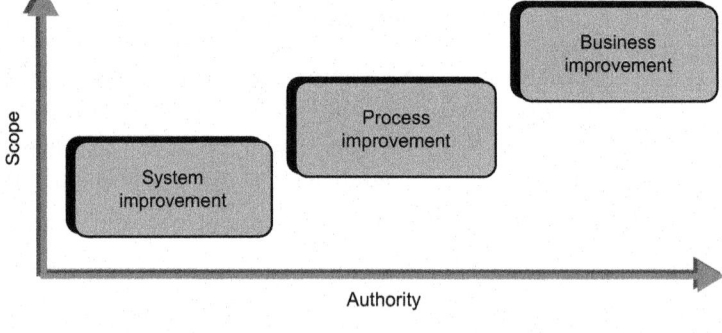

The consideration of these axes results in three, overlapping, levels of business analysis work. The movement from one level to the next is as a result of a progressive reduction in scope definition/constraint and an increase in the business analyst's authority. These three levels are described in Table 12.2.

Table 12.2 Description of the BAMM levels

BAMM level	Level description
System improvement	Clear scope that constrains the business analysis work; business analysts have limited authority
	The business analysis work at the system improvement level is concerned with the definition of requirements for an IT project where the scope is clearly defined. The business analyst may challenge the need for certain stated requirements and is responsible for evaluating the feasibility of the requirements and ensuring alignment with organisational objectives. However, their authority is restricted by the defined scope of the project and the responsibilities of their role
Process improvement	Scope is not entirely defined, particularly with regard to cross-functional business needs; business analysts have some authority
	Business analysis work at the process improvement level is concerned with a holistic view, as business analysts are not constrained to focus solely on the requirements for an IS project. Instead, they may take a view outside the project, possibly across an entire change programme, to ensure that all POPIT™ model elements have been considered. One of the key aspects of this work is the redesign of the business processes. This requires business analysts to take a cross-functional view of the organisation and the additional impacts relating to an IT project

(Continued)

Table 12.2 (Continued)

BAMM level	Level description
Business improvement	Scope is deliberately ambiguous; business analysts have significant authority
	Business analysis work at the business improvement level is concerned with defining the scope of a business change programme or project; while the scope is likely to include an IT project, this is not necessarily the case. The ambiguity will require business analysts to deploy a range of relevant techniques to understand the situation and to identify the root causes of problems that are to be addressed. The identification and evaluation of options to deal with the business situation is also a key part of business analysts' work at this level. Essentially, business analysts will focus on achieving beneficial business outcomes and ensure that any investment funds are spent wisely

The level of maturity of a BA Service in respect to scope and authority is influenced by the factors described in Chapter 1, including its position within the organisation and the structures in place.

The Capability Maturity Model Integration (CMMI)

The CMMI,[1] an overview of which is shown in Figure 12.3, provides an alternative framework for evaluating maturity. Rather than considering the different levels based upon an assessment of scope definition and authority, the CMMI considers the approach to the work and, in particular, the extent of standardisation, measurement and management.

Figure 12.3 Overview of the Capability Maturity Model Integration

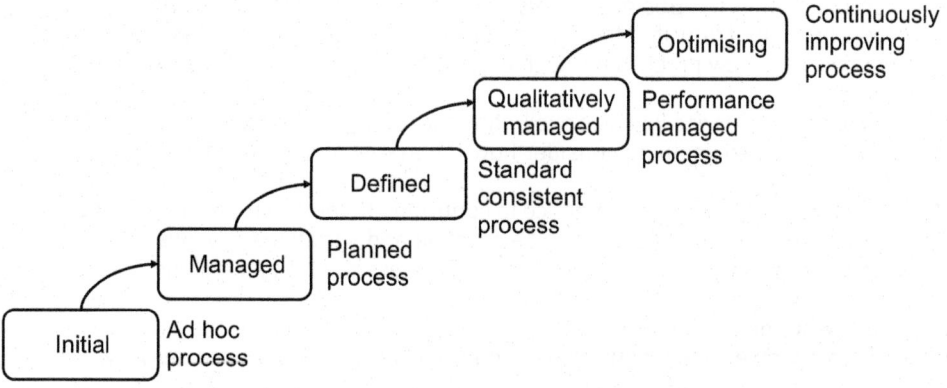

---

1   Developed by the Software Engineering Institute, Carnegie Mellon University.

The CMMI can be applied to the BAMM and thereby provide further insights into the analysis of business analysis maturity. For example, where an organisation is in the early stages of development for its BA Community of Practice, the business analysts may be employed solely on requirements definition work but there may be well-defined standards for this work that are consistently applied. Therefore, the BAMM level 1 work (system improvement) within the BA Service would be at CMMI level 3. Within the same BA Service, it is possible that the BAMM level 2 work (process improvement) is not as well defined, so is at CMMI level 2, and the business analysts conducting BAMM level 3 work (business improvement) are in the initial stages of developing their processes and standards, so are at CMMI level 1.

Paul, Cadle and Yeates (2014) also defined a customised version of CMMI that helps evaluate the maturity of the business analysis practice. This is shown in Figure 12.4.

Figure 12.4 The CMMI adapted for a BA Service

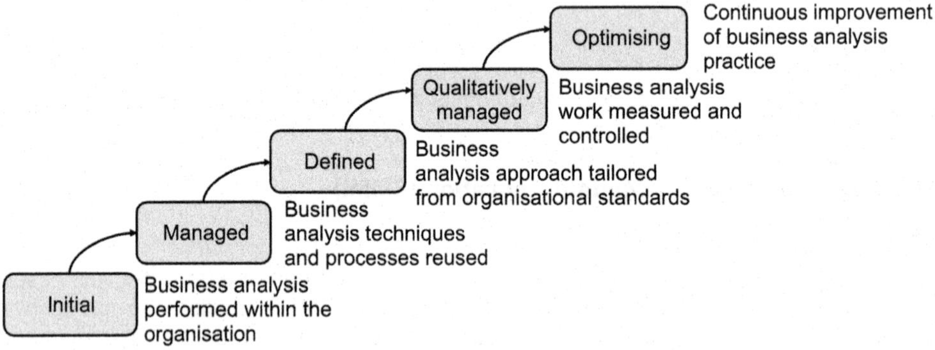

Optimising — Continuous improvement of business analysis practice

Qualitatively managed — Business analysis work measured and controlled

Defined — Business analysis approach tailored from organisational standards

Managed — Business analysis techniques and processes reused

Initial — Business analysis performed within the organisation

The BA Service Assessment

The combination of the Business Analysis Maturity Model, the BA Service Framework and the Capability Maturity Model Integration provides a basis for assessing the BA Service. The overview process for such an assessment is shown in Figure 12.5.

Assessing the BA Service involves evaluating the level of maturity for each aspect of the BA Service. It is also useful to consider how the assessment criteria will be evidenced.

Allowing all members of the BA Service to contribute to the service assessment process permits a common understanding to be reached and variations in views and practices to be debated. Common reactions to a service assessment might include feeling:

- **Overwhelmed:** the volume of improvement work identified by the assessment may seem unachievable alongside existing priorities and BA Service delivery.

- **Disheartened:** a great deal of work and effort may have been invested in service improvement, but the service assessment appears to show little improvement and considerable future effort is still required.

- **Motivated:** the assessment brings clarity and direction to the improvements that could be made to improve the overall service.

It is useful to reflect on the feelings evoked by the outcome of the assessment and consider questions such as:

- Are the target levels realistic?
- What is driving the target levels?
- Has the assessment been overly critical or overly optimistic?

Figure 12.5 Process for assessing the BA Service

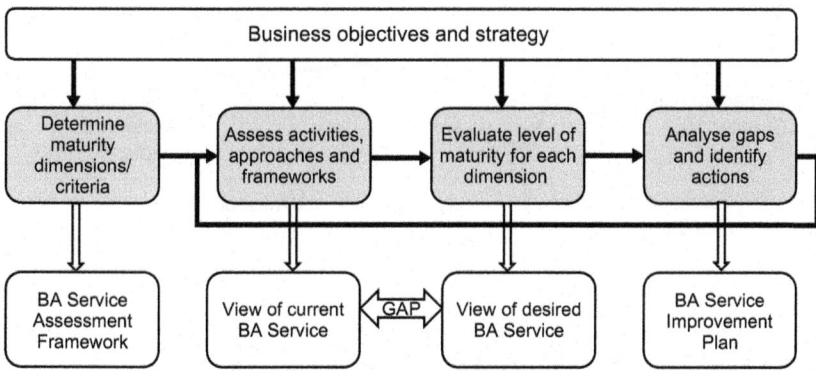

The dimensions and CMMI levels to be considered when assessing a BA Service are shown in Figure 12.6. Each of the dimensions of the BA Service are considered against the maturity levels, and the appropriate target level and current level are plotted for each dimension. The areas of the BA Service that have the most significant gap between the current and target levels may indicate areas to prioritise improvement activity.

The results of the service assessment can also be represented as a grid, with service dimensions shown against CMMI levels and with both current level and target level indicated, as shown in Figure 12.7. Both these examples show that it may not be possible or even desirable to achieve a single CMMI level for the whole BA Service, and the identified target state will depend on the needs and priorities of the Service and its customers. The 'gap' between current and target states is addressed via activities in the Service Improvement Plan.

Figure 12.7 could be extended to include dates, such as assessment dates for current assessment, and planned dates by which target states could be achieved, and therefore represent a high-level plan. The selection of the appropriate visual representation of the service assessment results will depend on the purpose and audience.

Figure 12.6 Example of BA Service Assessment Framework

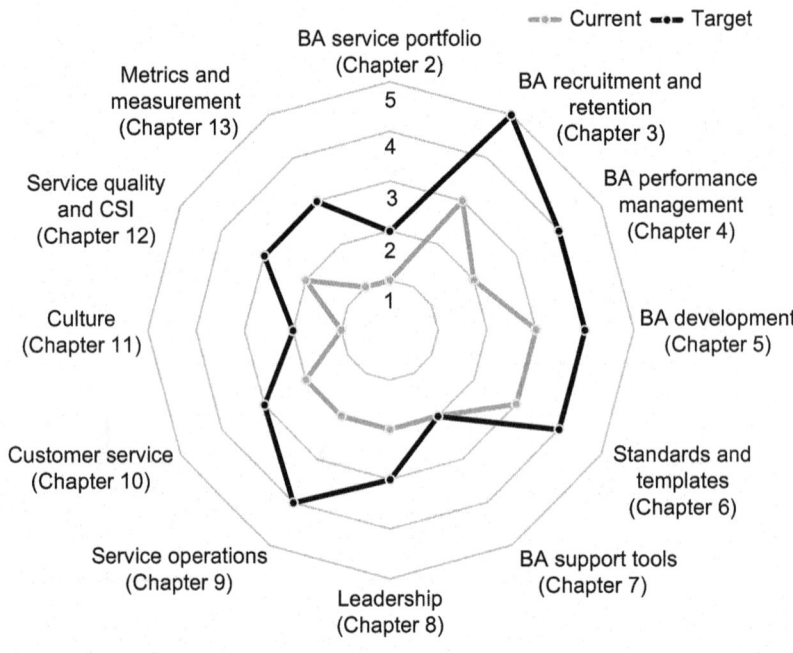

Figure 12.7 Example of BA Service Assessment Grid

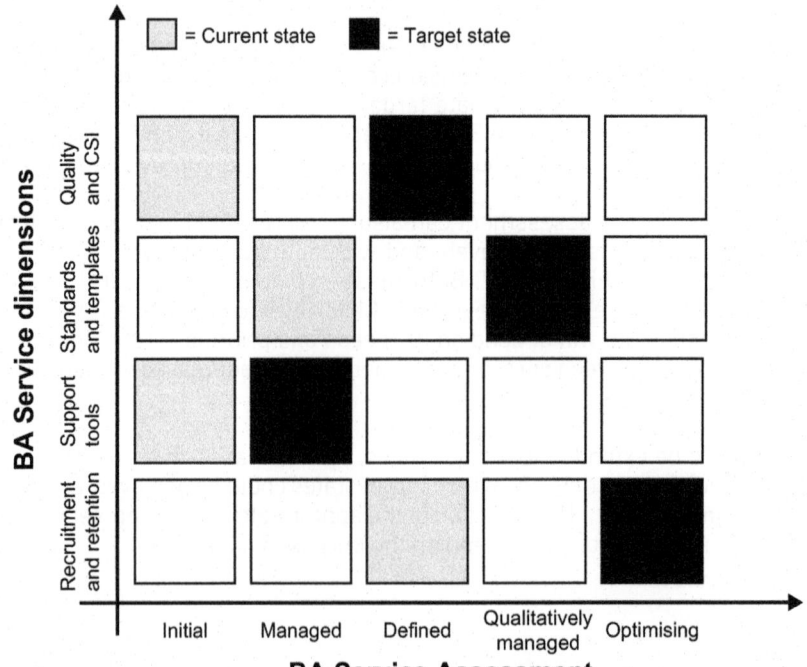

BA Service Improvement Plan

A Service Improvement Plan (SIP), discussed also in Appendix 12, shows the activities required to improve the quality and performance of the service and should focus on the areas of relative weakness highlighted when assessing the BA Service. The process of creating a SIP involves asking questions such as:

- What are the real CSFs for the service?
- What are the highest priority improvement areas?
- How do these align to organisation strategy?
- Is there agreement on priority?
- What are the options for improvement?
- Which activities will have the most impact?
- Who will benefit?
- Who will do them?
- When is this needed/When can this be achieved?
- How will progress be measured? What should KPIs be?

Progress towards the SIP can be shown visually using a milestone chart or a Kanban approach (covered later in this chapter). The aim of the plan is to create a coherent set of improvements providing a clear road map for the ongoing development of the service. Without this, the service may lose sight of why specific improvements are required and continue to 'tinker' with processes and metrics with no specific drivers or direction. It is always useful to consider 'Why are we planning to make this change/improvement and what will the service be able to achieve in future if this improvement is successful?' If there is no clear answer to this question, it is important to revisit the vision and goals of the BA Service before allowing further 'improvement' activity to continue.

BA Service Road Map

Creating a Service Road Map is an excellent way to engage with stakeholders, including business analysts, by visually representing progress towards the service objectives. It particularly focuses on new features and capabilities of the service.

> A roadmap is a plan that shows how a product or service is likely to develop over time.
>
> Gov.uk Digital Service Standard, 2017

A road map should be:

- **aligned:** it moves the service towards the vision and objectives. Every item on the road map should have a strategic justification;
- **clear:** easily understood with an appropriate level of detail;

- **maintained:** developed and updated regularly to reflect progress and changes in priority;

- **transparent:** available to anyone who has interest in the BA Service.

The road map shows a number of key themes or areas that the service needs to focus on, and time periods that are sufficient to show progress; this will vary between organisations and could be weeks, months, quarters or years. The road map must also be informed by the business case for the BA Service (see Chapter 2), so that the costs, benefits and potential return on investment into the BA Service are understood and agreed.

Figure 12.8 Example of BA Service Road Map

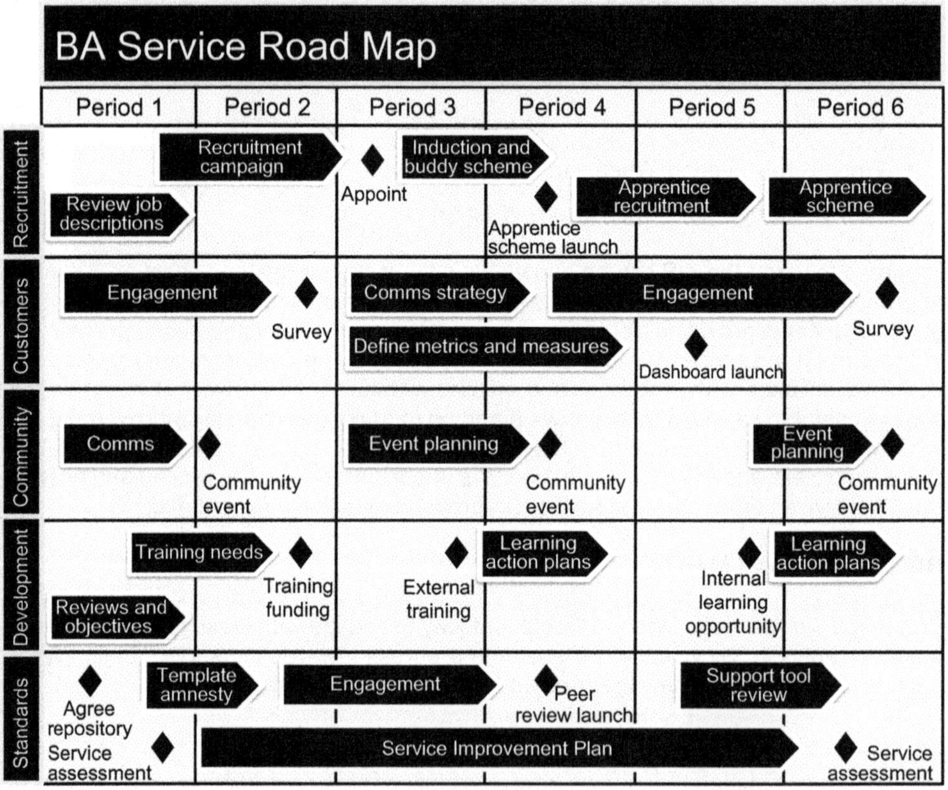

In the example shown in Figure 12.8, the road map shows activities and milestones that work towards six service objectives (shown in Table 12.3). Seeing the entirety of the service development work in this way allows BA leaders to ask questions such as:

- Does this order make sense and address priorities?

- When will the road map be reviewed to ensure it reflects reality and current priorities?

- Is there enough business analyst and management capacity to meet this?

- What are the impacts on customers?
- Are initiatives staggered appropriately?
- What level of change is being introduced? Is this manageable?
- Do the timings consider business peaks and troughs and holiday periods?

It can be discouraging to realise that an exciting improvement or initiative cannot start for many months, but it is more important for the BA Service to have a realistic road map and make progress towards it than to set a timeline than cannot be delivered.

Table 12.3 Example BA Service objectives mapped to road map targets

Area	Objective	Target
Recruitment	1. Increase capacity of BA Service	BA recruitment in period 2
	2. Introduce pipeline approach	Introduce business analyst apprenticeship scheme period 4
Customers	3. Improve customer satisfaction	Introduce customer survey period 2
		Implement BA Service Dashboard period 5
Community	4. Improve BA collaboration	Hold regular community events (starting period 2)
Development	5. Invest in development of BAs	Obtain funding for external accredited BA training
		Introduce internal development and knowledge-sharing opportunities
Standards	6. Standardise BA outputs and approach	Review existing templates, standards and processes period 1 and 2
		Engage with the BA community (ongoing)
		Introduce peer-review process period 4
		Carry out support tool review period 5 and 6

QUALITY MANAGEMENT

Quality management considers the standards, processes and activities required to achieve and maintain the desired quality levels for the BA Service. Establishing quality management includes the definition of quality objectives and targets, the communication of quality expectations and the design and deployment of processes that will ensure adherence to the quality management system and the opportunities to identify service improvements. Quality frameworks and principles provide a common language for quality management. Understanding quality cycles allows BA leaders to acknowledge that quality cannot be 'achieved and then forgotten'; quality management is an ongoing process of measuring, improving and learning.

The Deming Cycle

The Deming Cycle (see Figure 12.9) is a framework used for the continuous improvement of products and processes; it consists of four elements: Plan, Do, Study and Act (The Deming Institute, 1993; Sutherland and Canwell, 2004). The cycle starts with the **Plan** step, which involves identifying a goal or targets, formulating an approach and defining success metrics. This is followed by the **Do** step, where the components of the plan are implemented. Implementation activities are followed up with the **Study** step, where outcomes are monitored to assess the plan for signs of progress and success, or problems and areas for improvement. The **Act** step is the fourth stage in the cycle and brings together the learning generated by the entire process, which can be used to adjust the goal, change the approach, and inform future plans. These four steps are then repeated as part of the ongoing cycle of continual learning and improvement.

Figure 12.9 The Deming PDSA Cycle

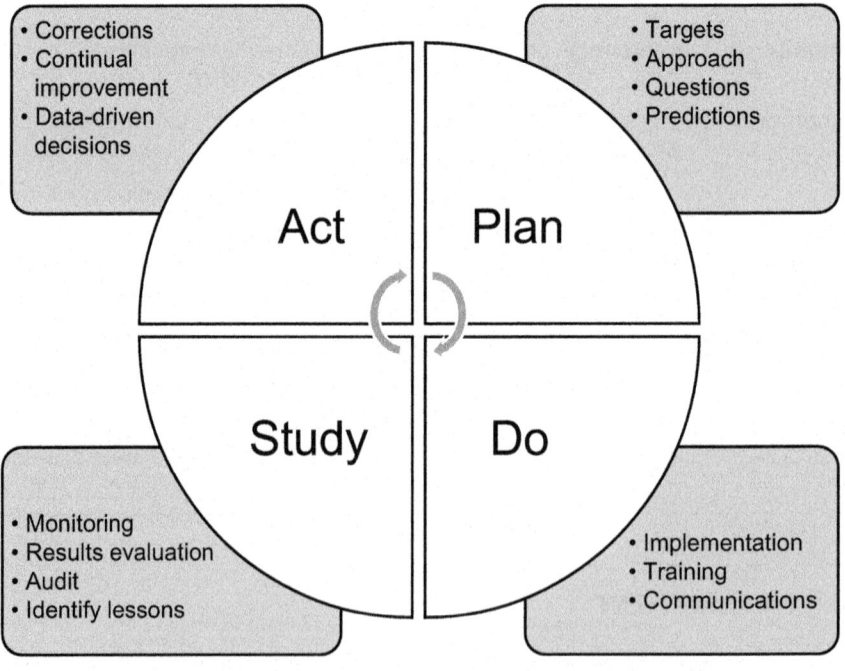

A related framework that is often used in conjunction with Six Sigma projects is known as Define, Measure, Analyse, Improve and Control (DMAIC). This cycle serves as a useful reminder that the driver may be to 'improve', but this must be set in context and there are number of steps that must be taken before the improvement can be made.

BA Quality Management Cycle

The Deming Cycle shown in Figure 12.9 has been expanded and adapted in order to provide a specific process for managing the quality of the BA Service as a whole and the quality of work undertaken by individual business analysts. This extended BA Quality Management Cycle is shown in Figure 12.10 and its elements are described in Table 12.4.

Figure 12.10 The BA Quality Management Cycle

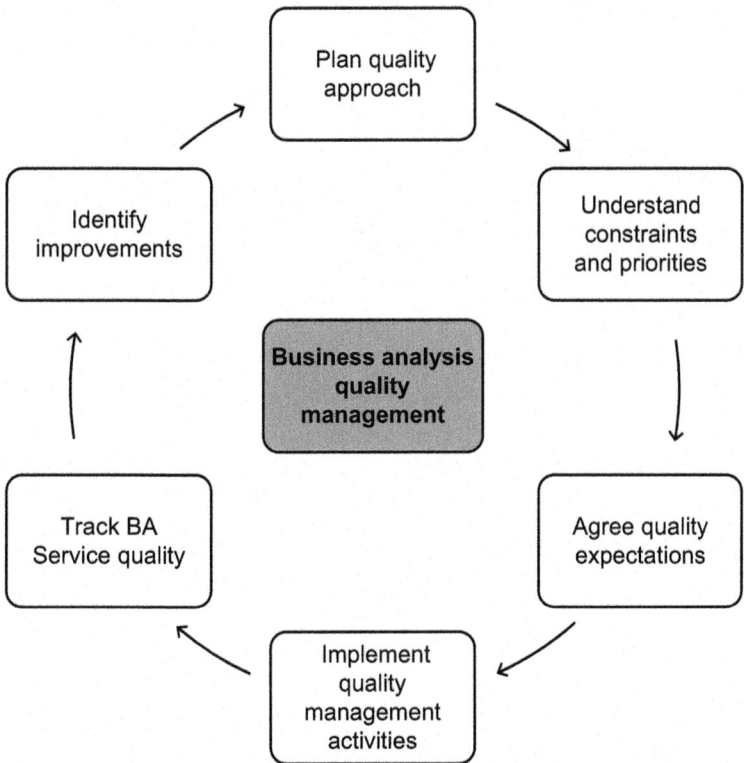

International Organization for Standardization (ISO) quality management principles

ISO[2] has developed a wide range of standards in relation to quality, including the ISO 9000 family.

2   See www.iso.org/iso-9001-quality-management

Table 12.4 Stages in the BA Quality Management Cycle

Stage	Considerations for the quality of the BA Service	Considerations for the quality of an individual business analyst's work
Plan quality approach	• Explore existing approaches to quality, including elsewhere in the organisation (for example, test practices often have well-established quality regimes) • Define the approach; this could be a document, diagram, statement, presentation or set of bullet points • Define the benefits of implementing a quality approach	• Consider existing best practice that is in use by business analysts • Consider the needs of customers
Understand constraints and priorities	• Be realistic about the current situation (e.g. apply SWOT in relation to quality) • Consider capacity and skills available	• Be realistic about the level of quality that can be achieved in the time frame. Understand whether TCQ is the key driver • Consider chunking work into essential and desirable elements and activities
Agree quality expectations	• Define CSFs and, where possible, KPIs and targets • Discuss expectations with business stakeholders and business analysts	• Define work packages with quality criteria • Set objectives
Implement quality management activities	• Communicate processes and activities that will support quality management • Communicate how this process and activities fit with the delivery process and activities	• Communicate roles and responsibilities in relation to quality assurance
Track BA Service quality	• Define metrics and measures • Create reports or dashboard to share findings	• Seek feedback • Use peer review • Apply checklists/quality compliance

(Continued)

Table 12.4 (Continued)

Stage	Considerations for the quality of the BA Service	Considerations for the quality of an individual business analyst's work
Identify improvements	• Invite specific feedback from customers and business analysts • Use root cause analysis on issues raised or targets missed	• Act on feedback • Encourage self-reflection on possible improvements • Set objectives for business analysts • Use buddying or peer review • Build into future work packages • Identify training and development opportunities

The standards provide guidance and tools for companies and organizations who want to ensure that their products and services consistently meet customer's requirements, and that quality is consistently improved.

www.iso.org

ISO provides a set of seven quality principles that underpin the standards, and which are relevant to both the quality of business analysis provided to customers and the importance of the continued improvement of the BA Service. These are set out in Table 12.5.

Table 12.5 ISO quality management principles

Principle	ISO statement	Implications for business analysis
Customer focus	The primary focus of quality management is to meet customer requirements and to strive to exceed customer expectations	Business analysts must seek to represent the needs of all stakeholders on projects and change initiatives The BA Service must be outward looking and ensure that customer expectations are regularly discussed and addressed
Leadership	Leaders at all levels establish unity of purpose and direction and create conditions in which people are engaged in achieving the organization's quality objectives	Business analysis can help to clarify the purpose and direction of the organisation The BA Service must clearly set out its quality strategy and processes

(Continued)

Table 12.5 (Continued)

Principle	ISO statement	Implications for business analysis
Engagement of people	Competent, empowered and engaged people at all levels throughout the organization are essential to enhance its capability to create and deliver value	Business analysts can champion an organisation-wide commitment to quality The BA Service should maintain an ongoing dialogue about quality with its members and customers
Process approach	Consistent and predictable results are achieved more effectively and efficiently when activities are understood and managed as interrelated processes that function as a coherent system	Process analysis and management can underpin an organisations efforts to improve consistency and efficiency The BA Service must act as a role model for this approach within the organisation by establishing consistent and repeatable processes that relate to the delivery of business analysis services
Improvement	Successful organizations have an ongoing focus on improvement	It is the role of business analysis to continue to help improve the organisation, its products, services and processes This principle applies equally to the BA Service itself, which must also focus on improvement
Evidence-based decision making	Decisions based on the analysis and evaluation of data and information are more likely to produce desired results	The quality of business analysis directly impacts the quality of organisational decision making The BA Service must role model this approach within the organisation by using information and analysis to make decisions about the direction and operation of the BA Service
Relationship management	For sustained success, an organisation manages its relationships with interested parties, such as suppliers	Investing in building internal and external relationships is vital to the ongoing quality and success of the BA Service This includes engagement with the business analysis professional community across organisational boundaries, sectors and countries

QUALITY MANAGEMENT TECHNIQUES

Quality management should include both proactive and reactive ways of encouraging and ensuring that appropriate levels of quality are being achieved. Proactive approaches are applied before something is produced and include the provision of adequate training and development (see Chapter 4) and the use of standards and templates (see Chapter 6).

There are numerous reactive techniques that may be used to enable effective quality management and provide quality assurance after something has been produced. This section discusses some of the techniques most useful for business analysis.

The review process

A defined review process is helpful when assessing and improving the quality of business analysis outputs and deliverables. An effective review process will:

- involve the right people;
- be clear on the purpose and expectations of participants;
- have defined stages, time frames and time commitments;
- be clear on the quality standard to be achieved and the criteria for assessing the quality of the deliverables.

Without an agreed review process, it is likely that time will be wasted, effort will be duplicated and people may become frustrated.

The review triangle
The review triangle (Figure 12.11) provides a representation of the different levels and types of review that may be conducted. The aim of reviewing business analysis outputs is to ensure that each output:

- achieves its agreed purpose;
- is appropriate for the audience;
- contains the correct content and is complete;
- is unambiguous;
- meets quality expectations.

There may be several people involved in conducting a quality review, but they do not all have the same review focus. The review triangle shown in Figure 12.11 reflects three levels of review and the differences in the breadth of the review conducted at each level.

1. **Self-review** is the first level of review, which typically identifies the most errors. This should be performed by the BA who created the output and should be conducted as a separate activity from the creation of the output. A review checklist (see also the Quality checklists section later in this chapter) for a specific type of deliverable can provide an invaluable mechanism in support of self-review.

2. **Peer review** is the second level of review and is carried out by another member of the BA Service or potentially by a member of the project team.

3. **Stakeholder review** is the third level of review. This level may require a number of separate iterations; for example, for project team or internal stakeholders, followed by external stakeholders. This level of review should yield the lowest number of errors. By this point, the only errors identified should concern scope and content (as opposed to technical) inaccuracies. Stakeholders should not be required to provide detailed comments; for example, regarding spelling, branding, notational inconsistency, grammatical error or use of language. (However, errors of this nature that are left in the documentation at this stage can undermine the stakeholders' confidence in the quality of the business analysis work.)

Figure 12.11 The review triangle

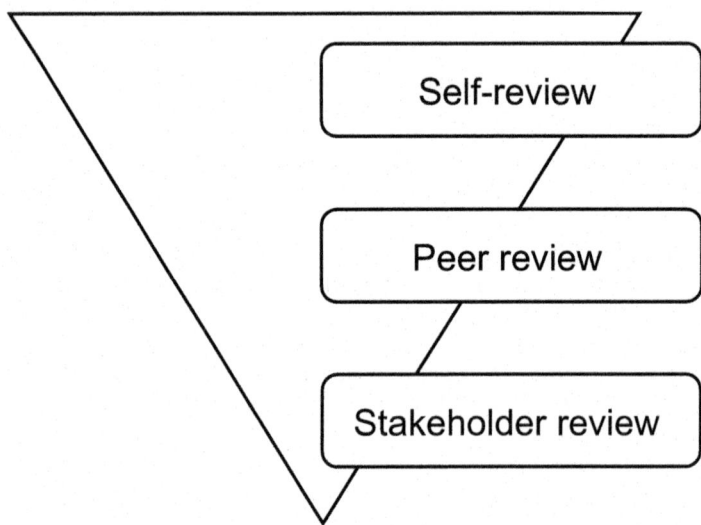

The three levels of review are clarified further in Table 12.6.

Table 12.7 shows an example of typical comments that may emerge from different types of review when reviewing a process model.

Business analysts are often expected to operate at a fast pace and with tight timescales for both the production and review of analysis deliverables. In this case it may be necessary to share outputs for review by stakeholders before/simultaneously with other reviews. In this case it is important to:

- **explain** to reviewers what they are seeing;
- **confirm** the purpose of their review;
- **assure** reviewers that any low-level errors (such as format, typos) will be addressed.

Table 12.6 The three levels of review

Review	Purpose of review	Review comments
Self	**Check:** • Deliverable makes sense as a whole • Gaps or placeholders are addressed • Meets quality criteria defined in work package • Meets quality defined in review checklist(s) **Sense check:** 'Is the quality of this sufficient to share?'	• Spelling and grammar • Consistency of notation/language/formatting
Peer	**Check:** • For small errors • Deliverable uses agreed formats (templates/standards) • Meets stated/agreed purpose • Appropriate for the intended audience • Standards for spelling and punctuation have been adhered to **Sense check:** 'If I can't understand this, how can we expect a stakeholder to?'	• Format errors • Typos (not easily spotted, i.e. word substitutions, transposed acronyms) • Suggest simplifications • Ask for clarifications • Highlight assumptions being made • Highlight possible alternative interpretations
Stakeholder	**Check:** • Content is correct and complete • Language used is correct, in business context • Come to an agreed understanding **Sense check:** 'Is this right?'	• Highlight omissions/gaps • Identify inaccuracies • Challenge content

Some stakeholders may be disconcerted by superficial errors in outputs and this can undermine their ability to trust the content. Other stakeholders may not notice these small errors and may just concentrate on conducting the required level of review. Discussing and agreeing quality expectations and reminding people of the purpose of their review will help to maintain the relationship and ensure the best use of each reviewer's time.

Table 12.7 Example set of review comments

Reviewer	Comments
Self	Sometimes 'admin team' used, sometimes 'support team' – is this the same thing? (find out and update)
	Moved to branded template
	Spelling errors corrected
	Final flows updated to use same notation throughout
	Added guard conditions to all decision flows
	Updated to verb/noun naming convention throughout
Peer	Add another final flow to prevent crossing lines/make it easier to read
	Include annotation to explain decision point logic?
	Shows that A OR B can trigger a notification, is this correct? Should it be it be BOTH A AND B?
	Is 'the notification' defined somewhere?
	Inconsistency of spelling of 'analyze/analyse'
Stakeholder	Task appears in swimlane X, but sometimes team Y performs this task
	Task Z can also trigger a notification to the customer
	Is business process D covered by another diagram?

Quality checklists

The purpose of a checklist is to act as a reminder when creating different outputs and to allow business analysts to review their own work objectively, or to assist in peer review. They remove personal preference and interpretation and move the BA Service towards consistent outputs, no matter who created the output.

Checklists are generally a simple way of ensuring quality. However, because they are simple to design and implement, more experienced practitioners sometimes assume they do not require them. On the contrary, research across industries as diverse as aviation, manufacturing and medicine has shown that a checklist applied at the right time can support those with even the highest levels of training and experience (Gawande, 2011).

Table 12.8 shows an example checklist for several business analysis deliverables. Checklists should not be too detailed and do not replace the need for standards, templates and appropriate training. Checklists should be updated regularly to reflect recurring issues identified during peer and stakeholder reviews.

Table 12.8 Example checklists for reviewing business analysis deliverables

Deliverable	Example checklist content
Documents	• Use of templates, branding, style guide
	• Date, page numbers, author
	• Use of standard sections: purpose, audience, review and approvals, executive summary for longer documents
	• Strong ending: next steps or recommendations clearly articulated
	• Spelling and grammar checks
	• Expand acronyms on first use and include in glossary
	• Language is appropriate to the audience (examples of words to use/not use)
	• File naming conventions and version control adhered to
Process models	• Agreed notation adhered to
	• Process flow is left to right
	• Only one trigger/start point
	• At least one target/end point
	• Activity naming convention: verb/noun
	• Use of colour is justifiable and explained
	• Layout is optimised for readability (crossing lines minimised)
	• Spelling and grammar checks
	• Appropriate documentation completed to support the model
	• Process model is cross-referenced with data model
	• Consistent naming of conventions across models (e.g. actors, entities and swimlanes that represent the same concept)
	• File naming conventions and version control adhered to
Data models	Agreed notation adhered to
	Data model is cross-referenced with process model
	Consistent naming of conventions across models (e.g. actors, entities and swimlanes that represent the same concept)
	Data definitions/data dictionary created to support the model
	Entities named as singular, not plural
	Entity naming convention: camel case
	File naming conventions and version control adhered to

(Continued)

Table 12.8 (Continued)

Deliverable	Example checklist content
Textual requirements	• Use of standard characteristics: numbering, name, description, source, owner, author, type, priority, acceptance criteria, rationale
	• Acceptance criteria are not simply a restatement of requirement
	• Acceptance criteria are consistent with requirements
	• No ambiguous lists ('including, but not limited to...')
	• Use of 'For example', 'e.g.' and 'i.e.' scrutinised
	• Use of 'and'/'or' within a requirement scrutinised
	• Relevant non-functional and standard requirements present
	• Opportunities for re-use of requirements/consistency with other projects explored
	• Life cycle of data, Create, Read, Update, Delete (CRUD) is covered in requirements
	• File naming conventions and version control adhered to
Use cases	• Use case diagram and description complete
	• Use case naming convention: verb/noun
	• When use case steps/alternative paths are complex, express as a process model
	• Use case is 'pitched' at the expected level of detail (e.g. summary/ user-goal/sub-function)
	• Actor location convention: primary (left), secondary (right)
	• Use of 'includes' and 'extends' scrutinised
	• Use of 'actor inheritance' is scrutinised
	• File naming conventions and version control adhered to
User stories	• Agreed format adhered to (e.g. stories are expressed in the format 'As a... I want to... So that...')
	• Story title describes an activity
	• Minimum and maximum word limits adhered to
	• Role is not 'user' or 'end user'
	• Benefit/rationale is not simply a restatement of the feature but a direct outcome of the story
	• Roles are defined in supporting documentation
	• Stories are a vertical slice of the system (e.g. includes both changes to user interface and back end to deliver the functionality)
	• Acceptance criteria meet agreed format and are defined as a list of scenarios with a clear pass/fail result
	• Solutions not suggested

Review mechanisms

There are several approaches that can be used by stakeholders to review business analysis deliverables. It is important to consider different factors in determining the right approach, such as the nature of the deliverable, the number and location of the stakeholders, the risk of non-review or limited review, and the timescales available.

Walk-through   The business analyst walks the reviewers through the output in a workshop, describing how the information was obtained, why it has been presented in this format and what it shows. provides the opportunity for them to ask questions or make comments. There is no expectation that a deliverable has been looked at in advance of the workshop.

This process may lead to updating the deliverable. A workshop can require a significant investment of time and may be used to acquire input from specific stakeholders. This approach is useful for gathering immediate feedback but is unlikely to deliver a 'deep' review.

Written review   Where it is not possible to gather stakeholders together (either face to face or using technology), or the priority of the review is relatively low, asking for written review comments is a suitable review approach. There are various technology-enabled approaches available to support this type of review including:

- updates/tracked changes to a shared version of the review item;
- updates/tracked changes to multiple versions of the review item;
- comments collated separately to the review item, via email or a review record.

It is important to consider the balance between allowing reviewers to use their preferred method of review and the overhead and potential risk for the business analyst who is collating their responses. Before distributing a deliverable for review, the business analyst should consider:

- What is the best approach? Is that approach likely to be adhered to?
- How experienced are the reviewers in the review process?
- Are the purpose of the review, the expectations of reviewers and the required time frames clearly articulated?
- Is it necessary for reviewers to build on or respond to each other's comments and, if so, how will they do this?
- Do reviewers expect or require responses to comments?

When the volume or complexity of comments received exceeds what was expected, this may point to the need for a review meeting. Equally, if very few comments are received, particularly when more have been expected, this may suggest that the mechanism (or time frame) was unworkable for reviewers.

Review meeting   The deliverable to be reviewed is shared in advance of an arranged meeting, and there is an expectation that comments and queries will be submitted and collated before the meeting. The meeting is used to address significant comments and agree corresponding updates. This approach is particularly valuable if stakeholders have provided conflicting comments.

Review summary   Senior stakeholders who are asked to approve key deliverables ultimately need assurance that an appropriate level of quality assurance and review has taken place. The completion of a formal review process that has included a peer and stakeholder review is a more compelling case for approval than suggesting that they also need to conduct a detailed review. The creation of a review summary is helpful to senior stakeholders; this sets out who has reviewed the deliverable, when the review took place, the main comments that were made, any quality controls such as checklists that have been applied and the actions taken to address the comments. It is also helpful to highlight any questions that remain to be decided by the senior stakeholder or group, such as issues related to scope or business strategy.

Kanban

The concept of Kanban originated from the Total Quality Management (TQM) approach developed at Toyota in Japan. It creates a visual representation that allows monitoring and limitation of work in progress, prevents build-up of excess inventory (see Table 12.1) and encourages a just-in-time (JIT) approach.

Figure 12.12 shows the three columns of the Kanban Board: 'To do', 'In progress' and 'Done'. Items in the 'To do' column are derived from an agreed backlog of potential work items. However, not everything from the backlog is represented – only items for which

Figure 12.12 Structure of a Kanban Board

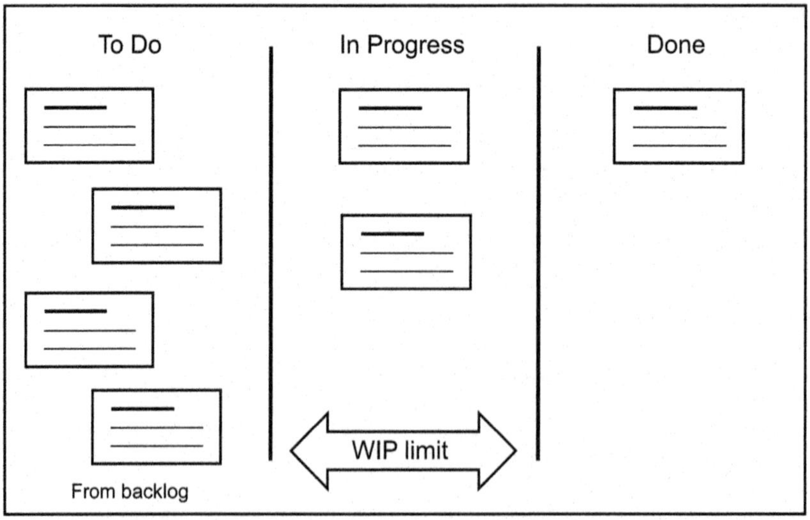

there is now (or in the near future) a work commitment should be entered onto the Kanban Board.

The aims of Kanban are to ensure that the work:

- is understood and agreed (transparent);
- meets agreed quality;
- in-progress limits are adhered to;
- flows through the columns.

Quality and acceptance criteria must be defined against which work items are assessed when deciding whether or not to move them from one column to the next. This ensures that work only starts on a particular item when there is clarity on what needs to be achieved and work is only considered complete ('Done') when it meets the defined quality criteria.

Where work remains 'In progress' for an extended period, this may indicate that the work has not been broken down into sensible, achievable chunks, or that barriers may be impeding progress towards meeting the agreed quality. These issues should be investigated and addressed in order to support the achievement of the quality criteria. Having too many items 'In progress' has been shown to impact efficiency and productivity (Sjøberg, 2018), so applying a limit on the amount of work in progress (WIP) encourages focus and flow.

Having WIP limits reduces time and effort wasted due to:

- context switching;
- excess meetings;
- working on lower priority deliverables;
- miscommunication;
- rework;
- duplicate effort;
- missed deadlines.

While business analysts may be most familiar with the use of the Kanban system to underpin product development, it can be used as a physical or virtual workload management tool for the service improvement activities identified for the BA Service. An example Kanban for suggested BA Service improvement activities is shown in Figure 12.13.

Using this approach, business analysts can see what service improvement activities are coming up, and therefore what they may be able to get involved in if capacity allows. This approach also shows that progress towards service improvement is being made.

Figure 12.13 Example Kanban Board for BA Service improvement activities

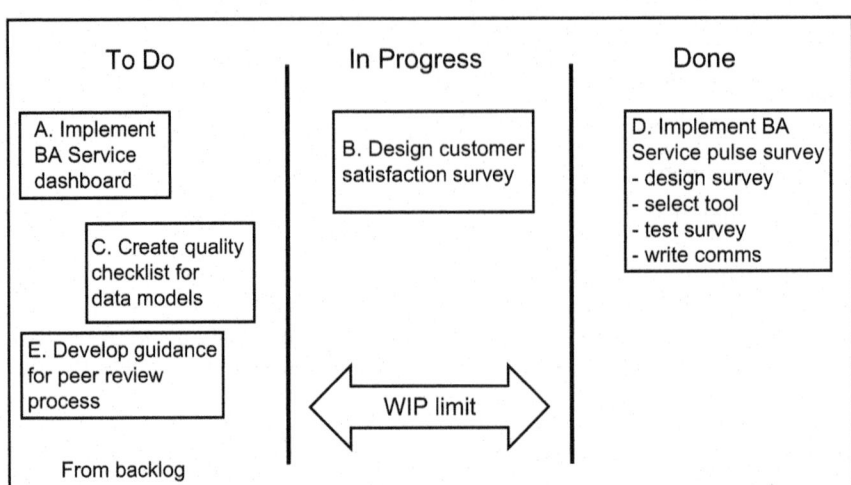

CONCLUSION

Delivering a high-quality BA Service will only happen through design and continued effort, and this requires a quality culture and a continual improvement mindset. It is the responsibility of every member of the BA Service to contribute to the development of service quality.

The provision of processes and approaches to assess the quality of business analysis deliverables will help to ensure that the artefacts produced by business analysts will be fit for purpose and will offer value to customers.

The maturity of the BA Service can be assessed, and potential areas for service improvement identified and managed, through use of approaches such as the BA Maturity Model, the BA Service Assessment, the BA Service Improvement Plan and the BA Service Road Map.

Various frameworks exist that help to improve service quality, including the Deming Cycle and the ISO quality management principles. Ongoing quality management, which encompasses formal processes and techniques, is needed to ensure that the BA Service maintains a focus on service quality.

CASE STUDY 8: INSTILLING A QUALITY FOCUS TO ENABLE BUSINESS ANALYSTS TO SUCCEED AND THRIVE

Charlie Payne, National Grid

Charlie Payne is a BA manager for a business area within the National Grid. He is also a regular presenter at business analysis events and the BA Conference Europe.

Charlie believes in having a clear vision and set of values for the BA team. He asks questions such as, 'How do we know that we are offering quality?' He doesn't believe in micro-managing his staff but in enabling them to succeed when performing their business analysis work. He is focused on achieving the required outcomes and answering the question, 'Why do we do what we do?'

His approach to measuring performance and improving the quality of business analysis work involves a combination of formal and informal mechanisms; for example, the IIBA Competency model has been used in workshops and discussions as a basis for exploring where the team has strengths and where there are gaps. Charlie believes in listening and understanding – whether working with customers or developing the BA team.

Charlie is very focused on the customer perspective and expects his business analysts to consider the customer view. One of the key questions from this perspective is: 'How does a customer know that the business analysts know what to do?' To address this question, he has instigated a new task that the business analysts need to work through when starting a project. This involves defining the approach that will be taken to the work and communicating with the customers to make sure that they understand the approach. At a later stage, Charlie contacts the customers to ask if they have signed up to the proposed approach and whether the approach was communicated effectively by the BA. He is keen that the BAs need to understand their stakeholders and think about what they need from the analysis outputs presented to them. 'Doing the right thing' and making sure that this has been thought through is very important.

The major challenge faced regarding performance measurement and quality improvement involves moving from non-measurement to measurement. Charlie feels that it is important to get to the point where people want performance and quality measurement rather than feeling that it has been imposed on them. He wants his team to embrace continuous improvement and feels that he needs to ensure that they are ready for this. He does this through co-creating a high-performance context with the BAs in the team.

Addressing the quality challenge has been accomplished by applying a formal process for working with the team. Providing time and space to discuss how performance measurement and quality might work is just one aspect. The other, more informal approach involves listening, supporting and coaching the team members. Charlie uses the analogy of an American football blindside tackler who protects the 'guys with the ball'. He sees his role as Chief Cheerleader, looking after the team members and instilling them with the confidence to do the work, knowing that he 'has their back'.

Charlie's BA team want to perform and want to offer great quality work. He wants to give them the ability to step up and succeed as BAs – or if business analysis doesn't suit them, to move into another role. He is currently trialling an approach whereby customers are asked review questions based on the IIBA Competency model:

1. How accurately has the BA captured the information for you to understand, review and validate?
2. How usable is the work that the BA has provided?

3. How effective is the format and presentation of the work?

4. How satisfied are you with how the BA communicates with you?

The BAs can ask these questions of their customers when they want. The idea is to learn and adapt, improving quality as they go, and to be the best BA they can be.

The key lessons are to be clear about what the team is trying to achieve, understand the purpose of the work (Simon Sinek's 'start with why') and know where you are going. Having a focus on the outcome is important, as this helps to pursue continuous improvement. Charlie believes in listening to customers 'relentlessly' and wants them to say, 'we are so glad we have your BAs here'. He also wants colleagues such as project managers to state how valuable the BAs are to the projects.

Charlie recognises that BAs work in the 'wicked mess' where there are lots of different people and multiple perspectives. The BAs have to bring those perspectives together. So, it is challenging work, but, with the right support and attitude, he intends to help the BAs in the team to succeed and thrive.

13 MEASURING THE PERFORMANCE OF THE BA SERVICE

INTRODUCTION

How do we know if we are delivering a good service? Service improvement is only possible if performance levels are monitored and understood. Performance can be evaluated in a variety of ways such as financial effectiveness and customer satisfaction. There is a range of areas that can be used to quantify the performance of a BA Service.

This chapter covers key topics relating the measurement of BA Service performance including:

- benefits and drivers for measurements (why measure);
- understanding service priorities (what to measure);
- sources and types of measurement (how to measure).

THE IMPORTANCE OF METRICS AND MEASUREMENT

There are two main reasons for creating meaningful metrics and measures for the BA Service. The first is to drive development and improvement; measurement is the only way to gauge performance and turn strategy into reality (see Figure 13.1). The second is that measurement provides the means to evidence the value offered by the BA Service.

This chapter refers to both metrics and measurements, terms that are sometimes used interchangeably but which actually refer to different levels of performance monitoring.

A **measurement** is a fundamental unit-specific term, such as a value that can be counted, timed or otherwise assessed. By tracking measurements over time, it may be possible to see trends, but single point-in-time measurements have no context and it is very difficult to draw conclusions from them.

A **metric** is a standard for measurement, often derived or calculated from one or more measurements. Metrics often require a baseline measurement to provide context and the opportunity to understand improvement or effectiveness.

The benefits of measurement

Without appropriate measurement the BA Service has no way of evidencing the value the service offers or the progress being made towards implementing agreed strategy. This

Figure 13.1 Turning strategy into reality

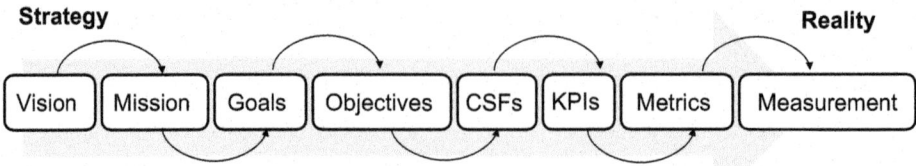

can be a precarious position to be in, when the direction of travel for most organisations is always to demonstrate efficiency and effectiveness and 'to do more with less'.

Robert Behn (2003) has researched and defined the purposes that managers have for measuring performance, and the questions that can be addressed through measurement; these are shown in Table 13.1.

Table 13.1 The purposes for measuring performance (Reproduced with permission from Wiley)

Purpose	Questions managers can answer through measurement
Evaluate	How well is my team performing? Are we meeting targets/objectives?
Control	How can I ensure that my team members are doing the right thing?
Budget	On which programmes, projects or people should my organisation spend money?
Motivate	How can I motivate the team, collaborators and stakeholders to do the things necessary to improve performance?
Promote	How can I convince senior management, stakeholders and customers that my team is doing a good job? How can we demonstrate that we are progressing towards or meeting strategic objectives?
Celebrate	What accomplishments are worthy of the important organisational ritual of celebrating success?
Learn	Why is that working or not working?
Improve	What exactly should we do differently to improve performance?

It is critical to select the right metrics and find efficient ways to measure them. This allows the BA Service to:

- deliver against strategy;
- make informed decisions;
- establish the case for change/investment;
- evidence improvement;
- allow objective assessment;
- celebrate individual and service success;
- allow meaningful comparison;
- inform future strategy.

Common challenges

Setting targets and tracking against them can seem like an unnecessary overhead, instead of an integral part of delivering an effective and efficient BA Service. This may be due to:

- limited data/data quality – 'not the full picture';
- monitoring the wrong things – 'doesn't tell me anything';
- monitoring too many things – 'not worth the effort';
- information not being timely – 'too late to influence anything'.

In addition, business analysts who have never been subject to any monitoring of their work may be suspicious or resistant to the introduction of metrics and measures. This can affect the ability to obtain the required information or its veracity.

Open monitoring can also have unintended consequences or drive undesirable behaviours. For example, counting 'how many' analysis products are generated in a certain time frame, or 'how long' it takes to generate a particular deliverable will put the focus on time rather than quality and may drive business analysts to avoid seeking peer review in an effort to 'save time'.

To overcome these challenges, start by focusing on a small number of metrics that can be accurately measured in a timely way. Develop the set of metrics and measures over time and encourage business analysts and other audiences to be engaged in the process of defining and improving metrics. Ensure that all stakeholders are shown the uses and usefulness of the information.

An approach to defining metrics

Going from a position of no monitoring or tracking to being able to set targets and have evidence available for decision making takes time and effort. It is an iterative process, which can begin with information that is easy to obtain to allow tracking against simple metrics and then expand to offer deeper insights into the BA Service and what are meaningful targets. Figure 13.2 shows that by starting to count simple things (monitoring) and building on this foundation, the BA Service can reach a position of informed decision making by setting and managing targets.

Figure 13.2 Approach to defining metrics

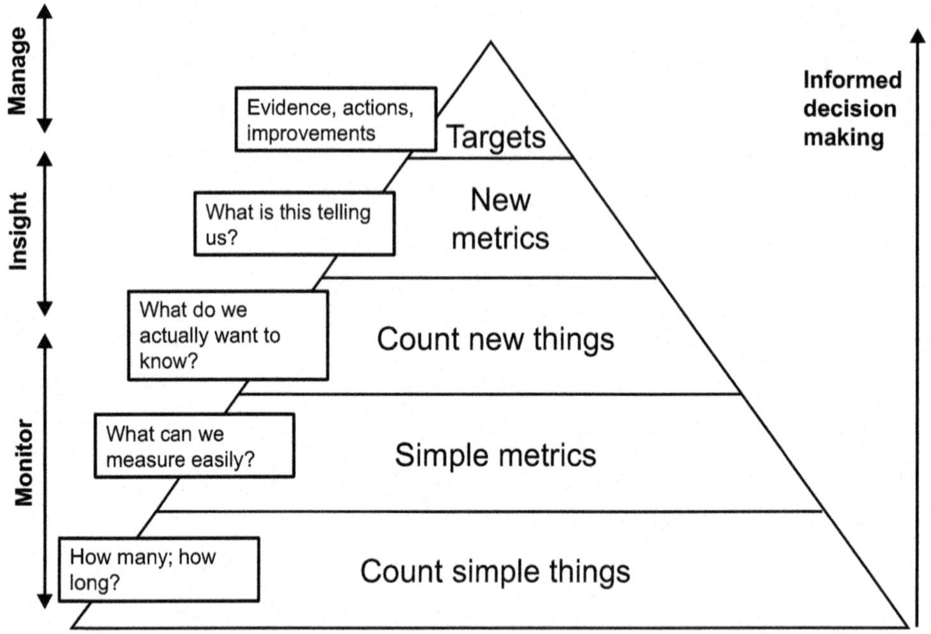

Table 13.2 shows the types of metrics that can be built up over time, starting with simple measures such as counting, moving to adopting new metrics and eventually setting targets.

Table 13.2 Increasing complexity of metrics over time

Metric type	Metric
Simple metrics (measures) *Information easy to obtain*	• How many business analysts do we have? • At what levels of seniority/grade? • On what employment terms? • How many projects are we supporting? • How many vacancies are there? • What future demand do we know about? • Who has attained professional certification?

(Continued)

Table 13.2 (Continued)

Metric type	Metric
New metrics *Introduced over time*	• How long is an average business analysis assignment/work package?
	• Which projects do not have business analyst support (and why)?
	• Customer satisfaction
	• BA satisfaction
	• Net Promoter Score®
	• Customer Effort Score
Targets *Used to track and manage performance*	• BAs support X% of project portfolio/business change initiatives
	• Employment type X% permanent, Y% contract
	• X% development (pipeline) business analyst roles in place
	• Customer satisfaction >X%
	• Net Promotor Score of >X
	• Customer Effort Score of >X
	• Vacancies <X% of total service size
	• X% business analysts hold professional certification

TYPES OF MEASURES

There are many types of measure that help to assess the performance of the BA Service. No single measure can give a complete picture and the greatest insights are gained by using a combination of measures to look at the BA Service from different perspectives.

Input and output measures

There are several things that may be measured, starting with inputs (things we need) and activities (things we do), moving on to outputs (things we produce), outcomes (things we deliver) and, finally, impacts (things we affect). Inputs and activities can be generally considered 'costs' of the project or service, whereas outputs, outcomes and impacts may be the 'benefits' it provides. Inputs are the easiest things to measure but don't always offer much insight or support for informed decision making; impacts offer the most interesting information but are much more difficult to accurately and confidently measure. The different areas of measurement are shown in Figure 13.3.

Having ensured that a range of input and output measures are in place, the BA Service can start to ask questions about value for money and efficiency. BA leaders can then see

Figure 13.3 Areas of measurement

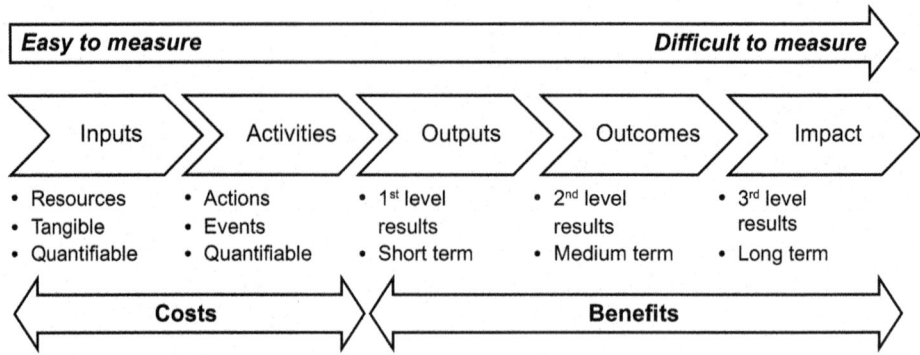

relationships between changing elements on the cost side (people, budget, time) and corresponding results on the benefits side.

Leading and lagging measures

Leading measures tend to be input orientated; they provide the opportunity to influence future performance. Lagging measures are typically output orientated and provide the ability to analyse past performance. Leading measures are often concerned with behaviours, relationships and attitudes.

If the Service focuses only on lagging measures, it will also be looking backwards 'Why did we miss that target?'; 'Why has our customer satisfaction dropped?', and so on. If appropriate leading measures are also in place, it increases the chances of 'keeping on track' and lagging metrics will not come as a surprise. Leading and lagging measures associated with core aspects of the BA Service are shown in Table 13.3.

Observable versus measurable

Not everything is measurable, and in many cases, the effort to measure something may outweigh the benefit of having the information. This is particularly true for leading measures; for example, what would 'increase levels of engagement between business analysts across projects' look like? What factors could be observed to support whether this was happening/not happening? Encouraging business analysts to attend each other's stand-up meetings, share work, share outputs of lessons learned or retrospectives might all be useful approaches, but actually tracking these things might not be sensible.

Consistently encouraging particular behaviours, actions and attitudes and highlighting/praising analysts when these are seen may impact measures down the line.

Table 13.3 Leading and lagging measures

BA Service area	Leading measure	Lagging measure
Customers	• All customers are offered weekly/monthly check-in calls • Customers are given opportunity to provide regular/ongoing feedback • % of work packages agreed	• Customer satisfaction • Net Promoter Score®
Timescales	• BA work packages have agreed timescales	• % projects on time
Business analysts	• Increase time/budget for business analysis training by X hours/£X • Hold one team event per quarter • All business analysts have monthly one-to-one meeting with manager or senior BA • Take-up of the business analyst buddy scheme	• Staff turnover • BA satisfaction
Quality of analysis	• All business analysts perform two peer reviews per month • All business analysts are working towards professional certification • Self-review using checklists is taking place • Adherence to processes	• Number of defects in downstream products • Customer satisfaction
Recruitment	• Expand number of advertising channels • Introduce employee referral scheme	• Conversion rate (recruitment metrics are discussed later in this chapter)
BA Service budget	• Adherence to processes • Potential business analysis demand that converts to actual demand • Time allocated for service improvement activities	• % re-charge target • Income ≥ BA Service budget

Service Level Agreements

It is useful for BA leaders, business analysts and customers to have a factual understanding of how long certain activities and processes take to accomplish. As business analysis starts to be seen as a service, thoughts may turn to the introduction of Service Level Agreements (SLAs). It may be difficult to guarantee SLAs for the BA Service, as there are so many interdependencies and aspects outside the control of the Service. There are some areas where SLAs or internal targets may be relevant if all factors can be controlled by the BA Service; these are covered in Table 13.4.

Table 13.4 Example business analysis service levels

BA Service area	Example service levels
Resource management	When the BA Service receives a request for business analysis support, customers will receive an acknowledgement within X days, the BA Service will aim to clarify the request within Y days and will provide a response to customers within Z days
	It may be difficult to provide a commitment to source business analysis capacity within a set time frame, unless other agreements with third parties (recruitment specialists, consultancies, etc.) are also in place
Absence management	When the BA Service becomes aware of planned or unplanned absence of a business analyst, the Service will provide short-term cover for any absences over X number of weeks
	This approach relies on some capacity being available within the Service, either by deprioritising improvement or management activities to enable delivery support or via access to additional business analysis capacity at short notice
Transition planning	When the BA Service becomes aware that a replacement business analyst is required (possibly due to the initial business analyst leaving, promotion or other moves that may arise) there will be a period of X weeks' notice to the customer
	It may also be possible to commit to a target handover period, but, as with resource management, this may not be possible unless other arrangements (notice periods and sourcing agreements) are in place

It is important to track the appropriate information before committing to an SLA in order to determine if measures are likely to be achieved – or breached. If the latter, a consequence must be defined. It may be more appropriate to set internal targets that are then tracked for a set period of time before making performance commitments to customers.

Setting time-based metrics for business analysis deliverables and activities are very challenging to achieve due to the myriad of factors that influence business analysis work on projects. These factors include the number of business analysts involved, the involvement of other roles, numbers of stakeholders, type of project, and development methodology, to name just a few. It is useful to track the actual time spent producing specific business analysis deliverables or performing business analysis activities. This information should then be used to inform future estimates rather than to set time-based metrics.

The Balanced Scorecard

The Balanced Scorecard (BSC) was developed by Kaplan and Norton (1996) as a means of defining a framework for performance measurement that would support the achievement of the vision for organisations, and the execution of business strategy (Cadle, Paul and Turner, 2014). Many organisations use the Balanced Scorecard to evaluate team and individual performance.

The emphasis of the BSC is to consider aspects of performance in a balanced way. It can be used as a visual reminder to ensure that when overall performance of the BA Service is considered, the metrics used do not all relate to one area, and that no areas are missing. It also shows that the elements are interrelated, and, by seeking to improve performance in one area, other areas will be impacted (see Figure 13.4). The 'balanced' part of the approach refers to the fact that, at any given time, managers have to make trade-offs between the various elements. For example, investing in learning and growth at the short-term expense of financial performance.

Figure 13.4 The Balanced Scorecard (after Kaplan and Norton, 1996)

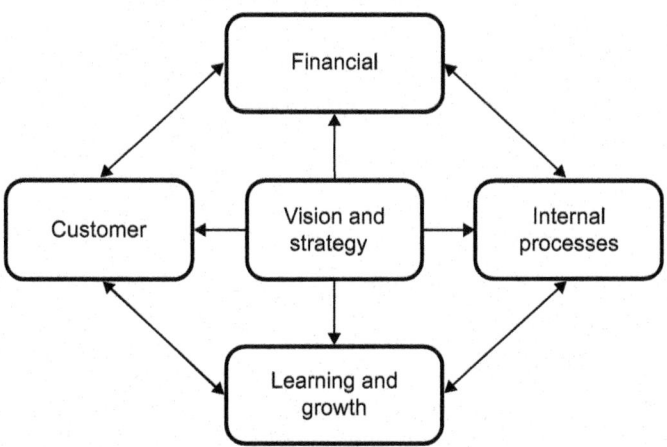

The elements of the BSC are shown in Table 13.5.

These four elements of the BSC are underpinned and driven by the vision and strategy of the organisation. It is useful to move through the levels shown in Figure 13.2 to identify suitable measures for each element of the BSC. The CSFs and KPIs should be linked to the vision and strategy for the BA Service and the wider organisation. This helps to provide the context for the metrics and measures that are to be monitored.

Critical success factors

Each objective of the BA Service will have a number of essential areas of activity that must be performed well in order for the objective to be met; these are the CSFs.

Table 13.5 Business analysis performance measures using the Balanced Scorecard

Balanced Scorecard perspective	Relevance to business analysis
Financial	The original Balanced Scorecard stated that the financial perspective was concerned with how the organisation appeared to the shareholders. When considering the financial perspective with regard to the BA Service, it is necessary to adapt how this perspective is applied. While the BA Service is typically seen as cost centre, rather than providing a profit margin, the financial perspective is still relevant and there are likely to be financial aspects to the expected performance. Key financial areas to be addressed by the BA Service are: • **Budgeting:** the ability to work within the budget set for the BA Service, meeting any income or recharge targets • **Feasibility:** providing support for the financial analysis for change initiatives and identifying where they are not financially feasible • **Options:** identifying options that ensure effective use of investment funds • **Efficiency:** defining changes to business processes that will increase the cost-efficiency of the processes
Customer	The customer perspective is concerned with how customers perceive the organisation. However, as discussed in Chapter 10, the BA Service has various different types of customer and their needs should be considered when setting customer performance measures Example measures include: • customer satisfaction (CSAT) • Net Promoter Score (NPS)®
Internal processes	The internal perspective is concerned with the areas where an organisation may excel. Internal areas for evaluation that are relevant to business analysis concern the following: • **Role:** the clarity of the business analyst role and service offering • **Requirements:** the accurate definition and management of requirements • **Deliverables:** the consistency and accuracy of the business analysis work, including the standards applied and products delivered • **Planning:** the effectiveness of the business analysis planning activities • **Recruitment:** the timescales and costs to recruit business analysts or conversion rates • **Resource management:** the supply and demand of business analysts

(Continued)

Table 13.5 (Continued)

Balanced Scorecard perspective	Relevance to business analysis
Learning and growth	The learning and growth perspective is sometimes referred to as 'innovation' and is concerned with how well an organisation is able to continue improve and offer value. Performance measures relate to the extent to which an organisation, such as a BA Service, is focused on improving the services offered and developing the service portfolio. Specific measures may relate to the following areas: • **Development:** the number of business analysts attending training or obtaining certifications • **Engagement:** the extent to which business analysts engage with the business analysis community, both within the organisation and external to the organisation • **Sharing:** the regularity and depth of sharing knowledge and insights with business analyst colleagues • **Extending:** the extent to which new developments in business analysis are introduced to the business analysis community • **Innovation:** the volume of ideas for business improvement offered by the business analysts • **Satisfaction:** the levels of morale and contentment reported by business analysts

It is necessary to differentiate between factors that are truly critical and those that are simply important to avoid overly burdensome measurement. Progress towards providing the CSFs allows the service to keep on track towards meeting objectives and, through these, achieving the vision (see Figure 13.1).

CSFs may evolve for the BA Service over time. During the early stages of Service maturity, raising awareness of the service offering and the business analyst role may be key CSFs to establishing the BA Service and meeting objectives. A more established BA Service may need to focus on the performance of the business analysts and the provision of a consistent service to meet the defined objectives.

Key performance indicators

I often say that when you can measure what you are speaking about, and express it in numbers, you know something about it; but when you cannot express it in numbers, your knowledge is of a meagre and unsatisfactory kind.

(Kelvin, 1883)

KPIs are quantifiable and provide a way of measuring whether or not a CSF has been achieved. Each CSF should have one or more associated KPIs, otherwise the service does not know whether that CSF is being performed well or not.

The process of defining KPIs follows the same iterative quality management process shown in Chapter 12 (see Figure 12.10). As time goes on, it is important to retest and confirm that:

- each KPI is providing meaningful information to the Service;
- each KPI is linked clearly to a CSF;
- the effort involved in obtaining the KPI information is justified.

FINANCIAL METRICS

The BA Service budget will primarily be concerned with staff costs, as discussed in Chapter 9. Depending on the charging model used, it may be necessary to set re-charge or 'income' targets for each business analyst and the BA Service as a whole. It is also useful to understand average costs and consider how cost savings or efficiencies could be achieved in each area. Typical areas to consider include average salaries, travel expenditure or software licence costs. For example, the average business analyst salary could be reduced by setting permanent staff to contractor ratios or by implementing new entry-level roles.

CUSTOMER METRICS

The customer perspective focuses on the people who use the BA Service. Surveys are often used to obtain opinion-based feedback and information about levels of satisfaction; for example, with performance. There are potential disadvantages to using surveys, such as the difficulty in reaching sufficient sample sizes, the possible bias of those completing the survey and the demand on people's time. However, surveys remain a reliable indicator for how people feel about the service they receive and using specifically targeted questions can provide significant insight. Surveys also offer a repeatable process – the same survey may be re-used, allowing responses to be tracked over time.

There are a number of established metrics to measure customer satisfaction that are described below.

Customer satisfaction (CSAT) survey

A CSAT survey provides a high-level customer satisfaction metric that indicates if customers' expectations are being met and they are happy with the BA Service. A low score can identify the need to carry out more detailed analysis via customer engagement, a root cause analysis or by utilising a more detailed service quality measurement survey.

Starting the conversation about satisfaction helps customers to appreciate that their opinion is valued and allows the BA Service to track if any continuous improvement activities that have been implemented have had a positive customer impact. Essentially a CSAT score helps the BA Service to answer the question, 'Is the Service focusing on improving the areas that matter to our customers?' Figure 13.5 shows an example of a CSAT score calculation.

Figure 13.5 Customer satisfaction survey example

Overall, how satisfied are you with the BA Service?

Extremely unsatisfied	Unsatisfied	Neutral	Satisfied	Extremely satisfied	Customer satisfaction (%) = (Sum all scores/number of responses) x 20
1	2	3	4	5	
☹	☹	😐	🙂	😊	

Net Promoter Score (NPS)®

NPS surveys are used to understand customer loyalty and are a good indicator of the potential for business growth; the higher the Net Promotor Score®, the more likely it is that demand for the BA Service will increase. It allows for easy comparison across teams, organisations and industries. Figure 13.6 shows an example NPS® score calculation.

Figure 13.6 Net Promoter Score®

How likely are you to recommend the BA Service to a colleague?

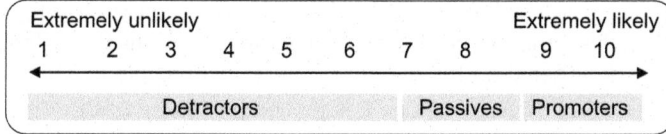

Extremely unlikely								Extremely likely		
1	2	3	4	5	6	7	8	9	10	NPS (%) = % Promoters–% Detractors
	Detractors					Passives	Promoters			

- **Promoters:** like working with the BA Service and will have a positive influence through word of mouth.
- **Passives:** are not particularly invested but are satisfied with the service they receive. These scores do not form part of the NPS® calculation.
- **Detractors:** have not particularly enjoyed working with the BA Service and will require proactive engagement to avoid reputational damage.

An NPS® of more than zero (i.e. any positive value) is considered good; a score of over 50 is considered excellent.

Customer Effort Score (CES)

This metric is used to understand how easy or difficult it is to be a customer of the BA Service; this will impact both CSAT and NPS® results.

Where business analysis is provided as an internal consultancy and customers effectively have no choice about using the Service or not, this metric can highlight the likelihood that customers will try to work-around or avoid using the BA Service. Customer statements such as 'We don't need a business analyst on this'; 'The business team have done their own analysis'; 'We'll bring in our own BA' can all be warning signs that the BA Service is not easy for customers to work with. Figure 13.7 shows an example CES score calculation.

Figure 13.7 Customer Effort Score

It was easy to work with the BA Service:

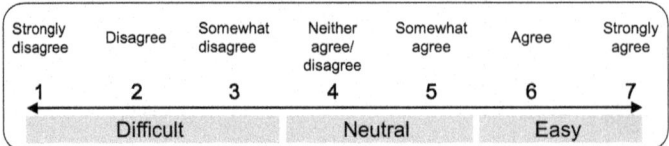

The same question can be used to calculate a similar indicator, the Net Easy Score (NES), which takes the same format as the NPS. In this scale, those who responded 6 or 7 find the service 'Easy to work with', those who responded 1, 2 and 3 find it difficult. The NES is calculated by % Easy – % Difficult.

Aggregating feedback

The customer metrics discussed in this section have all involved asking questions about the BA Service as a whole. However, customers may only feel able to provide feedback on the specific business analyst they have been working with and may not yet recognise the concept of a BA Service. In this situation, it is possible to phrase questions that relate to individual business analysts rather than the overall BA Service. Possible questions are:

- Overall, how satisfied are you with the work of (named business analyst)?
- Would you recommend (named business analyst) to a colleague?
- Is it easy to work with (named business analyst)?

The scores obtained can be shared with the individuals and aggregated to provide Service-level metrics. On first consideration, asking these questions about an individual can seem too direct but moving to the idea of delivering a customer-focused service requires a change in approach and attitude and a real commitment to continual improvement.

A recommendation for a named business analyst can be an indicator of good performance. However, accommodating requests for a specific business analyst is likely to present a challenge for the BA Service and may be demotivating for other business analysts. Requesting a specific business analyst may be driven by factors other than business analysis performance, such as business domain or system knowledge, or the willingness of the business analyst to provide support beyond the agreed role. It is even possible that a business analyst is popular with their customers because they do not challenge assumptions or assertions; in other words, that they are not performing the role effectively. The question of 'recommendation' is still useful to derive an aggregated Net Promoter Score®, but this could lead to unwanted behaviours from customers.

Scores and feedback provided at an individual level may also represent factors wider than the performance of an individual business analyst, such as:

- the clarity of the business analyst role (see Chapter 1);
- the nature of the customer expectations (see Chapter 10);
- other roles that are either present or not present.

In this case it may be appropriate to only use the aggregated metrics, to attempt to tackle the issues at a Service-level and not try to interpret or action scores for individual business analysts.

Complaints and compliments

It is unlikely that the BA Service will have a formalised 'complaints procedure', although this may be the case in some organisations. Complaints may be received in many ways, some of which may be subtle, requiring BA leaders to be alert to such approaches. For example, there may be a throw-away line in an email, a pointed comment made, facial expressions, corridor conversations or second-hand reports. There may also be more direct 'complaints', framed as concerns, feedback, lessons learned, general issues or even escalation requests.

These approaches may also be used to offer compliments about a business analyst or the BA Service. Compliments are unsolicited positive feedback, messages of thanks and appreciation. Compliments must always be acknowledged back to the provider and passed on to the relevant individual or group. Compliments should be shared within the BA Service as a regular agenda item in meetings or in a section of newsletters and updates. Creating a culture that openly celebrates success has been shown to improve performance (Behn, 2003).

All of this qualitative data may be tracked, and it can useful to create a log of both complaints (whether or not this term is used by the customer) and compliments that the BA Service or individual business analysts receive. The number of complaints will typically outnumber the compliments, as customers are far more likely to be motivated to raise issues.

LEARNING AND GROWTH METRICS

The learning and growth perspective considers the culture and development of the BA Service. Key questions the BA Service may wish to address from this element of the BSC are:

- What is the level of engagement for BA Service activities?
- Is knowledge management being applied consistently?

- Is the volume of knowledge assets of the BA Service expanding and being maintained?

- How much time are business analysts spending on learning and development activities?

- Is new learning being applied?

- Are business analysis support tools being used to their full potential?

- Are we seeing improvement in quality and performance after investment in training?

- What routes do we have for learning from outside the organisation and the sector?

It is important to consider how information to help answer these questions can be obtained. For example, the volume of files shared, accessed and updated may help to quantify knowledge management processes, and outputs of peer reviews may provide information about quality improvement after training. Some of the information will have to be obtained by asking the business analysts directly and surveys can again be an efficient mechanism.

BA pulse survey

The aim of a pulse survey is to get insight into how business analysts are feeling in relation to key areas such as workload, personal development, management support and wellbeing. It is quick to complete and can be repeated frequently (e.g. weekly or monthly). This snapshot of information can help inform decisions such as 'How urgent is this recruitment?' and 'Can the service take on an additional project?'

Asking for regular feedback promotes employee engagement. Pulse surveys offer the opportunity to highlight issues and can complement and even affect longer-term employee satisfaction. For example, employee satisfaction surveys may include questions about the opportunity to provide feedback, the ability to influence decision making and the employer's attitude to wellbeing, all of which may be answered more positively by the employee if pulse surveys are carried out regularly and the results are acted upon.

Pulse surveys have been shown to contribute to a more positive organisational culture (Mann and Harter, 2016), and provide a mechanism to remind employees of the areas that matter to the organisation. For example, being repeatedly asked about personal development reinforces the idea that personal development time is expected and encouraged, and that business analysts will be allowed time for this within their working week.

There must be a willingness to take action if pulse scores are low or drop, or if the results show wide-ranging results between different responders or from one survey to the next. Where this occurs, it is likely that the pulse survey has identified the need for more detailed engagement to determine underlying issues and identify possible remedial actions.

Before introducing a pulse survey, it is important to consider the following questions

- Will it be anonymous or identifiable?

- How will people be encouraged to complete the survey?

- What frequency will be applied or when will it be issued? (Tip – avoid Monday mornings and Friday afternoons as opinions expressed in these slots are not necessarily representative of the working week!)
- What results are expected?
- What routes of action are available if results are not as expected?
- How will aggregate information be shared back with the business analysts?

Figure 13.8 provides an example pulse survey.

Figure 13.8 Business analysis pulse survey

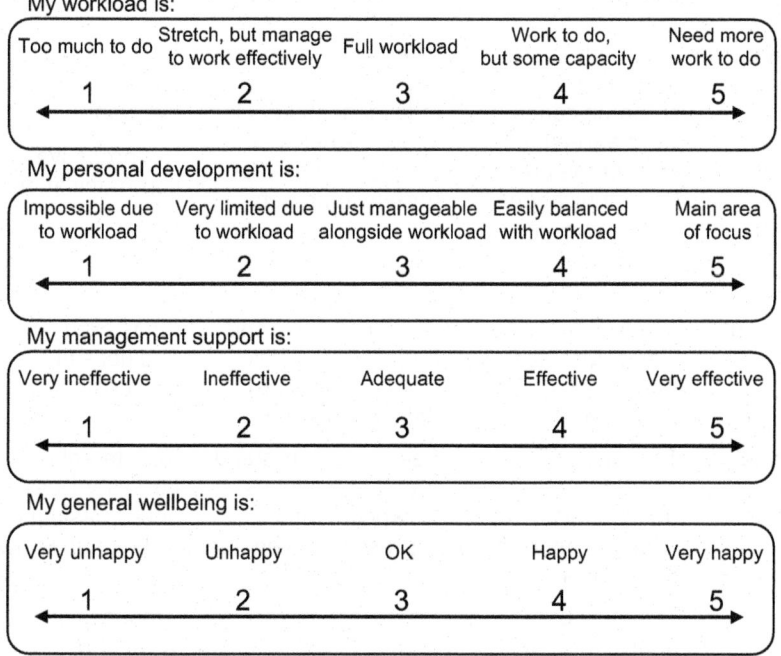

Business analyst performance measurement

Organisations typically have performance development and appraisal processes in place, though a generic process is unlikely to provide sufficient detail to assess the business analysts' performance and skill levels. The BA Service can survey customers about the business analysts they have worked with, either at the end of projects or assignments or on a pre-determined timing cycle (e.g. twice per year or annually). It is also useful for business analysts to assess themselves using the same parameters and scale as customers, as this will generate results regarding the business analysis CSFs and enable a comparison and consideration of two different views.

There are two possible uses for this data:

1. to aggregate the individual scores and obtain a view of the performance of the entire BA Service;

2. to support a performance evaluation for an individual business analyst.

The KPIs suggested (BA Manager Forum, 2015) in Table 13.6 may be asked as survey questions using a Likert scale (typically five points from 'strongly agree' to 'strongly disagree'). An example survey is also shown in Appendix 14.

Table 13.6 Potential CSFs and KPIs

Potential CSFs	Potential KPIs	Good performance	Poor performance
Communication	The method and frequency of communication were agreed at the start of the project. Communications were effective and were maintained throughout	Tailors communication approach to meet individual stakeholder needs rather than adopts a 'one-size-fits-all' approach	Expects the same approach to work for everyone Not proactive in communication
Commitment	The business analyst was committed to a successful project outcome	Concerned with the project as a whole, not just their own deliverables	Finds excuses and does not take responsibility
Knowledge	The business analyst understands the business and what is important to customers	Seeks to understand multiple business viewpoints and represent stakeholder interests	No interest or curiosity. Does not seek to ask questions or build up knowledge
Value	The business analyst produced outputs that were valued by customers	Produces artefacts that are seen as useful to the stakeholder	Produces artefacts without reference to how they will be used or the target audience; or does not appear to produce any artefacts
Teamwork	The business analyst encouraged collaboration within the project team	Engages others and fosters collaborative working	Creates boundaries and works in isolation

This list does not cover all aspects of business analyst performance that may be of interest to the BA Service. However, it is important to balance the areas that are measured, and the amount of time stakeholders are willing to spend providing feedback.

This type of performance feedback does not take into account the individual business analyst's different levels of seniority and experience, or that expectations may vary for different business analysts. Where the BA Service is sufficiently large and mature, it may be beneficial to construct a more complex measurement system that reflects differences in job descriptions. For example, the SFIA levels may be used for this purpose (see Chapter 4). However, starting with a straightforward mechanism that may be refined gradually is likely to offer the best approach.

INTERNAL PROCESS METRICS

The internal business processes perspective looks at how smoothly the BA Service is running. It gives the opportunity to consider process efficiency, reduce waste and identify where it is possible to work more quickly. The key processes required to operate the BA Service (see Chapter 9) will help to identify how baseline process measures could be defined and improved.

Recruitment metrics

There are two key recruitment metrics that should be used by the BA Service to plan the work effectively and respond to customer demand; these are recruitment timescales and conversion rates.

The most informative recruitment timescale metric is the average length of time from listing a business analyst vacancy to a new business analyst beginning work. There a several processes that contribute to this metric, including the length of time:

- adverts are listed for;
- recruitment agencies are given to source candidates;
- for the process of shortlisting, interviewing and making a decision; candidates are required to work as a notice period.

The BA Service cannot control all of these issues but should shorten time frames where possible, as this is likely to be of benefit to both customers and business analysts.

Conversion rates are a recruitment metric to help aid understanding of the end-to-end process. They provide opportunities to compare one round of recruitment with another or to compare recruitment exercises for different roles. They reflect the number of applications that are converted to interviews and how many interviews are converted to new business analyst appointments. Conversion rates should be tracked for all business analysis recruitment exercises, as this will develop helpful management information. This information is vital to inform the business analysis recruitment strategy (see Chapter 3) by addressing key questions such as:

- Which business analysis roles (senior, practitioner or entry level) have the highest conversion rates? Why is this? What are we doing differently at each level?
- How do business analysis conversion rates compare with other roles such as project management? What could explain the difference?

- At what times of year do we get more applications?

- Which advertising routes lead to more applications? Is the conversion rate affected?

Achieving a higher conversion rate without compromising on appointment standards indicates a more effective recruitment process. Table 13.7 shows an example of typical recruitment metrics that would provide a basis for informed decision making about the recruitment strategy and informed predictions about future recruitment. The data might lead to the following consideration:

'If we need to appoint 5 business analysts, based on our previous conversion rate (6.7 per cent) we would need to receive over 70 applications and see 20 candidates.' Is this feasible? How long would this be likely to take?

Table 13.7 Example business analyst recruitment metrics

Applications /CVs	Phone shortlist	Interview shortlist	Appoint- able	Offers made	Offers accepted	Application conversion rate	Interview conversion rate
30	11	8	3	3	2	2/30=6.7%	2/8=25%

The conversion rate could be calculated just from the number of applications (start of process) and the number of offers accepted (end of process). However, the intermediate information allows adjustment actions to be suggested such as:

- We rule out a lot of applications on paper. Should we be speaking to more applicants?

- We don't rule out many applicants via the telephone interview, is this working? Is it worth the effort?

- Why aren't all our offers being accepted? Are we tracking the reasons applicants give us?

It should also be possible to reflect ongoing performance of recently recruited business analysts against recruitment information:

- How do we feel about the recruitment decisions made once six months or one year have passed?

- Do our processes (e.g. questions, assessments) need to be updated to reflect the information we hold about gaps in applicants' knowledge and experience?

- What assumptions have we made that we didn't recognise?

- Did time pressures or customer demand affect our decision making? Was this successful or detrimental?

Where recruitment feedback from candidates suggests that the process is too slow, it may be useful to track candidate experience metrics such as:

- length of time between application and interview;
- length of time between interview and offer;
- percentage of offers not accepted.

These metrics will show where improvements can be made to avoid losing good candidates in a competitive market.

BA Service Dashboard

Presenting information about the metrics and measurements is vital to influence behaviours and encourage action.

> Information is only useful when it can be understood.
>
> (Cooper, 1994)

Developing a dashboard that can be used with different audiences is a useful approach, as it helps to present information concisely and clearly. The process of designing the dashboard needs to consider the following:

- the metrics and information to include;
- the target audience;
- the creation and maintenance process and resources;
- the support tools to be used;
- the dissemination mechanism(s);
- the frequency of updating the dashboard;
- the links to existing reports or other information.

Figure 13.9 shows an example dashboard.

The dashboard can use a number of different data visualisation techniques to make the content visually engaging. Displaying the dashboard in relevant physical and online locations sends the message that performance is taken seriously, and that the BA Service is making tangible steps towards ensuring that performance remains on track to meet the defined objectives and deliver the strategy.

The service gap

When a service is experiencing low customer satisfaction, there is a gap somewhere in the service provision. It is useful to understand where this gap is occurring. Are we providing the service we agreed, but the customer expects something different? Or, are we failing to meet the standards the BA Service has set? Were the standards correct in the first place?

Four dimensions that relate to customer service gaps are discussed in Table 13.8.

Figure 13.9 BA Service Dashboard

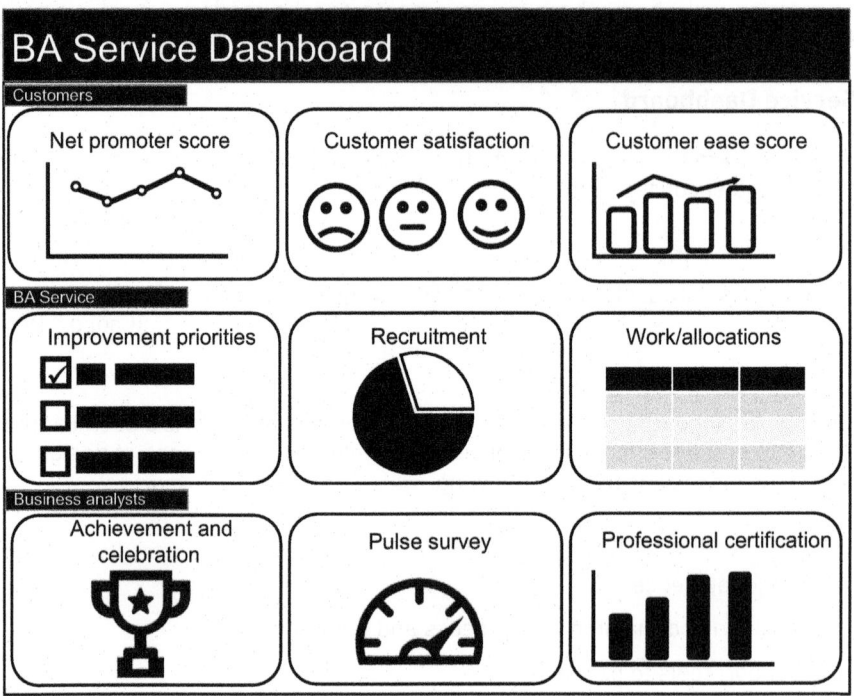

Table 13.8 Understanding the service gap

Gap	Description	Issue
Knowledge	**We don't know what customers expect from the service**	BA Service is providing what it wants to deliver, rather than finding out what customers need and expect
	The difference between the understanding of customer expectations of the BA Service, and actual expectations	To address this issue: • Start a two-way dialogue about the role of the business analyst and expectations of the BA Service • Review other internal consultancy models within the organisation and how they define and meet customer expectations

(Continued)

Table 13.8 (Continued)

Gap	Description	Issue
Standards	**Our standards don't meet customer expectations** Difference between the understanding of customer expectations and how these are reflected in BA Service definitions, standards and quality processes	The business analysis work is delivered to quality standards in the time that was agreed and meets the internal standards, but, for some reason, this is not what the customer expected or required To address this issue: • Improve communication and ensure that expectations are realistic • Use business analysis work packages to provide clarity on approach • Review standards and quality criteria • Involve representatives from customer teams in the development of definitions, standards and processes
Delivery	**We are failing to meet our standards** The difference between how the BA Service is defined and the service that is actually delivered	The business analysis work is not delivered to the quality standards or time that was documented. A business analyst may be under-performing, or has had insufficient training or supervision, or their work has had insufficient peer review This issue may also point to possible role ambiguity (see Chapter 1) To address this issue: • Ensure appropriate business analysis training, direction and oversight are in place • Consider the use of coaching and buddying

(Continued)

Table 13.8 (Continued)

Gap	Description	Issue
Communication	**We are failing to meet our promises** The difference between how the BA Service is communicated to customers and the service that is actually delivered	The business analysis is not delivered to the quality standards/time that was agreed. Business analysts may have over-promised, stating that quality could be achieved beyond usual standards, or that deadlines could be met within unachievable time frames. The business analyst may be over-optimistic, inexperienced or have competing priorities To address this issue: • Capture and share what was agreed, reflect in work packages • Ensure commitments are realistic – back up estimates with service-gathered data relating to previous similar projects • Ensure that the business analysts have support, can ask for help and that sufficient oversight is in place

CONCLUSION

This chapter has suggested a range of metrics relevant to the BA Service that explore each area of the Balanced Scorecard. Having used metrics to evaluate each of these areas, it is important to use the information gained to improve the performance of the BA Service. The four elements of the service gap – knowledge, standards, delivery, communication – provide a framework for considering where improvements may be made.

BA leaders need to invest resources in defining metrics and measuring performance against these metrics. This will enable them to understand whether the BA Service is improving and to demonstrate progress against the performance improvement strategy. This may seem a daunting task but, if a performance improvement exercise is initiated with a limited scope and using straightforward metrics, it is possible to build up confidence and capability in using a metric-based approach to improvement.

Ongoing monitoring and improvement of the BA Service may be facilitated through the use of performance metrics and the dissemination and publication of the survey results. The use of a BA Service Dashboard will help to highlight performance issues and clarify where changes need to be made in order to achieve the required performance improvements.

AFTERWORD

Our aim in writing this book has been to present the information, frameworks and approaches that we feel enable the delivery of a high-performing, effective BA Service.

The book is deliberately wide-ranging and includes guidance on the nature of service and value proposition, plus how to enable service performance and monitor customer satisfaction. The range of topics demonstrates the complexity of delivering an effective BA Service that is recognised as offering value to an organisation.

There is no 'one-size-fits-all' approach to delivering the BA Service but we suggest that BA leaders should start with ensuring that they understand:

- the BA services on offer: the value proposition, activities, techniques and skills available to the organisation;
- the BA team: the culture, capacity and capability of those that deliver the services;
- the variety of customers: their perspectives, drivers and expectations.

In many of the chapters, we have shown the benefits of applying business analysis techniques when developing a BA Service. It is hoped that BA leaders will adopt this approach and use their business analysis skills to ensure ongoing engagement with customers and continual service improvement.

Delivering business analysis as a service requires skills, knowledge and considerable effort. However, given the significant benefits to business analysts, their customers and organisations, it is effort that is well worth investing.

APPENDICES

Service name:	Situation investigation and problem analysis	

Service value proposition: State a clear definition of the problem to be addressed and the business needs to be met. Define the scope of the work to achieve this. Where a project is relevant, in outline, clarify the investment objectives and business benefits to be achieved by the project.

Service activities:
1. Investigate the situation and the problem or opportunity
2. Understand the strategic context for the situation
3. Identify and articulate the business needs
4. Define the problem
5. Define the scope of the business and IS project
6. Define the rationale for rejecting a project proposal

Service techniques:

Data modelling

Objectives: To represent the data required by an organisation or business area to support the delivery of services to customers (internal or external); to represent the business rules inherent in the structure of the data

Explanation: Data models provide a view of an information system from a data perspective. They may be developed at different levels of granularity; for example, an information concept or domain view consisting of high-level areas or a detailed data model encompassing elements such as data groupings, relationships between the groupings, business rules and individual data items. There are two major modelling approaches used to represent data or information. These are entity relationship modelling and class modelling. While they represent similar concepts, there are differences in the ways these concepts are modelled and in some of the detail represented

Techniques: Entity relationship diagram, class diagram, data definition, domain definition

(Continued)

353

Service name:	**Situation investigation and problem analysis** 

Environment analysis	**Objectives:** To analyse the external business environment over which the organisation has little, if any, control; to analyse the factors within the organisation that must be considered when deciding on the strategy to respond to external factors
	Explanation: Environment analysis techniques provide a rigorous basis for developing a SWOT analysis. However, this may result in a large number of factors to be considered in each quadrant of the SWOT and a degree of prioritisation is often required. The strengths and weaknesses are the internal factors that will help to determine the strategic choices available to an organisation. The threats and opportunities are the external factors facing the organisation; these need to be distinguished from the strategic choices made on the basis of the SWOT
	Techniques: PESTLE analysis, Porter's 5-forces, SWOT analysis, Balanced Scorecard, critical success factor, key performance indicator
Investigation	**Objectives:** To explore situations with the aim of uncovering issues, problems, opportunities and other relevant information; to clarify the root causes of problems
	Explanation: Investigation techniques are concerned with understanding a situation from a holistic standpoint. Information that may initially seem irrelevant, such as the climate of a business area or ad hoc comments, is gathered and noted in case it illuminates the root causes of problems or helps to identify opportunities for change. A variety of techniques are available to business analysts when investigating situations. Many of these techniques overlap with those used during requirements elicitation. However, the application, stakeholders and focus are different in line with the often ambiguous and vague business situations that business analysts encounter
	Techniques: Interview, workshop, survey, observation, focus group, document analysis, prototyping, wireframing
Problem definition	**Objectives:** To identify the root cause of a business problem that is to be addressed by the BA Service; to create a statement setting out a clear definition of the problem
	Explanation: Problems that are identified to require investigation and resolution are often found to be symptoms or manifestations of an underlying problem. Business analysts are required to investigate situations, challenge statements and take a holistic view in order to identify the root causes of problems and ensure that these are addressed

(Continued)

Service name:	Situation investigation and problem analysis

Techniques: Rich picture, mind map, problem statement, Ishikawa (fishbone) diagram, five whys, context diagram, brainstorming/brainwriting, Post-it™ exercise

Requirements engineering

Objectives: To elicit tacit and explicit information from stakeholders regarding their requirements; to analyse this information with a view to understanding and recording why something is needed, what is needed, when it is required and who requires it

Explanation: Different levels of requirements may be required for a project. For example, a senior executive may request a feature at an overview level of definition; this may need to be explored in further detail with operational business staff. Different techniques may be applied when recording requirements. These techniques record different aspects of the requirements and may be applied at different levels of detail

Techniques: Requirements elicitation, requirements analysis, traceability matrix, requirements documentation, requirements management, prioritisation

Stakeholder management

Objectives: To identify stakeholders with concerns relevant to a proposed business change; to analyse stakeholders' levels of power and interest, and their values, beliefs and priorities; to determine stakeholder communication and management approaches relevant to the situation

Explanation: Stakeholder management techniques are an essential part of the business analysis toolkit because of the volume and range of stakeholders likely to be interested or affected by proposed business changes. These techniques help to ensure that stakeholders are not overlooked and that their concerns are understood, considered and addressed where possible

Techniques: CATWOE, root definition, worldview analysis, stakeholder wheel, stakeholder map, power/interest grid, social network analysis, RACI

User role modelling

Objectives: To explore the customer community, in particular the business user, to identify and clarify the requirements of a particular user role; to explore concerns specific to user roles with defined characteristics and needs

Explanation: User role modelling helps to understand the perspectives, viewpoints and needs of different categories of customer

Techniques: Use case diagram, scenario, user story, persona, UX diagram, storyboard, empathy map, customer journey

Service name:	Feasibility assessment and business case development
Service value proposition:	Define the rationale for a proposed business change, generate, describe and evaluate the options to achieve the business requirements, and quantify and/or describe the investment objectives and predicted business benefits
Service activities:	1. Generate and describe options to resolve the problem
	2. Remove unviable options
	3. Identify and analyse impacts and risks for each option and what may be done about them
	4. Identify and analyse costs and benefits for each option
	5. Evaluate financial, technical and business feasibility of options
	6. Evaluate alignment of options with strategic goals
	7. Support comparison and selection of solution

Service techniques:

Business case development	**Objectives:** To identify, define and evaluate options for business change; to ensure there is a financial case for a proposed change
	Explanation: Business case development techniques are concerned with the analysis of options to address business problems or realise business opportunities. This is necessary to ensure that an organisation is going to invest financial and other resources in viable projects. These techniques consider four aspects relevant to options: the costs, benefits, impacts on the organisation and risks. They also examine the likely business acceptance of an option
	Techniques: Cost/benefit analysis, investment appraisal, force-field analysis, risk analysis, benefits review, impact analysis, business impact assessment
Data modelling	**Objectives:** To represent the data required by an organisation or business area to support the delivery of services to customers (internal or external); to represent the business rules inherent in the structure of the data

(Continued)

Service name:	Feasibility assessment and business case development

Explanation: Data models provide a view of an information system from a data perspective. They may be developed at different levels of granularity; for example, an information concept or domain view consisting of high-level areas or a detailed data model encompassing elements such as data groupings, relationships between the groupings, business rules and individual data items. There are two major modelling approaches used to represent data or information. These are entity relationship modelling and class modelling. While they represent similar concepts, there are differences in the ways those concepts are modelled and in some of the detail represented

Techniques: Entity relationship diagram, class diagram, data definition, domain definition

Environment analysis	**Objectives:** To analyse the external business environment over which the organisation has little, if any, control; to analyse the factors within the organisation that must be considered when deciding on the strategy to respond to external factors

Explanation: Environment analysis techniques provide a rigorous basis for developing a SWOT analysis. However, this may result in a large number of factors to be considered in each quadrant of the SWOT and a degree of prioritisation is often required. The strengths and weaknesses are the internal factors that will help to determine the strategic choices available to an organisation. The threats and opportunities are the external factors facing the organisation; these need to be distinguished from the strategic choices made on the basis of the SWOT

Techniques: PESTLE analysis, Porter's 5-forces, SWOT analysis, Balanced Scorecard, critical success factor, key performance indicator

Gap analysis	**Objectives:** To examine a current and target state in order to determine where there are differences; to identify the actions required to move from a current to a target state

Explanation: Analysing the differences between current and target states might involve examining different representations of these states. For example, a popular approach is to compare 'as is' and 'to be' business process models; an alternative is to use a BAM as a conceptual view of a possible future state that may be compared with a representation or description of a current situation. Frameworks such as the POPIT™ model help to structure the gap analysis

Techniques: Gap analysis, 'as is' and 'to be' comparison, BAM, POPIT™ model

(Continued)

357

Service name:	Feasibility assessment and business case development	

Requirements engineering

Objectives: To elicit tacit and explicit information from stakeholders regarding their requirements; to analyse this information with a view to understanding and recording why something is needed, what is needed, when it is required and who requires it

Explanation: Different levels of requirements may be required for a project. For example, a senior executive may request a feature at an overview level of definition; this may need to be explored in further detail with operational business staff. Different techniques may be applied when recording requirements. These techniques record different aspects of the requirements and may be applied at different levels of detail

Techniques: Requirements elicitation, requirements analysis, traceability matrix, requirements documentation, requirements management, prioritisation

Stakeholder management

Objectives: To identify stakeholders with concerns relevant to a proposed business change; to analyse stakeholders' levels of power and interest, and their values, beliefs and priorities; to determine stakeholder communication and management approaches relevant to the situation

Explanation: Stakeholder management techniques are an essential part of the business analysis toolkit because of the volume and range of stakeholders likely to be interested in or affected by proposed business changes. These techniques help to ensure that stakeholders are not overlooked and that their concerns are understood, considered and addressed where possible

Techniques: CATWOE, root definition, worldview analysis, stakeholder wheel, stakeholder map, power/interest grid, social network analysis, RACI

Service name:	**Business process improvement**

Service value proposition:

Define the required enabling changes through describing and redesigning business processes, and identifying the actions to be undertaken to deploy the improved processes

Service activities:

1. Model existing processes
2. Define required (new or revised) processes
3. Identify gaps between existing ('as is') and required ('to be') processes
4. Analyse gaps between existing and required processes
5. Identify and analyse business process measures
6. Identify actions to implement new processes
7. Ensure alignment between IT systems and processes

Service techniques:

Gap analysis **Objectives:** To examine a current and target state in order to determine where there are differences; to identify the actions required to move from a current or target state

Explanation: Analysing the differences between current and target states might involve examining different representations of these states. For example, a popular approach is to compare 'as is' and 'to be' business process models; an alternative is to use a BAM as a conceptual view of a possible future state that may be compared with a representation or description of a current situation. Frameworks such as the POPIT™ model help to structure the gap analysis

Techniques: Gap analysis, 'as is' and 'to be' comparison, BAM, POPIT™ model

Investigation **Objectives:** To explore situations with the aim of uncovering issues, problems, opportunities and other relevant information; to clarify the root causes of problems

Explanation: Investigation techniques are concerned with understanding a situation from a holistic standpoint. Information that may initially seem irrelevant, such as the climate of a business area or ad hoc comments, is gathered and noted in case it illuminates the root causes of problems or helps to identify opportunities for change. A variety of techniques are available to business analysts when investigating situations. Many of these techniques overlap with those used during requirements elicitation. However, the application, stakeholders and focus are different in line with the often ambiguous and vague business situations that business analysts encounter

Techniques: Interview, workshop, survey, observation, focus group, document analysis, prototyping, wireframing

(Continued)

Service name:	Business process improvement	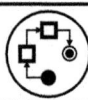

Process modelling	**Objectives:** To represent processing conducted by an organisation or business area to deliver services to customers (internal or external); to provide a diagrammatic view that is a basis for improving business processes
	Explanation: Process models provide a view of an information system from a process perspective. They may be developed at different levels of granularity; for example, an organisational view of the value chain consisting of high-level activities or a cross-functional diagram showing detailed elements such as process flows, actors, decisions and tasks. The fundamental aspects of process modelling techniques are very similar as they show activities or tasks and the flows between them. However, the level of detail represented will differ depending upon the context, and the modelling notation is variable depending upon the standard adopted within an organisation or by the BA Service
	Techniques: Business process model, swimlane diagram, BPMN diagram, business process map, decision modelling, value chain, activity diagram, event analysis
Stakeholder management	**Objectives:** To identify stakeholders with concerns relevant to a proposed business change; to analyse stakeholders' levels of power and interest, and their values, beliefs and priorities; to determine stakeholder communication and management approaches relevant to the situation
	Explanation: Stakeholder management techniques are an essential part of the business analysis toolkit because of the volume and range of stakeholders likely to be interested or affected by proposed business changes. These techniques help to ensure that stakeholders are not overlooked and that their concerns are understood, considered and addressed where possible
	Techniques: CATWOE, root definition, worldview analysis, stakeholder wheel, stakeholder map, power/interest grid, social network analysis, RACI
User role modelling	**Objectives:** To explore the customer community, in particular the business user, to identify and clarify the requirements of a particular user role; to explore concerns specific to user roles with defined characteristics and needs
	Explanation: User role modelling helps to understand the perspectives, viewpoints and needs of different categories of customer
	Techniques: Use case diagram, scenario, user story, persona, UX diagram, storyboard, empathy map, customer journey

Service name:	Requirements definition

Service value proposition:

Define the required enabling changes through eliciting, analysing, describing and managing requirements for business and IT changes at the level of detail relevant to the context

Service activities:

1. Define requirements definition approach and quality standards
2. Elicit and interpret the requirements
3. Record requirements
4. Build models and prototypes to represent the requirements
5. Collaborate and communicate with internal stakeholders in the business and IT functions, and external stakeholders to clarify requirements
6. Analyse, prioritise and assure the quality of the defined requirements
7. Support stakeholder review of requirements
8. Conduct user analysis and profiling
9. Ensure requirements are aligned with project scope and strategic business goals
10. Establish traceability of requirements from the business need to the solution

Service techniques:

Agile development	**Objectives:** To apply Agile principles to a software development project; to govern the work of an Agile software development project
	Explanation: Agile software development projects adopt techniques and ceremonies that align with the Agile philosophy and principles. There are established techniques used to apply Agile effectively
	Techniques: Product/solution backlog, Kanban Board, daily stand-up, retrospective, sprint/iteration

(Continued)

Service name:	Requirements definition

Data modelling	**Objectives:** To represent the data required by an organisation or business area to support the delivery of services to customers (internal or external); to represent the business rules inherent in the structure of the data
	Explanation: Data models provide a view of an information system from a data perspective. They may be developed at different levels of granularity; for example, an information concept or domain view consisting of high-level areas or a detailed data model encompassing elements such as data groupings, relationships between the groupings, business rules and individual data items. There are two major modelling approaches used to represent data or information. These are entity relationship modelling and class modelling. While they represent similar concepts, there are differences in the ways those concepts are modelled and in some of the detail represented
	Techniques: Entity relationship diagram, class diagram, data definition, domain definition
Investigation	**Objectives:** To explore situations with the aim of uncovering issues, problems, opportunities and other relevant information; to clarify the root causes of problems
	Explanation: Investigation techniques are concerned with understanding a situation from a holistic standpoint. Information that may initially seem irrelevant, such as the climate of a business area or ad hoc comments, is gathered and noted in case it illuminates the root causes of problems or helps to identify opportunities for change. A variety of techniques are available to business analysts when investigating situations. Many of these techniques overlap with those used during requirements elicitation. However, the application, stakeholders and focus are different in line with the often ambiguous and vague business situations that business analysts encounter
	Techniques: Interview, workshop, survey, observation, focus group, document analysis, prototyping, wireframing

(Continued)

Service name:	Requirements definition

Process modelling	**Objectives:** To represent processing conducted by an organisation or business area to deliver services to customers (internal or external); to provide a diagrammatic view that is a basis for improving business processes
	Explanation: Process models provide a view of an information system from a process perspective. They may be developed at different levels of granularity; for example, an organisational view of the value chain consisting of high-level activities or a cross-functional diagram showing detailed elements such as process flows, actors, decisions and tasks. The fundamental aspects of process modelling techniques are very similar as they show activities or tasks and the flows between them. However, the level of detail represented will differ depending upon the context, and the modelling notation is variable depending upon the standard adopted within an organisation or by the BA Service
	Techniques: Business process model, swimlane diagram, BPMN diagram, business process map, decision modelling, value chain, activity diagram, event analysis
Requirements engineering	**Objectives:** To elicit tacit and explicit information from stakeholders regarding their requirements; to analyse this information with a view to understanding and recording why something is needed, what is needed, when it is required and who requires it
	Explanation: Different levels of requirements may be required for a project. For example, a senior executive may request a feature at an overview level of definition; this may need to be explored in further detail with operational business staff. Different techniques may be applied when recording requirements. These techniques record different aspects of the requirements and may be applied at different levels of detail
	Techniques: Requirements elicitation, requirements analysis, traceability matrix, requirements documentation, requirements management, prioritisation

(Continued)

| Service name: | Requirements definition |  |

Stakeholder management	**Objectives:** To identify stakeholders with concerns relevant to a proposed business change; to analyse stakeholders' levels of power and interest, and their values, beliefs and priorities; to determine stakeholder communication and management approaches relevant to the situation
	Explanation: Stakeholder management techniques are an essential part of the business analysis toolkit because of the volume and range of stakeholders likely to be interested or affected by proposed business changes. These techniques help to ensure that stakeholders are not overlooked and that their concerns are understood, considered and addressed where possible
	Techniques: CATWOE, root definition, worldview analysis, stakeholder wheel, stakeholder map, power/interest grid, social network analysis, RACI
System requirements specification	**Objectives:** To create a detailed specification of the requirements to be delivered by an information system; to provide a basis for the development of an information system
	Explanation: Some systems development projects require detailed specification of the requirements and, in some organisations, business analysts may conduct or contribute to this work. For example, this may be for specific features or for non-functional requirements such as security and access. Techniques defined by the UML are often used to provide a detailed level of specification
	Techniques: Sequence diagrams, state charts, CRUD matrix
User role modelling	**Objectives:** To explore the customer community, in particular the business user, to identify and clarify the requirements of a particular user role; to explore concerns specific to user roles with defined characteristics and needs
	Explanation: User role modelling helps to understand the perspectives, viewpoints and needs of different categories of customer
	Techniques: Use case diagram, scenario, user story, persona, UX diagram, storyboard, empathy map, customer journey

Service name:	Business acceptance testing	

Service value proposition:

Collaborate with stakeholders to support business acceptance of the solution

Service activities:

1. Agree scope for testing activity

2. Define test scenarios and test cases

3. Provide support to stakeholders when testing for business acceptance

Service techniques:

Agile development	**Objectives:** To apply Agile principles to a software development project; to govern the work of an Agile software development project
	Explanation: Agile software development projects adopt techniques and ceremonies that align with the Agile philosophy and principles. There are established techniques used to apply Agile effectively
	Techniques: Product/solution backlog, Kanban Board, daily stand-up, retrospective, sprint/iteration
Stakeholder management	**Objectives:** To identify stakeholders with concerns relevant to a proposed business change; to analyse stakeholders' levels of power and interest, and their values, beliefs and priorities; to determine stakeholder communication and management approaches relevant to the situation
	Explanation: Stakeholder management techniques are an essential part of the business analysis toolkit because of the volume and range of stakeholders likely to be interested or affected by proposed business changes. These techniques help to ensure that stakeholders are not overlooked and that their concerns are understood, considered and addressed where possible
	Techniques: CATWOE, root definition, worldview analysis, stakeholder wheel, stakeholder map, power/interest grid, social network analysis, RACI
User acceptance testing (UAT)	**Objectives:** To design and conduct test scenarios with a view to identifying where a product fails to meet the needs of the business user; to support the business user community in ensuring that a product is of a sufficient level of quality to be accepted for deployment
	Explanation: The confirmation that a product is acceptable is the responsibility of the business users. However, business analysts are often required to support the business users during user acceptance testing. This requires planning of the approach to the UAT and deciding the techniques and data that will be used during this process
	Techniques: User acceptance scenario, test case

Service name: Business change deployment

Service value proposition:

Collaborate with stakeholders to support the deployment of the required business changes and enable their adoption

Service activities:

1. Assess business readiness

2. Support transition planning

3. Support the adoption of the IT and business changes

4. Develop and deliver training in the new IT and business systems

5. Support the benefits and post-implementation reviews

6. Support the realisation of the business benefits

Service techniques:

Implementation **Objectives:** To prepare affected business areas for the implementation of business changes; to deploy business changes successfully; to review the business change processes and outcomes

Explanation: Implementation of business changes requires comprehensive planning and preparation. Typically, this includes consideration of areas such as communication, training, infrastructure set-up and data migration

Techniques: Training needs analysis, training material development, CPPOLDAT, post-implementation review

Stakeholder **Objectives:** To identify stakeholders with concerns relevant to a
management proposed business change; to analyse stakeholders' levels of power and interest, and their values, beliefs and priorities; to determine stakeholder communication and management approaches relevant to the situation

Explanation: Stakeholder management techniques are an essential part of the business analysis toolkit because of the volume and range of stakeholders likely to be interested or affected by proposed business changes. These techniques help to ensure that stakeholders are not overlooked and that their concerns are understood, considered and addressed where possible

Techniques: CATWOE, root definition, worldview analysis, stakeholder wheel, stakeholder map, power/interest grid, social network analysis, RACI

(Continued)

Service name:	**Business change deployment** 

User role modelling	**Objectives:** To explore the customer community, in particular the business user, to identify and clarify the requirements of a particular user role; to explore concerns specific to user roles with defined characteristics and needs
	Explanation: User role modelling helps to understand the perspectives, viewpoints and needs of different categories of customer
	Techniques: Use case diagram, scenario, user story, persona, UX diagram, storyboard, empathy map, customer journey

Service name:	**Stakeholder engagement** 

Service value proposition:

Support the achievement of business and IS project success through stakeholder collaboration, communication and effective stakeholder relationship management

Service activities:

1. Challenge and inform stakeholders
2. Negotiate stakeholder conflicts
3. Engage with stakeholders
4. Communicate with stakeholders verbally and in writing
5. Support stakeholders
6. Facilitate meetings and workshops and record outputs

Service techniques:

Stakeholder management	**Objectives:** To identify stakeholders with concerns relevant to a proposed business change; to analyse stakeholders' levels of power and interest, and their values, beliefs and priorities; to determine stakeholder communication and management approaches relevant to the situation
	Explanation: Stakeholder management techniques are an essential part of the business analysis toolkit because of the volume and range of stakeholders likely to be interested or affected by proposed business changes. These techniques help to ensure that stakeholders are not overlooked and that their concerns are understood, considered and addressed where possible
	Techniques: CATWOE, root definition, worldview analysis, stakeholder wheel, stakeholder map, power/interest grid, social network analysis, RACI

APPENDIX 2
BA RECRUITMENT STRATEGY

Explanation: A recruitment strategy for the BA Service sets out what the service needs to achieve via recruitment, the internal and external context and the approach that has been selected to meet the objectives. This will be particularly important for organisations with a large number of BAs, but even a small BA Service needs to consider a mix of grades, gaps in skills and knowledge, future demand and budget constraints and how these issues can be addressed through recruitment.

SUGGESTED CONTENT FOR BA RECRUITMENT STRATEGY

Document controls

Service name		Sponsor/customer	
Author		Date and version	

Context

Purpose of the BA recruitment strategy	Why has this been created?
Audience	Who will contribute to and use the BA recruitment strategy?
Glossary	Key terms used, with descriptions
Related documents	For example role profiles, job descriptions, career pathways, pay scales, industry research, BA demand forecasts

Detail

Purpose/goals(s) of the strategy	What is the BA Service hoping to achieve with the recruitment strategy? For example, increase the number of BAs from X to Y, change the mix of grades/levels of experience, introduce a pipeline approach, change the ratio of contract to permanent staff, bring certain skills into the organisation, meet budget targets, etc.
Demand for business analysis	What is the current level of BA resource in the BA Service?
	What is the predicted demand for business analysis capacity and capability for the next X months/years? What is the level of certainty in the demand? What could influence this?
	What attrition/turnover rates does the service experience?
Organisational context	What internal information is relevant to the BA recruitment strategy? For example, organisation growth or reduction, creation or removal of other related disciplines, location strategy, any changes in direction that may impact BA resources
Internal routes into business analysis	How might people join the BA Service? What are the related roles? Can relationships be built to facilitate this? How could awareness of the BA career path be raised?
Local market analysis	What organisations are key competitors for BAs?
	Market pay and other attraction factors
	May include PESTLE analysis
Pipeline approach	Is a pipeline approach suitable? What approaches are in use elsewhere in the organisation?
	Which factors may suggest one pipeline approach over another (e.g. remote location; apprenticeship route aimed at existing residents of the local area; nationally recognised brand – nationwide graduate search and expect people to relocate)?
Attracting candidates	How will the BA Service be presented? Are the benefits of working here clear? What has worked well/not worked in the past?
Channels	Which routes are available to communicate with and attract candidates? Select primary channels to be used
Specialist recruiters	What specialist help is available? What has been successful in the past? (provide evidence)
Time frame	For what period is the strategy expected to apply? How quickly do the goals need to be met?
Constraints	What other constraints exist that may impact the strategy?
Costs	What are the cost implications of different channels, routes and specialist help?

APPENDIX 3
BA INDUCTION CHECKLIST

Explanation: An induction checklist is used to ensure a smooth and consistent experience for business analysts joining the BA Service.

Pre-arrival:

- ☐ Agree start time
- ☐ Consider location
- ☐ Arrange equipment
- ☐ Arrange access
- ☐ Prepare welcome pack
- ☐ Follow organisational processes (HR/payroll, etc.)
- ☐ Add email to distribution lists
- ☐ Add to relevant meeting invites
- ☐ Plan first week agenda
- ☐ Send new job card
- ☐ Announce new arrival to relevant colleagues
- ☐ Keep new BA informed

First day:

- ☐ Outline the plan for the day
- ☐ Agree finish time
- ☐ Welcome activities and key introductions
- ☐ Provide welcome pack
- ☐ Discuss working practices and culture
- ☐ Discuss organisation and BA Service strategy
- ☐ Organisation requirements including health and safety
- ☐ Arrange office tour
- ☐ Explain practicalities (parking, entry, desk arrangements, kitchens, drinks, bathrooms, etc.)
- ☐ Set up equipment
- ☐ Overview of phones, printers, etc.
- ☐ Signpost to support
- ☐ Make lunch plans
- ☐ Assign buddy
- ☐ Discuss employee benefits
- ☐ Remember to listen to the new person too!

First week:

- ☐ Provide assignment details
- ☐ Provide background reading
- ☐ Confirm plan for the week
- ☐ Identify shadowing opportunities
- ☐ Continue appropriate introductions
- ☐ Arrange regular check-in sessions
- ☐ Overview of key systems and tools
- ☐ Explain performance review process and objective setting

First month:

- ☐ Corporate induction activities
- ☐ Set clear objectives
- ☐ Discuss progress
- ☐ Discuss and agree training, support and development
- ☐ Get feedback on recruitment and induction

APPENDIX 4
BA LEARNING ACTION PLAN

Explanation: A learning action plan provides a mechanism to encourage business analysts to commit to three actions they will each take in response to a learning and development opportunity. The intention is that these actions will help to embed the learning and share the knowledge. The learning action plan applies equally to all types of learning activities, such as reading a book, watching a webinar, attending formal training or a conference, or attending internal development sessions.

The actions can be categorised as:

Find it: Investigate this learning point further (e.g. follow up references or reading list provided), which may lead to additional action.

Make it: Create or update a template or guidance material to support future use within the BA Service.

Use it: Apply this learning on a project or BA Service activity.

Share it: Promote the learning through a business analysis meeting, development event, shared area or other method of dissemination.

SUGGESTED CONTENT FOR BA LEARNING ACTION PLAN

Document controls

Business analyst		Location	
Development activity		Date and version	

Detail

Learning point	Learning point description	Learning action type	How will the action be achieved?	Does this link to current objectives?	Target date
Encourage 3 points per activity	What is the key learning point/area of interest?	Find it, Make it, Use it, Share it.	What action will be taken as a result of the learning/ development activity? (activities, resources, support required)	Y/N – state which development objective this relates to	
1					
2					
3					

APPENDIX 5
BA COACHING/MENTORING AGREEMENT

Explanation: Where a BA has a mentor, either from within the BA profession or another discipline, it is good practice for both mentor and mentee to discuss what they hope can be achieved through the mentoring process and document this via a mentoring agreement.

It is important to define a time frame for reviewing the agreement and to identify questions to be discussed during a review. These questions could include:

- Are these goals still relevant?
- What progress has been made?
- Is this relationship still useful/working/needed?
- Are we able to commit appropriate time for this relationship?
- What are the goals/actions going forward?

Open-ended mentoring relationships can cease to be useful or fizzle out. Agreeing in advance that these potentially difficult subjects will be discussed makes the prospect of ending or changing the mentoring relationship easier.

The same approach could be used to agree specific outcomes and ways of working in a coaching relationship.

SUGGESTED CONTENT FOR BA MENTORING AGREEMENT

Document controls

BA (person being mentored i.e. 'mentee')		Status	(draft/agreed)
Mentor		Date and version	

Detail

Initial learning objectives/goals	What has instigated the mentoring relationship? What does each person hope to achieve through the relationship? What will be the broad areas of focus/ themes?
Ways of working together/ground rules	Confidentiality, professionalism, consideration regarding cancellation or rescheduling meetings
Responsibilities of the mentee	Behaviours/actions/information
Responsibilities of the mentor	Behaviours/actions/information
Support	Other people or resources that may be called upon to support the mentoring processes
Logistics	Frequency and duration of sessions. Location or communication mechanism (e.g. face to face, online, telephone, etc.)
Date to review mentoring agreement	At this point, the mentor and mentee will reflect on the process and relationship, consider progress and discuss future objectives. The mentoring relationship could end or change following discussion

APPENDIX 6
BA SERVICE SUPPORT TOOLS STRATEGY

Explanation: There may be a number of different tools in use to support the delivery of the BA Service. A support tools strategy should determine which tools will be used to provide the functionality required by the BAs. The aim is to streamline the technology used while ensuring that the tool support is available when required. The support tools strategy may also include requirements where a support tool is not currently available, but a BA service or activity has been defined that could be supported by a tool at some point in the future (possibly following an assessment, development or procurement exercise).

SUGGESTED CONTENT FOR BA SERVICE SUPPORT TOOLS STRATEGY

Document controls

Service name		Sponsor/owner	
Author		Date and version	
Reviewer(s)		Change log	

Context

Purpose of the BA Service support tools strategy	Why has this been created?
Audience	Who will contribute to and use the BA Service support tools strategy?
Glossary	Key terms used, with descriptions
Related documents	For example, documentation relating to contracts, licences agreements, organisational support tools strategy or principles, industry whitepapers

Detail

Tool name	
Functionality	What does the tool offer?
	What is actually in use?
Users	Number and type of users (e.g. particular individuals, teams, roles) who use and advocate the use of this tool
Support	What support, guidance, training is available for the tool?
	Has training been invested in previously? If so, what courses/ suppliers?
Costs	What are the direct costs/ training costs/ licence costs/ hosting costs, etc.
Owner	Who pays for the tool and the licences?
	Who has the supplier relationship?
	Who could make the decision to replace?
Strategy	What is the intention for the use of this tool?
	(A) strategic tool
	(B) interim tool: review by X date
	(C) tactical tool: replace by X date
	(D) legacy tool: no longer in use

APPENDIX 7
BUSINESS ANALYSIS WORK PACKAGE CONTENT

Explanation: A work package is used to agree and document the business analysis work to be carried out, the boundaries, activities and outputs/deliverables. It should cover:

Why the analysis is required (purpose and goals).

What analysis will be carried out (activities and details of deliverables).

Who will do the analysis and who will be involved (named BA and stakeholders).

When the work is required (deadlines, dependencies and constraints).

How the analysis will be done (methods, approach to review, sign-off arrangements).

The creation of the work package facilitates a conversation about the business analysis service to be provided and records the agreements about the business analysis activities and deliverables. This enables shared expectations and outcomes to be defined. A tension about work packages may arise regarding the business analysis activities required to address the business need and the limitations of a fixed time frame.

SUGGESTED CONTENT FOR BA WORK PACKAGE

Document controls

Project/programme/ work area		Sponsor/customer	
Author		Date and version	

Context

Business analyst(s)	Whole-time equivalents/number of BAs required
Requestor	Who is asking for the business analysis work to be carried out?
Target start date	
Target completion date	
Assumptions	What assumptions are being made by the requestor/author? Examples are: availability of BAs, complexity of the work, number of stakeholders, availability of stakeholders, prior knowledge or level of experience of the business BAs
Related documents	For example, previous or related work packages, budget or recruitment approvals, statements of senior support, evidence of prioritisation, relevant plans

Detail

Purpose and goal(s) of the wider project/work	What is the context for this work package? How does this work package contribute to the wider aims of the project?
Purpose and goal(s) of the business analysis work package	What are the analysis activity and deliverables trying to achieve? What business questions are being addressed via the analysis? (What is the focus of the analysis: fact-finding, developing and exploring options, enabling informed decision making, risk mitigation, enabling communication, relationship building, documenting information, assessing impact...?) **This information is key to selecting the appropriate business analysis outputs and methods**
BA(s) allocated to carry out the work	Who will carry out the work package?
Stakeholders involved	Who will the BA(s) need to work with?
Outputs to be delivered	What is the work package going to produce? What will it create or modify? What will these deliverables look like in terms of format, content, scope? It may be worth considering minimum outputs and possible subsequent or nice-to-have deliverables if time allows

Target audience for outputs	Who will receive the outputs?
	Recipients, beneficiaries, consumers. How will they use the outputs?
Out of scope	Is anything specifically excluded from the business analysis activities?
	Groups of stakeholders, business areas, systems, deliverables
Sources of information	Have any sources of information for this work already been identified?
	Subject matter experts, business areas, documents, policies, regulations, existing systems, other projects, lessons learned logs from previous projects
Related activities	What other activities will be taking place in parallel, or which will impact this work package, or which could be impacted by this work package? What are the dependencies (in terms of people, activities and timescales)?
Quality	What quality checking method(s) will be used?
	Consider both format and content (peer review, team review, use of templates, quality criteria, review checklists)
Configuration management	What controls will be used to ensure different versions of the products are properly maintained? Where should work package outputs be stored?
Sign-off arrangements	Who will approve or accept the work? What conditions must be met for this to happen? Relevant governance groups and boards? How should completion be communicated and to whom?
Time frame	What is the agreed time frame for this work package?
Constraints	What other constraints exist?
	Consider POPIT™, as well as financial, timescales, policy or legal constraints on the work
Progress reporting arrangements	How should progress on the work package be reported?
	To whom, how often, by what means

APPENDIX 8
BUSINESS ANALYSIS APPROACH

Explanation: A business analysis approach is used to agree and document the business analysis methods, priorities and ways of working. The breadth of potential areas for business analysis could be very wide, with many techniques available to BAs. The business analysis approach sets out a rationale for the areas of focus and techniques to be applied. This could take the format of a document, diagram, presentation, plan or structured conversation.

By considering the business analysis approach up front, the needs of the customer will drive the business analysis activities. This will ensure that the business analysis effort expended, and the deliverables produced, will help the business to make informed decisions and do not simply represent the analysis the BA wanted to deliver. The approach should not be 'set in stone'; it may need to be refined or updated as more information becomes available or there are project changes.

SUGGESTED CONTENT FOR BA APPROACH

Document controls

Project/programme/ work area		Sponsor/customer	
Author		Date and version	
Reviewer(s)		Change log	

Context

Purpose of the business analysis approach	Why has this been created?
Audience	Who will receive and review the business analysis approach
Glossary	Key terms used, with descriptions
Related documents	For example, BA Service standards and guidance, related work packages, related project documentation, relevant plans

Detail

Influencing factors	The business analysis approach will be influenced by which business analysis services are being provided, needs of stakeholders, capacity and capability of BAs, BA Service maturity, internal and external context for the organisation, timescales, cost, risk appetite, existing analysis work, organisational priorities, access to stakeholders, supplier landscape, IT development approach as well as physical and logistic constraints (co-location, geography, time zones)
	It is useful to confirm with stakeholders and business analysts what the business analysis approach will be for this project and the key factors influencing the approach
Business analysis planning	Which business analysis services are most relevant? What are the stages of analysis?
	Who will define and deliver the business analysis activities? How will estimating and prioritising be carried out? How will progress be monitored? What are the dependencies?
Stakeholder management	How will stakeholders be identified? What stakeholder analysis techniques will be used? How will the analysis inform stakeholder engagement?
	What will be the methods and frequency of communication between BAs and stakeholders?
Process management	What is the level of process maturity in the organisation? Existence/role of process owners? Approach to process improvement? What will the processes be used for? How will processes be documented and managed? Levels of process to be documented? What supporting documentation is needed in addition to models?
Requirements engineering	Relationship to scoping? What will the requirements be used for (for example, organisational change, procurement, system development)?
	Agree a requirement hierarchy and life cycle. What elicitation techniques will be used? How will requirements be documented and managed? What estimation and prioritisation mechanisms will be used? How will traceability be achieved?
Data analysis	What will the analysis be used for? What is the level of data maturity in the organisation? Existence/role of data owners? How will data be documented and managed?
	What supporting documentation is needed in addition to models?

Business analysis resources	What are the roles and responsibilities? What support and development needs do the BAs have?
	How will analysis work be allocated? Will work packages be used? How will additional resource be accessed if needed?
	Charging/funding considerations and mechanisms
Risk and issue management	How will risks and issues arising from the business analysis work be communicated, captured and managed?
Scope and change management	How will questions relating to the scope of business analysis work and the scope of the project be addressed?
	What are the processes and the level of formality/ documentation related to change management?
Reporting lines and BA management	What are the reporting lines to project roles and for BA oversight?
	What project meetings or mechanisms will be used for reporting on business analysis progress? How will issues be addressed or escalated?
Business analysis tools and methodology	What tools will be used? What are the implications of using the tool (access, training licensing)?
	What (if any) methodology will be followed? Why is this appropriate?
Quality management	What quality control processes will be applied?
	(Peer reviews, walk-throughs, review tracking and response mechanisms, use of product descriptions to set and manage expectations, adherence to standards, use of checklists, etc.)
Business analysis standards	What BA Service standards are applicable and will be adhered to? How will compliance to standards be monitored?
Governance	What approaches will be used for approvals and sign-off? Who needs to be involved? What is the level of formality/ documentation?
Benefits management	What are the responsibilities of the BAs in relation to benefits analysis and management? How will benefits be documented, categorised, measured and tracked?
Business architecture	What are the responsibilities of the BAs regarding business architecture? How will existing business architecture information be accessed and re-used? How will new architectural and design information and decisions be documented and shared?
Conclusion, recommendations, next steps	What are the outstanding questions that need to be resolved, decisions that need to be made, or recommendations in relation to moving forward with the analysis? What happens now?

APPENDIX 9
BA SERVICE COMMUNITY EVENT CHECKLIST

Explanation: Successful events require careful planning. To facilitate the smooth running of BA Service community events, it is useful to create a checklist, assign responsibilities and track progress. Events involving large numbers of people or external speakers need sufficient lead-in time (approximately 12 weeks). Smaller internal events will require less time (approximately four weeks).

It is essential to consider common issues that may arise and, where possible, make contingency arrangements. Also consider the circumstances under which the event may have to be cancelled.

4–12 weeks before:

- ☐ Book venue
- ☐ Send invites
- ☐ Draft agenda
- ☐ Approach speakers
- ☐ Promote event

Contingency planning:

- ☐ Speaker cancels
- ☐ Technology fails
- ☐ Venue unavailable
- ☐ Key person unavailable

2 weeks before:

- ☐ Confirm venue
- ☐ Confirm speakers
- ☐ Confirm numbers
- ☐ Send reminders
- ☐ Send agenda
- ☐ Plan exercises
- ☐ Consider printing
- ☐ Consider security/access
- ☐ Arrange refreshments
- ☐ Arrange technology
- ☐ Arrange equipment/resources
- ☐ Assign roles for the event

On the day:

- ☐ Arrive early
- ☐ Provide signposting
- ☐ Set up room
- ☐ Provide refreshments
- ☐ Test technology
- ☐ Arrange security
- ☐ Set up sign-in

Within 1–2 weeks:

- ☐ Thank speakers
- ☐ Send notes/summary
- ☐ Send actions
- ☐ Confirm next date(s)
- ☐ Seek feedback
- ☐ Analyse feedback

APPENDIX 10
BA SERVICE COMMUNICATIONS STRATEGY

Explanation: To ensure that the right stakeholders are engaged throughout the year, the BA Service needs to consider creating a service communications strategy. The strategy provides the opportunity to consider and document the types of information needed by different groups (internal and external), the frequency and the channels that can be validated with stakeholders and translated into a communications plan.

SUGGESTED CONTENT FOR BA SERVICE COMMUNICATIONS STRATEGY

Document controls

Service name		Sponsor/owner	
Author		Date and version	
Reviewer(s)		Change log	

Context

Purpose of the service communications strategy	Why has this been created?
Audience	Who will contribute to and use the BA Service communications strategy?
Glossary	Key terms used, with descriptions
Related documents	

Detail

Purpose of communications	What is the service trying to achieve through this communication?
Audience	Which individuals or groups will be contacted? Consider using the stakeholder wheel
Key messages	What are their main areas of interest/concern that the communications need to address?
Channels	What mechanisms will be used?
Frequency	How often does this need to occur?
Owner	Who will produce the communications?

APPENDIX 11
BUSINESS ANALYSIS EXPECTATION MATRIX

Explanation: Stakeholders may have expectations of the BA Service, or possibly regarding individual business analysts, which are unspoken and often not addressed. Facilitating a discussion about expectations at an early stage helps to ensure that future work packages and agreements about roles and responsibilities are built on a foundation of shared understanding.

SUGGESTED CONTENT FOR EXPECTATION MATRIX

Document controls

Project/programme/ work area		Sponsor/customer	
Author		Date and version	
Reviewer(s)		Change log	

Context

Purpose of the expectation matrix	Why has this been created?
Audience	Who will contribute to and use the business analysis expectation matrix?
Glossary	Key terms used, with descriptions
Related documents	For example, stakeholder analysis, relevant work packages and plans

Detail

Stakeholder type	Name of stakeholder or stakeholder group (e.g. customers, sponsor, testers, etc.)
Expectation	What do they want? (**what** and **how**)
Experience	Are we meeting the expectation? What is their current experience?
KPIs	How can we measure and monitor?
Objective	What can we do to **either** meet the expectation **or** change it?
CSFs	Factors that influence achieving the objective
Importance	Prioritise the stakeholders and actions

APPENDIX 12
BA SERVICE IMPROVEMENT PLAN

Explanation: The BA Service Improvement Plan exists to turn the outcomes from a business analysis service assessment into a set of tangible actions that will be carried out over a defined period of time. Possible improvements may also be suggested via customer feedback, business analysis events, a quality review process and as a result of learning and development activities. A key aspect of the plan concerns traceability, showing how service improvements contribute to service or organisational strategic objectives and tracking the origin of improvement suggestions.

Some improvements may not be practical, possible or considered a priority for the service and it is reasonable to reject some suggested improvements.

SUGGESTED CONTENT FOR BA SERVICE IMPROVEMENT PLAN

Document controls

Service name		Sponsor/owner	
Author		Date and version	
Reviewer(s)		Change log	

Context

Purpose of the Service Improvement Plan	Why has this been created?
Audience	Who will contribute to and use the BA Service Improvement Plan?
Glossary	Key terms used, with descriptions
Related documents	For example, any previous improvement plans, service assessment outputs, customer feedback, organisational or service strategy, improvement suggestions captured by BAs

Detail

POPIT™ or strategy area	What does this improvement relate to?
	Which service or organisational objectives would this improvement contribute to?
Ref/ID	Unique reference
Improvement description	What is the improvement that has been identified?
	What are the options for making an improvement?
Impact assessment	What would be the impact of this improvement?
	Who would benefit?
	Could there be any negative or unintended consequences?
	How easy will it be to implement the improvement?
	What are the cost implications?
	Are these justified?
Source	Where did this suggested improvement originate?
Priority, timescales	How big an issue is this?
	How quickly does it need to be addressed?
	Accept/reject?
	Target completion date
RACI	Who will carry out the activity?
	Who is accountable?
	Who needs to be consulted and informed?

APPENDIX 13
BA SERVICE RISK ASSESSMENT

Explanation: There may be a number of risks that could significantly impact the delivery of the BA Service. A risk assessment provides the opportunity to assess and document those risks, to define actions and plans to address the risks, and to decide how to respond should the risk occur.

SUGGESTED CONTENT FOR BA SERVICE RISK ASSESSMENT

Document controls

Service name		Sponsor/owner	
Author		Date and version	
Reviewer(s)		Change log	

Context

Purpose of the service risk assessment	Why has this been created?
Audience	Who will contribute to and use the BA Service risk assessment?
Glossary	Key terms used, with descriptions
Related documents	

Detail

POPIT™ area	What does this risk relate to?
Risk ID	Unique reference
Risk description	What could occur (challenges **and** opportunities)
	Why might the risk arise?
Impact assessment	What would happen if this risk occurred?
	Who and what would be affected?
	How would they be affected?
	(score if applicable)
Probability	How likely is the risk to occur?
	(score if applicable)
Countermeasures	Actions in relation to each of the potential risk action types:
	Avoidance
	Mitigation
	Transference
	Acceptance
	Plans to be put in place if risk occurs
Owner	Who owns the risk, who is assessing options and defining plans?

APPENDIX 14
BUSINESS ANALYSIS PERFORMANCE SURVEY

Explanation: It is useful to seek feedback from customers on a regular basis, and at least at the end of a business analysis assignment to enable reflection and growth. The categories shown below were created with input from a large number of BA managers and senior BAs, via the cross-industry BAMF. The categories are considered to be most relevant to customers, reflect the key aspects of the BA role and to be applicable for many settings (e.g. project, business as usual, work package) and different development methodologies (e.g. Linear/Waterfall, Agile).

The method and frequency of **communication** were agreed at the start, and were maintained:

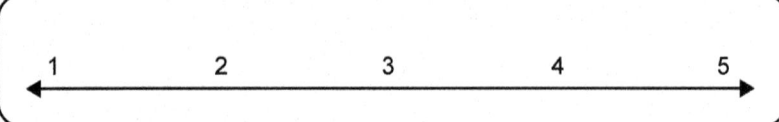

The BA was **committed** to a successful project outcome:

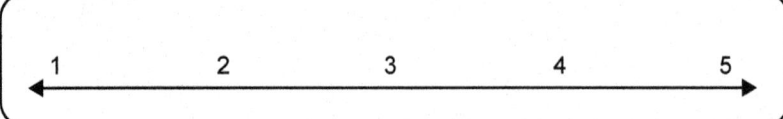

The BA **understands** my business and what is important to me:

The BA produced outputs that were **valuable** to me:

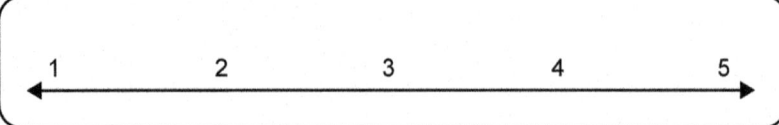

The BA encouraged **collaboration** within the project team:

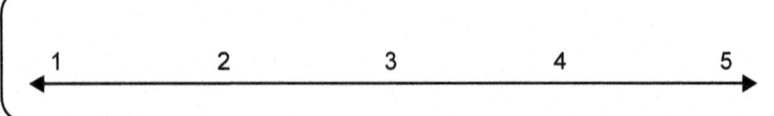

REFERENCES

All URLs are correct at the time of first publication.

ACAS Guidance (2016) Employing younger workers. Available from: www.acas.org.uk/media/pdf/0/i/Employing_younger_workers_Nov.pdf

Adair, J. (2009) *Effective Leadership*. London: Pan Books.

Allee, V. (2002) *The Future of Knowledge: increasing prosperity through value networks*. Burlington, MA: Routledge.

Argyris, C. and Schon, D. A. (1974) *Theory in Practice: increasing professional effectiveness*. San Francisco: Jossey Bass.

Artz, B., Goodall, A. and Oswald, A. (2016) 'If your boss could do your job, you're more likely to be happy at work', *Harvard Business Review*. Available from: hbr.org/2016/12/if-your-boss-could-do-your-job-youre-more-likely-to-be-happy-at-work.

Baddeley, S. and James, K. (1987) 'Owl, fox, donkey or sheep: political skills for managers'. *Management Education and Development*, 18 (1). 3–19.

Behn, R. D. (2003) 'Why measure performance? Different purposes require different measures'. *Public Administration Review*, 63 (5). 586–606.

Berger, C., Blauth, R., Boger, D., Bolster, C., Burchill, G., DuMouchel, W., Pouliot, F., Richter, R., Rubinoff, A., Shen, D. and Timko, M. (1993) 'Kano's methods for understanding customer-defined quality'. *Center for Quality of Management Journal*, 2 (4). 5.

Business Analysis Manager Forum (2012) Skills coverage model. Available from: www.bamanagerforum.org/events/

Business Analysis Manager Forum (2015) Measuring BA performance. Available from: www.bamanagerforum.org/events/

Business Analysis Manager Forum (2016) The tools of the trade. Available from: www.bamanagerforum.org/events/

Cadle, J., Paul, D. and Turner, P. (2014) *Business Analysis Techniques*. Swindon: BCS Learning and Development Ltd.

Checkland, P. (1999) *Systems Thinking, Systems Practice: includes a 30 year retrospective*. Chichester: John Wiley and Sons.

Cialdini, R. B. (2007) *Influence: the psychology of persuasion*. New York: Harper Business.

CIPD (Chartered Institute of Personnel and Development) (2017) Employer guide: apprenticeships that work. Available from: www.cipd.co.uk/Images/apprenticeships-guide-2017_tcm18-10897.pdf

Collins, J. (2001) *Good to Great*. London: Harper Collins Business.

Cooper, M. (1994) Director of the Massachusetts Institute of Technology (MIT) Press, interview with J. Abrams. *International Design Magazine*, Sept/Oct issue.

Dweck, C. (2017) *Mindset: changing the way you think to fulfil your potential*. New York: Ballantine Books.

Gable, S., Reis, H. T., Impett, E. A. and Asher, E. R. (2004) 'What do you do when things go right? The intrapersonal and interpersonal benefits of sharing positive events'. *Journal of Personality and Social Psychology*, 87 (2). 228.

Gawande, A. (2011) *The Checklist Manifesto*. London: Profile Books.

Girvan, L. and Paul, D. (2017) *Agile and Business Analysis*. Swindon: BCS Learning and Development Ltd.

Goleman, D. (2013) *Leadership: the power of emotional intelligence*. Northampton, MA: More than Sound.

Goodall, A. (2012) A theory of expert leadership, IZA Discussion Papers, No. 6566, Institute for the Study of Labor (IZA), Bonn.

Gorman, M. E. (2010) 'Trading zones, normative scenarios, and service science'. In: Maglio, P. P., Kieliszewski, C. A. and Spohrer, J. C. (eds). *Handbook of Service Science*. New York: Springer. 665–675.

Gov.uk (2017) 'Digital service standard'. Available from: www.gov.uk/service-manual

Hall, E. T. (1976) *Beyond Culture*. New York: Anchor Books.

Handy, C. (1993) *Understanding Organisations*, 4th edition. New York: Oxford University Press, Inc.

Harvey, J. (Summer 1988). 'The Abilene Paradox: the management of agreement'. *Organizational Management*. American Management Association. 17 (1). 19–20.

Henderson, L. S., Stackman, R. W. and Lindekilde, R. (2016) 'The centrality of communication norm alignment, role clarity and trust in global project teams'. *International Journal of Project Management*, 34. 1717–1730.

Himmelman, A. T. (2002) Collaboration for a change. Definitions, models, roles and a guide for collaborative process. Minneapolis: Hubert Humphrey Institute of Public Affairs, University of Minnesota. Available from: https://depts.washington.edu/ccph/pdf_files/4achange.pdf

Hofstede, G., Hofstede, G. J. and Minkov, M. (2010) *Cultures and Organizations: software of the mind: intercultural cooperation and its importance for survival*, 3rd edition. USA: McGraw Hill.

IIBA UK (2015) Annual report. Available from: www.iibauk.org/documents/survey/basurvey2015.pdf

Jakob, D. (1986) 'The design of integrated information systems using business analysis'. Case study 4. *Journal of Information Science*, 12. 311–315.

Jiang, J. and Klein, G. (1999) 'Software development risks to project effectiveness'. *The Journal of Systems and Software*, 52. 3–10.

Johnson, G., Whittington, R., Scholes, K., Angwin, D. and Regner, P. (2017) *Exploring Corporate Strategy*, 11th edition. Harlow: Pearson.

Kahler, T. (1975) 'Drivers: the key to the process of scripts'. *Transactional Analysis Bulletin*, 5 (3). 280–284.

Kano, N., Seraku, N., Takahashi, F. and Tsuji, S. A. (1984) 'Attractive quality and must-be quality'. *Journal of the Japanese Society for Quality Control* (in Japanese), 14. 39–48.

Kaplan, R. S. and Norton, D. P. (1996) *The Balanced Scorecard: translating strategy into action*. Boston: Harvard Business Review Press.

Kaplan, R. S. and Norton, D. P. (2008) *The Execution Premium: linking strategy to operations for competitive advantage*. Boston: Harvard Business Press.

Karau, S. J. and Williams, K. D. (1997) 'The effects of group cohesiveness on social loafing and social compensation'. *Group Dynamics: Theory Research and Practice*, 1 (2). 156.

Kelvin, Lord (1883) 'Lecture "Electrical Units of Measurement"'. Published in Popular Lectures Vol. I, p.73. UK

Lovelock, C. (2018) 'When BAs go BAD!' In: *Business Analysis Conference Europe 2018*, London, 24–26 September 2018.

Lovelock, C. and Wilford, S. (2014) 'Grow your own business analysts'. In: *Business Analysis Conference Europe 2014*, London, 22–24 September 2014.

Luft, J. and Ingham, H. (1955) 'The Johari window, a graphic model of interpersonal awareness'. *Proceedings of the western training laboratory in group development*. Los Angeles: University of California.

Lusch, R. F. and Nambisan, S. (2015) 'Service innovation: a service-dominant logic perspective'. *MIS Quarterly*, 39 (1). 155–176.

Mann, A. and Harter, J. (2016) 'Amid rapid-fire workplace change, pulse surveys emerge', *Gallop Business Journal* (March).

Mashek, D. and Nanfito, M. (2015) People, tools and processes that build collaborative capacity. Available from: www.researchgate.net/publication/284672867_People_Tools_and_Processes_that_Build_Collaborative_Capacity

Michela, J. L. and Burke, W. W. (2000) *Handbook of Organizational Culture and Climate*. Thousand Oaks: Sage.

Mitchell, R. K., Agle, B. R. and Wood, D. J. (1997) 'Toward a theory of stakeholder identification and salience: defining the principle of who and what really counts'. *Academy of Management Review*, 22. 853–886.

Musselwhite, C. and Plouffe, T. (2012) 'What's your influencing style?' *Harvard Business Review*. Available from: hbr.org/2012/01/whats-your-influencing-style?autocomplete=true

Osterwalder, A. and Pigneur, Y. (2010) *Business Model Generation: a handbook for visionaries, game changers, and challengers*. Hoboken, New Jersey: John Wiley and Sons.

Parasuraman, A., Berry L. L. and Zeithaml, V. A. (1991) 'Understanding customer expectations of service'. *Sloan Management Review*, 32. 39–48.

Patel, H., Pettitt, M. and Wilson, J. R. (2011) 'Factors of collaborative working'. *Applied Ergonomics*, 43. 1.

Paul, D. E. (2013) 'Business analysis – the Third Wave'. In: *Business Analysis Conference Europe 2013*, London, 23–25 September 2013.

Paul, D. E. (2018) Defining the role of the business analyst, published doctoral thesis, Henley Business School, 2018.

Paul, D., Cadle, J. and Yeates, D. (2014) *Business Analysis*, 3rd edition. Swindon: BCS Learning and Development Ltd.

Porter, M. (1985) *Competitive Advantage: creating and sustaining superior performance*. New York: Free Press.

Portnova, I. and Peiseniece, L. (2017) 'Leaders' competencies for successful leadership of invention and implementation of innovation: a conceptual model'. *Journal of Business Management*, 13. 40–55.

Reed, A. (2018) *Business Analyst: careers in business analysis*. Swindon: BCS Learning and Development Ltd.

Reivich, K. J., Seligman, M. E. P. and McBride, S. (2011) 'Master resilience training in the U.S. Army'. *American Psychologist*, 66 (1). 25–34.

Rogers, E. M. (2003) *Diffusion of Innovation (innovation adoption lifecycle)*. New York: Free Press.

Salovey, P. and Mayer, J. D. (1990) 'Emotional intelligence'. *Imagination, Cognition, and Personality*, 9 (3). 185–211.

Sanford, N. (1966) *The American College*. USA: John Wiley and Sons.

Schein, E. (2016) *Organizational Culture and Leadership*, 5th edition. Hoboken, New Jersey: John Wiley and Sons.

Senge, P. (2006) *The Fifth Discipline*, 2nd edition. London: Random House.

Sinek, S. (2011) Available from: www.simonsinek.com

Sjøberg, D. (2018) An empirical study of WIP in Kanban teams. *12th ACM/IEEE International Symposium on Empirical Software Engineering and Measurement*. Oulu, Finland, 11–12 October 2018. New York: ACM. Article 13.

Srinivasan, A. and Kurey, B. (2014) Creating a culture of quality. *Harvard Business Review*, 92 (4). 23–25.

Stone, D. and Heen, S. (2014) *Thanks for the Feedback*. New York: Portfolio Penguin.

Sutherland, J. and Canwell, D. (2004) *Key Concepts in Management*. Basingstoke: Palgrave Macmillan.

Swieringa, J., Wierdsma, A. and Swieringa, J. (1992) *Becoming a Learning Organization: beyond the learning curve*. Wokingham: Addison-Wesley.

The Deming institute (1993) Plan, do, study, act. Available from: www.deming.org/explore/p-d-s-a

Thomas, P., Paul, D. and Cadle, J. (2012) *The Human Touch*. Swindon: BCS Learning and Development Ltd.

Ury, R. and Fisher, W. (2012) *Getting to Yes*. London: Random House Business.

Vargo, S. L. and Akaka, M. A. (2009) 'Service-dominant logic as a foundation for service science: clarifications'. *Service Science*, 1. 32–41.

Ward, J. and Daniel, E. (2012) *Benefits Management: how to increase the business value of your IT projects*, 2nd edition. Chichester: John Wiley and Sons.

Wenger, E., McDermott, R. and Snyder, W. (2002) *Cultivating Communities of Practice*. Boston: Harvard Business Review Press.

Whitmore, J. (2009) *Coaching for Performance: growing people, performance and purpose*, 4th edition. London: Nicholas Brealey Publishing.

Wrzesniewski, A., Berg, J. M. and Dutton, J. E. (2010) 'Managing yourself: turn the job you have into the job you want'. *Harvard Business Review*, 88 (6). 114–117.

INDEX